# RHETORIC and STYLE

## Strategies For Advanced Writers

**NEVIN K. LAIB**

*Director, The Writing Program*
*Franklin & Marshall College*

PRENTICE HALL, Englewood Cliffs, New Jersey 07632

Library of Congress Cataloging-in-Publication Data

LAIB, NEVIN K.
    Rhetoric and style : strategies for advanced writers / Nevin K.
Laib.

        p.       cm.
    Includes bibliographical references and index.
    ISBN 0-13-478967-9
    1. English language—Rhetoric. 2. English language—Style.
I. Title.
PE1408.L24   1993
808'.042—dc20                                    92-22827
                                                    CIP

---

*This book is dedicated to my wife,
Catherine A. Curtis, to my
parents, and to Frank O'Hare.*

---

*Acquisition editor:* Phil Miller
*Editorial/production supervision and
    interior design:* Hilda Tauber
*Prepress buyer:* Herb Klein
*Manufacturing buyer:* Robert Anderson
*Cover design:* Miguel Ortiz

Printed in the United States of America

10   9   8   7   6   5   4   3   2   1


ISBN 0-13-478967-9

Prentice-Hall International (UK) Limited, *London*
Prentice-Hall of Australia Pty. Limited, *Sydney*
Prentice-Hall Canada Inc., *Toronto*
Prentice-Hall Hispanoamericana, S.A., *Mexico*
Prentice-Hall of India Private Limited, *New Delhi*
Prentice-Hall of Japan, Inc., *Tokyo*
Simon & Schuster Asia Pte. Ltd., *Singapore*
Editora Prentice-Hall do Brasil, Ltda., *Rio de Janeiro*

# Contents

## Part Four: THE PRESENTATION OR DELIVERY

# Preface

Unlike most texts, *Rhetoric and Style* is less concerned with *how* to write than with how one *could* write. The book does not prescribe a particular style or presume to judge which style is best. Instead it describes the wide range of stylistic possibilities, examines their respective strengths and weaknesses, and leaves it to the reader to determine which strategy is most suited to the occasion. Thus, in the widest sense, *Rhetoric and Style* is about how to be an effective, interesting, informed, and attractive person—both on paper and off. These attributes are the essence of style and the aim of rhetorical training.

## *Organization of the Book*

Decisions about style fall into three general categories: (1) those related to the situation or circumstances to which you are responding; (2) those related to the subject about which you are writing; and (3) those related to the performance or "delivery" of the material, to the manner in which you present the subject and yourself to an audience. After reviewing the nature of rhetoric and style in the opening section, the book discusses each of these dimensions of stylistic choice in succession.

In Part One, rhetoric is presented as a social art, a means of maintaining and changing the fabric of society. In the form of education and proselytism it preserves and transmits culture. In the form of inquiry, invention, and criticism it provides the means of transforming culture. Style is discussed as a system of values, a complex pattern of judgment, belief, and behavior which is reflected in discourse and perceived as our identity, stance, or public image.

In Part Two, the various dimensions of the rhetorical situation or the context of discourse are studied. These include the author, the audience, the events that lead you to write, the occasion when your speech is delivered or your writing is read, the forum in which it is presented or appears, and the conventions of discourse that are pertinent to the context. Also covered in Part Two are fundamental questions about how to respond to a situation that calls for writing and how to gauge the level of assertiveness appropriate for the occasion.

Part Three discusses variations in style that can be traced to the nature and selection of the subject, to the author's sources of information, to the author's perspective or point of view, and to the author's objectives, meaning, or intent. The chapters focus on the significance, originality, and relative complexity of topics, and on methods of interpreting, representing, researching, observing, and evaluating the subject.

Choices related to presentation are essentially matters of performance, the manner in which you display and support your point of view in the finished essay. Part Four examines the different forms of presentation or delivery available to writers, the various ways that ideas and feelings can be represented in prose.

Individual chapters discuss alternative methods of beginning and ending a presentation, the effect of varying the length of the discussion, the kinds of evidence or support one can use, the nature of organization or arrangement, the stylistic resources of language, and the effects of planning, revision, and spontaneity on style. It is in the act of presentation or delivery that all the diverse skills of writing are focused and realized. In the performance of an idea, belief, or state of mind we recognize its worth.

A good writer responds to the moment, knowing when to trust the facts to speak for themselves and when to force an interpretation upon them, when to use rational argument and when to use emotional appeal, when to be ingratiating and when polemical, when to be distant and when to reveal some personal truth, when to make concessions and when to resist compromise. In this calculation and wit lies the art of rhetoric.

**A Note About Method.** Frequently in *Rhetoric and Style* I explain the nature of writing in terms of oral communication, comparing it with the conventions and intent of casual talk, academic and professional discourse, and public debate. In fact, the terms "writing" and "speaking," "readers" and "audience" are used almost interchangeably. After all, writing, although confined to the page, arises from dialogue. Its motives, structure, and style are ultimately defined by the habits and practices of conversation and speech.

## Acknowledgments

My thanks to those who have helped with this book: to Phil Miller at Prentice Hall for his support of the project, and to the various editors at Prentice Hall who have contributed advice and guidance; and to those who reviewed the manuscript at different stages in its development and revision, among them Kathleen Boardman, University of Nevada; Sandra Clark, Anderson University; Nan Johnson, University of British Columbia; Larry Mapp, Middle Tennessee State University; Andrew McLean, University of Wisconsin, Parkside; and Nancy Cole Yee, Fitchburg State College.

# The Nature of Rhetoric

Rhetoric [is] the *science of speaking well*. . . . This definition includes all the virtues of oratory and the character of the orator as well, since no man can speak well who is not good himself.　　　　　—Quintilian

Rhetoric may be defined as the faculty of observing in any given case the available means of persuasion.　　　　　—Aristotle

Oratory is the art of enchanting the soul.　　　　　—Plato

## *Functions of Rhetoric*

Rhetoric is a social art, a system of conduct, and a method of inquiry. We use it

- to convey and challenge beliefs
- to transmit and change our culture
- to create alliances and friendships
- to influence the behavior of those around us
- to further our interests within the community

Rhetoric is related to leadership, ethics, and logic. It is the means through which we make decisions, form agreements, inspire confidence, attract a following for ourselves and our ideas, and build consensus. Rhetoric is concerned with how we should treat an audience, how we should behave in different situations, how we should perceive and interpret the world around us, and how we should represent ourselves to others. Rhetoric is the means through which we support, explain, debate, and even discover ideas.

1

The goal of rhetorical training is excellence in citizenship, scholarship, and the social graces. Effective communication is an important part of this, but rhetoric is as much the art of living well as it is the art of speaking well. Rhetoric is the means through which a person creates an attractive and convincing persona. It is the process through which we define and discuss our beliefs. It is the mechanism through which we organize information, channel the efforts of society, and get things done.

"Eloquence," says Cicero, "is so potent a force that it embraces the origin and operation and developments of all things, all the virtues and duties, all the natural principles governing the morals and minds and life of mankind, and also determines their customs and laws and rights, and controls the government of the state" (*De Oratore* III. xx. 76).

We use rhetoric to improve social conditions and personal status; to negotiate, bargain, command, and compromise; to proselytize and teach; to foster mutual respect, understanding, and trust; and to express our emotions and thoughts. It shapes and reshapes us.

## *Personal Rhetoric*

We are all intuitively aware of rhetorical principles and strategy. We use rhetoric to gain attention or to avoid being noticed, to assert ourselves or defer to others, to publicize our accomplishments and to make excuses for our shortcomings. It is through rhetoric that we explain our ideas and actions, seeking approval for ourselves, for our opinions, and for our beliefs, inspiring others to trust and agree with us and to work with us in getting things done. And it is through rhetoric, as well, that we criticize the way things are, acknowledging the need for change.

No one older than three is unfamiliar with rhetoric. Small children are adept at manipulating their parents to get what they want. Students know they can get attention in class either by answering questions well or by answering sarcastically. Although no one likes a know-it-all, show-off, or complainer, people learn quickly that complaining, showing off, and cockiness are often rewarded.

From an early age we begin to form extremely complex habits of expression—some designed for self-defense, some for earning respect, some for controlling the behavior of others, some for pleasing employers or peers, some for coping with stressful circumstances, and some for participating in social events and situations. There are strategies for storytelling and for reporting; strategies for requesting money, permission, or use of the car; strategies for defending one's actions, ideas, and interests.

These habits of expression eventually form a consistent and recognizable pattern of discourse and behavior, an agenda for communication or system of preferences and tendencies that we conventionally use to represent ourselves and our ideas to the world around us. This system might be called an individual style, a persona, or a "personal rhetoric." Its consistency arises from the habits, values, and principles that underlie all of a person's writing and speaking.

A personal rhetoric does not necessarily stay the same from day to day, task to task, or year to year and may or may not reflect the author's true identity. It may be based on one or more character traits or on a particular role in which the person is comfortable. It can be to some extent a fabrication, a public image or veneer that conceals what we really are or that conflicts with the way we would like to be. It may be an *ad hoc* style, developed for a particular situation though still based on essentially the same rhetorical agenda as the person's usual discourse.

We develop our personal rhetoric from a combination of many factors. Our culture and beliefs limit or shape our discourse. Education teaches us accepted views of a subject and conventional styles for discussing it. Professional experience forces us to refine our discourse and practice new roles. Observation provides us with models to imitate. Individual talents and inabilities may determine the stylistic options available to us.

But we learn much of our rhetoric by trial and error, by experimenting with different approaches and styles to see what works, what we are capable of, what we can get away with, and how people react to our attempts. The process has its advantages, allowing more scope for variety and choice, enabling some people to arrive at styles more suited to their talents, not pinning them down to styles imposed by tradition, family, or profession or styles that are contrary to their personalities.

But trial and error can also create inflexible and self-defeating styles. Working on trial and error alone, we tend to repeat discourse strategies that worked before, no matter how much the context has changed, or to let subconscious needs control or distort our style and message. We may try, for instance, to use the same rhetorical ploys on teachers, managers, and spouses that we used against our mothers and fathers. We may base our rhetoric on unattractive motives, like fear or egotism. Or we may expect that our assertions will receive the same respect and acquiescence in written form that they get when spoken among friends. A trial-and-error rhetoric is simply not able to adapt quickly to new situations and audiences.

The result is frustration. If one relies on trial and error, success often seems more a product of luck and guesswork than talent and hard work. Only after a long apprenticeship of attempts and mistakes can one arrive at any degree of confidence about controlling the effect of one's writing. But it does not need to be that way. To some extent we can escape the cycle of trial and error by learning to make our rhetorical choices more consciously and by learning what choices are, in fact, available to us.

Our personal rhetoric is often based on a set of principles or assumptions about discourse that are simply too limited to be useful in all situations. Often, for instance, we put too much faith in good ideas and plain, clear, informative writing. The assumption is that good ideas will speak for themselves, that straightforward presentation of the facts will automatically persuade others to listen to us, hire us, or change their ways. But other people have good ideas, too.

Even when the facts have been clearly presented, it may not be enough. There is no guarantee that readers might not willfully misunderstand you or prefer not to listen. After all, the reader who accepts one of your ideas must do so at the expense of his or her own. You must overcome the inherent competitiveness of people. And you must overcome the inertia of the status quo. People would rather stick with what they already know and keep things pretty much the same. Change, as reflected in new ideas, can threaten their security, position, identity, and beliefs.

In every business, every court of law, every scientific and academic pursuit, more voices are raised than there are audiences to hear them. As a result the competition for attention, respect, and reward is intense. Under such circumstances, you cannot afford to rely on trial and error. You need to know what the alternatives are and what effect each might have before you write.

## EXERCISE A

Which of the following values and intents might influence the rhetoric of the listed occasions for discourse? Which intents might seem inappropriate? What other considerations might affect the author's style?

### VALUES AND INTENTS

a. being accurate
b. being thorough
c. being entertaining
d. being organized
e. expressing oneself
f. getting attention

g. staying safe
h. helping others
i. being honest
j. achieving success
k. being spontaneous
l. being brief

m. creating understanding
n. looking attractive
o. working together
p. discovering the truth
q. avoiding problems
r. exerting control

### OCCASIONS FOR DISCOURSE

1. The evening news
2. A daytime talk show
3. An instruction manual for a microwave oven
4. Instructions on the box of a new game
5. An excuse for missing a deadline
6. An excuse for a bad decision you made or some public failure
7. A party

8. A business lunch
9. Picketing or any other public demonstration
10. A traffic sign
11. A report on a chemistry experiment
12. A report to the police on a traffic accident you were involved in
13. Arguing with a friend, spouse, or relative
14. Applying for a job
15. Advertising a new breakfast cereal
16. Advertising a charity
17. Description of a fossil
18. Description of a sporting event
19. Running a meeting
20. Writing a law
21. Writing a poem or story
22. Writing a research paper

## *The Arts of Rhetoric*

Rhetoric has five constituent arts:

- Invention
- Arrangement
- Style
- Memory
- Delivery

Classical authors call these arts the "offices" or "canons" of rhetoric.

**Invention** is the art of discovering things to say. It encompasses all theorizing, perception, and imagination, including the processes through which we form opinions, accumulate data (whether through experience, observation, discussion, or experimentation), and develop hypotheses. It also includes reasoning, logic, interpretation, and criticism, since these processes "create" more content, more ideas and development. And it includes our ability to envision alternatives and consequences, to conceive of solutions to problems, and to develop plans for action.

**Arrangement** is the art of organizing behavior, events, and information. It includes any kind of structure, form, order, pattern, or procedure. The methodology of an experiment is a pattern of arrangement. So are rules of order for public debate and for legal proceedings.

Arrangement is part of the "staging" of events—the sequence in which things are meant to occur or to be seen. It is apparent in the progression of ideas in an essay and in the logical, associative, or conceptual structure of the material.

**Style** is the manner of expression. It is seen in our choice of words and in the structure of our sentences. It reflects the values we live by and our attitudes toward the subject and audience.

Style conveys a sense of the author's character, status or authority, and stance toward an issue. It represents and embodies the role an author is playing in a given situation. Considerations of style also include the medium one chooses for expressing oneself—whether language, action, resistance, imagery, or music—and its constraints. Constraints include the relationship that exists or is asserted between the author and audience (the relationship between a mother and son or between an employer and a prospective employee, for example, affects the style of their respective discourse).

**Memory** is the art of recall or the ability to draw on education and experience when speaking or writing.

In classical rhetoric, this art was restricted to the mechanical process of memorizing speeches for later presentation. But it is now perceived as a more active and complex skill, involving the ability to identify and explain common knowledge about a subject (the collective wisdom we all share and "remember"), to comprehend and apply concepts learned from library research (the memory of what various experts have had to say about the topic), and to call on one's own collection of experiences, stories, arguments, set pieces, maxims, and observations.

Memory includes the ability to repeat and paraphrase ideas and to report vividly or thoroughly what one has seen. It includes our respective vocabularies and our knowledge of the language. It includes the patterns of expression we habitually use and the various forms of discourse we remember and imitate.

The art of memory is related to one's knowledge of the subject. Developing a fund of ideas is one of the primary objects of formal education. Memory of these ideas is a prerequisite for expertise.

**Delivery** is an art of performance or presentation, the ability to dramatize an idea, belief, emotion, situation, or state of mind.

In classical rhetoric, which was concerned primarily with oratory, this art was equated with the ability to modulate one's pace, tone, and voice and to control one's body language. It was seen as similar to acting, with the difference that the orator was expected not just to "act out" an emotion or scene but genuinely to "feel" it. It was not enough to be believable; one's delivery was supposed to reflect actual and sincere conviction. Posture, carriage, and facial expression had to appear natural, appropriate, and attractive.

The art of delivery is more difficult to perceive in writing, but its importance there cannot be overstressed. If anything, delivery in writing carries a heavier burden, since it must compensate for the absence of many features of speech we take for granted: volume and emphasis, pitch, emotional displays and inflections, rapidity of expression, hesitations and pauses, gestures, questions or reactions from the audience, the effect of the setting, and the sheer visual impact of seeing the author or seeing the object referred to (which an orator or lawyer might hold up for display).

Delivery in writing therefore includes the ability to make the subject seem authentic, sincere, immediate, or vividly "present." It includes the ability to imply tone, voice, and pace and to evoke a sense of the location, time, and circumstances of the discussion.

Above all, delivery is a creative art. It does more than just convey or encode information. It "represents" or portrays events and ideas, making us feel that we are participants in the discovery or debate rather than distant spectators.

Delivery creates a sense of urgency or dialogue. It gives shape and significance to ideas, bringing concepts to life—not listing facts and arguments but "showing" us the subject whole and complete.

## EXERCISE B

Which of the five arts of rhetoric is/are reflected in each of the following cases? Explain.

1. Using a chart or picture to illustrate an idea
2. Following the scientific method (to observe, hypothesize, experiment, replicate the experiment, and revise or discard the hypothesis)
3. Conducting a survey or questionnaire
4. Reading a book
5. A child with a skinned knee crying only when his or her parents are in view
6. Interrupting someone else who is speaking
7. Quoting a favorite author to support your contention
8. Telling a friend what happened at a meeting or social event
9. Pounding your fist on a table to emphasize a point
10. Underlining a word in an essay you are writing
11. Phrasing your idea as a question, rather than asserting it outright
12. Changing your mind about something
13. Exceeding the 55-mile-per-hour speed limit
14. Writing a shopping list

**15.** Retelling a joke

**16.** Starting a letter with a complaint

## *Rhetoric and the Composing Process*

Even when it seems spontaneous, good writing does not just "happen." It is the result of extended practice, general familiarity with the subject, an intuitive or deep understanding of people, and a well-trained sense of appropriateness and timing. Preparing oneself to speak or write effectively takes years. It is a process of social and cognitive development.

The process of writing has three modes or stages:

- Prewriting
- Writing
- Revision

These stages do not necessarily occur in sequence. They may be simultaneous events, or the entire process may be recursive, with each activity repeated many times during the composing of an essay.

**Prewriting** is the conceptual mode of discourse, including all research, invention, hypothesizing, and speculation. In some sense it may be said to begin long before one ever decides to write about a particular subject. The preparation for writing includes your education, experiences, and observations, as well as the immediate work that goes into developing an essay.

**Writing** is a performance mode, the process of "publishing" or presenting your thoughts. It includes finding the right words, constructing sentences, and organizing the material—calculating your style to suit the audience, intent, and occasion.

The performance may be mental, verbal, or written. Drafts and other "practice publication" may be thought through, tried out in conversation, or actually set down on paper.

**Revision** is a mode of criticism, testing, and reconsideration. During revision one examines the projected work, the evidence, and the finished performance and decides whether the argument is sound, the hypothesis valid, and the presentation effective.

Revision has two dimensions: (1) refinement or rethinking of the concept, and (2) refinement or change in the presentation.

In sum, the process of writing an individual essay is parallel to and part of the wider processes of intellectual discovery and social deliberation. An individual essay is one voice in a cumulative dialogue.

## The Rhetorical Situation

There are seven basic components to any communication:

- The subject or circumstances to which your speech refers
- The exigence, need, or justification for speaking
- The occasion on which you decide to speak
- The forum, setting, or context within which the speech occurs
- The audience you address
- The self
- The medium of expression

These components are usually referred to collectively as elements of "the rhetorical situation."

Each element presents unique problems. A change in any single component of communication affects the entire transaction. People who know us well are much different from an audience of strangers, and we address them differently. A private conversation in an office or restaurant may lead to different topics and solutions than public discussion in a committee meeting. If you become more knowledgeable about a subject or are promoted to a supervisory position, your relationship to the audience is changed, and so is your style.

Being able to recognize and respond to the complexities of the situation can improve your writing and speaking.

The **subject** is more than just the topic you write about. It represents something that is important to you—something so significant, interesting, rewarding, or meaningful that you are willing to devote time to discussing and studying it—and something you feel should be important to your audience. The choice of subject reflects not only your values, character, and beliefs, but also your perception of your audience.

Dimensions of the subject include its familiarity (to you and to your audience), the attitudes and emotions associated with it, and the state and extent of knowledge about it. Subjects may be of general interest to you, or they may be connected to a specific event, object, person, phenomenon, or set of circumstances that attracts your attention and leads you to write.

The **exigence** is the reason for speaking. It may be a problem that needs to be resolved or an awkard silence that needs to be filled. It may be an important discovery or a need for attention.

The exigence must be strong enough to force you to speak up, and it must appear to the audience to be sufficient justification for speaking.

Exigence may be found in external circumstances, in the author, or in the audience. External exigence comes from the rhetorical situation itself, as when some crisis or threat exists that must be dealt with.

Exigence comes from within the author when he or she is motivated to speak by emotional needs, doubt, curiosity, the will to power, or the desire for self-expression. Internal exigence is also found in personal goals, wishes, dreams, fears, and ideals.

Exigence comes from the audience when the audience poses a question or assigns a task, when it seeks to be informed or entertained, or when the author feels that the audience needs to be changed in some way, as when he or she wishes to change the audience's opinions, actions, or attitudes, or to persuade them to buy or believe something.

Multiple motives for discourse are more the rule than the exception. And clear distinctions between external, internal, and audience-based motives can be difficult to make. For example, a person's desire to be noticed and advance his or her career may find expression in an attempt to personally resolve a business crisis and thereby please his or her employer, who has in the past encouraged initiative. In such a case, the internal, external, and audience-based motives work together.

The **occasion** is the actual moment when you choose to write or speak. Some of the considerations that affect the choice of occasion are the immediacy of the crisis, your emotional state, your maturity, your status in the community, your relative knowledge of the subject, the emotional and cognitive state of the audience, the choice of a proper forum, the existence of an opportunity to speak (or to enter the conversation, get on the agenda, or join the community), and the strategic advantage of different occasions for speaking.

Classical rhetoric defines three different relationships between oratory and the occasion: *kairos, tō prepon,* and *tō dynaton.* The first choice is to defer speech until the right moment (*kairos*) comes along or until you are absolutely ready to speak.

The second option is to adapt to the present occasion for speaking, to make your style appropriate (*tō prepon*) to the occasion at hand.

The third option is to change (*tō dynaton*) the present occasion—in a sense, to make present circumstances adapt to you rather than you to them. Rather than adapting to a lecture hall setting, for instance, a speaker might choose to walk out into the audience, breaking down the barriers of distance and formality implied by the forum. Rather than accommodating some form of prejudice in his or her audience, a speaker might choose to attack and confront it. The audience would not perceive this attack as appropriate, but the tactic might be necessary and effective in forcing a change.

The **forum** is the actual place where you speak or the manner of publication. You might choose, for instance, to convey the same message during a meeting, in casual conversation, in a memo, in a report, over the phone, at a social gathering, on a business form, or in a formal article written for experts in the field.

Dimensions of the forum include its relative formality; its privacy; its status; its traditions, rules, and ceremonies; and the permanence of the message in such a format.

The **audience** is not just the people you choose to address. Considerations of audience include its relationship to you and to the subject; its attitudes, knowledge, emotions, and beliefs; its maturity, position, and status; its motives and psychology; its values and standards; its perspective; and more.

There may be multiple audiences for a given speech (for instance, newspeople chatting with each other on television are indirectly talking to the viewing public), mixed audiences of diverse people, and homogenous audiences. The audience may consist of a single person; it may be large; or you can talk to yourself.

The **self** is who you are and what you know. Self includes the role you play and the stance you take on an issue. It includes your psychological and cognitive state of mind, your emotions and interests. It includes your abilities, identity, experience, perceptions, perspective, reputation, and appearance. These and other facets of the self affect your style.

The **medium of expression** is the vehicle through which a message is conveyed. We most commonly associate rhetoric with the medium of language, but meaning can be embodied in other media, as well—in action, in gestures and facial expressions, in music and noise, in silence, in visual images, in dance, in mathematics, and in models and charts, for instance.

Dimensions of the medium of expression include the author's facility, the audience's knowledge of the medium, the existence of conventions and expectations, and the inherent limitations and strengths of the form.

## EXERCISE C

Analyze each of the following rhetorical situations as it might pertain to you. Fill in details with information drawn from experience, observation, conjecture, and imagination.

Discuss how each rhetorical situation presents different problems to different speakers.

1. Answering a tough question in a calculus class
2. Shopping for a personal computer
3. Seeking election to a campus or public office
4. Telling your employer that other workers are malingering
5. Asking someone you have just met for a date

6. Teaching a three-year-old to stay away from electrical outlets
7. Criticizing a friend's manner of dress
8. Complaining to city hall about conditions in your neighborhood
9. Disagreeing with a social or political opinion that everyone else in the room seems to hold
10. Telling neighbors that their son has been stealing tools from your garage
11. Writing a report about your own family and upbringing for a sociology professor
12. Writing an essay to convince people that they should give more money to charities

## *The Forms of Discourse*

Classical rhetoric recognizes three basic forms of persuasion:

- Forensic or legal discourse
- Deliberative or governmental discourse
- Epideictic or ceremonial discourse

These are concerned, respectively, with deciding guilt or innocence, with determining the best course of action, and with assessing praise or blame.

These categories are still in current use, and not just as they apply to law, government, and public ceremonies. Forensic discourse can be seen to include not only questions of law but also any dispute over fairness, propriety, due process, and justice. Deliberative discourse can be said to encompass all questions related to administration and leadership, including decision making, problem solving, and policy setting. Epideictic discourse, originally limited to speeches given on ceremonial or ritual occasions (like funerals, awards ceremonies, and retirements), might be extended to include any form of criticism and appreciation, any discourse that evaluates a subject or determines worth.

Many kinds of discourse, however, are still not explained by these categories. Technical and scientific reports, teaching, instruction manuals, casual conversation, literature, explanatory essays, preaching, advertising, public relations, and news commentary are some major examples.

For this reason, attempts have been made to categorize writing in other ways. In the late nineteenth century, Alexander Bain suggested that there were four basic "modes of discourse." More recent attempts to classify discourse have been made by James Kinneavy, James Britton, and James Moffett, among others. While their respective systems are far more complex than can be shown here, the basic similarities should be apparent:

| Bain | Kinneavy | Britton | Moffett |
|------|----------|---------|---------|
| persuasion | persuasive | informative | persuasion |
| exposition | referential | persuasive | exposition |
| description | expressive | poetic | narration |
| narration | literary | expressive | drama |

*Source:* Adapted from James L. Kinneavy, "A Pluralistic Synthesis of Four Contemporary Models for Teaching Composition," *Reinventing the Rhetorical Tradition,* ed. Aviva Freedman and Ian Pringle (1980): 37–52.

The categories are fairly obvious. They reflect consistent and familiar aims, styles, and genres of discourse.

The problem is that while any written text will generally fit into one or another of these classifications, writing often has multiple intents. An essay that seems to be purely descriptive in content may be intended to persuade (as, for example, in a description of a strip mine meant to persuade people to favor land reclamation). A courtship poem may be simultaneously literary, persuasive, and self-expressive (as is Marvell's "To His Coy Mistress"). To avoid confusion, it might be helpful to distinguish between the surface mode of the presentation and the underlying mode of the author's intent.

Our intent for writing may be to

**REPRESENT,** illustrate, or portray
**REPORT,** describe, recount, or paraphrase

**INSTRUCT,** counsel, deliberate, warn, or advise
**INTERPRET,** explain, and analyze

**PERSUADE,** legislate, or command
**CRITICIZE,** evaluate, judge, and assess value

**BUILD CONSENSUS OR COMMUNITY,** create identification, amuse, or ingratiate
**ATTRACT ATTENTION,** promote or publicize, or express one's emotions and identity

The means by which each of these ends is accomplished—the mode of the presentation—can be the same as the intent, or very different. You can, for instance, use description or narration to instruct, persuade, create identification, or criticize. You can use criticism to amuse or attract attention, as well as to evaluate. It all depends on whether you want to pursue your aims directly or indirectly, whether you want to conceal or reveal your motives.

## *The Forms of Rhetoric*

It has recently become common to speak of any *situation, discourse community, culture, profession,* and *field of study* as having its own rhetoric. This means that each is associated with a recognizable style or pattern of discourse.

Different roles, organizations, and circumstances call for different kinds of evidence, different patterns of presentation, different stances toward the subject, and different vocabularies. Knowing this can help us understand each other better and make it easier for us to adapt our style to suit different audiences and subjects.

### SITUATIONS

Situations that commonly recur have often developed highly conventional rhetorics. Political campaigns, for instance, focus on images, simple issues, and easy answers, trying to keep their messages catchy and short in length but long on emotional connotations. Taking a complex view of problems can seem indecisive. Stated agendas can alienate people. The idea is to sound forceful without committing to anything.

Politicians want the audience to identify with them and to feel alienated from the opponent. Attack on or criticism of the opponent is rarely far from the surface.

There are situational rhetorics associated with social phenomena like parenting, job interviews, and dating, and with everyday events like asking directions (or giving them), borrowing a tool, answering questions in a classroom, cheerleading, and splitting a check in a restaurant.

### DISCOURSE COMMUNITIES

People who commonly associate with each other develop their own special "language." They share a common fund of experiences and examples, use particular words and phrases in a specialized manner, and know each other's foibles and personalities. Often a characteristic manner of discussion is followed and disputes are resolved by idiosyncratic methods.

Examples of discourse communities include people in the same town or region, employees at a business, students in the same class or at the same school, people in a club or social organization, and members of a committee.

### CULTURES

Cultures have their own unique styles of communication, the result of long traditions, communal beliefs, and accepted preferences. Some cultures appreciate vocal display and virtuosity, for instance. Some respect facts and plain talk. Others admire circumspect discourse and reasoned silence.

These are not just matters of taste. They reflect culture-specific habits of argument and discussion. A society that values confrontation and self-promotion resolves disputes in a different manner than does a society that values deference and respect for authority.

## PROFESSIONS

Professions or vocations require a person to learn their particular rhetorics and styles. To be an insurance salesperson, a stockbroker, a doctor, a coal miner, or a newspaper reporter, one has to be familiar with the special subject, vocabulary, manner of presentation, and method of inquiry associated with the job.

While some careers put more emphasis on discourse than others—public relations, psychological counseling, and teaching, for instance, require very complex rhetorical skills—even in relatively physical occupations like farming or construction you have to know how to talk about the work in order to coordinate people's efforts, learn new techniques, and make decisions.

## FIELDS OF STUDY

Often parallel to specific professions, fields of study are in some ways defined by their rhetorical situations and choices. A few examples follow.

**Physical Sciences.**    The rhetoric of science embodies belief in objectivity, induction as a means of discovery, and experimentation as a means of validation and support for contentions. Science relies on thorough inspection of very limited topics—often focusing on objects like bones, leaves, or grains of sand that might seem trivial or commonplace to the layperson. The audience, in theory at least, is not an adversary but a disinterested colleague.

**Business and Management.**    Discourse in business reflects a belief in competition or advantage, in justifying one's opinion through concrete results, in efficiency and monetary worth as measures of authority or rightness, and in the appropriateness of charging a price for helping others or providing things they need.

**Education.**    Instruction assumes that the audience is relatively unfamiliar with the subject. The author therefore occupies a higher rank based on knowledge rather than social status, position, age, or wealth. The emphasis, particularly at introductory levels, is on teaching general skills and conveying, through report and illustration, concepts widely accepted by experts as true or significant.

**Law.**    Legal rhetoric implies faith in adversarial debate as a means of discovery. It is confrontational in tone and in its procedures. Arguments are largely deductive, based on the correlations between the factual evidence and existing laws or principles. The pretense is maintained that in each case there is only one "right" interpretation. The emphasis is on winning rather than compromise.

**Engineering and Technology.**    The rhetoric of engineering is focused on solutions to problems. It is highly pragmatic, focusing on the properties of matter and energy as they are useful, rather than for the sake of knowledge. The basic measures of success are accuracy, efficiency, and effectiveness. The language tends to be highly specialized, assuming that the audience has considerable knowledge of the subject.

**The Arts.**    The arts are more representational, expressive, and entertaining than analytic. The study of art, however, emphasizes interpretation and criticism.

Expertise in art criticism is predicated on both perceptive interpretation of particular artworks and on extensive knowledge of general and historical cases. It presumes a refined sense of taste. The author's relationship to the audience may be advisory or instructive, as in the case of movie critics. Or the author may speak to other experts. Unlike law or science, the arts may encourage multiple interpretations of the same object.

**The Humanities.**    The humanities take a philosophical and interpretive stance toward society, emotions, beliefs, and events. They are likely to focus on the uniqueness of individual cases but to see the particular instances in terms of values, premises, ideologies, and beliefs.

Individual cases are interpreted in the broadest sense, not just to explain their nature but also to explore their connotations and emotional significance. As in the arts, multiple interpretations are not only possible, but likely. It is not a question of one opinion being as good as another, however. Different perspectives give rise to different truths. These are constrained and validated by the available evidence.

**The Social Sciences.**    The humanities and social sciences study essentially the same subjects—human nature, social interaction, and culture. The social sciences do so, however, from an analytic and empirical perspective. The rhetoric of social science depends on experimentation, direct observation, and quantitative data for evidence. General cases are more important than specific instances or exceptions to the rule.

Like all science, the social sciences are concerned with predicting behavior. Theories are validated by how well they explain what will happen or what will be found in a given set of circumstances.

In conclusion, every forum for discourse has its own underlying principles, its own conventions, its own particular audience, its own particular focuses and patterns of emphasis, and its own standards for measuring success. Learning these is part of knowing a subject, joining a group, and building a career. Until we become adept in the form of rhetoric appropriate to a given situation or procession, we are at a disadvantage.

## Goals of Effective Writing

To be "good" at rhetoric requires more than being clear or being understood, more than "knowing how to write" or simply getting the job done. Writing well is inextricably entwined with how well we know our subject, how well we have mastered the style of our profession, and how well we think and observe. It is dependent on how well we know ourselves and our audience; how authoritative, attractive, and ethical we look in print; and how appropriate our response is to the situation at hand.

More specifically, the goals of rhetoric include knowing when to speak and when to keep silent, what to say and what not to say, how to portray oneself and how to detach oneself from the issue, how to present one's thoughts effectively and how or when to defer to the thoughts of others, and when to prefer action to words. The ideal rhetorician is not to be described only in terms of linguistic fluency or facility (sometimes, in fact, a lack of fluency can be more effective). Good writing calls on many diverse abilities and traits, such as

- verbal facility
- appropriate vocabulary
- knowledge of the subject
- knowledge of the audience
- self-awareness
- assertiveness
- perceptiveness
- originality
- skill in interpretation and criticism
- an awareness of conventional patterns and forms of discourse
- the imagination to create new patterns and forms
- previous experience with the situation
- maturity or composure
- the ability to distance oneself from emotional involvement with events and beliefs
- leadership, management, and organizational skills
- showmanship, dramatic flair, or promotional skills
- a sense of what might be attractive or aesthetically pleasing in style and action

- a good ear
- an ability to get things done
- a sense of one's role or position
- familiarity with professional standards and procedures

Well-crafted writing convinces the reader that the author is an informed, effective, entertaining, ethical and interesting person, someone who values or respects his or her audience—or can justify showing it some disrespect. Good writing seems to be shaped, refined, and regularized in accord with some plan, creed, or vision. Where it is shapeless or eccentric, some sufficient rationale or excuse for the shapelessness must be apparent. Good writing conveys a sense that the author's personality, outlook, and behavior elsewhere are equally coherent or consistent (or equally strange), that the author intentionally writes as he or she does or that the style reflects the writer's personality.

Note that it is not enough to *be* informed, effective, clever, and ethical; one must also convey the corresponding good impression. Inarticulate knowledge is largely wasted. Quiet effectiveness often goes unnoticed. And unspoken wit is unappreciated.

We should not make the mistake of thinking that there is only one right way to be effective as a speaker or writer, just one ideal that all should aspire to, or one ideal pattern of behavior and speech for a given occasion and subject. On the contrary, there are many ways to be good, and the approach that is right for one person will fail miserably for another.

Effective writing depends on so many different factors—and we all bring such varied abilities and experience to the task—that each person must find a different way of putting it all together, a different and personal "ideal" of expression suited to his or her own talents, personality, perspective, knowledge, and skill and to the situation as he or she sees it.

## Conclusion

Rhetoric is more than a system of rules for writing. It is salesmanship and negotiation, courtship and complaint, teaching and proselytism, advertising and diplomacy. It is embodied not just in what we say but in our culture, actions, beliefs, and personalities. It is a part of who we are, how we behave, and how we deal with evidence, ideas, and other people.

## ASSIGNMENT:   Exhortation and Dissuasion

Write an essay that responds to one of the following rhetorical situations. An analysis of the first rhetorical situation is provided as an example of the kinds of thinking that would prepare you for writing the essay.

1. Find a situation that might call for warning others not to do something, despite their conviction that they are doing the right thing and/or what seems like evidence to the contrary (for example, warning people to move to higher ground when there is no visible evidence of rain in the area, much less a flood, and the weather reports are all favorable).

## PARTIAL ANALYSIS OF THE RHETORICAL SITUATION

SUBJECTS: Physical and sudden disasters are easier to argue than intellectual, emotional, or moral crises. People will respond, at least initially, to warnings about danger to life, limb, and property. But they become desensitized by repeated warnings, especially if the threat has not materialized in the past or if the forecast disaster struck somewhere else. The threat must be personally experienced to seem valid.

It is difficult to make a "slow" disaster seem credible, dangerous, and imminent. Decay, degeneration, decline, and gradual change are readily ignored. When the subject is abstract, as in moral failings, decadence, growing ignorance, and even economic recession, people may react with surprising haste and determination, since these subjects may damage our pride or engender strong emotional reactions, including indignation. Usually this determination is focused on changing other people instead of oneself. If the abstract crisis is common enough, readers may be entertained but not persuaded. Some abstract crises are constantly being proclaimed.

There is an element of entertainment to all crises. People are fascinated by disasters in the same way that they are fascinated by horror stories and by natural wonders like the Grand Canyon.

AUTHOR: When you warn others, they may perceive you as self-important and self-righteous. Warning implies that you know better than others what is going on or how to behave. It may be perceived as "talking down" to readers, treating them like children. Expertise, inside knowledge, or past experience can help make you more credible. Otherwise you will, like the outspoken child in "The Emperor's New Clothes," be silenced.

AUDIENCE: You can expect your audience to doubt that any crisis exists, especially if they are reaping benefits from the behavior you are warning against—like the pleasure of owning beachfront property in an area prone to an occasional hurricane, or the enjoyment of continued prosperity in spite of unsafe banking practices, or the satisfaction in a successful war when the political consequences and responsibilities still seem remote.

OCCASION AND SITUATION: People often listen to warnings only when the danger is visible—and sometimes only when it is too late. Writers use some visible sign or example of impending disaster as the excuse for speaking up.

2. Admonish or reprove some behavior you regard as rude, improper, incautious, or counterproductive.

3. In a situation where an apparent crisis exists, try to dissuade people from acting rashly or from pursuing a course of action you think is wrong. You might consider, as one part of the argument, contending that the crisis is illusory or exaggerated (as is sometimes the case in headlines proclaiming that there is a crisis in education, the quality of American-made products, and funding for the sciences or arts, for instance).

# The Nature of Style

Our defects [in style] usually spring . . . from the same sources as our good points.
—Longinus

True grace arises from some kind of independence of mind.
—Mary Wollstonecraft

The style is the man.
—Dionysius of Halicarnassus and
—George Louis Leclerc de Buffon

## Functions of Style

Style is the external expression of your values and beliefs, your personal or social rhetoric. It is your persona or role as an author—a public image you project, a mask you wear, or a stance you take toward the subject and audience.

An admirable style reflects an admirable person. To refine and develop your style is to develop character. This is no easy task.

We admire people who are

- interesting and attractive
- knowledgeable and inventive
- witty and charming
- powerful and effective
- experienced and mature
- responsible and self-assured
- trustworthy and principled
- helpful and sincere
- mysterious and compelling

A style must convey at least some of these qualities to earn respect and appreciation.

## Misconceptions About Style

These are some common *mis*conceptions about style:

- Correctness is all that matters.
- Correctness is a basic skill.

- Clarity alone can make a style effective.
- Clarity is just a matter of saying what you mean.
- Self-expression is the same thing as style.
- Self-expression requires no art or effort.

- What you say is more important than how you say it.
- If you know the material, the style comes naturally.

### CORRECTNESS AND STYLE

The tendency to equate correctness with style is unfortunate. People think that because they have not written badly, they have written well—that fluency and effectiveness are the same thing. Knowing the language is important, but it does not by itself make a person articulate.

Nor is correctness easy to come by. It is hard enough at the level of grammar and syntax. Completely "clean" copy is the exception rather than the rule. It requires a professional editor's knowledge of language, conventions, and manuscript form.

But correctness is all the more difficult when we recognize that it includes being socially and situationally "correct." People expect that what we say and do will be proper, suitable, and appropriate.

Correctness is not a basic skill, but something to aspire to.

### CLARITY AND STYLE

We like to think that clarity makes a good style. If people seem to understand us, we are satisfied. But being understood does not make a person effective.

It is easy to convince yourself that being clear is a simple matter. All you have to do is "say what you mean." But clarity is extremely difficult to achieve. Often we do not know what we mean. We may believe that our meaning is clear when it is, in fact, muddled. We blame others for not understanding us when the fault is our own.

And what good is clarity when the point being made is simplistic or wrong? Clarity in the widest sense requires an accurate, complex, and thorough comprehension of the subject. It requires expertise and clear-sightedness, a coherent and valid interpretation of the subject.

Making oneself understood is not as easy as it seems.

### SELF-EXPRESSION AND STYLE

We prefer to think that character develops naturally or should be allowed to find its own shape and direction. To be self-conscious about it seems a contradiction. To teach it seems invasive and unethical.

In this romantic perspective, all we should have to do to be interesting is to express our "true" selves, to show our emotions and feelings or to explore and explain our private opinions and beliefs. If style is related to self, then creating a style should be no more than a process of revealing one's personality.

There can be considerable truth in this viewpoint. An intelligent process of self-discovery is essential in reflective and speculative writing. That does not mean it is easy. Self-expression requires a certain amount of self-knowledge, self-doubt, and willingness to change. It may require a kind of honesty and courage that is beyond us.

But self-expression is not the complete answer to the problem of style. It can lead to idiosyncratic and self-indulgent writing, focused more on attention seeking than communication. And the "inner self" an author expresses may turn out to be tedious, shallow, and incoherent.

Style includes not only self-expression but also self-creation, the ability to refine, change, and portray one's role, character, or stance.

### CONTENT AND STYLE

It is tempting to separate style and content, to think that the substance of an essay precedes or is more important than the stance. This seems intuitively obvious, considering our experience with people whose style is "full of sound and fury" but signifies nothing.

But style and content are interdeterminate. They develop simultaneously and affect each other. How you say something is part of the message. What you say is part of the style.

The absence of significant content is a particular case, one of many possible relationships between stance and substance. It is just as likely that someone will have something important to say but not be able to express the concept in a way that conveys its significance.

Knowing the subject is no guarantee of an effective style. In fact, a complex and sophisticated understanding of a subject may make it all the more difficult to express oneself clearly and cogently. There are as many inarticulate experts as there are eloquent fools.

## Stylistic Values

Style is a system of values. A person's characteristic manner of speaking reflects what he or she regards as important or worthwhile. For example,

- If we value self-expression and openness, our style tends to include more self-revelation, more reference to doubts and wishes, more emphasis on emotions, speculation, and personal experience.
- If we value learning and knowledge, our style may incorporate more testimony, conventional wisdom, and citations from sources. It will avoid opinion. We will emphasize evidence more than arguments.
- If we value control and power, our style may be more imperative or assertive, emphasizing position or rank, principles, and rules as sources of authority and support. There may be a tendency toward monologue, polemic, criticism, and harangue. The style may evince our confidence in the rightness and truth of our personal vision.

These and other relationships between style and the value structure they represent are not, however, rigidly fixed. People learn to conceal their motives. And the overt style may be maladroit, an inaccurate reflection of a person's true nature.

Nevertheless, from among the possible elements of style—the ways we *could* write—each person, community, discipline, and culture assembles a characteristic palette of choices—an individual, social, professional, or national style, a perceived identity.

## Writing Well

I find it impossible to say with assurance that any particular style is "right" or "wrong." What is ineffective or awkward in the hands of one author will seem adroit and efficient in the style of another. What seems in the abstract an inappropriate or ill-advised stylistic choice can be *made* appropriate by circumstances or force of character.

No element of style is necessarily good or bad. No particular style is intrinsically superior to another. Each is simply an option or possibility, a potential way of expressing oneself—with its own attendant drawbacks and advantages. Tentativeness can seem either wisely cautious or pathetically indecisive. The thorough development that is a virtue in one case seems a vice in another. The assertiveness that impressed us yesterday may offend us the next, seeming arrogant or self-conceited.

The uncertainties of style can be frustrating. To understand them better and cope with them, it is useful to distinguish between (1) possible styles, (2) realized or expressed styles, and (3) perceived styles.

### POSSIBLE STYLES

A possible style is a way you *could* express something, apart from any considerations of correctness, appropriateness, attractiveness, or effect. Possibilities are neither good nor bad.

"The possible" includes *all* of the options available to a writer or speaker, all of the ways a message could be conveyed. This includes saying it well and saying it badly, choosing to act or saying and doing nothing. It includes ways of expressing oneself that are familiar and unfamiliar, attractive and unattractive, conventional and unconventional, or common and uncommon, and styles that are grammatical and ungrammatical, learned and unschooled, permissable and forbidden, pleasant and unpleasant, simple and complex, and previously tried or unprecedented.

The author must choose from this vast range of possibilities in responding to a given situation and in developing his or her own personal rhetoric.

### OPPOSITE STYLES

One of the best ways to explain and understand stylistic possibilities is in terms of opposites. Each element of style has its antithesis: meaning can be expressed either directly or indirectly, organization can be imposed on your subject or derived from within it, your presence as the author or observer can be emphasized or hidden in the essay. The following are some of the most important stylistic opposites.

|              |                  |
| -----------: | ---------------- |
| quiet        | outspoken        |
| assertive    | deferential      |
| conventional | unconventional   |
| expressive   | dramatic         |
| monologic    | dialogic         |
| focused      | diffuse          |
| inventive    | scholarly        |
| interpretive | representational |
| critical     | reportative      |

| | |
|---|---|
| self-contexting | dependent on context |
| formally structured | dramatically structured |
| concise | thorough |
| logical | persuasive |
| plain | ornate |
| planned | spontaneous |

### EXPRESSED STYLES

The expressed style is the actual manner of presentation you choose, the way you perform or deliver the message. The execution can be good or bad, whatever manner is chosen: well written, well calculated, and meaningful or clumsy, ill considered, and insignificant.

It is important to avoid preemptive value judgments. Prejudging a possible style as "bad" may prevent you from trying any number of effective alternatives. For example, if you assume that all ungrammatical styles should be avoided, you will not allow yourself to write a line of poetry like Dylan Thomas's "Do not go gentle into that good night" or a musical refrain like "Is you is or is you ain't my baby."

If you assume that the only "good" writing states its message directly or stays narrowly on the subject, you will not permit yourself to be gracefully (or strategically) indirect or to offer intelligent digressions for the sake of interest. Most polite conversation digresses. To force people to stay on the subject in casual discussion can seem downright unfriendly, rude, and condescending.

Direct statement can be good *or* bad, depending on the performance and situation. Digression can be good *or* bad. Assertiveness can be good *or* bad, well executed and effective or badly written and pretentious.

### PERCEIVED STYLES

The perceived style is the reception your writing gets from an audience. The distinction between expressed and perceived styles is important in understanding the effect you have on others. Figure 2.1 may help you visualize the relationship between possibilities, performance, and reception. However good your expressed style may be, the reception may be bad. Conversely (and perversely), a poor presentation might earn some praise.

A beautifully written, balanced, and objective report might be perceived as an attempt to hide the author's opinions or play it safe. The balance might be interpreted as fence-sitting and the objectivity as a lack of

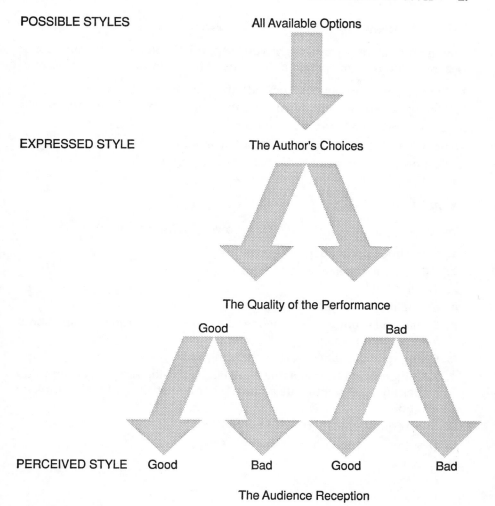

POSSIBLE STYLES          All Available Options

EXPRESSED STYLE          The Author's Choices

The Quality of the Performance

Good                                    Bad

PERCEIVED STYLE    Good          Bad          Good          Bad

The Audience Reception

**Figure 2.1**

initiative. In the same circumstances a pointless, bureaucratic report might be appreciated, if not admired. The pointlessness may be seen as solid and conservative thinking and the bureaucracy as appropriateness and decorum, the voice of experience.

Expressed expertise may be seen as aggressive or helpful. Questioning may seem intrusive or deferential. Advice may be welcome or offensive. The use of allusions may seem witty or elitist. Straightforwardness may seem open and honest or crassly blunt, however it was intended.

## EXERCISE A

How many different ways might you respond to the following situations? Describe a number of options and discuss which would be best and why.

1. Getting people to notice or pay attention to you
2. Making consumers more familiar with a brand name your company sells
3. Convincing people to recycle plastic
4. Building support for a law you want enacted
5. Responding to someone who has insulted your family

## EXERCISE B

How do you perceive and judge the following stylistic choices?

1. Using quotes from popular songs
2. Using quotes from classic authors
3. Talking fast
4. Changing the subject frequently
5. Remaining silent when someone else expresses a strong opinion about a controversial subject
6. Giving someone advice about changing a tire
7. Keeping a child from making a mistake by telling him or her not to do something (e.g., not to date a much older person or not to start drinking alcohol)
8. Asking questions frequently in class
9. Disagreeing with everything people say
10. Cursing
11. Openly expressing anger
12. Using big words

## *The Dimensions of Style*

Style has six primary dimensions: (1) the effective, (2) the accurate or representational, (3) the efficient, (4) the attractive, (5) the appropriate, and (6) the ethical.

### EFFECTIVE STYLES

Effectiveness is a measure of whether or not the style chosen is successful in achieving its desired result. Flamboyant, rebellious, or shocking behavior can be effective if the goal is to attract attention. If the goal is to sell a house, then the style is effective if it achieves that end, no matter how ugly or disreputable it may be. If the goal is to correct an injustice, the style cannot be considered effective, however eloquent it might be, unless the injustice is redressed.

Sometimes our desire to be effective leads us to write in ways that, strictly speaking, we would not normally regard as ethical or attractive. But sometimes the most attractive style also turns out to be the most effective. And unethical behavior, while it may offer short-term benefits, is often less effective in the long run than an ethical style.

### ACCURATE STYLES

Accuracy, representation, or verisimilitude is the relation of style to reality or truth. It includes the extent to which style is shaped by a desire to portray correctly and exactly the author's ideas, perceptions, or beliefs. It includes the effort to make theories as "adequate" as possible, to develop and refine scientific and technical explanations to fit the facts or conform to reality. And it is related to the degree of realism we perceive in description, narration, and dramatization, our sense that a depiction is either "true to life," abstracted, exaggerated, or interpretive.

### EFFICIENT STYLES

Efficiency in style refers to the amount of time and effort it takes to achieve one's goal. It includes the processes of bargaining, lowering our sights, cutting corners, cutting our losses, and settling for less—the ways we compromise our goals and ideals to get the job done. At the opposite extreme, efficiency includes painstaking study, careful methodology, detailed development, and attentive administration—the effort expended in order to make things run more smoothly and efficiently on a daily basis.

Efficiency is important when the matter at hand is trivial (like a shopping list or a note reminding oneself to do something) or when time is pressing. We make little effort on such occasions to make our prose beautiful, grammatical, or thorough, concentrating instead on adequateness or ease to the detriment of other stylistic dimensions.

Efficiency is also important when the subject is complex or repetitive or generates a large volume of information.

### ATTRACTIVE STYLES

Attractiveness in style is the aesthetic dimension of discourse, character, and appearance. It is concerned with the relative beauty of the language and delivery, whether the message is expressed in a way that is pleasant or unpleasant, graceful or clumsy, plain or ornate, and so on.

An attractive style may please the audience but do so at the expense of efficiency and effectiveness. It takes a great deal of effort to produce some of the refinements we associate with beautiful prose. Effectiveness may suffer because in listening to the sound of an essay, the reader may lose track of its meaning, not comprehending the message the author intends to convey.

### APPROPRIATE STYLES

Appropriateness in rhetoric is the principle of decorum, which involves adapting one's style and approach to the situation at hand. If one is speaking to children, for instance, one tends to use words and examples familiar to them, "appropriate" for the audience. Similarly, in speaking to a new acquaintance we usually consider it inappropriate to offer deep personal revelations. The content changes to fit the situation.

An effort to be appropriate in style might gain a person the reputation of being courteous, disciplined, and even mature or experienced (since someone who knows how to respond to a given situation may seem to have spent time learning the ropes). But writing that is appropriate and nothing more is drab, uninspired, and conventional to a fault. In being appropriate one may lose the effectiveness and attractiveness that comes from surprise.

Both attractiveness and appropriateness may serve to build social ties and create a sense of community.

### ETHICAL STYLES

A sixth characteristic of style is its relative morality, immorality, or amorality—or more precisely, the ethics, rectitude, conduct, and manners an author demonstrates in his or her discourse. This should not be confused with the choice or avoidance of offensive words and topics, which are more directly questions of appropriateness in style.

The ethics of a style are measured by the degree to which it is honest or dishonest, engaging or distant, manipulative or straightforward, fair or unfair; they are related to the way an author treats or mistreats an audience. Is the author considerate or inconsiderate, patient with us or rude, brutally frank or helpfully blunt, evasive or politely indirect? Does the author appear arrogant or deferential, tyrannical or willing to listen? Does he or she try to entertain and please us or to intimidate us into submission? Make us feel good about ourselves or unnecessarily guilty about something? Play on our emotions or help us resolve emotional distress? Treat us like equals, experts, superiors, or children? Is the author more interested in getting noticed than in being right?

The answers to these and similar questions describe the ethical dimension of a style. Attention to ethics can make writing more appropriate and socially acceptable, but it is unfortunately true that an overemphasis on being "ethical"—in the sense of being moral, humble, or good—can make style less effective and less attractive. People are sometimes drawn to those who mistreat them, impressed by self-serving displays of eloquence, and enamored of arrogance. At the same time, the strength or authority of one's style may be damaged by excessive courtesy or by deference to the audience. And much that is aesthetically pleasing—wit, linguistic virtuosity, and clever exaggeration, for instance—may be lost in the effort to be overly nice or punctilious.

## Conclusion

Ideally, the dimensions of style discussed here should work in concert. We like to think it possible to be simultaneously effective, accurate, efficient, attractive, appropriate, and ethical. We like to assume that accurate writing will automatically be attractive; that appropriate writing will automatically be effective, ethical, and efficient; that ethical writing will automatically be effective and interesting.

But the various attributes of style more often work against each other than in harmony. The dictates of ethics contradict the impulse to make style attractive, since attractiveness is a kind of manipulation. Pursuing effectiveness can make one's style seem pushy and inappropriate. At times efficiency detracts from effectiveness, accuracy, and propriety.

Stylistic vices can be profitable. If you are abrupt and arrogant, your style may be effective. If you are a tentative thinker, your style may seem accurate. If you are careless of the facts, your style may look engagingly unconstrained. If you are vain and self-important, your style may appear fluent and dramatic.

Stylistic virtues may be penalized. A gracious manner can seem weak. A wide vocabulary and a love of attractive language can seem precious and self-important, distracting us from the message. Deference to the opinions, ideas, and beliefs of others, though ethical, may be perceived as an absence of confidence, content, and personal authority.

People are too diverse and complex to be satisfied by a single ideal style. They have different skills and weaknesses, different values and tastes, different experience and knowledge, and different perspectives or viewpoints. There are too many possible ways to present any subject and too many possible audiences to address. The best we can do is to seek some tenable synthesis of the various elements of style, some balance between the competing aims.

There are no guarantees. A style that sounds attractive to part of an audience may seem pretentious to everyone else. An approach that works on one occasion may fail the next time it is tried. The attempt to makes one's style as appropriate as possible, even if genuinely successful, can be interpreted by the audience as too obvious an attempt to solicit favor, to try to fit in. You cannot please everyone.

This can be taken as cause for despair or as an excuse for not consciously studying and refining one's own rhetoric and style—on the theory that whatever you try will fail or however much you labor over it you still cannot take everything into account. The impossibility of pleasing everyone can be taken as reason for simply "being oneself," for avoiding premeditation of style, for just responding intuitively or responding in a habitual manner. And in fact an unconsidered or unself-conscious approach is sometimes effective. But sometimes it isn't.

## EXERCISE C

Which dimensions of style might be emphasized in each of the following situations? Should the author stress ethics, effectiveness, attractiveness, appropriateness, efficiency, or accuracy? Why? What might happen? And what might be gained by changing the emphasis?

1. Selling life insurance
2. Asking for a raise
3. Describing a physics experiment
4. Conversing at a formal garden party
5. Complaining about an improper charge on a phone bill
6. Discussing with friends the football game you are watching
7. Taking notes in an engineering class
8. Interviewing at a major accounting firm
9. Chatting with a neighbor about the weather
10. Discussing the weather on a news broadcast
11. Discussing the weather with other farmers
12. Arguing about a family decision
13. Escaping a bore
14. Taking a day off from work
15. Quieting a child
16. Haggling about the price of a car
17. Keeping a record of the performance of your employees
18. Describing Italian architecture to art historians
19. Describing a miserable trip to Italy to a group of friends
20. Describing the same trip to people of Italian descent

## ASSIGNMENT A:     Politeness and Euphemism

1. Address a subject that your audience is sensitive about or finds difficult to confront and cope with. Be delicate, but don't pussyfoot too much and don't avoid the obvious questions. Try to speak openly and firmly without being blunt or giving offense.

2. Take the role of someone asked to give bad news to the audience. This need not be a hypothetical case. You could speak in your own voice, and the message could be a fairly conventional misfortune, like reminding people of their own shortcomings or calling attention to a continuing recession. Or you could recall an actual situation where you or someone else received bad news, and reflect on the moment, discussing a painful subject with grace and good humor.

3. Take a disastrous event or ugly topic and put a good face on it, serious or comic. But be careful. At worst, this process can lead to evasion and doublespeak. And even when the intent is less blameworthy and unethical, the results can be patently ridiculous. There are occasions, however, when it is necessary, if only for psychological reasons, to make the best of a bad situation. We need to think well of ourselves. We need to recover from disasters. We need hope.

Ethical speakers sometimes acknowledge the worst even as they attempt to cast a good light on things. Or they find a more uplifting context for the subject: a military build-up is talked about in terms of the patriotic defense of one's country and culture (which it is, but not exclusively); a humiliating athletic defeat is written off as a learning experience.

## ASSIGNMENT B:     Advice and Guidance

Select a skill or craft about which you are something of an expert, either from direct experience or from observation and reading. Put yourself in the role of giving advice on the subject to a specific person, to a specific group of people, or to a more general audience.

### *PARTIAL ANALYSIS OF THE RHETORICAL SITUATION*

AUTHOR: At its best, advice is disinterested and constructive, intended to help someone unfamiliar with a situation or process. The author of the advice is presumed to be someone who has been through the process before or knows how to deal with the situation. At its worst, advice becomes a means of controlling the audience, channeling it toward objectives and outcomes that please the person giving the advice rather than the person receiving it.

AUDIENCE: Often the audience already knows more about the subject than you give it credit for. And the audience may be capable of better work than you give it credit for. The evidence of one mistake may not give a true measure of the audience's skill. People prefer to be their own critics (and to let themselves off the hook). Advice is likely to seem unnecessary and intrusive.

OCCASION AND SITUATION: Advice is often given immediately after someone has just made a mistake. It is, under such circumstances, generally unwelcome, implying criticism, superiority, and the presence of an observer of someone's embarrassment. Advice given to prevent someone from making a mistake is often equally offensive. People need to make their own mistakes and find their own solutions to problems. The trick is to know when to intervene and to do so in such a way as to seem nonjudgmental and unintrusive.

# 3

# Reticence and Outspokenness

To every thing there is a season, and a time to every purpose under the heaven. . . . A time to rend, and a time to sew; a time to keep silence, and a time to speak.                                                    —ECCLESIASTES 3:1,7

Be silent always when you doubt your sense.          —ALEXANDER POPE

He who knows does not speak. He who speaks does not know.
                                                                     —LAO-TZU

Authentic thinking, thinking that is concerned about *reality*, does not take place in ivory tower isolation, but only in communication.
                                                                 —PAULO FREIRE

## *Getting Involved*

To write well you have to take an interest in something. You have to see its meaning, significance, or humor. You have to understand it. The subject does not have to be a passion or cause, but it does have to matter to you. It has to catch your eye and hold your attention.

Those who do not speak up are not heard. They let other people make the decisions. They accept the way things are. They do not ask questions. They take what comes to them.

Yet there are times when it is better to avoid attracting attention, when keeping your mouth shut is politic, intelligent, and polite. The problem is that both silence and outspokenness can be misconstrued. Reticence can be interpreted as a good or bad quality; likewise outspokenness can be seen as either an asset or a liability.

35

### ◀ RETICENCE ▶

| Good Qualities | Bad Qualities |
|---|---|
| judicious reserve | shyness |
| depth | apathy |
| diplomacy | evasiveness |
| enigmaticness | aloofness |

### ◀ OUTSPOKENNESS ▶

| Good Qualities | Bad Qualities |
|---|---|
| openness | attention seeking |
| involvement | meddling |
| fluency | loquacity |
| taking charge | being pushy |

As shown in Figure 3.1, there is a circular relationship between silence, reticence, outspokenness, and action. Increasingly outspoken styles tend toward taking action. Styles associated with taking action tend toward silence, and so on.

## *Deciding Whether to Write*

We write or speak when we want to establish some relationship with the audience, or when we think that what we have to say is so amusing, interesting, important, or worthwhile that others ought to hear it. Even casual discussion has its purpose. Conversation reaffirms acquaintances and builds friendships. It reinforces alliances and beliefs.

Deciding whether to speak is part of getting involved with people and the community. It is part of taking action and pursuing an occupation, part being productive, effective, and content. To write or speak is to accept responsibility. Like casting a ballot, it registers your vote on the issue.

Considerations regarding whether to write include the following:

- The exigence, the need for writing
- Your knowledge of the subject
- Your place in the discourse community
- Your "readiness" to speak out on the matter
- Your audience's needs and interests

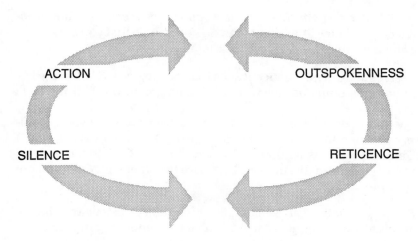

**Figure 3.1**

- The occasion or opportunity to speak
- The potential losses and gains

## *Being Reticent*

The reticence of a style is measured by how little the author says and how long he or she takes to respond. Note that even a fairly lengthy and glib response can be essentially reticent if there is little substance in the presentation.

If you wish to appear reticent, the following strategies can be helpful:

*1. Be Concise.*   The appearance of reticence may be produced by a concise and measured style, with little amplification and repetition and a minimum of digression.

*2. Speak Only on the Immediate Subject.*   We may perceive a writer to be reticent when everything said pertains directly to the issue at hand. Digressions and personal commentary are avoided.

*3. Avoid Expressing Emotion.*   Emotion, self-revelation, humor, and reference to personal experience are often suppressed in reticent styles.

*4. Speak Only When Necessary.*   A reticent writer usually reserves comment for only the most extreme and urgent subjects or waits until his or her opinion is solicited or debate on the issue has gone on for some time.

*5. Be Silent When You Know Little About the Subject.*   Do not write about subjects you know little about. And do not assume that you are knowledgeable about a subject just because it is familiar to you.

*6. Reserve Judgment.*   Reticent styles can be very assertive, but the author usually forms opinions slowly, reserving judgment until all the facts are in.

The writer does not feel constrained to answer every question or address every problem the moment it is presented. One can, in effect, say, "I would like to study the situation and respond later." Or "It's too early to reach any conclusions in this matter." Or "I have to confer with others before saying any more."

*7. Study the Subject at Length.*   Study a subject extensively before making absolute assertions about it. And consider mentioning in your essay the time spent studying the issue.

Reticent styles often refer to or describe the process and extent of research.

*8. Make Every Word Count.*   After studying and evaluating a subject carefully, you might want to state your response rather forcefully, almost as a principle or maxim.

There is a tendency in reserved styles to invest what little is said with heightened significance, presenting it as "the last word" on the subject or as the product of some special vantage point—experience, long observation, review of the preceding dialogue, or expertise.

*9. Avoid Confrontations and Emotional Issues.*   There is good reason to refuse to respond to idle questions and aggressive inquiry, and to sidestep comment on volatile or emotional issues. This averts antagonism and leaves you with a clean slate. If social or political fortunes change, neither side will be able to blame you.

*10. Delegate Speaking.*   You can avoid talking if you have someone else speak for you, a spokesperson or agent.

Although it is effective in many cases, this ploy may backfire if the person who speaks for you does too good a job. And you have to be careful about which opportunities for speaking you delegate.

If the subject is trivial, consider asking a subordinate to handle it. If the subject or occasion is ceremonial and significant, you should usually handle it yourself.

If the subject is dangerous, weigh the risks and rewards carefully. Speaking up yourself may win you credit for strength, decisiveness, and courage but may also draw fire. Yet asking an expendable subordinate to speak for you on dangerous occasions might look cowardly.

One alternative is to refer the problem to a higher court, disclaiming personal authority to address the issue and deferring to your superiors or to some higher agency.

*11. Take Action.*   Instead of talking or writing, you can take action. The message may be clearer. Or you can use actions to support your meaning, to take the place of evidence.

It is not simply a matter of "actions speaking louder than words." It also concerns how deeds and words are related to each other. People who do not practice what they preach are seen as hypocrites. Those who talk a lot but do nothing lose our respect.

*12. Be Tentative.*   If you do not have time to study a subject at length, describe your findings as tentative, your decisions as still under review.

A reticent style may be purposely inconclusive. Opinions may be stated with various qualifications, as in "It appears to me that . . ." or "My initial reaction would have to be that. . . ."

*13. Use Silence to Your Advantage.*   Remember that silence can convey meaning. Silence in the presence of any behavior effectively condones it. Silence when you are asked to support someone's opinion may be more effective than speaking against it.

Avoiding communication with someone can be an insult, a punishment, or a means of ostracism. It can imply that you have greater status or rank, that others must come to you and wait until you are willing to be addressed.

Reserve about a subject may also signal its importance or gravity or lend it an aura of mystery.

*14. Listen and Doubt.*   Listen to and respect the opinions of others. Do not assume that you are the first or the only person who recognizes the truth about an issue.

But be cautious about believing everything you hear or read. Always express reservations or doubts.

## Being Outspoken

The relative outspokenness of a style is inferred from how much important or significant information it reveals, including so-called inside information and aspects of the author's identity, beliefs, or emotional state.

How *much* an author says is also relevant, but a reticent style may also be lengthy at times. And thoroughness is not necessarily a feature of loquacity.

A better measure of outspokenness is how frequently an author speaks and how many subjects the author speaks on. People who seem—or claim—to know something about everything are obviously outspoken, as are people who speak or write with no provocation.

The following strategies can increase the outspokenness of your style:

*1. Speak Often.*    If you wish to attract favorable attention, you should seek out opportunities to contribute to the discussion, to express your ideas in words and print.

How often and how long you should speak depends on the circumstances, but obviously you should not monopolize the floor, even when you have been asked to speak or have much to offer.

The same is true in writing. Readers have to be given opportunities to contribute to the essay as they read it, to fill in ideas you have sketched out or to reach their own conclusions.

*2. Bring up New Subjects.*    Outspoken people propose topics for discussion. They control the agenda of debate by focusing the groups' attention on the issues that they feel are important.

Even irrelevant or impertinent topics may serve. In friendly conversation, the person who brings up strange, inappropriate, or surprising subjects may seem witty and interesting.

*3. Fill Silences.*    An outspoken person does not let the conversation lapse. Silences are filled.

At worst, this process may result in empty chatter. At best, it represents very polite and ethical behavior. The speaker relieves awkwardness and tension with wit. Other people's lame remarks are rescued. Remarks that have trailed off into inarticulateness are gracefully rephrased and finished.

*4. Emphasize Diversity.*    Outspokenness works best when the writer has many different ideas, presents information in different styles, or can vary the focus. Though it may be clearer and more accurate to stay on the same subject and develop it at length, thoroughness is more likely to become tedious.

*5. Do Not Talk About Yourself Unnecessarily.*    Much unpleasant outspokenness is based on self-promotion and self-interest. The writer talks exclusively about himself or herself.

Effective speaking and writing leaves the impression that the author has the interests of the audience at heart, even when the author's personal experience and private goals are the immediate focus.

*6. Do Not Be Afraid to Make Mistakes.*    One does not earn a reputation for outspokenness by being cautious. Speak up even at the risk of failure.

The potential damage can be limited by taking a performer's stance. Try out "material" on an audience. Perfect the style by changing the presentation to get a better response. Distance yourself from the reception the material or ideas receive.

Risk taking is important because ideas you keep to yourself do you no good. You do not get credit for things you do not say.

*One note of caution:* Some discourse communities are less tolerant of mistakes than others. You have to gauge the situation carefully.

If the audience appreciates risk taking, then speak your mind freely. Some mistakes, commonplace wit, and pointless conjecture will be accepted as a normal part of the creative process. Unfortunately, audiences will sometimes encourage risk taking at first, and then turn on you once you have spoken.

If the audience is intolerant of error, then reticence is the preferable style.

*7. Avoid Perfectionism.*  If you never speak until you have absolute control of the subject, you may well miss the best moment for speaking. Someone else will beat you to the mark. They may not express themselves beautifully or completely, but they will get credit for the idea nevertheless.

If you never show your writing to others until it is absolutely perfect, you may end up writing one piece while everyone else is writing ten. And quantity counts for something. On the job, a person who writes ten good reports seems more productive than a person who writes one that is excellent. In creative writing, the quantity written or, to be more accurate, the copiousness of the author's imagination is one measure of quality.

In the attempt to be "perfect," you may lose perfection, sacrificing the attractions of spontaneity for the sake of precision and refinement.

*8. Speak on Whatever Subject Is at Hand.*  An outspoken writer will find something to say about anything.

Don't assume too quickly that you know nothing about a subject. Many topics that appear highly abstract or inaccessible can be intelligently and effectively addressed on the level of common sense and everyday experience.

## Readiness

The choice to speak is not always one's own. We are often called on to make decisions before we feel ready to, to discuss matters not entirely familiar to us, and to report on subjects that require study. Crises do not wait for our convenience. In such instances, the question is not *whether* to speak but how to *prepare* oneself for discourse as quickly and effectively as possible.

Responding to these situations effectively requires skills of memory, invention, and judgment. We will discuss these areas further in subsequent chapters.

Here are some suggestions for handling difficult subjects and situations:

**1. *Cut Through Technical Jargon.*** Sometimes you can find something to say about an unfamiliar and difficult topic when you replace the technical terminology with everyday terms.

**2. *Focus on Particulars.*** If you do not entirely understand the concepts and abstractions being discussed, try focusing on particulars—on specific instances or individual cases.

**3. *Change the Forum.*** If you feel unable to speak in a particular setting, consider changing the forum, situation, or medium in which the communication will take place. For example, a more private, confidential, or "intimate" discussion might seem safer than discourse in a public forum.

Another example: Instead of airing your opinions in a widely distributed form—and thereby attracting too much attention and opposition—you might choose to write to or talk with just one or two key people, especially at first. If the smaller audience responds favorably, you might then feel better able to address the larger audience.

**4. *Wait Until Someone Else Has Spoken.*** After someone else has spoken, you can often speak with less fear of contradiction. But you have to be careful.

It always sounds lame and self-congratulatory to say "that's exactly what I was thinking" after someone else has ventured an idea. You seem to be trying to share the spotlight.

More effective stances include (a) criticizing what the speaker has said; (b) contradicting what the speaker has said; (c) supporting or seconding the speaker (see item 5); (d) refining the speaker's ideas; and (e) discussing implementation.

**5. *Support Other People's Ideas.*** It is safer to pose as a supporter of others' ideas than as a proponent of your own views. You can speak at length and not be blamed for it if you appear to be seconding someone else.

Gossip, rumors, and slander are often spread in this manner, but more sophisticated discourse may use the same device. One approach is to offer opinions not as your own but as accepted wisdom, as the standard practice in such cases or as the historical and general view of a subject.

**6. *Limit the Topic.*** Outspokenness is easier if you focus on some small or limited aspect of the subject, either one you already know something about or a part of the subject you can study and research more quickly than the entire issue.

*7. Take a Speculative Stance.* If the topic is relatively unfamiliar, take an avowedly speculative stance. Raise questions and discuss the range of issues involved rather than attempting to offer solutions.

*8. Characterize the Subject as Complex.* You can speak up with greater impunity if you characterize the subject as difficult and complex or describe the situation as unsettled and fluid. No one can fault you for failing to define an ill-defined problem.

*9. Limit the Agenda or Focus of the Debate.* It is possible to limit the agenda of debate, to focus attention on "safe" topics and to keep more dangerous issues off the floor. This can be extremely effective, though of course its ethics are questionable.

A clever (or devious) speaker will draw our eyes to a particular interpretation of the subject, knowing how difficult it can be (once the assertion has been made) for audiences to see the subject any differently or to add more questions to the agenda the speaker has framed.

You see this happening in statements like "It is primarily a question of unfair trading practices on the part of our competitors" (omitting discussion of our incompetence in management or lack of vision), or "The report will outline the most productive uses of the land" (omitting emotional and environmental considerations).

*10. Pursue Tangents.* Channel conversation onto tangential topics you feel comfortable discussing. If the immediate topic is a statistical analysis of the stock market, for instance, try to shift the focus toward investments in real estate, which you understand better, or toward the deceptiveness of statistics.

*11. Shift the Focus.* Recast the subject within a wider perspective that allows you to address it safely. For example, if the immediate topic is baseball, about which you know little and care less, change the focus to "entertainments" or "sports as an industry."

*12. Change the Subject.* Learn to change the subject gracefully. This strategy may be difficult with a topic recently addressed, since people may not feel that they have said all they wanted to say about it yet. And the person who introduced the topic originally will probably try to draw discussion back to it.

But after an issue has been "on the floor" for some time, a change may be welcome. If the subject of extended discussion and interest has been Mayan burial practices, find an opportunity to introduce a somewhat related topic—like the ritual nature of play or the recent rediscovery of an ancient crop. Extreme changes of topic may seem rude. Shift gradually to something more congenial. (After talking about the ritual nature of play, you could safely bring up lacrosse or soccer.)

Strategies for redirecting the conversation apply to writing as well as to speaking. Ongoing written debate in a field of study or a discourse community tends to focus on some current issue at length until the topic is exhausted, the problem resolved, or someone changes the subject.

*13. Confess Ignorance.*   You can speak safely on almost any subject if you begin by professing a degree of ignorance. After that you can present your opinions and ideas without the burden of posing as an authority.

Expressing a degree of doubt or uncertainty can be fairly attractive, and it protects you from harm should your comments attract wide criticism. If the original statement was only conjectural or speculative, it is easy to retrieve the situation by disavowing belief in the statement, saying something like "It was just a suggestion" or "That was just for the sake of argument."

*14. Focus on Personal Experience.*   You can speak safely on a wide range of subjects if you limit your comments to whatever personal experience you have with the subject. It is hard to attack such remarks, since no one can be more of an expert about an experience than the person to whom it happened.

*15. Express Emotions.*   State, show, or describe your emotional response to the subject. One can have feelings about anything. Expressing emotions also makes you seem more open or self-revelatory.

Like experiences, emotions are personal property, not especially susceptible to question or doubt.

## EXERCISE A

Rephrase the following passages to make them sound more reticent.

1. *The Maltese Falcon* is a great movie.
2. I saw a new movie last night that I really liked.
3. Interferon therapy has not fulfilled its promise as a cancer cure.
4. People will never recycle plastic until there is profit in it.
5. We should send in the army.
6. Sell petrochemical stocks immediately.
7. The man is obviously neurotic.

8. The welfare system needs better management and better funding.
9. That new chemistry professor is awful.
10. It's not every day that you can get quality office space for such a low cost per square foot. We have to move fast. Interest rates are likely to rise. And there are other potential buyers. This opportunity could disappear overnight.

## EXERCISE B

Rephrase the following passages to make them sound more outspoken.

1. The possibilities of public health insurance need closer study.
2. I have no opinion about how much professional football players are paid.
3. What a lovely child.
4. Our studies show that in the period between 1955 and 1975, the incidence of electrical fires was greater in houses with aluminum, rather than copper, wiring.
5. I'm really not familiar with the phenomenon of "split personalities."
6. There are a number of options. We could provide tax incentives to businesses willing to move into the district. We could condemn properties and raze them. We could try to establish an arts and crafts center in some of the abandoned warehouse space. Or we could wait for supply and demand to run its course. Private citizens might take advantage of bargain prices and decide on their own to renovate houses in the area. We should consider all the possibilities.
7. Waste not, want not.
8. Some experts claim that an increase in carbon dioxide in the atmosphere will lead to global warming—the so-called greenhouse effect. But this is still largely a matter of conjecture.

## *WHEN TO BE RETICENT*

Saying little or nothing can be an ethical, attractive, and pragmatic style. You should consider being reticent

- when doing nothing is preferable to action or change
- when you have no opinion on the subject
- when you are uninformed
- when times are perilous
- when outspokenness would be inconsiderate
- when speaking would reopen wounds

- when you are new to the community or group
- when the subject is complex and needs study
- when others are speaking

## WHEN TO BE OUTSPOKEN

We admire people who are outspoken when the cause, content, style, or situation seems to justify their outspokenness. Speaking up is appropriate

- when the cause is significant or the circumstances pressing, as in a crisis
- when the content is original, amusing, or interesting
- when you want to be heard or noticed
- in response to an inquiry
- when others have previously offered opinions or made revelations
- when you wish to be helpful or forthcoming
- when you are faced with a dilemma

---

### GAINS AND LOSSES

---

#### ◀ RETICENCE ▶

| **Advantages** | **Disadvantages** |
|---|---|
| Relatively safe and easy | Attracts little attention |
| Buys time | Not interesting |
| Lets others commit first | Less opportunity for success |

---

### GAINS AND LOSSES

---

#### ◀ OUTSPOKENNESS ▶

| **Advantages** | **Disadvantages** |
|---|---|
| Attracts attention | May be dangerous |
| Earns credit | Receives blame |
| Actively creates change | Creates antagonism |
| Tests ideas and styles | May be criticized |
| Makes space on the agenda | May lose strategic advantage |
| May make you a leader | Creates responsibility |
| May create interest | May be boring |

---

## EXERCISE C

In the following situations, should you be reticent or outspoken? Why?

1. A friend cheats on a test.
2. A friend cheats on her income tax.
3. Your new car isn't as good as it was claimed to be, though nothing is mechanically wrong with it.
4. There is a small but obvious flaw in your new car's upholstery.
5. You figure out an easier way to manage a routine procedure at the office.
6. You discover a more economical way to produce something at work. It could be very profitable.
7. You notice that a friend is doing something the hard way.
8. You notice that a total stranger is doing something the hard way.
9. You have been asked to design or implement a new procedure.
10. You have found a nice restaurant—excellent food, service, and atmosphere, and never too crowded.
11. You have seen a movie you enjoyed very much.
12. You have an opportunity to retell an off-color joke you heard recently.
13. You find an early American spear point at a site much older than any previously documented prehistoric settlement.
14. While working at an observatory, you notice a blotch on a photographic plate. It could be either a new asteroid or a mistake you made in photo-processing.

## EXERCISE D

Analyze each of the following situations and decide what you should do—specifically, (a) whether you should act, keep silent, or speak up; (b) to whom you should speak and why; (c) when you should speak; and (d) how you should behave or how you should phrase your comments to achieve the best effect.

1. You have heard your neighbors cursing, threatening, and screaming at their children. You suspect child abuse.
2. You see some fellow students vandalizing your school.
3. You find that your tires have been slashed.
4. You see the results of recent vandalism and are annoyed that people would be so pointlessly destructive, though you suffer no personal loss.
5. You notice that certain run-down buildings in a downtown area seem to be architecturally interesting. They have been recently condemned and are likely to be demolished soon.

6. You run into someone you would like to meet, but at the moment they look busy or preoccupied. Variations: the person is well known, popular, or influential, and you are not; or you are selling stocks, real estate, or artwork the person might be interested in.

7. A colleague severely criticizes a project you have been working on, without directly mentioning or criticizing you.

8. You have no fixed opinion about advertising aimed at selling toys to children, but you are asked to comment on the subject.

9. You strongly believe that abortion is wrong (or a right).

10. You are new to an organization, but after a few months on the job you are confident that you know a better way to get things done or have found the answer to a problem that your superiors (or people who have been with the organization longer) have been trying to solve for some time.

11. You don't know exactly how to say what you mean, or you haven't quite figured out what you think about the subject being discussed.

12. Based on your research, you have come up with a theory that seems to contradict generally accepted ideas about psychological depression (or management style, or the decline of empires, or upward mobility in society).

13. On a previous occasion you have been ridiculed or criticized by the group for your opinion of a certain candidate for public office, but you think he or she is misunderstood. You find yourself discussing politics with the same audience again.

14. You know little or nothing about the funding of public services, but you feel strongly that your local police officers are overpaid and underworked. You have seen a number of them in the doughnut shop down the street for hours at a time.

## *Wider Implications*

Reticence and outspokenness are partially questions of secrecy, privacy, copyright, and access to information. They are related to property, privilege, and power.

We are all justifiably suspicious of decisions made behind closed doors. They seem to exclude us from determining our own fate and from judging the propriety of the decision makers. People who do not explain their actions or support their opinions both fascinate and appall us.

To be denied information is to be ostracized. Without knowledge of procedures within an organization, you cannot get things done. Without knowledge of others' values and beliefs, you do not know how to approach them. You are constantly off balance, uncertain about what to say and what reaction you will receive. It is like playing a game where everyone else knows the rules.


CONFIDENCE

Outspokenness and reticence are both motivated by the writer's security, authority, and self-confidence.

Impetuous writers either feel secure in their authority or do not fear contradiction and criticism. More cautious writers may arrive at the same ends by a different route. In order to develop confidence and expertise, they wait and learn and think before writing.


RETICENCE AND THE COMPOSING PROCESS

The sense that one knows the right answer is a state of mind, with no necessary relationship to true knowledge, expertise, or wisdom, to age or intelligence, to social standing or practical experience, or to perceptiveness and provincialism. Age, scholarship, and insight can make it easier to speak. Or they can reduce us again to silence—as experience shows us how little we actually do know or how well informed others can be.

We prepare all our lives for the occasions when we will be called on to speak or write or act. What is said or written, even spontaneously, is directed and channeled by our cumulative past, influenced by what we have said and done previously in similar circumstances, what we have heard others say or seen in their responses, and how we have wished to sound and wished to be perceived.

An essay is not written in the time it takes to put words on paper, but in the hours and years of experience and education that shape our opinions and character, our knowledge of the subject, our habits of thinking and patterns of behavior. The time actually spent in writing or speaking our minds is miniscule compared to the time it takes to get ready to speak or write.


RETICENCE AND EXPERTISE

Reticence is related to becoming an expert on a subject. In that sense, all one's education, research, observation, experience, and thoughts about a subject are part of the writing, or "composing," process. Writing and speaking skills are not just the narrow concerns of English and speech courses, but the wider ends of education and self-improvement. "Expertise" is a fund of ideas that permits one to discourse about a subject, whether in the spoken word, on paper, or through meaningful action. "Expertise" is also the *ability* to discourse about a subject, since concepts and facts alone do not make an expert.

The true expert tests, refines, and restructures concepts, arriving at new ideas, developing new solutions to problems, and creating new interpretations of the facts, making sure that he or she has something worth saying before communicating the finding to colleagues. These mental and physical processes are no different from the processes involved in writing. The scientist's hypothesis or theory is just a particular species of assertion, in the same class with thesis statements and logical propositions.

### RETICENCE, RESEARCH, and REVISION

Like education, research is a slow process, a reticent behavior. Researchers take time to study the subject in detail. They are cautious about drawing conclusions. They constantly revise their conclusions as new evidence and ideas are found—hence the meticulousness of experimental research and the time-consuming nature of scholarly reading. These activities contribute to both the development of expertise and the development of an essay. They give substance to a writer's authority and provide part of the body of an essay.

Both reticence and research imply ongoing revision, not just of the author's understanding of the subject, but also of the view of the subject held by the discourse community.

### CERTAINTY AND DOUBT

Underlying the decision to be reticent or outspoken is an inherent paradox. If we wait until we are absolutely prepared to speak about a subject, completely ready to respond to a situation, we may never speak at all. One can never feel totally secure that all the facts are in hand. One can never be sure that every factor has been considered, every expert consulted, every mishap foreseen. Yet if we speak too soon, we run the risk of seeming unprepared, ignorant, foolhardy, or naive. And the dilemma is compounded with an irony: we can never be ready to speak unless we have already spoken.

### RETICENCE AND SOCIAL READINESS

The question of when to speak or write is not just based on knowledge. It is influenced by maturation, by the level of acceptance one receives from one's audience, and by the development of a sense of identity, both in general and with respect to one's social or professional role. We speak when we are ready to—socially, psychologically, and professionally—or as ready as we can hope to be. Because our knowledge is always incomplete and our spirit perpetually unready, we find ways to do the best we can.

### RETICENCE AND *"KAIROS"*

As discussed in Chapter 1, *kairos* is the term in classical rhetoric for the moment when it is propitious for a person to speak—"the right time" for addressing an issue. For the Greek philosophers, *kairos* was an almost mystical convergence of the ideal occasion, forum, audience, and state of knowledge. One remained silent until all of the circumstances and signs were favorable, until the time was ripe.

The alternatives to *kairos* were *tō prepon*, the skill of adapting to existing circumstances or making one's speech appropriate, and *tō dynaton*, which might be construed as the art of changing circumstances to suit the orator.

### OUTSPOKENNESS, *"TŌ PREPON,"* AND *"TŌ DYNATON"*

Outspokenness is related to appropriateness and action. It does not wait until the right time for speaking arrives—preparing for it through study, practice, and observation—but attempts to adapt to the present moment, speaking up in spite of unfavorable circumstances or limitations of knowledge. Or it attempts to change the situation—restructuring the occasion to suit the speaker rather than changing the speech to suit the occasion.

## *Conclusion*

Much of what can be said about reticence and outspokenness seems to be common sense, and well it should. Common sense tells us when we are ignorant or insecure and should keep our mouths shut. Common sense tells us when it is better to say nothing. Common sense tells us when we should stop talking and start doing something about a problem. But common sense can be uncommon. And there are times when common sense should be ignored.

Your interests and ideas have no better or more appropriate advocate than you yourself. Don't expect others to stand up for you.

## ASSIGNMENT A:   Rising to the Occasion

1. Write about a person, group, belief, institution, creature, or object that does not get the respect or attention it deserves, taking the role of some-

one motivated to speak for the underdog. Make sure you choose a genuinely needy cause. Do not presume, for example, that "the flag" or "patriotism" need defense if your audience does not truly disrespect them. The absence of visible or vocal support does not imply disrespect. It may simply reflect a perference for avoiding ostentation and chauvinistic display.

2. Identify what seems to you to be a clear and continuing injustice— either a familiar injustice or one commonly overlooked. Focus on a general case rather than a specific instance. Take the role of advocate, calling people's attention to the problem and arguing for some remedy of the situation. You do not need to be an expert on the subject to perceive injustice. And you do not need to have a ready or simple solution to the problem. Persistent injustices seldom have any simple remedy.

3. Consider a situation where speaking up on an issue may result in some harm to your position, reputation, or well-being (or that of the profession, family, or group you represent) or may focus unwelcome attention on you. Either write directly on the issue, speaking in your own voice, or find a way to address the matter while at the same time distancing yourself from any harmful effects or unwelcome associations.

For example, an author might wish to speak on behalf of a conservative or liberal cause without being considered either liberal or conservative. Or an author might wish to question the business practices or environmental responsibility of a local employer without damaging either the firm or the employment status of a relative who works there.

## ASSIGNMENT B:   Deliberative Discourse and Problem Solving

1. Identify a problem that lends itself to some practical solution (for example, a long commute that could be shortened by the construction of a bridge, or multiple forms to fill out that could be consolidated into a single master form). Describe the problem and argue on behalf of the solution you are proposing, to the exclusion of other possible solutions or the continuation of the status quo.

2. Contribute to the local or national political debate on a fairly concrete issue (as opposed to a matter of human rights or justice). Propose a course of action or support one already proposed by someone else. You may need to demonstrate that your course of action is more expedient than others.

## ASSIGNMENT C:   Promises, Professions, and Avowals

1. Explain and defend in writing the degree of commitment or adherence you feel to a particular idea, belief, institution, group, or point of view. Doubt, irresolution, and uncertainty are also acceptable stances.

2. Write an essay that defines, explains, and argues on behalf of some goal for yourself or for the community at large, or that makes some personal or public guarantee, promise, or resolution, discussing its importance, meaning, applications, and consequences.

What would you have to do to meet the goal, and is it likely you will be able to follow through on the promise? You might also wish to discuss the general role and character of such promises and the degree of faith we should have in their validity (as in the case of campaign promises, or promotional claims for products, or a dream of making one's fortune or becoming famous).

You could focus on some limited and personal goal, if you are able to make it relevant and important to your audience, or on a more public or familial responsibility or objective. It is important to appear credible and self-aware.

3. Discuss the role of interpersonal commitments, trust, or shared goals in some aspect of discourse or the community.

# 4

# Assertiveness and Deference

A soft answer turneth away wrath. —Proverbs 15:1

Confidence often labors under the disadvantage of being regarded as arrogance. —Quintilian

I wish to persuade women to endeavour to acquire strength, both of mind and body, and to convince them that . . . soft phrases, susceptibility of heart, delicacy of sentiment, and refinement of taste, are almost synonymous with epithets of weakness. —Mary Wollstonecraft

## Speaking With Authority

Sometimes those who speak the loudest have the least to say, and those who speak with the least confidence are most worth listening to. It is a paradox of authority that diffidence comes with knowledge; the more you know about a subject the less certain you may be of your conclusions. And yet you can't be an authority without being sure of yourself.

This is a stylistic problem. We associate assertiveness with both good *and* bad qualities.

### ◀ ASSERTIVE ▶

| Good Qualities | Bad Qualities |
| --- | --- |
| leadership | autocracy |
| strength | arrogance |
| expertise | bias |

We also associate nonassertive or deferential voices with good and bad qualities.

### ◀ NONASSERTIVE ▶

| Good Qualities | Bad Qualities |
|---|---|
| openness | submissiveness |
| politeness | weakness |
| humility | uncertainty |

The trouble is that you can't always tell which kind of assertiveness or deference you are dealing with. Is an assertive person truly knowledgeable or simply opinionated? Is a deferential person mature and open to new ideas or youthfully indecisive?

There are further complications. People who are otherwise sure of themselves may be intimidated by the circumstances or audience and, as a result, behave and speak submissively. People who are intimidating or dramatic may impress us in spite of intellectual mediocrity.

The danger lies in dismissing the one group outright and falling for the other. The worth of the person, idea, and perspective may have nothing to do with the worth of the style.

## Finding a Voice

When you speak, your tone of voice is crucial. You can make a compliment sound like criticism. A suggestion can sound like a command. If the intonation is wrong, an important discovery can seem commonplace. The same is true in writing, though intonation, volume, and accent must be suggested in other ways.

This is partially a matter of emphasis—the degree of assertiveness shown in the presentation. It is affected by your

- character
- rank or status
- maturity
- conviction
- emotional state
- confidence
- relationship to the audience,

as reflected in your style.

Once you decide to speak up, you have to decide what level of assertiveness is appropriate, what level will be effective or attractive, and what level you can manage.

## *Being Assertive*

The relative assertiveness of style is determined by how weakly or aggressively it promotes the author's view of the subject, the author's status, or the author's place in our attention and consideration. This can be very difficult to gauge. Although the appearance of assertiveness may be gained by making strong, unqualified statements or by choosing an exceptionally flamboyant, loud, or peculiar mode of delivery, quiet insistence and patient, considerate explanation can be as emphatic and effective in their own right as the most absolute generalizations and the most dramatic presentation.

In general, if you wish to emphasize your point, the following strategies can be helpful:

*1. Reduce or Eliminate Weak Qualifiers and Self-Depreciation.*    Do not minimize your own ideas or express doubt in your own authority. Do not undercut your assertions with weak qualifiers like *maybe, sometimes, perhaps,* or *in some cases.*

If you have a good idea, don't undersell it or apologize for it. You can present it inoffensively without also qualifying it out of existence.

*2. Increase the Force of Your Assertions.*    Use strong qualifiers like *always, most, necessary,* and *must* to characterize your claims. Of if that seems too strong, use slightly weaker qualifiers like *many, probably,* and *ought.*

There is an "all or nothing" attitude behind assertiveness, a feeling that the author's position on the matter is the only right way of interpreting the facts or resolving the dispute.

*3. Increase the Level of Generality.*    Extend the applicability of your claim from individual cases to the general case. Instead of saying "I like river rafting," say "River rafting is fun" or "Many people enjoy active pastimes."

*4. Use Direct Statements.*    Do not be indirect in expressing your ideas. State your opinions straightforwardly and explicitly. In extreme cases, use direct address and commands or warnings.

Conciseness may also be important. Complex verbiage can decrease the force of your assertions.

*5. Take the Role of Spokesperson or Authority.*    Present your view as representative of what "we" all believe or feel: "It has become clear to many in the profession that conventional explanations of this phenomenon are inadequate. We have for some time questioned accepted theories without being able to offer any viable substitute."

6. *Characterize Your Own Point of View Favorably.* Assertiveness may be expressed through positive characterizations of the author's opinions or stance: "It should be obvious that . . ." or "It is hard to avoid the conclusion that . . ." or "The most careful and systematic dissection revealed no sign of. . . ."

7. *Take an Objective Stance.* An impersonal stance can be authoritative if it assigns credit for the claim to some process that seems unassailable, not the result of human interpretation: "The experiment demonstrated that. . . ."

8. *Criticize or Ignore Other Points of View.* An assertive style may emphasize attack or antagonism. It may imply or describe the existence of organized opposition. It may pointedly attempt to refute other possible points of view or simply refuse to acknowledge that other points of view are possible. It tends to be inherently competitive and combative.

9. *Highlight the Main Issues.* Reducing the problem to fewer issues or simpler terms can make your style more emphatic, though perhaps less accurate. Complexities and details seem academic or bureaucratic. We expect leaders to cut through Gordian knots and petty complications.

Sometimes, however, we mistake reductiveness for vision.

10. *Express Strong Emotion.* Highly emotional or obviously committed styles are often more assertive. They imply direct advocacy, that the speaker is willing to fight for his or her point of view.

Even seemingly "weak" emotional outbursts like crying can at times have this effect. And anger, ironically, can imply a loss of control, undercutting the authority of the speaker. Usually, however, anger serves to intimidate or emphasize.

11. *Decrease the Focus on Evidence and Support.* The more you have to defend and explain your ideas, the more it seems that they need defense. Extensive evidence starts to sound like rationalization.

Substitute vivid examples, images, and anecdotes. State assertions as maxims, axioms, laws, or principles.

12. *Change Terminology.* Do not automatically state your ideas in words you have heard before. In doing so, you may suppress or simply not express original thoughts and perceptions.

Do not automatically accept the phraseology of others. The words other people use may support their own point of view, implying perspectives and attitudes you do not agree with.

Sometimes inventing your own terminology can heighten the impact of your style—and convey the impression of originality, whether or not it is warranted.

*13. Focus on Differences Between Your Ideas and the Status Quo.*   Do not immediately assume that your ideas are the same as everyone else's, even when you agree with truisms about the subject or with commonly held opinions. Look for and exploit the areas where your views differ from, extend, or refine common knowledge.

*14. Don't Fear Giving Offense.*   Do not try to please everyone or be too safe. At the price of avoiding negative reactions, we often sacrifice quality. In order to please people, we water down our ideas and style so much that nothing distinctive is left.

*15. Be Polite but Stand up for Your Ideas.*   Don't confuse social deference with intellectual deference. Politeness and respect do not require you to stifle your voice and vitiate your ideas. If your audience expects that of you, then your audience does not particularly deserve politeness and respect, though perhaps some caution would be in order.

Respect for the audience can be separated from the issue at hand, so you can both defer to the audience and disagree with its views on a particular subject.

*16. Do Not Be Intimidated by Criticism.*   Sometimes criticism reflects social pressure rather than constructive advice. In such cases, you should try to ignore or attack the criticism and defend your ideas. Do not respond by qualifying or understating your claims (unless personal safety, emotional well-being, and your position are at stake).

Listen to criticism and take it into account. Sometimes critics help you refine your ideas. Sometimes they show you where you have claimed too much or too little, or where you need to do further research. Sometimes they tell you what point of view you should try to refute more directly. Sometimes they represent an audience you never intended to address, and therefore can discount.

And sometimes they are wrong.

*17. Demonstrate Authority.*   The most ethical form of assertiveness, of course, comes from true authority.

Assertiveness may be implied or expressed in terms of knowledgeability, scholarship, and objectivity. Authors may strengthen and amplify their statements by backing them up with extensive evidence, testimony, and corroboration.

## *Being Deferential*

Deference is not necessarily a matter of being unassertive. It involves respect for the ideas of others and distance from one's own beliefs, as well as polite understatement. Deference reduces the emphasis on the author and the author's opinions.

The following strategies can help you reduce the assertiveness of your style:

**1. *Decrease the Level of Generality in Your Claims.*** An unassertive style often refuses to generalize about the subject, presenting isolated cases as unique with no reference or relevance to other, similar circumstances.

The same effect might be achieved by emphasizing personal opinion or personal experience: "Well it's only my opinion, but it's seemed to me that . . ." or "The one time I had to deal with that we decided to. . . ."

**2. *Qualify Your Assertions.*** An unassertive style often qualifies or undercuts its own assertions. Words like *maybe, perhaps, possibly,* and *seems* become common.

Assertions may be criticized even as they are made: "I'd like to think that a media blitz is the best option, but of course it might just annoy people."

Qualifying or limiting the applicability of your assertions can make them more palatable. Instead of saying "Lawyers are the scavengers of justice" say "Lawyers may in some respects seem like scavengers" or "There are, of course, some lawyers who are little better than vultures."

**3. *Acknowledge Other Points of View.*** Try to include some appreciation of other points of view in your discussion. Show the connections and distinctions between your ideas and those with which your audience is familiar.

Even if they do not appear in the finished essay, weigh alternate opinions and shades of interpretation carefully. Do not settle on one opinion to the exclusion of all others and assume that it is completely true. This process of weighing and testing ideas is the essence of research, education, consideration of others, and revision.

**4. *Do Not Fake Authority.*** Admit the limitations of your knowledge and experience. Say what you can comfortably support and no more.

If you have no particular opinion about a subject, do not try to hide that fact behind assertive platitudes or a cringingly deferential style. Study the issue and form an opinion (see Part III of this book), or excuse yourself from discussing it.

**5. *Seek Common Ground.*** You can often avoid giving offense by by finding some common ground with the audience: "We all share a common interest in the economic well-being of the country, despite our differences about how it might be achieved" or "We all respect the importance of free speech."

*6. Include the Audience in Your Viewpoint.*    You can make assertions more acceptable by putting the audience on your side of the issue, as in "We all suffer when frivolous lawsuits cause insurance rates to go up." Since no one is likely to regard their own lawsuit as frivolous, everyone gets to side with you in blaming a hypothetical third party for the problem.

The same effect can sometimes be achieved by sharing the blame, as in "Every profession preys on its clientele; lawyers are no different from the rest of us."

A similar tactic can be seen in a statement like "Those familiar with the case are aware of the flaws in Wickersham's research design." This presumes that at least part of the audience shares the author's criticism, and it silences people unfamiliar with the situation.

These strategies can be especially useful when you feel otherwise compelled to state your claims in strong terms.

*7. Be Humble.*    Assertiveness can be tempered with humility. Be diffident about your accomplishments and give credit to others.

*8. Do the Work Meticulously.*    Patient attention to detail can justify assertiveness. It shows a willingness to do the menial labor of supporting and explaining a point, and therefore it seems deferential.

*9. Associate Your Work With Some Wider Goal.*    Any hint of personal profit or egotism can compromise your work and undercut your effectiveness.

You can reduce the self-interest of your claims by submerging them in a larger and admirable endeavor or by channeling your efforts toward benefiting the community. Personal distress about noise pollution in your neighborhood can be euphemized in a campaign to create a better environment for children. Advancing science can be the excuse for South Sea excursions and mountain-climbing expeditions. Children and science may be helped by these activities, but the individuals involved also profit.

This applies to expository and persuasive writing as well as to actions. If you write exclusively about yourself, your experiences, your ideas, or your beliefs, people may get annoyed. Incorporating a wider interest deflects this criticism.

*10. Be Indirect.*    If deference seems called for, you can still make your point by being indirect in expressing it. State ideas obliquely or metaphorically. Imply rather than assert. Use graceful ambiguity. Offer suggestions rather than present demands.

Avoid, however, expressing yourself in such muted terms that it becomes hard to recognize the point being made.

**11. *Use Questions.*** You can soften assertions by phrasing them as questions. The effect of this is to defer to the audience, leaving final judgment to others rather than attempting to offer a final judgment yourself.

**12. *Avoid Assertions.*** A deferential style may avoid assertion entirely, shifting the emphasis to report or description. Like questions, report and description leave interpretation and judgment to the audience. They provide and perhaps classify data, but do not explain it.

One variation of this is the research report, which recounts or describes other people's ideas but offers none of its own.

**13. *Focus on Common Knowledge.*** You can deemphasize your ideas by focusing on their similarity to common knowledge or accepted theory.

Do not go too far, however. Sometimes authors afraid of criticism suppress their ideas, substituting bland recitations of common knowledge and noncontroversial repetition of platitudes and truisms.

**14. *Be Hypothetical.*** Rather than asserting a point directly, you can state it as an appearance, hypothesis, or theory. For example, you might say "It is possible . . . ," "It appears . . . ," "It seems to me . . . ," or "One theory would be. . . ." If the claim is disproven or attacked, you can easily disassociate yourself from it.

Hypothetical statements are inherently less assertive than direct claims.

**15. *Build Authority.*** Consider beginning on a more quiet note and gradually building toward greater assertiveness as authority is established.

**16. *Distance Yourself From the Subject.*** Maintaining objective distance from the subject or issue can be a deferential posture as well as an assertive one. It protects authors from having to assert anything on their own authority, thereby removing the element of competition or threat from any pursuant discussion.

Distance also removes emotional involvement from the discussion, making it easier to discuss the matter rationally. It reduces the need to tread lightly around people's feelings.

**17. *Displace Assertions.*** Try displacing assertions. Express them as "possible" views or as the view a particular group might hold. For example, you could say "Lawsuit victims tend to regard lawyers as opportunistic vultures." If you agree with another author, present your case by supporting his or her opinions.

*18. Borrow Authority.*    If you are not regarded as enough of an authority to be safely assertive yourself, you can use such displacement to "borrow" expertise. Citing a respected authority in effect uses an expert witness to speak for you and deflects attention from yourself.

*19. Use Self-Depreciation.*    Self-depreciation can be used to qualify your assertions and to reduce the threat you pose to the ideas of others. For example, "I'm no expert, but it seems to me that . . ." or "In my limited experience, I've observed that . . ." or "This may seem superficial or simplistic, but could it be that . . . ?"

The self-criticism implied in such a stance may disarm the audience and deflect additional criticism or attack.

*20. Use Humor.*    Humor (other than ridicule) may serve to defuse potential argument and confrontation. It reduces tension and builds community. It can lower barriers of rank and expertise. And it undercuts the author's own authority by putting him or her in the somewhat submissive or deferential position of entertaining the audience.

## EXERCISE A

Rank the following statements from most to least assertive. Explain your rankings (differences of opinion are acceptable and likely).

1. The television news format is far too inflexible.
2. The formats of most television news programs are essentially the same.
3. Television news broadcasts bore me to death.
4. It would appear that the basic format of television news has become more and more settled, evolving to a point where there is little need for ingenuity.
5. The news usually starts out with major crime stories or tragedies. Then it covers public affairs. After that you get sports news and weather, or weather and sports news. Most of the time the show ends with some kind of human interest story.
6. Some might suggest that for all their superficial differences, television news programs are pretty much alike.
7. Doesn't it seem that the television news format has become less and less spontaneous—more predictable than it once was?
8. The television news format is fairly inflexible.
9. It seems like changing the channel doesn't make much difference. One television news show is a lot like another. But I'm no expert.
10. Most experts would agree that the television news format has become a settled genre, with little experimentation in the order or style of presentation.

## EXERCISE B

Rewrite the following statements to make them more assertive. Tell which strategies you used. Discuss the difference the revisions make in the statements' effect.

1. I don't like meatloaf.
2. The recent attempt to take over Mattel Corporation seems ill advised.
3. It seems to me that there could be some reason for disagreement here.
4. How could I help you?
5. I believe that the folder you just picked up might be mine.
6. According to some experts, the conventional interpretation of Michelangelo's frescos in the Sistine Chapel was based more on accumulated dirt and grime than on intentional gloominess in the painter's worldview.
7. Camaros have acquired the reputation, perhaps undeserved, of being showy but underpowered, with poor handling characteristics. They certainly look like performance cars, but some people claim that they aren't.
8. I wish you would stop disagreeing with everything I say.
9. Three presidents in a row were Republican. Social welfare budgets were cut. The economy became weak.
10. One rather gloomy hypothesis attributes the persistence of poverty to inevitable social stratification. If I understand this theory correctly, it implies that there will always be an impoverished class, that society is organized in "strata" or layers that function almost like ecological niches. As one group escapes poverty, another moves in (or is forced by circumstance) to fill the gap.

## EXERCISE C

Rewrite the following statements to make them more deferential. Tell which strategies you used. Discuss the difference your revisions make in the statement's effect.

1. Superconductivity will transform not only electronics but also our culture.
2. This was the most stupid and insane kind of military adventurism imaginable.
3. We think you blew it.
4. Dinosaurs were warmblooded.
5. There is no rest for the weary.
6. Business success is a simple matter of maximizing profits and minimizing expenses.
7. I'm serious. If you don't get your act together now, if you don't start

getting the work done on time, if you don't show some initiative and effort, you're fired.

**8.** Look out!

**9.** Guns don't kill people. People kill people.

**10.** "These are the times that try men's souls."

## WHEN TO BE ASSERTIVE

You should consider being assertive

- when there is immediate or pressing danger
- when you are an acknowledged expert
- when you occupy a position of leadership
- when your audience is set in its ways
- when you wish to challenge social and professional barriers

## WHEN TO BE DEFERENTIAL

Deference may be appropriate

- when you are being informative
- when you are unsure of yourself or the role expected of you
- when your position or status is weak
- when addressing those worthy of respect
- when communication and compromise are more important than "winning"
- when the evidence is unassailable
- when your position and authority are high or you wish to remove any social and professional barriers

---

### GAINS AND LOSSES

---

#### ◀ ASSERTIVENESS ▶

| Advantages | Disadvantages |
|---|---|
| Silences opposition | Polarizes discussion |
| Seems coherent and significant | Oversimplifies |
| Emotionally satisfying | Alienates part of audience |
| Hard to attack | Easy to dismiss |
| Extremely persuasive | Unethical or inconsiderate |
| Establishes strong bargaining position | In the long run, gives way to more moderate views |

## GAINS AND LOSSES

### ◀ DEFERENCE ▶

| Advantages | Disadvantages |
|---|---|
| Hides author's views | Limits originality |
| Pleases audience | Sacrifices individualism |
| Builds community | Offers little obvious leadership |
| Avoids competition | Invites attack |
| Deflects criticism | Elicits little respect or support |
| Encourages communication and compromise | May get nothing done |
| Gives audience a voice in decisions | Audience may take credit for decisions |

## EXERCISE C

Should you be assertive or deferential in the following situations? Why and how?

1. You are interviewing for a job at an old, established engineering firm and your credentials are weak.
2. You are interviewing for a job at a new engineering firm and have twenty years' experience in the profession.
3. You have been helpful and considerate to a friend who has not returned the favor. This person is important to you and is socially prominent. Now he or she is asking for further assistance—help with preparations for a social event–at a time when you have a business deadline to meet.
4. Your interpretation of a particular novel, movie, or essay contradicts accepted opinion but seems well supported by the evidence. You are writing for a teacher.
5. You have discovered what is almost certainly a new species of insect. Although you are well informed about the subject, you are not a professional entymologist.

## *Wider Implications*

Social order is in many ways dependent on patterns of assertiveness and deference. The fabric of society is a web of relationships, interweaving mutual respect with expressions of personal authority and status.

### ASSERTIVENESS AND ARROGANCE

There is no necessary correlation between assertiveness and arrogance or between deference and weakness, though people often confuse these qualities. And even though an assertive style may sound more expert to the layperson, there is no necessary correlation between assertiveness and knowledgeability.

### MASCULINE AND FEMININE STYLES

It is tempting, and not uncommon, to associate assertiveness and deference with masculine and feminine styles, even to argue that they are sex-linked and genetically programmed behaviors. However, one can see deference at work in any situation where the speaker or writer feels lower in status, authority, or age than the audience, regardless of sex.

### ASSERTIVENESS AND LEADERSHIP

Although it also might seem natural to equate assertiveness with leadership ability, many respected leaders are considered effective largely because of their willingness to listen, to learn from others. Assertiveness can be tyrannical and closeminded. And deference need not be submissive.

Assertiveness by itself is no qualification for leadership, no assurance that the speaker knows what he or she is doing, and no reason for putting trust in a person.

### ASSERTIVENESS AND CONTENT

Assertiveness and deference are perceived not just as the expression of your personality or voice, but as the visible reflection of confidence or doubt about your own opinions. We are suspicious of unassuming and unemphatic styles. If the cook doesn't eat the food, why should we?

But the author's assertiveness or deference is no measure of the validity of the concept presented. Lies can be emphatically stated. Truths can be stated shyly.

### THE QUESTION OF RANK

A deferential style implies that the audience has equal or higher "rank" or authority on the subject, that the author respects their opinion and defers to it. It is dialogic. Deference pays attention to the audience and invites discussion.

An assertive style, by contrast, implies that the author's status and knowledge is equal to or greater than the audience's. It favors monologue, requiring the audience to listen without responding.

Since people are very sensitive about matters of status and worth, the relative assertiveness of one's style is not likely to go unnoticed.

### ASSERTIVENESS AND CIRCUMSTANCE

Assertiveness is relative. It varies with the situation and circumstances. For example, the statement "It looks like rain" is more assertive when spoken by a meteorologist than by a philosopher. If you say "The freeway system is badly designed" while stuck in a traffic jam, it has a much different effect than the same assertion made in a formal report to the state legislature. The more public forum increases the assertiveness or force of the charge being made.

### LEARNED ASSERTIVENESS

Assertiveness or deference can be a learned behavior. We may acquire the habit from long experience and conditioning.

If our views are continually challenged and ridiculed, we may become less willing to assert them, less sure of ourselves. If people take us seriously, listening patiently to what we have to say no matter how ridiculous it may seem, we may acquire a high estimation of our own authority and worth and be more confident and assertive as a result.

## *Conclusion*

Both assertiveness and deference can defeat their own ends. In being assertive about our ideas, we may antagonize the very people we wish to convert. In being unassertive and deferential, we are apt to find ourselves not favored but poorly regarded—our ideas misunderstood or their significance unrecognized.

But assertiveness, when properly managed, is part of true authority and effective leadership. And a pleasing deference is not subservient but is the essential mechanism for debate, growth, and change, for the continuing discussion and revision of knowledge.

## ASSIGNMENT A:   Respect, Uncertainty, Fear, and Diffidence

1. Write on a topic or issue on which you are least somewhat uncertain and insecure, with no fixed opinion and limited experience. Try to keep the audience's attention and interest and attain some credibility.

2. Write for an audience that is confident of its opinions and authority on the subject you address, and possesses greater stature, age, and reputation than you. Without seeming presumptuous or seeming to challenge the audience, attempt to express and gain attention for your point of view.

3. Address an audience that might be antagonized by your proposal or point of view on an issue, and attempt to avoid generating unpleasantness or conflict without seeming too weak or sacrificing principle entirely.

## ASSIGNMENT B: Self-Confidence, Certainty, and Assertiveness

1. Write about some aspect of your own experiences, attitudes, possessions, family, and/or feelings—something on which no one can question your authority. Portray and discuss this subject without qualification or apology. Do attempt to make it interesting and significant, but to a certain extent let your subject speak for itself. Trying too hard to generate interest can actually suggest a degree of doubt.

2. Try to express one of your opinions in the strongest possible terms, and see how well you can sustain this extreme stance.

## ASSIGNMENT C: Complaint

1. In retrospect, assert your rights against some annoyance, private nuisance, irritation, humiliation, or bore (or boor) you have suffered from, or someone who has taken advantage of you, recently or in the distant past. Re-create or report enough of an incident for an audience to appreciate and understand your position. Avoid putting blame on yourself. Express anger, frustration, and other emotions openly.

2. Write a formal complaint about some public nuisance, problem, or state of affairs that affects and upsets you.

3. Complain about the performance of some product, employee, supervisor, clerk, public servant, or company.

## ASSIGNMENT D: Questions and Inquiries

1. Interview an audience no more expert about a subject than yourself. Write out in advance a series of questions intended to elicit a fairly complete and interesting portrait of the audience's experience with and thoughts about the matter. Write a coherent account of what you discovered, characterizing, interpreting, and organizing the information.

2. Prepare for (and actually conduct, if possible) an interview of an audience, perhaps another student, that has considerable expertise on a sub-

ject or experience with something you know little about. Your purpose is threefold: to educate yourself on the matter; to pass on the information you acquire to your own audience; and to convey to your audience a sense of the character and history of the person interviewed. Contrive in advance questions that will help you meet these ends. Since you are uninformed on the matter yourself, be sure to ask some questions that are more open ended, allowing the person interviewed to tell you things you would not have thought to ask about.

3. Ask questions of yourself, exploring what you know and think about a particular issue or topic. The questions should be challenging and comprehensive, not limited by what you feel comfortable or secure in saying or by familiar ideas. They should reveal not only what you already know but where your knowledge is limited and lacking in real support or evidence. If this self-interrogation is not hard work, you have not asked the right questions.

Write up what you have discovered, reporting and interpreting your findings. Your purpose for writing might be to explain a conclusion you have arrived at (like some perception about the validity or shortcomings of common knowledge), some new (to you) awareness about the process of education, or some recognition of the internal obstacles to understanding. And/or you might wish to make yourself look interesting, amusing, or personable.

## ASSIGNMENT E:   Requests, Pleas, Appeals, and Applications

1. Make some request of or appeal to an intimidating audience, someone whose reputation or character makes him or her difficult to approach.

2. Deal with a situation (a specific instance or general case) in which you have been at fault and must ask for pardon, reprieve, or indulgence.

3. Appeal to someone or some group for support, attention, or guidance in some matter.

4. Make a case for a prospective employer to hire you for a job you are interested in but are not qualified or trained for.

# 5

# Convention and Nonconformity

Be not the first by whom the new are tried,
Nor yet the last to lay the old aside.
                                                —ALEXANDER POPE

Break any of these rules [of writing] sooner than say anything outright
barbarous.
                                                —GEORGE ORWELL

Impropriety is the soul of wit.
                                        —WILLIAM SOMERSET MAUGHAM

## Saying the Right Thing

Saying the right thing is an art. It is the ability to find the right words and
sentiments for the moment, to be able, for instance, to respond to success
graciously, to present original ideas without seeming to attack the status
quo, or to give advice without also giving offense. It is the ability to console
people without being irritating, to comment on events without irrelevance
or condescension, or to tell people what to do without making them feel
subservient.

It is not necessarily a matter of being polite or pleasant. There are times
when "saying the right thing" might require you to be insulting, one-sided, or
angry, when politeness would invite further abuse and pleasantness would
be seen as a lack of substance and authority. You have to know how to respond to rudeness and heckling, to defend yourself as well as to be nice to
others. You have to know how to deal with arrogance and presumption.

These are considerations of appropriateness and conventionality in style. Determining what is appropriate for the moment is no simple matter. What the audience perceives as an appropriate style for you may not serve your best interests. The audience may prefer that you keep silent or say what they want to hear. And a truly inappropriate, even offensive style is sometimes extremely effective. It may actually seem attractive to some people. To say what is expected or appropriate may be seen as either good or bad. An unexpected or unconventional style may also be perceived as good or bad.

### ◆ APPROPRIATE ◆

| **Good Qualities** | **Bad Qualities** |
| --- | --- |
| socially adroit | overrefined |
| traditional, classic | old fashioned |
| well mannered | conformist |
| dignified | restrictive |
| proper | unimaginative |

### ◆ UNCONVENTIONAL ◆

| **Good Qualities** | **Bad Qualities** |
| --- | --- |
| active | childish |
| different | eccentric |
| surprising | radical |
| courageous | lacking restraint |
| visionary | threatening |

## *Choosing an Appropriate Style*

Appropriate styles are often conventional. They conform to the audience's expectations or adhere to traditional formats and stances. A style is perceived as unconventional when it does not use familiar patterns, meet our expectations, or conform to standard practices and norms. It may, in extreme cases, satirize or directly attack tradition. But an unconventional style is not necessarily radical or inappropriate. It may only be different from what we would normally expect.

Appropriateness is influenced by

- traditions
- formats
- norms of behavior
- conventions

- audience expectations
- proprieties
- etiquette

- protocol
- accepted practices or methodologies
- ethics

The choice between a conventional and unconventional style is, to some extent, a choice between correctness and breaking the rules, between decorum and impropriety. But is would be a mistake to limit a discussion of conventionality in style to such terms.

A style can be creative and surprising within the bounds of convention. And it can forge its own rationale, an internally coherent vision, out of unconventional material and methods. There is no need to be extreme or strange to be interesting, no need to be rigidly conventional to be effective and socially acceptable. Though related to propriety, decorum, courtesy, and conventionality, appropriateness is more than a matter of etiquette. It is also a matter of diplomacy and discretion.

## *Being Appropriate*

A conforming or conventional style attempts to follow as closely as possible traditional patterns, formats, and prescriptions for discourse. It uses familiar syntax, diction, genres, forms of evidence, stances, and perspectives.

The following strategies can help you make your style more appropriate:

*1. Imitate the Conventional Style.*   If you are called on to write a kind of essay or report you have not written before, seek out examples written by someone else in identical circumstances—by your predecessor in the job or someone else in the same field or profession.

Developing your own style for a particular essay can be time-consuming and even counterproductive. A style too different may be badly received, however well written it is. People may prefer a banal and unoriginal report because that is what they are used to. Contemptible though this may be, familiarity is comforting.

A useful means of learning a conventional style is to paraphrase it, rephrasing an essay you admire to practice and internalize the style. Transcribing the essay word for word can have the same effect, as long as you pay attention to the writing as you copy it. Many subtleties of style elude analysis, but in the process of paraphrasing the example or copying it word for word they can be absorbed and learned.

For the same reasons, it is valuable to try to apply the style and form of a model essay to a different topic or situation.

*2. Use a Conventional Format.* If there is an established format for the kind of writing you are doing, learn to follow it before attempting to personalize or change it. Look for patterns in essays that the discourse community respects, and present the same kinds of information in the same sequence.

If obvious subheadings are commonly used, it may be easier to perceive conventional formats. But in many writing situations conventional sections and subtitles are neither appropriate nor traditional.

*3. Follow Standard Rituals, Procedures, and Methodologies.* The basic rule of propriety is to "go by the book." If there are accepted rules or procedures for the kind of research you are doing, your style will appear more attractively conventional if you follow them to the letter. Any deviation from the norm will make your work seem less meticulous, less precise, and less valid.

*4. Use Familiar Syntax and Diction.* Styles seem more appropriate when they use familiar words and phrases, or the characteristic diction and sentence structure of the profession or role the author represents.

*5. Support and Develop Your Claims in the Accepted Manner.* Appropriate styles use standard patterns of development and support. They follow accepted procedures for reporting data and ideas. The kinds and extent of evidence cited corresponds to the occasion and circumstances. For example, in formal discourse more exacting evidence is usually expected than when conversing with friends. And emotional appeals would seem inappropriate when discussing a problem in electrical engineering.

*6. Adapt to the Situation.* A conventional style makes every effort to suit the discourse to the situation, to adapt the presentation to the time, audience, and place. It will seem "appropriate" in the sense of being decorous or proper, well mannered and unsurprising.

*7. Make Your Writing More Stylized or Formulaic.* Conventional styles are more prescriptive or contrived. The style is more obvious and self-conscious, even when wit is intended. Conventional wit is formulaic, patterned, or courtly.

*8. Be Predictable.* Conventional styles do not surprise the audience. They either follow patterns the audience is familiar with or create expectations about what will come next, and fulfill them.

*9. Conform.* A conventional style will sound and look very much like everyone else's style. There tends to be less emphasis on the individual person or personality and more on the subject or the role the author is taking.

*10. Choose Conventional Topics.* Topics tend to be constructive and socially acceptable. Issues and material not considered pertinent to the discussion are omitted.

*11. Be Straightforward.* The whole tenor of the discussion in a conventional style may be more serious and disciplined, if not more cautious. There is a no-nonsense attitude about it.

*12. Be Correct.* There is an emphasis on grammatical and formal "correctness" in the conventional style. Conventional styles are judged in part on how well the author follows the rules.

## *Being Unconventional or Inappropriate*

An unconventional or nonconforming style avoids or contradicts traditions and norms. It may break "rules," make new ones, and surprise or shock us, violating our expectations about what should be said, how it should be said, and to whom. It emphasizes the unique, different, and uncommon in both self-expression and subject.

To make your style less conventional, use the following guidelines:

*1. Do the Unexpected.* Unconventional styles emphasize shock and surprise. They keep the audience off balance and even uncomfortable, saying the opposite of what people would normally expect.

*2. Choose Uncommon Topics or Perspectives.* Unconventional styles tend to violate not only our expectations but our sensibilities. They may bring up subjects usually regarded as taboo or issues usually sidestepped or ignored.

The topics may be unusual in other ways: oddly trivial or personal, for instance, or addressed from a strange perspective.

*3. Use Unfamiliar Diction and Syntax.* An unconventional style may use words and phrases that would generally be thought inappropriate to the circumstances. It may, for example, use everyday speech in a technical report or highly poetic diction in discussing a sporting event.

*4. Show Little Respect for the Audience or Its Knowledge.* Unconventional styles show little respect for the status, position, or role of the audience, or for conventional wisdom. They are likely to be irreverent, rebellious, or polemical.

*5. Overstep Your Authority or Exceed Your Charge.* The author may overstep what we perceive as his or her authority, place, role, or status, addressing subjects or audiences usually denied him or her. For instance, we regard it as inappropriate for people to speak on subjects they are largely unfamiliar with, for children to advise their elders, for employees to criticize management decisions, and for teachers or judges to campaign for particular attitudes or beliefs.

6. *Violate Restrictions of Place and Time.* An unconventional style will sometimes violate restrictions based on place or circumstance, introducing topics or setting a tone considered inappropriate for the occasion. For example, it would be unconventional to sell life insurance at a wedding or to introduce humor at a funeral (though selling life insurance at a funeral might be oddly appropriate, in a darkly humorous way).

7. *Ignore Proprieties.* An unconventional style may be rude, offensive, impolite, or improper. For example, it is rude to insult people, especially in public. But an unconventional comedian might do so and be considered entertaining.

8. *Avoid or Satirize Conventional Formats and Styles.* If there is an accepted norm, fashion, or format, the unconventional style will avoid it, use it ironically, or use it in an inappropriate context.

9. *Avoid Patterns and Continuity.* The unconventional style may avoid not only traditional formats but any semblance of order, pattern, or continuity. It may attempt to be random. It may change tone and direction repeatedly, tending toward digressiveness and incoherence. It may change topics, venue, and perspective without warning.

If a pattern emerges, the author may undercut it with self-referential irony, calling attention to the style's own contrivances or form.

10. *Break the Rules.* Unconventional styles break rules. They may be purposely incorrect or ungrammatical. This incorrectness may be effective if there is sufficient and clear reason for it. Otherwise it may be regarded as a sign of ignorance, laziness, or lack of fluency.

11. *Invent Words or Meanings.* An unconventional style may use words in unfamiliar ways, extending their usual meaning or emphasizing an archaic, provincial, or personal connotation. It may assign new meanings to familiar words or invent new words and terminology.

*A Word of Caution.* For the most part, writers choose to be only moderately unconventional in style. They might introduce some element or degree of nonconformity, but seldom to an unqualified extreme. For instance, an author who introduces new topics suddenly, without immediate transition, might compensate for this unconventionality by later explaining or strongly implying the connections between the various issues, by tying up the loose ends, or by establishing continuity in the essay through some means other than logical progression—with an obvious and consistent tone or attitude, perhaps, or with a recurrent motif.

## Dealing With Difficult Situations

Problems with appropriateness occur when your objectives and your style do not suit each other, as, for instance, when you must use a highly conventional format but wish to attract attention, or when you wish to appear traditional and conservative but no clear conventions exist for the occasion.

You can deal with such problems in the following ways:

*1. Make One Part of the Presentation Unconventional.*   You can compensate for a conventional format by applying it to an unconventional topic or by playing a role as author that does not conform to our expectations.

*2. Be Self-Conscious About the Conventions.*   Conventions can be made to seem more original if you call attention to them as you write, self-consciously referring to or discussing their use or mocking the conventions even as they are used.

*3. Rediscover the Conventions.*   More difficult in many respects is the practice of revivifying the conventions, using them seriously and wholeheartedly as if they were not conventions at all—not clichéd responses to the situation but creations of the moment, with their original vitality, appropriateness, and immediacy restored. This may take study, imagination, or a habit of taking things personally, feeling the relevance of conventions to one's own emotions and thoughts.

The trick is to find the reasons why a certain style or pattern of presentation has become conventional in the first place. Instead of blindly following the conventions, you have to develop a convincing rationale for them, a valid reason for writing in that style.

*4. Adapt Conventions From a Different Situation.*   Sometimes you can borrow conventions from a different situation. Doing so may make your job easier, bolster your authority, or (if applying the borrowed conventions to the new circumstances seems clever) provide interest.

This practice can be as simple and obvious as taking from one office a standardized form or a tried-and-true procedure and using it in another. It includes good and bad adaptations we make without consciously thinking about them, like using a conversational style in a formal meeting or treating employees like children (a bad adaptation).

You can impose the structure or style of one kind of discourse on another: for example, you can use a series of letters to develop a novel or use a news-documentary style of presentation in a business report. The conventions of allegorical writing could be used in a political essay. The conventions of psychological analysis might be applied to movie criticism or to conducting a job interview.

*5. Emphasize One Convention to Conceal an Impropriety.*   Use of one convention can conceal the absence of another.

For example, youth or lack of experience can be concealed by an assertive tone, an emphasis on knowledge and scholarship, or the simple device of "dressing the part"—wearing a pinstripe suit to business meetings or using letterhead paper and a highly formal and distant stance in correspondence.

A conventional style can be used to dignify unusual or strange ideas, compensating for their inherent "nonconformity." An important issue may help justify and sustain an otherwise inappropriate tone and manner.

*6. Mix Conventional and Unconventional Styles.*   There are obvious benefits to starting conventionally and gradually becoming more unconventional or startling the audience with an unconventional opening and (relatively quickly) resolving any qualms the readers might have by reverting to a more traditional approach. The former maintains interest; the latter seizes attention.

You might also consider interspersing unconventional passages throughout the essay, or including an unconventional section in an otherwise conventional essay—perhaps a passage of dialogue within a formal report, for example, if it served to highlight a crucial difference of opinion.

*7. Justify an Unconventional Style.*   It is possible to start with an unconventional approach and pursue it so diligently, consistently, and well that it takes on the solidity of a convention itself and begins to look natural, predictable, or familiar on its own terms.

This self-justification can also be attained through careful and objective analysis of the rhetorical situation; such analysis can provide the basis for a new approach to the situation, one equally or more appropriate than the conventional response would be.

## EXERCISE A

On a scale of 1 to 10, rate the appropriateness of the following passages, with 1 being most inappropriate or unconventional and 10 being most conventional and proper.

Note that the relative appropriateness depends not only on the situation but also on which audience you are addressing.

Explain your answers.

1. [*To a close friend*] Good morning. How are you?
2. [*To a close friend*] Hi, there. How's it going?
3. [*To your employer*] Hi, there. How's it going?
4. [*To a stranger*] Good grief, you look awful. What hit you?
5. [*On the evening news*] Get out your umbrellas. It's gonna rain.
6. [*On the evening news*] The low tonight will be 35 degrees, the high tomorrow 42, with a 70 percent chance of rain.
7. [*On the evening news*] Rain, rain go away. Come again some other day.
8. [*To a neighbor*] Looks like rain.
9. [*In a story*] Rain it might. It could. It will. It ought to rain.
10. [*In a newspaper*] Old man Marley bought the farm.
11. [*In a newspaper*] The deceased is survived by a wife and three children.
12. [*In a poem*] Death and gloom and desperation. Dust to dust. The dying take our breath away.
13. [*In a newspaper*] That stiff Jacob Marley. He got what was coming to him, the greedy beggar.
14. [*To an office acquaintance*] Marley died. Can't say as I'll miss him. He only cared about money.

## WHEN TO BE CONVENTIONAL

Conventional writing is expected or appropriate

- when the occasion is routine
- when the occasion is ceremonial
- when you support the status quo
- when you want to fit in or be part of the group
- when you want to avoid attracting attention
- when you wish to conceal your intentions

## WHEN TO BE UNCONVENTIONAL

We are often amused and awed by unconventional behavior, even when we do not respect it. Sometimes we are jealous. People who are able to flout convention seem more free, more unconstrained. They take more risks than we care to, but we find ourselves wishing we could comfortably act as they do.

Restrictions on behavior that we personally accept and society depends on can nevertheless be chafing. We enjoy seeing them mocked; it reminds us that we are as much in control of the restrictions as they are of us. But we would not want them destroyed.

It may be "appropriate" to be unconventional

- when the audience is close-minded
- when your ideas might otherwise be misread
- when the audience admires unconventional behavior
- when the subject is unconventional
- in a crisis or emergency
- at a celebration
- when tensions are high
- when you seek to entertain
- when your ideas are stale or commonplace
- when you seek to attract attention

## GAINS AND LOSSES

### ◀ CONVENTIONAL STYLE ▶

| Advantages | Disadvantages |
|---|---|
| More easily defended | Less memorable |
| Gains readier acceptance | Limits options |
| Reassures the audience | May reinforce preconceptions |
| More accessible | Blends in too well |

## GAINS AND LOSSES

### ◀ UNCONVENTIONAL STYLE ▶

| Advantages | Disadvantages |
|---|---|
| Entertaining | Shocks or disturbs |
| Puts people off balance | Loses credibility |
| Stands out from the crowd | Distracts from message |
| Memorable | Hard to understand |
| Individualistic | Doesn't wear well |
| Hard to answer, logically or conventionally | Harms productive dialogue |

## *Wider Implications*

When we refer to conventions in discourse, we are talking about a wide and not entirely understood range of traditional habits or patterns in communication. At one level these include conventions of punctuation, spelling, and grammar. But they extend to conventions that dictate how an audience or subject should be approached, how we should present ourselves, what form the communication should take, what should be included in or left out of the message, what matters are regarded as important or significant, what kind of authority is valued, how information or ideas are typically assembled, what patterns of thought are typically used, and what standards of evidence are generally expected, among other things.

These conventions are part of our familial, social, and professional culture. While the more obvious or superficial conventions are often directly taught and followed, many of the rest are acquired partly through trial and error, apprenticeship, imitation, and intuition and are used almost subconsciously—artfully rather than mechanically—as much by nature or "feel" as by self-aware intent or in accord with any explicit principles and prescriptions.

### CONVENTIONS AS DRAMATIZATIONS

The public conventions of a given situation, genre, or field are often oversimplified or "sanitized," a conventionalized version of how things are done that removes some of the messiness, some of the infighting, some of the politics and impoliteness, some of the amoral or unethical behavior, and some of the imagination from the process.

The scientific method, for instance, is not as neat and straightforward in practice as it is in theory. In much the same manner the conventions of scholarly writing and bibliographic citation suggest that library research is a clean, direct, and logical procedure rather than the scavenger hunt it often is. Standard advice about managing a store (another rhetorical situation) or teaching a class is often sketchy at best, merely indicative of the ways that persons typically conduct themselves or communicate in the professional context.

### EFFICIENCY AND CONVENTIONAL STYLES

Although it is tempting to regard following conventions as the easiest way of writing—since it seems less work to "fill in the blanks" in a conventional format—all discussion of the relative "difficulty" of various styles is dangerous. You can make anything as easy or as difficult as you wish. And what is easy for one person in one situation may be extremely difficult for another, who comes to the writing task with different attitudes and skills and a different relationship to the audience.

Furthermore, in saying that one style is more or less difficult than another, one may not be adequately taking into account the difference in result or effect; if a particular style takes more work than others but persuades more people, it may be more than worth the extra effort.

In terms of simple efficiency or competence, a conventional style can indeed make writing easier. But to truly understand, exploit, and work creatively within a demanding set of conventions can be more difficult than simply following one's own taste or whim.

Likewise, nonconformity in style can be easy or difficult.

### FAMILIARITY AND APPROPRIATENESS

Conventional style evokes a "recognition" response in the audience. it *looks* familiar, and consequently readers tend to think it must be good, its message must be respectable, and its author must be credible and expert. Style that conforms to professional standards and patterns is one of the badges of authority. It lends weight and significance even to trivial observations. It can make nonsense sound respectable.

If we are writing a letter or memo, for instance, we use conventional headings and formats because people might be surprised or annoyed if the conventions were not followed. It would take longer for them to figure out what kind of message they were receiving, what it pertained to, who it was from, and therefore how to respond to it. If we are writing a scientific or technical report, we conventionally leave out expressions of personal emotion and feeling, since it has become traditional to regard the affective dimensions of the subject as irrelevant in reportative or "referential" writing.

### DANGERS OF CONFORMITY

In conformity, one risks becoming purely bureaucratic, being perceived as a creature of convention without substance or purpose. Convention can become empty ritual, dogmatic, the pointless reiteration of formulae and preconceptions. No real communication occurs because nothing is really said; the "message" is no more than unexamined belief, ideas reported rather than understood. A conventional style can lead to conventional thinking. One ends up looking like, sounding like, and saying the same thing as everyone else, staying carefully within the boundaries of accepted doctrine or theory, confirming or disproving details but never questioning the traditional way of interpreting them.

Audiences may interpret conformity in style (whether the writing is good or bad, appropriate or inappropriate, effective or ineffective) as a sign that authors conform in other aspects of their lives—that they do not question the values and beliefs of the culture or establishment within which they work, that they accept their place and role within it, that they are the functionaries and representatives of the system, institution, or group whose style they adopt.

This, in turn, is often falsely interpreted as knowledgeability or reasonableness. We suspect that anyone who knows the forms and style of a profession or trade must also know its substance, must be well informed in all other respects. We assume, often without cause, that anyone who represents the status quo must be reasonable (and conversely, that anyone who attacks it must be unreasonable).

### INDIVIDUALISM

To be unconventional is to associate oneself with individuality and "breaking the rules." It is associated with humor, personality, and escape from constraints. Unconventional conduct and discourse can be extremely attractive. It can represent the best kind of self-expression and communication: open and healthy, unhampered by neurosis or guilt. On the other hand, it can represent individualism at its worst: antisocial and self-indulgent.

### ATTENTION SEEKING

The motives behind nonconformity are not always pure. People desperate for attention may choose to be unconventional because it offers the greatest reward for the least effort. It is easy to shock people.

Not all attention is beneficial. A speaker can get noticed by shouting in a library or by insulting a police officer, by undressing in public or weeping in the streets. But although one can conceive of occasions that would justify such behavior, for the most part the negative consequences outweigh the potential gains.

Even attention directed at less extreme behavior is not necessarily worth having. A quirk of style like an oft-repeated phrase or the habit of digressing into personal matters can attract ridicule. A proclivity toward humor can garner attention but create a reputation for being superficial or insufficiently serious.

### RESPECT FOR NONCONFORMITY

It is easy, but often unfair, to dismiss the unconventional as evidence that the author is self-indulgent, inept, young, immature, radical, flamboyant, uninformed, or ignorant of the rules. Slight divergences from the norms are often regarded as accidents or mistakes, unintentional slip-ups, as if the authors didn't know what they were doing. Readers conclude that the writers were not skillful or hardworking enough to follow the rules and formats appropriate to the situation.

In that respect, extremes of unconventionality are sometimes easier to carry off, easier to justify. The audience can see almost instantly that the author "meant" to violate the norms.

Nonconformity in style is apt to be considered eccentric and threatening, a sign that the authors regard themselves as better than the rest of us (who have chosen to accept the conventions being flouted).

The unconventional style may be admired, however, for its originality—even when little admiration is deserved. To an uncritical audience, anything shocking or surprising may seem original.

### RESPECT FOR CONFORMITY

In the long run, we tend to believe or respect more those people who seem to have earned our attention rather than stolen it, whose message, experience, or effort appears to justify a hearing. An advantage of conventional style is that it lends itself to this interpretation, to being perceived as earnest, hard won, and tested by time. It conveys an aura of credence and truth.

Conventional styles are likely to win approval from colleagues, parents, employers, and the community. They are strongly supported by our social and cultural values, by our own modesty and self-depreciation, and by our interest in discerning scientific, legal, and philosophical truth—separating opinion from fact and distinguishing appearance, impression, and prejudice from reality.

The conventional style tends to deemphasize personality and personal gain, subordinating these to the goals of the organization, the state, a system of belief, or a social group.

### SOCIETY AND ESTABLISHED BELIEFS

People associate even superficial conventions with things they believe in, principles by which they live, and values to which they ascribe. A writer who sidesteps them may seem, in some small or considerable manner, to be scorning or criticizing commonly held beliefs.

Breaking away from convention implies disrespect and disregard for things we value and ideas we identify with closely. The norms are part of our self-image; any flouting of convention seems like criticism of our identity and knowledge.

### CONFORMITY AND POWER

In some fairly complex fashion, the conventions of discourse and style are associated with the relative authority, status, wealth, and reputation of the speaker. This is not to say that a "power" style will make you a leader or that a high-status style will confer actual rank and privilege. It does not mean that people with great reputation, social standing, or wealth are necessarily endowed with a corresponding grace in discourse, or that such grace is denied to others.

But it does suggest that the ability to imitate and eventually take on a particular business, professional, or social style, to be consummately "conventional" in discourse, may ease one's progress, aid success, and contribute to the maintenance of good fortune once it has been achieved.

### FAIRNESS AND EFFICIENCY

Conventions keep things running, save us from constantly having to reinvent procedures and styles. They allow us to concentrate on ideas rather than presentation, to be efficient and consistent, to be fairer in evaluation of competing arguments or theories.

Following conventions reduces the scope of debate: a scientist who meticulously follows conventional methodology in an experiment will generally have to defend only his or her interpretation of the findings, not the means through which the data was accrued.

### CONFORMITY AND INTEREST

Conformity in discourse and style is sometimes thought of as unavoidably drab, uninteresting, and unrewarding. This unfair assessment is perhaps based on the observation that many drab and boring people use highly conventional styles. There are, however, many tedious nonconformists. And there are many people we find interesting whose professional and social styles are highly traditional.

### ORIGINALITY AND APPROPRIATENESS

Anything inherently new, original, or different inevitably seems unconventional—until people become used to the idea or familiar with the style, until it has been widely accepted and imitated, until it has become so commonplace that it becomes conventional itself and replaces the norms or consensus of opinion it originally threatened.

It is important to note, however, that the unconventional is not necessarily original, not in all cases destined to supplant the norms of behavior and style, and not necessarily or even most probably "better" than the conventions it violates. The burden of proof is on nonconformity rather than on tradition.

## THE SITUATIONAL NATURE OF CONVENTIONS

Appropriateness varies with the situation. A style that is proper and effective on one occasion may be inappropriate in another, however similar the occasions may be. What may be appropriate in the confined circumstances of a particular debate may not seem appropriate in the long run, in the wider perspective, in retrospect, or when reported on the street.

Multiple, even conflicting conventions may apply to the same situation. It may be almost impossible to decide which audience, time, and occasion to conform to. Audiences are complex. What pleases part of an audience may be offensive and seemingly inappropriate to others. It may even seem simultaneously appropriate and offensive to the same person. Mixed feelings are common.

There may be multiple audiences. What is the "true" audience of a congressional debate, for instance? Other legislators? The news media? Television viewers? Political scientists? One's home constituency? One's age group or members of one's faith? One's fellow conservatives, liberals, lawyers, or businesspeople? Or is the ultimate audience comprised of future generations? It can be all or several of these at once. The definition of *appropriateness* changes accordingly.

## REPETITION AND CHANGE

Conventions can themselves change. They exist only because a community agrees to observe them, and they are subject to refinement, replacement, distortion, and neglect. The more superficial conventions—those representing fads or fashions in expression and style—are often ephemeral or transitory, since their effect and existence is based on appearing "new" and uncommon—a characteristic they lose by becoming too successful.

We tire of repetition. As a result, stylistic fashion and fashionable opinions tend to change in a cyclic pattern, with one convention giving way to another and another until eventually the first returns again to favor, having become so unfamiliar that it can once more seem fresh.

In an odd way, defying conventions can be just another kind of conformity; the author "conforms" to the audience's desire for scandalous, surprising, or outrageous behavior and does so by breaking a set of rules or conventions that the audience itself has little respect for.

### EVALUATING APPROPRIATENESS

How we measure appropriateness is subject to question. What may be appropriate by the standards of social propriety may be totally inappropriate if judged by the standard of effectiveness. What may be appropriate in terms of business practices may be inappropriate if measured by the criteria of a particular faith or creed. What may be legally appropriate may be aesthetically unpleasant.

To put it differently, the criteria by which we judge conformity and nonconformity are contradictory and redundant. They overlap and disagree. Should we conform to the standards of aesthetic beauty? To the principles of scientific and academic reasoning? To statistical validity? To tradition? To ethical ideals? To common practice? To social or personal values? We are always caught in the middle.

### CREATING AN INDIVIDUAL STYLE

Nonconformity for its own sake is little more than attention seeking, so easy that a child can do it. But a well-conceived and disciplined nonconformity, a unique and effective personal style, can be hard to create and maintain.

By definition, an individual style cannot follow habitual patterns or standard formulas. Consequently, more thought must go into it. There is no simple format to rely on. Every detail of the text and style may have to be consciously weighed and selected. Nothing can be left to tradition. And an unconventional style is also more dangerous, more likely to draw fire. The author is forced to work harder to justify both the style and the message, to protect against attack and to respond to criticism.

### SOCIETY AND THE INDIVIDUAL

The question is whether to adapt your discourse to the proprieties of the occasion or to create your own style. Is it better to accept the norms and conventions of the forum or to try to force your own style and personality on the situation?

At its heart, this dilemma is defined by the conflict between social and individual values. Appropriateness is a social good, a virtue based on the norms and interests of the community. Nonconforming or unconventional behavior tends to favor and benefit the individual.

You are confronted with the choice of fitting into society or standing apart.

## *Conclusion*

In essence, the dilemma of conventional and unconventional styles is a manifestation of our contradictory nature: we like things to stay the same but we also like change. Continuity in style suggests stability, consistency, security, and timelessness. It suggests calmness and coherence, fixity, the absence of debate and factionalization. Changeability in style suggests both freedom and license. It implies excitement and stress, progress and revolution, dialogue and conflict, discovery, surprise, and continuing uncertainty.

## ASSIGNMENT A:   Courtly and Rude Styles

1. Discuss what would be the most diplomatic or courteous things to say on a difficult occasion.

2. Write a gracious but effective response to someone who has directly or indirectly criticized you, offended you, or challenged your authority.

3. Gracefully acknowledge and accept received support or appreciation—as from friends, parents, teachers, colleagues, or those interested in your work or ideas. On the occasion of receiving some compliment or award, of course, it is considered polite to thank those who have contributed to your success.

4. For comic effect, write about the things people don't say (but should?) on a particular occasion or in some particular context.

5. Take advantage of hindsight, and write out what you wish you had said on some occasion, perhaps as part of an essay or narrative about the event.

6. Discuss rude or purposely shocking comments and behavior, citing examples.

7. Use a certain degree of abruptness or bluntness in addressing an audience or organization that has abused your courtesy, or for some clear reason deserves no civility. Or write to a third party or neutral audience and speak uncivilly about someone else.

## ASSIGNMENT B:   Entertainments, Eccentricities, and Surprises

1. Analyze the style, message, and persona of a performer or public figure who is regarded as something of a renegade, eccentric, or scandal.

2. Write about something in a very unconventional manner. For example, you could write a lab report as if it were a detective mystery or a horror

movie (as seen through the eyes of a white rat?); or use a purposely odd verbal style to attract attention and entertain while writing about an otherwise routine subject, like how to get a car loan or how to apply to college; or write a literary analysis in the form of a letter from a purposely obtuse reader to a long-dead author.

3. Begin with, and clearly establish, some conventional style or format, but within this framework do something unexpected and try to make it work (that is, try to make it seem justified or try to create some useful effect). For example, write what seems to be a memo or job application letter, and within it incorporate a commentary on the state of the economy or on business ethics; or write what seems like a last will and testament, in legal jargon, and quickly begin to intersperse satire on a comic strip character, whose will this proves to be; and so on.

4. Use illogic or purposely unconventional evidence to support a contention.

## ASSIGNMENT C:   Dissent, Rebellion, and Rejection of the Status Quo

1. Challenge some entrenched position, attitude, or widely accepted point of view that you regard as wrong.

2. Challenge, question, or criticize some aspect of an existing organization, law, or power structure by which you are affected. This need not take the form of open revolt or angry confrontation. Nor does it necessarily imply complete rejection of the status quo or automatically set you outside the political process. (It is often, but not always, a mistake to move too quickly to an extreme or confrontational stance, since doing so may reduce your credibility, solidify your opposition, and limit your options.) Challenging the power structure may simply be an assertion that you need more latitude, that you need more respect or wish to be on more equal terms with those in authority, or that you would prefer to have others in power in place of the present establishment or the incumbent officeholders.

3. Take strong exception to a judgment so well established that questioning it seems shocking (like saying that *Citizen Kane* is a terrible movie or that becoming militarily involved in South Vietnam was actually the right thing to do). Be prepared to defend your contention well, and be ready to bail out, moderating your view by the end of the essay, if you want to. Or do the same with some common practice.

4. In an essay or letter to the editor discuss a subject usually considered taboo.

CONVENTION AND NONCONFORMITY **89**

# ASSIGNMENT D: Confirmation, Encouragement, and Reassurance

1. In writing, offer support and reassurance to a point of view, person, or group that appears in need of it. Avoid condescending to those you purport to help.

2. Cite, reiterate, and explain another person's idea, proposal, or theory. And offer evidence, arguments, and examples from your own experience to support it. If your own opinions coincide with that of the source, take the role of "seconder," joining the group of those who adhere to the concept.

# 6

# Audience: Dialogue and Monologue

In the tragic view, people speak essentially in monologues. Listeners get from these monologues what is useful to them, often the opportunity to begin a monologue of their own. —Phyllis Rose

Writing, when properly managed (as you may be sure I think mine is) is but a different name for conversation. —Laurence Sterne

Every scientist has to learn the hard lesson, to respect the views of the next man—even when the next man is tactless enough to express them. —Jacob Bronowski

## Establishing Rapport

We like people to listen to us, to consult our wishes and consider our feelings. We like to be coaxed and coddled, courted and entertained. If the subject does not please us, we avoid it. If the reading is difficult, we put it down. Yet we appreciate a challenge. Writing that makes us think enlarges our understanding of the world. It stretches the imagination.

Styles that challenge the audience are lecture based, oratorical, and monologic. One-sided and authoritative, they locate control of the subject and agenda in the author. At best, a monologic style may be charismatic and compelling. At worst, it is self-indulgent and authoritarian, pointlessly arcane and contrived or hopelessly self-centered. A monologic style may be considered either good or bad.

### ◀ MONOLOGIC ▶

| Good Qualities | Bad Qualities |
|---|---|
| independent | inconsiderate |
| commanding | autocratic |
| resolute | dogmatic |
| self-assured | self-serving |

Styles that court the audience are open, interactive, and discussion centered, or dialogic. They try to accommodate readers, to make the presentation relevant, accessible, or engaging. At best, such a style may seem not only considerate, but ethical and democratic. At worst, it reinforces complacency, pandering to the audience's interests and beliefs. A dialogic style may also be perceived as good or bad.

### ◀ DIALOGIC ▶

| Good Qualities | Bad Qualities |
|---|---|
| considerate | servile |
| eager to please | exploitable |
| engaging | unctuous |
| supportive | uncritical |

## *Treating People Well*

Part of one's style is determined by the nature of the audience. It is embodied in the author's relationship to the readers, the author's understanding of their interests, values, and beliefs, and the way the author conceives of and treats his or her readers.

The relationship between the author and the audience is fundamentally one of control and concession. Either the readers concede the floor to the writer, or the writer concedes it to his or her audience. It is a question of responsibility and ethics, acquiescence and power.

The dilemma comes from our ambivalence. We like to call the shots, but we want people to tell us what to do. We hate to be preached at, but we resent having to make all the decisions ourselves. We consider ourselves independent and self-determining, but want someone else to tell us who we are. We depend on others to define or confirm our identity.

Discourse reflects an interplay of vanity and courtship. The speaker plays up to and parades before the audience. The readers expect to be placated and enthralled.

The effectiveness of your style may depend on how well you understand the audience and how you decide to approach it. Considerations include the following:

- your status or authority
- the status of the audience
- how sure you are that you are right
- the attractiveness of your ideas and style
- the degree of resistance from the audience
- the need for efficiency
- the audience's values and beliefs
- the audience's experience, status, and age
- the audience's emotions and state of mind
- the present circumstances or interests of the audience

## Being Monologic

Styles appear one-sided or monologic when authors leave no room for the audience to speak or respond, no space for opposing points of view. This is the style of lecturing and pontification.

Here are a number of ways to make your style appear monologic:

*1. Be Highly Assertive.*   Monologic writing is usually forceful and unqualified. There are few indications of doubt and probability. Qualifiers like *maybe, perhaps, many,* and *in some cases* are rare. In their place the author expresses conviction and certitude—with unqualified generalizations, for example, and with modifiers like *invariably, all, most,* and *without question.*

*2. Control the Floor or the Agenda.*   Monologic authors may attempt to dominate conversation, controlling the agenda and dismissing, criticizing, or ignoring (rather than taking up) issues that others in the group have raised.

*3. Close off Further Discussion.*   Your writing will appear more monologic if you attempt to forestall any further discussion of the issue. This may be accomplished in a number of ways, some more ethical than others: (a) by presenting a seemingly comprehensive view of the subject; (b) by presenting your position as absolute and definitive; (c) by limiting the scope of the discussion (as in controlling the agenda so other points of view may not be contemplated or admissible); and (d) by not allowing others to speak.

*4. Develop a Self-Contained Logical System.*   Style can be made to appear more monologic if the essay develops a unified system of belief—an ideology, creed, theory, logical system, or plan of action. This is inward-looking or centripetal writing. Since the author's aim is to present and explain the internal workings of a specific theory, the immediate need for discussing alternative points of view is reduced.

*5. Be One-Sided.*   A monologic style often presents only one side of the issue. Other points of view are presumed to be irrelevant or wrong, not worth mentioning.

A monologic style tends to reflect a black-and-white view of truth. Monologic writing implies by its very nature that there is only one way to see the issue, only one correct answer, only one version of truth.

*6. Build a Strong Case.*   The bias of monologue is toward argument or adversarial discourse. It assumes that the opposition must fend for itself. Present your side of the case as strongly as possible. Pile up arguments and evidence. And leave your opponents to do the same from their perspective. If the opposition cannot defend itself, the point is won.

If the situation is not adversarial, or if the burden of proof rests on the author (as in legal prosecution), the stance is more likely to emphasize thoroughness and proof, even to the point of plodding through the evidence.

*7. Refute, Ridicule, or Criticize the Opposition.*   When other points of view cannot be ignored or suppressed, a monologic style may criticize or refute them, finding fault with their conclusions and arguing against the validity of their arguments. It is more likely to ridicule than consider.

*8. Use Invective or a Torrent of Words.*   Monologic styles may attempt to bury the opposition beneath a torrent of words. The tone of a monologic style may be polemical, if not openly emotional and angry. There is a tendency to rail at the opposition.

*9. Cast the Audience in a Passive Role.*   If you cast the audience in a passive role—as students, apprentices, children, employees, attendants, clerks, or lieutenants, for example—your style will appear more monologic. People in such positions are often expected to do as they are told, and not to question. (Of course, this may not always be the most effective or enlightened way to get the best effort from subordinates.)

*10. Be Self-Centered.*   A monologic style may be egocentric, focusing only on the author and his or her experiences and viewpoints. Obviously, this suggests a bias toward first-person singular address (*I, me,* and *my*), especially in informal writing.

In more public or polemical discourse, "I" and "we" may be used to rally the crowd, to organize the faithful against the threat of a perceived "they"—the adversaries or opposition. The author's self-interest becomes a "representative case," purporting to embody the wrongs and injustices endured by others.

**11. *Emphasize Ideology and Principle.*** Monologic styles tend to reason from the top down, applying laws, principles, and beliefs to specific cases. The "truth" is seen as residing in the belief system rather than in particular instances. Monologic styles may be more inflexible, as a result.

**12. *Make the Readers Come to You.*** Do not attempt to generate interest or dramatize the ideas. A monologic style expects readers to come to the author, to provide their own interest. It assumes that the author and his or her topic are intrinsically interesting.

**13. *Suit Yourself.*** A monologic style emphasizes pleasing the author. It usually reflects his or her personal taste and interests. No effort is made to include topics that appeal to the audience or to present information in a way that readers might find attractive.

In extreme cases a monologic style may be quirky and idiosyncratic, following whims and associations rather than the needs of debate or necessities of coherence.

Of course, suiting oneself may be quite interesting and attractive when authors are good audiences for their own work, challenging themselves to be more creative and thoughtful.

**14. *Avoid Explanation.*** Style appears more monologic when the author makes little or no attempt to accommodate any limitations in the readers' knowledge and understanding—assuming that his or her message is of sufficient merit to warrant the additional effort. Complexities and contradictions are not explained.

**15. *Exploit Crises.*** Monologic writing can be justified by the existence of a crisis. If there is a need for immediate action, the author may not be expected to leave room for dialogue.

**16. *Stand on Authority.*** If you are an expert or can claim to be the spokesperson for a widely accepted point of view, you may not have to leave room for dialogue. When people wish to learn from authorities, they do not expect to do the talking themselves. The situation presumes that the audience has nothing to say.

Claims to authority, however, can be abused. The speaker may use supposed expertise as an excuse for cutting off debate and as a substitute for evidence. Even when the expertise is real, it is usually more polite to listen as well as speak.

## *Being Dialogic*

Writing appears more dialogic when it seems to invite or embody continued discussion of the subject. These are some of the many ways to make your style appear more dialogic:

*1. Anticipate Questions.*   In a dialogic style, authors often show some awareness of the potential response to their presentation. Instead of refuting the opposition, they may anticipate and answer questions or objections, try to avoid hurting people's feelings, and recognize potential confusion or mis-understanding.

*2. Show Respect.*   Give others credit for being—in their own eyes— reasonable and sane about the issue. Do not assume that they are ridiculous or ignorant, unsophisticated or irrational. Treat the audience with respect.

*3. Reconstruct the Audience's Point of View.*   To make your writing seem more dialogic, try thinking through the audience's point of view. Suspend judgment for a moment. Try to see the subject from the readers' perspective.

*4. Include the Audience's Point of View in Your Writing.*   A dialogic style may incorporate the audience's point of view within the essay, either synthesizing it with the author's or showing the relationship between the two views. If that is not possible, the author may at least try to show his or her understanding and appreciation of the audience's beliefs.

*5. Establish the Relevance of the Subject.*   To make your style more dialogic, explain the relevance of the subject to the readers and show how it relates to their experience or interests.

Try to make the issue seem immediate and pressing. Through argument or emotion, for example, establish the overriding and necessary significance of the issue. Put it before the readers as if it were unfolding now, in front of them.

*6. Seek Topics That Interest Your Audience.*   Dialogic writing may cater to the audience, focusing exclusively or at least initially on topics the readers are interested in. The author is less likely to force on readers a topic he or she thinks they ought to pay attention to.

*7. Tell Readers What They Want to Hear.*   Catering to the audience may include reinforcing the readers' beliefs, telling them what they want to hear. This may, in its worst form, be flattery and pandering. But the practice also encompasses much legitimate and important discourse.

We reinforce existing beliefs when we endorse or extend existing theories, provide additional evidence for accepted points of view, or show the significance and applications of the audience's ideas.

*8. Explain the Subject in Familiar Terms.*   A dialogic style makes every effort to explain the subject. It may offer illustrations and examples, extended paraphrase and amplification, or comparisons to familiar subjects and ideas.

*9. Use an Accessible Vocabulary.*   Writing seems more audience-aware when technical terms, concepts, and words you use with specialized or personal meanings are carefully explained as they are introduced. This does not apply, however, when your audience is already familiar with the diction and subject in question. If the readers are experts on the subject, attempting to explain words and concepts they already know may seem condescending and rude.

*10. Listen and Be Patient.*   Your style will appear more dialogic if you avoid being adversarial and confrontational, answering quietly and with restraint even when provoked. A dialogic style is more patient and conciliatory. It listens closely to what others have to say, trying to understand their point of view.

*11. Talk to the Audience or Mimic Conversation.*   Styles may appear dialogic when they permit the audience to ask questions or when they follow a question-and-answer format (even if the author provides the questions). Use of colloquial language and style may further this effect.

The use of dialogue itself may make the presentation seem more two-sided. The dialogue may be incorporated within the essay, with the author imagining the different "voices" in the conversation. Or dialogue may be built into the discourse event, as in a panel discussion, a meeting, a seminar, or a television talk show.

*12. Avoid Closure and Exclusion.*   Keep the channels of communication open. Do not cut off discussion or artificially focus the debate. Do not attempt to have the last word on any subject. Do not put deadlines or all-or-nothing demands on the audience. Leave room for negotiation and compromise.

Most important, allow room for other points of view. Do not exclude them from the community or discussion.

*13. Accept Differences of Opinion and Perspective.* A dialogic style is usually more tolerant and accepting. The author shows respect for other opinions and beliefs, not feeling obliged to change other people's ideas and behavior to conform to his or her own notion of correctness.

This tolerance may arise from personal security or from a relativistic, situational, or pluralistic view of truth. What is "true" may be seen as a matter of probabilities and degrees, as something defined by and only valid for the individual or for the particular circumstances, or as a compilation of many ("plural") points of view.

*14. Try to Please the Audience.* An audience-aware or dialogic style may attempt to be entertaining, clever, or intellectually stimulating, to involve the audience in thinking as it reads or listens. The concerns and interests of the audience become the center of attention.

The author may attempt to play up to his or her readers, flattering and cajoling them, indulging their tastes and even their prejudices. He or she may try to be ingratiating or friendly.

*15. Avoid "Selling" Your Own Interests and Taste.* A dialogic style may suppress or understate the author's own beliefs, ideas, and preferences. It operates on the principle that readers are more interested in themselves than in others, preferring to hear their own ideas and beliefs reinforced.

*16. Qualify Your Assertions.* It also appears more dialogic and audience-aware when you qualify, undersell, or depreciate your own ideas. This seems deferential and modest. It invites the audience not only to determine the worth of your claims, but to assess them at a higher value than you yourself have granted them.

*17. Avoid Sketchiness.* Authors writing purely for themselves tend to omit detail. They were witnesses to the events. They observed the subject and arrived at the conclusions. They do not need extensive narration or description to fill in the background or explain the outcome. The reasoning is clear to them.

The result is sketchy and egocentric writing. It may seem wonderful and complete to the writers personally, but only because they can fill in the missing information, meaning, events, and emotion from memory. The writing is in fact more like a diary or notebook, intended more to remind the author of events and ideas than to explain and present the same events and ideas to an audience.

Don't assume that your observations and experiences are shared, that readers can see through your eyes or intuitively understand everything you meant to say.

*18. Re-Create the Events and People.* Writing may seem more audience-aware if it attempts to re-create events, conveying a sense of what happened and who was involved. It makes the presentation more dramatic and immediate and can make readers feel like participants in the experience.

*19. Re-Create Places.* Graphically describing the setting has the same effect. It provides context for the events, locating them against a backdrop or panorama. It allows readers to visualize the action more effectively, making them spectators rather than passive listeners.

*20. Re-Create Emotions.* Re-creating or evoking emotions can help the audience to understand your point of view. Part of the worth of an idea or the significance of an event is embodied in how it makes us feel. If the emotion is not included or conveyed, the audience cannot really know what value to place on the subject or how to react.

Evoking emotions is a way of breaking down the distance between reader and event or reader and idea. If the readers are emotionally involved in the issue, they cannot help but feel that they have a personal stake in the success of the essay.

*21. Re-Create Thought Processes.* Patiently constructing or reconstructing a sequence of ideas is like providing the audience with a roadmap to your thoughts. Instead of presenting readers with a collection of vaguely associated conclusions and expecting them to see the same connections in the material that you do, the sequence of ideas actually provides the connections.

*22. Be Thorough and Meticulous.* Careful scholarship or thorough presentation of pertinent evidence can also help the audience follow your reasoning. It assembles the data and ideas that led you to your conclusions, enabling the reader to understand why you believe as you do.

The danger is that excessive thoroughness is itself inconsiderate, implying that the audience is slow-witted and dull.

*23. Avoid Impassioned Discourse.* Give yourself time to calm down or reflect before speaking. If you are highly involved in or emotional about the topic, your first draft may appear too egocentric and self-serving. Consider setting this draft aside for a while until you are more objective about the subject. Rewrite it and tone down the invective, effusiveness, or emotionalism.

Writing emotionally is not the same thing as evoking or re-creating emotion.

*24. Appear Disinterested or Altruistic.* You may appear more dialogic if your objective does not appear to benefit you personally, if your goals seem directly to benefit others or the community and any personal gain is indirect and unmentioned. Likewise, you appear less egocentric if you share the credit for your work or success with others. This implies that you have listened to other people, and it increases the credibility and authority of your claims, since they are represented as the combined efforts of several experts or workers.

*25. Study the Audience.* Spend almost as much time studying your audience as you spend studying the subject. This can tell you not only how to present your subject but also more about the topic itself. Businesses and advertising agencies do market analyses to see what will sell and how to sell it. But the wider goal of audience analysis is not just effectiveness, or even communication, but understanding.

A thorough audience analysis goes far beyond the immediate case, trying to find out what the readers are like, what motivates them, and how they see the world. It might include studying their

- beliefs
- knowledge of the subject
- general knowledgeability on other matters
- education
- interests
- social status
- short-term and long-range goals
- dreams and aspirations
- moral stance
- hypocrisies

- habits
- preferences
- expectations
- feelings and attitudes
- fears and aversions
- values
- upbringing and family history
- cultural background
- personality and perspective
- maturity
- appearance

The list is not all inclusive. Even seemingly irrelevant information can be useful.

## EXERCISE A

Describe or study one of the following audiences in detail, noting individual characteristics as well as traits typical of or ideal for the role or category in question. Note cases where there might be more than one target audience, but focus on just a single group of readers.

1. The typical highway litterer, a person you want to persuade not to throw trash out the car window
2. Eighteen-year-old high school seniors you want to persuade to enlist in the armed services or in the Peace Corps

3. People you might want to hire as security guards or members of the police force
4. People who might contribute to charities for the homeless
5. People concerned about fitness and exercise

## EXERCISE B

Sketch out a role or self-image that would appeal to one of the audiences listed in Exercise A—how they would like to see themselves in the given situation. Contrast this with the way the group really is or conceives of itself at present.

## EXERCISE C

For one of the situations listed in Exercise A, write out two different discussions of the subject, the first monologic in tone and the second dialogic.

### WHEN TO BE MONOLOGIC

Although they are conventional and effective in argument, monologic styles are not just adversarial. They can be essential in teaching and research, as well. Monologue is appropriate

- when writing for yourself
- when expressing strong emotion
- when responding to injustice and threat
- when building a case or formulating a theory
- when establishing a strong bargaining position
- when closing off debate
- when the audience is confrontational or monologic
- when lecturing or preaching

### WHEN TO BE DIALOGIC

A discussion-centered style is expected in deliberation and polite discourse. It is appropriate

- when exploring a subject
- when the audience is uninformed
- when the status of the audience is higher than yours
- when you want to be polite or ethical

- when seeking a favor or courting an audience
- when conversing

## GAINS AND LOSSES

### ◀ MONOLOGIC STYLES ▶

**Advantages**

Closes out opposition

Controls the agenda

Makes author seem like someone
to be reckoned with

Fills power vacuums

Displaces existing points of view

Gives full scope to author's ideas

**Disadvantages**

Suppresses dissent

Limits range of ideas on the floor

Creates fear or antagonism

Subordinates the group to the
individual who speaks

Leaves no room for consensus or
compromise

Reveals scope and weaknesses of
author's ideas

## GAINS AND LOSSES

### ◀ DIALOGIC STYLES ▶

**Advantages**

Gives audience a role

Opens the forum to discussion

Encourages independent thinking

Invites compromise and consensus

Shares the responsibility and work

**Disadvantages**

Divides authority

May allow preconceptions to persist

Allows mistakes and
misunderstandings

Distorts author's message

Limits scope and force of author's
ideas

## *Wider Implications*

Most of the time we combine the features of monologue and dialogue. The distinctions break down quickly. A monologic style can be engaging and conversational. Dialogue can be subverted and channeled, becoming little more than a set speech in dramatic form.

It would be a mistake to assume that monologue is inevitably egotistical, autocratic, and unethical, or that dialogue is necessarily more interesting and friendly. The two stances reflect the underlying aims of the author, the mode of his or her intent, rather than the mode of the presentation.

### ETHICAL BEHAVIOR

Discourse can be used to intimidate, harass, and antagonize, violating the audience's trust and frustrating their wishes. It can aid, enlighten, and inspire, empowering the readers and uplifting their spirits. Style can be ethical or unethical.

An ethical style is considerate and open. It neither conceals motives nor withholds information. In monologue and dialogue alike, it listens to and accommodates the audience. An ethical style does not prejudge others or attempt to control and manipulate them. It accepts people for who they are and tries to understand and work with them.

Unethical styles disenfranchise the audience. Whether through deception, concealment, abuses of power, or emotional pressure, they take from us the right to make our own choices.

### PLEASING BEHAVIOR

However careful you are to be ethical, misunderstanding is possible. Readers may choose to interpret ethical behavior as subservience, an attempt to please them. And they may mistake pleasantness for morality.

Ethicalness should not be confused with attractiveness or avoiding offense. A pleasing style, if it panders to us or subverts the truth, may be unethical. The author may be more ethical, in the true sense of the word, who is difficult, one-sided, and obtuse, who antagonizes us and challenges our beliefs.

### COURTESY

Nor is courtesy the same as acquiescence. Being polite does not imply agreement or even "being nice" to one's audience. In fact, there may be greater need for the politeness and repartee of a dialogic style when author and audience are at odds. Adapting to the audience means suiting the insult to the occasion, as well as the pleasantry.

Monologue can be a blunt instrument, by comparison—pointless and impenetrable.

## AUDIENCE AWARENESS

Effective writing takes great knowledge of people. One must understand at some level the complexities of human nature and imagination, the rational and nonrational, the normal and aberrant mind. One must understand at some level the complexities of human behavior and motivation.

This does not necessarily mean being sensitive or sympathetic. Satire and ridicule may show as much, or more, understanding of human nature as sentiment.

## INDEPENDENCE

Independence is partially a matter of originality. But it also depends on the author's relationship to the audience. Neither monologue nor dialogue is ultimately attractive if the writer seems subservient. To be independent, however, does not mean to be different or disagreeable. Monologue does not presume independence, and dialogue does not prevent it.

As an expression of the individual spirit, monologue may be intrinsically independent. But monologue that does not challenge us is really restatement of the status quo. The author is speaking for and from established beliefs.

Independence in dialogue may seem obvious in criticism and contradiction, in courageous opposition to injustice and public dissent. But when the author dissents on the basis of prejudice or unexamined beliefs, his or her independence of mind is more stylistic than actual.

## YOUTH, EFFECTIVENESS, AND EGOCENTRICITY

In some ways, self-serving or egocentric writing is a function of youth and aspiration. It seems immature to regard oneself as inherently interesting, the center of the universe. But monologue is as much a result of our natural pride and preoccupation with self. People naturally place as high an estimate on their own significance and worth as the market will bear.

A lack of audience awareness is often perversely effective. A self-centered style may demean and demoralize the opposition. Because it is blindly confident, inconsiderate, uncompromising in debate, and arrogantly assertive, an egocentric style is often successful in achieving its objectives.

## CONGENIAL AND CHALLENGING AUDIENCES

Egocentric writing persists because there is an audience for anything. However strange or eccentric, however different or off the wall, however contrary or antagonistic your message might be, there are others who share the same opinions and would welcome hearing them.

Although this is reassuring (in the sense that it promises an audience and applause for anyone), it can be taken as an excuse for self-serving discourse of the worst or most feeble sort—defending prejudices and justifying stupidity, the kind of self-righteousness and self-congratulation that is apparent in people who assume that they are always right, who never question the validity of their preconceptions, the correctness of their actions, and the inherent attractiveness of their personalities.

The message is to be suspicious of too-ready success, to discount compliments from a friendly audience. Neither should be accepted as validation of your opinions. A challenging audience is a better test and more equal opponent.

### CLOSE-MINDEDNESS AND MONOLOGUE

The difference between prejudice and conviction can be slight. A monologic style can reflect either a closed mind or an extremely well-thought-out and coherent perspective. A rationalized point of view looks much like expertise, and a well-considered and supported theory can sound like rationalization. In either case, the author has "closed the book" on the subject.

### EXPERTISE AND MONOLOGUE

Each authority on a subject develops his or her own version of "the truth." This complex account is a mental monologue on which the expert draws in writing and debate. It might be said to constitute the substance of the person's expertise.

The same thing happens in particular cases. Each commentator or authority develops a different "reading" of the event. The result may be a battle of expert witnesses—who from the same evidence arrive at opposite conclusions.

### DIALOGUE, OPEN-MINDEDNESS, AND DOUBT

Dialogue tends to reflect either open-mindedness or doubt. A dialogic style may even engender doubt. The more we listen to and credit the opinions of others, the less secure we are likely to feel in our own opinions. There are just too many good arguments on all sides, too many intelligent ways of perceiving an issue, too many other people preempting our ideas. The more we listen, the more our confidence erodes and the less willing we are to speak and write ourselves: our own ideas seem fatally weak by comparison, ill informed and unoriginal, conjectural and incomplete.

### THE SPOKESPERSON

We often rely on others to speak for us. We accept monologue if the author's concerns, taste, and objectives truly mirror our own. We seek as our representatives those who can be trusted to act on our behalf, observe on our behalf, and comment for us, to say what we would have said or would like to say.

The importance and pervasiveness of this role in society is often over-looked. Lawyers and legislators are professional spokespersons. Advertising and public relations firms speak for companies and institutions. We hire speechwriters, ghostwriters, and technical writers. We listen to critics. We grant proxies and powers of attorney. We applaud those who second our views and express our feelings, who speak for inarticulate causes and disen-franchised dreams.

## Conclusion

Ultimately we seek in good writing to combine the virtues of dialogic and monologic styles. The goal is to treat the audience well, but not at one's own expense, to be impressive without becoming repressive, to delight *and* in-struct.

## ASSIGNMENT A:   Listening, Reading, and Paraphrase

1. Listen to and take extensive notes on a lecture, a meeting, a television talk show, or the like. Write a report that reflects accurately and in your own words what was said and the direction of the discussion. Occasional quotes are acceptable, but for the most part avoid giving a word-for-word transcript. Paraphrase the lecture or debate, clearly attributing it to the speaker or speakers as appropriate (even if you can only say "A man from Helena, Mon-tana, said that . . ." or "A self-proclaimed expert on the subject reported that . . .").

You might frame the report like a newspaper story, by giving an ac-count of when and where the communication took place and some indica-tion (from you) of the significance of the occasion and message. Light com-mentary might be useful, but it should be plainly and gracefully indicated that such comments come from you, and not from your source.

2. Read a nonfiction book or an extended essay, taking extensive notes as you do so. Then summarize, paraphrase, and comment on the author's

ideas, taking care to report them as accurately, intelligently, and fairly as possible. Perceive yourself as something like a teacher or reporter, transmitting your understanding of the subject to an audience that has not read the book.

## ASSIGNMENT B:   Polemic and Compromise

1. Address an audience that is extremely stubborn and complacent about its views on a subject. Write a one-sided polemic designed to shake the readers out of their ruts, to disturb their complacency and open their minds.

2. Confront a one-sided point of view, an opinion that does not allow for any discussion or compromise. Think of yourself as talking not directly to the adversary, but to an audience familiar with the opposition's perspective but more neutral on the subject. Choose between discussing the subject as if you were absolutely and completely right on the issue and granting some validity to other points of view.

3. Address an audience that represents multiple points of view on a subject. Try to advance your own perspective without challenging too directly what others believe. Allow room for other points of view. Grant validity to other perspectives. Qualify your own opinions.

## ASSIGNMENT C:   Ridicule, Reprimands, and Rebukes

1. While maintaining some good humor and perspective, make fun of the stance your opposition takes on a subject. Focus on arguments and evidence rather than persons or actions.

2. Attack a group or point of view by caricaturing or satirizing it, depicting the group or viewpoint in action and exposing its weaknesses and absurdities. You do not need to support the opposite position or even to disagree entirely with the point of view being satirized.

3. Reprimand or rebuke someone or some group for its stance on an issue, for its behavior, or its inaction.

## ASSIGNMENT D:   Ingratiation, Empathy, and Identification

1. Address a group or organization as though you were an outsider, stranger, or newcomer, a person seeking acceptance, recognition, or entry into the community. Though it is important that you have some message to convey, your primary objective might be either to make yourself pleasing to the audience or to establish an attractive persona. It might be important to

demonstrate your sympathy with or understanding of the audience's perspectives and beliefs, to identify yourself with some cause or goal they share, to take on the appearance and style conventional in the group, and to cater to the audience's wishes and whims without seeming too spineless.

2. Try to imagine yourself in the position, role, or circumstances of another person, reflecting in your writing some understanding of the person's motives, attitudes, feelings, and beliefs.

# 7

# Author: Self
# and Rhetorical Stance

Every man's work, whether it be literature or music or pictures or architecture or anything else, is always a portrait of himself.    —Samuel Butler

The essayist . . . can pull on any sort of shirt, be any sort of person, according to his mood or his subject matter—philosopher, scold, jester, raconteur, confidant, pundit, devil's advocate, enthusiast.    —E. B. White

## *The Presentation of Self*

One of the goals of all communication is to make the author attractive to the audience—so interesting, informed, ingratiating, impressive, or adroit that readers are either drawn in by the sheer force of the author's character or are disarmed by the author's integrity, good nature, and good sense. This is true even in very distanced, objective, and scientific writing, which tries to convince us that the author is a distanced, objective, and dedicated scientist, well-read and highly skilled at both formulating experiments and interpreting the results of observation and testing.

When you write, you are forced to choose between two different modes of self-portrayal, between self-expression and self-dramatization, between being yourself and playing a role. Being yourself means dropping any pretense, revealing your motives, and setting aside restrictions you would normally place on your demeanor and discourse. It means "acting naturally."

We appreciate people who are genuine, open, and sincere, who speak their minds without contrivance or subterfuge. They seem spontaneous and trustworthy, incapable of lying to us. Their naturalness is attractive as a style because it seems direct, innocent, non-threatening, or self-revelatory, free of manipulation and concealed self-interest. But artlessness may be equated with a lack of art, skill, sophistication, or experience.

Playing a role means projecting a conventional or contrived stance, conveying a personality or character that is somehow different from the "real" you. This persona may be a role associated with your profession—like "tough-as-nails attorney" or "self-promoting and enthusiastic sportscaster"—or with your philosophy—like "liberal" or "conservative." It may be an adaptation to situations you typically find yourself in or a role—like "victim"—forced on you by circumstances. It may be a conventional social role, like "parent," "friend," or "critic." Or it may be a stereotype, like the "strong, silent type," "scholar," "flake," or "bureaucrat."

We respect self-awareness and professionalism. We admire people who know what is expected of them, who play their part in an exemplary manner. But we fear the impersonality and injustice that can occur when people play a role in a mechanical fashion, without regard to either humanity or the individual case. And we tire of people who seem to have no identity beyond that provided by their role, function, or profession.

Trying to "be yourself" may be perceived as good or bad.

### ◀ BEING YOURSELF ▶

| Good Qualities | Bad Qualities |
| --- | --- |
| straightforward | folksy |
| friendly | overly familiar |
| informal | inexpert |
| honest | provincial |
| unpretentious | egocentric |

Playing a role may also be perceived as good or bad.

### ◀ PLAYING A ROLE ▶

| Good Qualities | Bad Qualities |
| --- | --- |
| official | obstructionist |
| authoritative | distant |
| complex | evasive |
| conservative | defensive |
| rational | dogmatic |

## *Making a Good Impression*

You have relatively little time in an essay to make an impression. People draw conclusions quickly, inferring your character, position, and knowledge from whatever limited evidence they find in the writing. Their judgment of you is based on

- the way you treat them
- their previous experience with you or with someone else playing the same role
- the topics you choose
- your ideas or opinions
- the way you present the subject
- your emotions and attitudes
- your manner of speaking

It is tempting to leave this to chance, assuming that your personality will automatically show through. But much can go wrong. The cues you give your audience may be misinterpreted or may give an incomplete and warped view of your character. Inappropriate emotions or attitudes may show through. The writing may leave no distinct impression of your personality. The impression you make may not be as good as you think it is.

## *Being Yourself*

The expressiveness of a style is measured by how much it reveals about the author's emotions, attitudes, ideas, and beliefs. It is affected by our sense of the author's genuineness or sincerity, our impression that we are talking to a "real" person and not a robot, bureaucrat, or sophist.

The following strategies will help you make your style appear more natural:

*1. Be Informal.*    Styles that are more informal may appear more natural. Formality implies barriers or distance between the author and audience. Increased intimacy or closeness seems more personalized and human, whether or not the closeness is welcome.

*2. Use First- and Second-Person Address.*    Writing sounds more genuine when it employs *I* and *you,* the first-person singular and second-person address. Both are more dialogic; they put the author and audience into the text and force interaction on the reader.

*3. Be Conversational.*    Use the intonations and rhythms of oral speech. These include short or incomplete sentences, the use of informal diction (including common words, popular terms, idiomatic expressions, and slang), and the use of the active voice. The style may show greater emphasis on syntactical balance and repetition, which are distinctly oral in effect.

These features are not, however, prerequisite to or exclusively reserved for role-neutral writing. An author may intend and accomplish a personal style without using these linguistic devices.

*4. Claim Sincerity and Directness.*   Claiming that you are honest, sincere, and genuine may make it appear that you are acting naturally. The same effect may arise from claiming that you are plainspoken, direct, or straightforward.

*5. Don't Overestimate Your Charm.*   Although it is tempting to take the easy route, to "act naturally," making no effort to adapt to your audience or fit into the situation, don't assume that just being yourself is enough. For the most part, we consider ourselves far more clever, witty, informed, and entertaining than we actually are.

*6. Simplify or Speculate.*   To some extent, we regard people as "natural" when they are uncomplicated, when they react without analyzing or see life in simple terms. But acting naturally does not necessarily mean being simpleminded.

Style also seems natural when the writer appears to be honest with himself or herself and with us. That may be evinced in sincere speculation and self-doubt or in the author's careful appraisal of his or her own motives. When authors realistically analyze and openly reveal their motives, we feel that the authors are both genuine and self-aware.

*7. Base Arguments on Personal Experience.*   It may appear that you are acting naturally when you emphasize personal experience, telling anecdotes and stories related to the subject.

If you are writing about automobile quality and design, it explains who you are and why you are writing if you tell that a car you owned slid into a busy intersection because of a brake failure. Omitting reference to personal experience would suggest a more formal role—that of consumer advocate, perhaps, or (if the presentation is unemotional and reportative) that of impartial industry analyst.

Personal styles tend to use the "historical argument," the rationale that because something was believed or done in the past it should still be valid. The author may reason that because something was tried in the past and failed, or because something was not done or not believed in the past, it should not be tolerated in the present. Historical arguments are often based on personal experience, on the premise that the speaker "was there" and for that reason knows what he or she is talking about.

*8. Limit Generalizations.* Personal styles tend to avoid excessive generalization and abstraction, except in the form of truisms and common knowledge. Generalizing implies both expertise (and therefore the role of authority) and distance. It removes you from the particular event.

But a personal style can be very assertive in more indirect ways. In avoiding generalization and focusing on particular cases, it may imply that experience is more valid than formal study, academic or scientific research, and accepted theories.

*9. Reveal Confidences.* We expect more self-revelation in a personal style. Disclosing secrets, revealing intimate details, offering private or "inside" information, and telling personal anecdotes can make it seem like the author is being himself or herself or leveling with us. Done well, this self-revelation can reduce distance between the author and audience, creating a sense of intimacy or sharing. We tend to trust people who tell us secrets about themselves, and we feel constrained to answer them with revelations of our own.

Sharing private information is like shaking hands or dropping one's guard: it gives the audience some advantage over the speaker and therefore inspires confidence that the speaker will treat us kindly.

**Ethics and Self-Revelation.** Although normally it is an ethical strategy, self-revelation can also be a means of "forcing" relationships more quickly to a level of intimacy, whether or not the intimacy is welcome. Private information is usually not disclosed until people are fairly well acquainted. Early or aggressive self-revelation presumes a level of intimacy that may not be justified or appreciated.

**Status and Self-Revelation.** Rank or status is also a consideration. When a person of higher status discloses personal information, the result is a lowering of barriers. The revelation puts the author on a more equal footing with his or her subordinate. Disclosures from a person of lower rank or status may, on the other hand, be perceived as offensive attempts to create unwanted intimacy.

*10. Reveal Emotions.* The emotional dimension of persona is often overlooked. People often feel that emotion is not proper "content" for an essay. And showing emotion can be regarded as a weakness or an impropriety. But even the suggestion of an emotion can be very effective in defining your character. There is no need to seem openly demonstrative or effusive.

If you wish to be perceived as emotionally affected by the subject, you can directly say so and explain how, you can describe your emotions, you can mention your appearance as it reflects your emotion, or you can choose words that obviously suggest emotional involvement.

*11. Reveal Attitudes.*   Attitude, perspective, or stance can be indicated by describing your point of view directly or by characterizing the "angle" or position from which you are viewing the subject. You could, for instance, express disappointment or commitment or characterize your perspective as panoramic, cursory, or humorous or your stance as critical, objective, advisory, or hortatory.

Attitude, perspective, and stance may also be implied by the material you select for inclusion in the essay and by the choice of words.

*12. Identify Yourself in the Essay.*   Part of the content of an essay is self-identification, telling the audience who you are and why you are speaking. The misconception that essays only transmit "data" has tended to obscure this fact.

**Revealing Identity in Conversation.**   In verbal communication, we can usually tell a great deal about a person from physical mannerisms and bearing, from dress and appearance, and from the context in which we find them. People also are more likely to tell us explicitly in conversation who they are and what they represent. Sometimes this is rather rude, a way of telling us that they know more than we do or that they are "better" than us.

Rude or not, it is common for people to identify themselves (by their manner of employment, for example) and to make some fairly direct claims to authority and experience. If the topic is the stock market, for instance, one person might identify himself or herself as a bank manager and indicate that he or she has ten or twenty years of experience with stock transactions. This tells us that the person is something of an expert and that if he or she talks about the market, we should listen.

**Revealing Identity in Formal Writing.**   In writing, the process of self-identification is usually more subtle. In formal essays, expertise is established indirectly by citing ideas and sources of information only an expert would be familiar with, or by demonstrating (in the quality and depth of the discussion) an extensive knowledge of the subject. Character is indicated by such features of style (discussed elsewhere in this book) as assertiveness, degree of outspokenness, choice of support, treatment of the audience and the opposition, and so on.

**Revealing Identity in Informal Writing.**   In more informal writing, the manner of self-identification may be closer to the pattern of conversation, though still somewhat indirect. Stories, anecdotes, or other first-person accounts are often used to suggest a person's rank and authority. Reporting an incident in the lab may obliquely tell us that the author is a chemical engineer. A description of a national park may be salted with technical words that tell us the author is a professional biologist or geologist. A story about a ruined shipment of appliances might identify a businessperson.

## *Playing a Role*

Styles that involve role-playing may conform to recognizable character types. Or they may create a unique and consistent character that we perceive as a self-dramatization.

To play the role expected of you, or to construct an effective and appropriate persona, use the following strategies:

*1. Study Role Models.* Study the role appropriate to a situation carefully. Determine the behavior and personality traits that the audience admires and attempt to duplicate them in your discourse. Do not, however, confuse admired traits with admirable traits. Sometimes the behavior that people admire and respect in practice is anything but admirable in the abstract.

*2. Imitate Those Around You.* People commonly advise that you should imitate the style and behavior of those familiar with the occasion or those to whom you are accountable. This is wise insofar as it allows you to fit in more quickly and to acquire conventions without having to analyze them. It may be subliminally or directly flattering to the people imitated.

The danger is that imitation can be taken as an insult as well as a compliment. It may also seem like "scene stealing," as if you are trying to share in another person's success by copying his or her style. And it is more difficult to master than you might think. The nuances of a role you wish to copy may escape casual observation. The manner may simply be beyond your scope or ability.

*3. Imitate Conventional Roles.* There are stereotypic roles for many situations. Imitating these stereotypes may serve you well or ill. They may be effective because they represent how people expect you to act. But they also reflect prejudices and misconceptions. If you embody the stereotype completely, you confirm prejudices and become a caricature.

*4. Acknowledge Unfamiliarity With New Roles.* If you are new to the group and largely unfamiliar with the role that seems to be expected of you, do not attempt to play it. It is usually better in such circumstances to hold back, to keep quiet for a while or to make an effort to act naturally, to be yourself. Sometimes it is polite to acknowledge your unfamiliarity with the situation and to use that to excuse and justify your acting naturally.

*5. Seek Advice.* Ask people what they expect of you. Seek advice from acquaintances who have dealt with similar situations. The problem, of course, is that roles are difficult to articulate. People may not be able to explain adequately how you should act. There may be wide differences of opinion. Suggestions about parenting, for instance, may range from advising relative permissiveness to advising strictness. And what people think you should do may not be the same as what you ought to do.

Often there are books that offer advice about how to handle specific roles and occasions.

*6. Standardize Your Responses.* Role-based styles are formulaic. They follow prescribed patterns. There is more standardization in the way the author responds to similar situations.

*7. Be Self-Conscious Only When Necessary.* Self-consciousness can be useful when you are uncomfortable with the role you are cast in. It can make you seem more human. People are more likely to forgive the formality, awkwardness, or distance of your stance when they feel you are aware of the problem and regret it.

But there is a danger of overdoing it. Excessive self-consciousness undercuts your role, making it seem that you disagree with what your persona says and does. It can make the role seem all the more contrived and artificial.

*8. Define a Character.* You can actually script your role, creating and practicing a "party platform" of beliefs, concepts, anecdotes, and standard answers you can call on at will. Doing so is commonly advised for job seekers. Politicians, teachers, and entertainers script their performances carefully, often down to the moments when they seem most spontaneous. But for some reason we are otherwise reluctant to script ourselves. For one thing, it is more work. And it seems manipulative and unnatural. But the benefits should not be overlooked.

Even for an individual essay, you can script the kind of character you wish to play. Doing so may contribute to the unity, method, and coherence of the performance.

Defining a character is much the same thing as a job description, which defines your role, duties, and responsibilities at work.

*9. Develop the Character Around a Dominant Motive or Ruling Passion.* Part of scripting your role is deciding your persona's motivation. The motives reflected in the essay may determine whether you are seen as shallow or deep, socially aware or pragmatic, decisive and goal directed or speculative and content, among other things.

It may be wise to select and emphasize a dominant aim that your audience can readily understand and appreciate. To a certain extent, this means developing a caricature rather than a character, but people are more likely to remember and grasp the obvious trait than the subtle or complex persona.

A politician, for example, might choose to emphasize a concern for creating jobs or a love of family. A manager might emphasize an interest in efficiency or quality control. A humorist might exploit people's unexpressed anger or focus on not getting any respect.

Unattractive motives, motives too obviously self-indulgent, and motives that if known would defeat themselves are usually suppressed or openly refuted—more often suppressed, since even mentioning unattractive motives can create an unfavorable impression.

*10. Develop an Image.*   Envision the image you would like to project, the way you would like others to see you. Then make an effort to match your behavior and style to the model you have created. Though it should go without saying, it is important that your self-image be realistic, believable, and attainable.

Image building also applies to companies, products, social groups, political parties and institutions, and even ideas.

*11. Use Allusions and Associations.*   Allusions to well-known characters, roles, or people may help define your role or stance. You can parallel your situation to theirs, imply a contrast, or suggest that such people are your exemplars. The danger is that if the people named are particularly famous or impressive, associating yourself with them may seem pretentious.

*12. Create Distance.*   A role-based style will likely place more distance between the author and audience, emphasizing the difference in their respective status, position, or knowldege of the subject. For example, a judge speaking to the jury might say, "The jury should recognize that in point of law such circumstances do not constitute sufficient proof."

*13. Define the Audience's Role or Relationship to You.*   Part of your own identity or status is suggested by the nature of the audience. If you imply in your writing the role you expect of your readers, you can indirectly confirm the persona you want to project. Casting them as supplicants, for instance, supports your right to dispense favors.

*14. Generalize.*   In role-based writing, we expect more emphasis on the general as opposed to the specific case, especially when the author speaks as a member of an established group or clearcut occupation, as a spokesperson, perhaps, or as someone cognizant with a body of knowledge inaccessible or unfamiliar to the rest of us.

## EXERCISE A

Discuss the social and intellectual characteristics associated with the following roles. Evaluate the advantages and disadvantages of each persona.

1. The teacher's pet
2. The young rebel
3. The "yes man or woman," the person who uncritically agrees with and supports whatever the employer, leader, or organization proposes
4. The movie critic
5. The television weather person
6. The electrical engineer
7. The strict father
8. The mother who tries to be a friend to her daughter
9. The aspiring artist
10. The football coach
11. The biologist
12. The police officer

## EXERCISE B

Write about a fairly neutral subject—like the weather or the city you live in—and try to project one of the following stances or personas.

1. The overcritical complainer
2. The cheerleading enthusiast
3. The moody, dark, ironic dreamer
4. The poetic sentimentalist
5. The objective observer

## EXERCISE C

Write about a potentially inflammatory subject—gun control, politics, drug abuse, or child support, for example—and try to avoid playing any role. Don't be an advocate. Don't repeat the party line. Don't play the expert or the offended citizen. Just be yourself.

### WHEN TO ACT NATURALLY

You might wish to act naturally, to "be yourself,"

- when the occasion is informal

- when the role is unfamiliar
- when you want to be polite or deferential
- when popularizing a technical subject
- when you want to be more honest with the audience

*A Note About Nonroles.* Confusion is possible at this point because often (or perhaps inevitably) the nonrole you choose is itself a role. This is true of the popularizer stance. And it is true of many familiar modes of behavior: the "just plain folks" and "aw shucks" personas, for example. Conventional nonroles are also apparent in trying to be plainspoken or straightforward and in going along with the crowd.

Even confusion, apathy, randomness, immaturity, and professed ignorance can be poses. There can be apologetic ignorance, rebellious and scornful ignorance, ignorance from lack of opportunity, and ignorance eager to learn.

People play these roles because they offer some advantage in discourse. If you act helpless, people help you. If you are apathetic, you do not have to think or take on responsibilities. If you are random and immature, people expect nothing of you. They may even be entertained by your actions.

## WHEN TO PLAY A ROLE

You should consider playing a role

- when it is familiar and comfortable
- in situations related to your employment or profession
- on ceremonial occasions
- when the situation is unstable
- when the situation or subject is unfamiliar
- to be entertaining

*A Note About Revising Conventional Roles.* There are times when the conventional pattern of behavior may prove inappropriate or ineffective, and "being yourself" is not an option. The alternatives include the following:

**Revising the Conventional Role.** If you respect the uniqueness of each new situation, you have a certain obligation to vary your response and role to suit it. This does not necessarily mean evolving a totally new stance or persona. What people typically do is to make reasonable accommodations and revisions in their manner to adapt it to different people, different cases, and different surroundings. The basic form or role remains intact.

**Ad Hoc Roles.** There are, however, times when it can be appropriate to redefine your image or to calculate an ad hoc stance for a particular situation or for a new set of circumstances. For instance, it would be wise to consider redefining your image if your previous persona has not been working, if it has not been achieving the desired results. Changes may be in order, as well, if you are unhappy with how others perceive you and you acknowledge the aptness of their judgment.

An ad hoc stance may be necessary when you address a topic unfamiliar to you, when you begin a new job, or whenever you must speak in a medium and context that differs considerably from what you are used to. The strategies that were effective in a seminar may prove ineffective in a lecture hall. The persona that sold well in formal reports may be ill suited to management directives. The role that seemed attractive in scholarly prose may be awkward in more informal writing.

---

**GAINS AND LOSSES**

---

### ◀ BEING YOURSELF ▶

| Advantages | Disadvantages |
|---|---|
| Creates empathy | Calls attention to self |
| Breaks down barriers | May force unwanted intimacy |
| Creates social ties and obligations | Confuses the issues with personal information |
| Reduces need for concealment | May give away secrets |

---

**GAINS AND LOSSES**

---

### ◀ PLAYING A ROLE ▶

| Advantages | Disadvantages |
|---|---|
| Efficiency | Repetitiveness and routine |
| Neutralizes social factors | Depersonalizes communication |
| Creates distance | Sacrifices identification of audience with author |
| Hides personality and emotion | Replaces substance or content |

## *Wider Implications*

Writers often consciously or intuitively create a character or role that suits the occasion, portraying themselves in their writing in a way that is sympathetic, effective, or readily understood. This dramatization of the author is called a persona. Slightly different is the practice of defining a particular stance, a perspective or position relative to the subject or audience. A stance (or rhetorical stance) is the attitude the author takes toward the subject—critical, polemical, objective, or assertive, for instance—or the posture an author takes with respect to the audience—deferential, authoritarian, egalitarian, or friendly, for example.

### REPUTATION

The audience's collective interpretion of a person becomes the person's reputation, his or her public image or perceived personality. Reputations are not just high or low, good or bad. They include nuances and complexities—fear tempered with appreciation, for instance, or admiration without respect. They include the manner in which an author wears his or her reputation—with self-depreciation or arrogance, for example.

Technically, persona and stance are part of the public image one projects, the overall reputation a person attempts to build. All are distinct from true identity, the essence or complex whole of a person's character. A persona may reflect or contradict a person's identity. It may convey only a simplified or two-dimensional view of the author's beliefs, ideas, and character. Nevertheless, persona, stance, public image, identity, and role are all part of the same phenomenon, related to and dependent on each other.

The distinctions blur, of course. Stances may depend on the author's identity. In particularly open or guarded people, identity may be hard to distinguish from public image. As we acquire new roles, we internalize them and make them part of ourselves. They cease to be masks or personae and become second nature to us.

### CHARACTER AS AN ART

Putting together a role or persona is an artistic process. It takes time, testing, and revision. In our daily lives we gradually evolve complex roles appropriate to our jobs, to the people we work with, and to our social circle. It may take years, for instance, to prepare for the profession of legislator, lawyer, or teacher and become comfortable in the role. It may take years to sort out the respective stances of two people in a relationship or a group of people in an organization. These things are not simple—in life or in writing an essay.

## MOTIVES AND IDENTITY

We have a tendency to judge people by their motives or goals. But motives can be misread.

For example, an author's motives may seem readily apparent when he or she is asking for a raise or complaining about mistreatment. If we are favorably disposed toward the person or if the evidence supports his or her cause, we perceive the person as an underpaid employee or an abused victim. If we are not favorably disposed, we perceive the person as a complainer.

Neither judgment may be accurate. The writer's objectives may be unclear or covert. The request for a raise may be occasioned more by a desire for respect than for money. The complaint may be a veiled attempt to manipulate the audience's emotions.

Writing often has diffuse or complex motives. A discussion of the status of the social security system may, for instance, have multiple aims: to improve the system, to warn people of impending problems or soothe their fears, to make people better informed on the issue, to develop and enlarge a conservative or liberal voice in national policy, to gain adherents for the author's views, to increase the author's reputation, to encourage others to speak out, to anger and annoy the opposition, and to attack bureaucracy in general. Our impression of the author may depend on which of these many aims seems most predominant.

## IDENTITY AND EXPERTISE

Part of our assessment of character is based on the author's relationship to the subject. There are different kinds of expertise and different kinds of ignorance.

Expertise can appear to derive from hands-on experience, from formal or informal observation, from emotional involvement and belief, from various shades of hearsay (inside information, folklore, what friends and relatives have told you, and so on), or from academic learning, for example. At the opposite end of the spectrum, a person can pose as a well-read layperson, a person with no direct experience of the matter, an interested but confused spectator, a person aware of his or her limitations, and so on. Each level and manner of knowledge is perceived as a different stance.

## METHODOLOGY AND CHARACTER

A person's method of observation and study is perceived as part of his or her character. We respond to the manner in which the author accumulates and presents information.

Some people seem to be patient and thorough. Others are careless and messy or serendipitous and insightful. If the data is systematically developed, it conveys an impression of care, thoroughness, and validity. If the same information is presented in a graphic and opinionated manner, it may convey an impression of force, emotional involvement, and lack of control.

### STATUS AND POSITION

The author's status or position affects our evaluation of character. Status includes not only the actual job title or professional and social rank, but also the author's place in our hearts, in our minds, in our priorities, in the belief structure of the community, and in the power structure of the profession.

### SINGLE AND MULTIPLE STANCES

Although an essay may be easier to write or more intelligible with just one stance portrayed within it, the writer's viewpoint may be more complex than that implies. We are simultaneously one person and many selves. We may be of two minds about a subject or perceive it in several ways. We may combine several roles in our approach to the subject.

### SELF-DECEPTION

Even when we are confident of our opinions and knowledge, we are often deceiving ourselves. A particular stance may be easy enough to portray but not "ring true" either to us or to the readers. The audience may sense the disparity between the role we are playing and our real but unarticulated attitude toward the subject and situation.

## *Conclusion*

Writing calls for both the expression and denial of self. It requires the writer to promote and portray an identity—a personality for others to see and respond to. And it demands the suppression of personal motives, ego, and beliefs. There must be both hubris and negative capability, both excessive pride and the capacity to "disappear" behind the text, to give the message, subject, or style such complete preeminence that the author's presence is forgotten.

The paradox is that you cannot write until you know who you are and you cannot know who you are until you have written, until your audience has, so to speak, confirmed that you are who you think you are.

## ASSIGNMENT A:   Self-Expression and Self-Revelation

1. Without being too confessional or intimate, try to give a sincere and honest account of your attitudes and emotions about a particular issue or on a particular topic. You want to appear as if you are giving us the inside story, not holding anything back or veiling your true feelings.

2. Describe and analyze your own public image—how you believe you are generally perceived by others, and why. You might wish to distinguish between what you consider to be your "true" self and the identity you project or find imposed on you. You might also discuss various personas you project in different circumstances or with different audiences. And you might consider your motives for appearing as you do, or the sources of particular character traits.

3. Discuss the effect that some change in your appearance might have on your public image, style, or the reception of your ideas.

4. Write a "self-introduction," trying to explain to an audience of strangers who you are and what you represent. You want to make yourself memorable without appearing self-important or lacking in self-awareness.

5. Write a "personal statement" as if addressed to a school or program you wish to attend or to a prospective employer. This personal statement should not only acquaint the audience with who you are, but also make some graceful and perhaps indirect attempt to make your application more attractive. You should spend more time on subjects and skills that matter to the audience than on peripheral issues.

6. Try to represent and convey to your audience a complex emotional state you have found yourself in, or an assemblage of complex and conflicting attitudes and ideas you are dealing with. The point is not so much to resolve the issues as to reflect the condition you are in. Some speculation on or description of the causes of this state of mind could be relevant and useful.

You might want to suggest or imply that your condition represents how others like you must also feel. Avoid using easy and obvious generalizations to describe your mental state, since these tend to make your account appear less original, less authentic, and less perceptive.

## ASSIGNMENT B: Autobiography

1. Write about the origins and development of your ideas and your understanding about a particular subject.

2. Write about a particular incident that greatly affected your attitudes or beliefs on an issue or had a strong emotional effect on you.

3. Write an account of some crucial or pleasant period in your life, a time that is memorable for its effects on you or its appeal. Try to make learning about this part of your life seem important, interesting, or entertaining to your audience.

## ASSIGNMENT C: Dialogue and Drama

1. Script answers to questions you might receive on a particular issue or issues, as if you were preparing to be interviewed.

2. Write both sides of a debate or dialogue on a subject, dramatizing the issues and reflecting or creating the characters, scenes, and situation involved.

3. Re-create from memory and imagination a discussion you actually participated in , heightening issues and style for effect , if it seems warranted.

4. Dramatize a situation or incident that exemplifies or sheds light on an issue, conflict, relationship, or state of affairs you are interested in.

## ASSIGNMENT D: Roles and Role-playing

1. Develop, describe, and defend a persona that might be used to sell a particular product or to promote a particular institution or point of view.

2. Describe and analyze the persona of a spokesperson, of someone in public life, or of someone in the public eye. Discuss its attractions, effects, and significance.

3. Describe and discuss a persona that is conventional for or stereotypical of particular profession, public office, way of life, or role. Consider whether the stereotype is apt, what intentions have shaped its development how effective the persona is in meeting its goals, and what variations or alternatives exist.

4. Develop two distinctly different personas and strategies for approaching someone who has offended you, infringed on or misused your property or damaged something belonging to you, or made some threat to your person or property. Describe these personas in detail, scripting or gen-

eralizing about what each might say. Discuss how the intended audience might respond to each persona and what its liabilities and advantages might be.

5. Assume that you have been asked to teach a particular concept or skill to a specific audience. Define the audience and topic, and then consciously shape and script a role for the occasion that is suited to your knowledge of the subject, your abilities, your appearance, your audience, your relationship to the audience, and the effect you wish to achieve. You might wish to contrast this with some of the alternatives.

# 8

# Context: Occasion and Situation

Remember that there is a local propriety to be observed in all companies; and that what is extremely proper in one company may be, and often is, highly improper in another.　　　　　　　　　　—Lord Chesterfield

The occasion may be one for sorrow or for rejoicing, the time at our disposal may be ample or restricted, and the orator must adapt himself to all these circumstances. It, likewise, makes no small difference whether we are speaking in public or in private, before a crowded audience or in comparative seclusion, in another city or our own, in the camp or in the forum: each of these places will require its own style and peculiar form of oratory.　　　　　　　　　　　—Quintilian

## Acceptance and Change

The way things are and the way they ought to be are never quite the same. Our dreams are more perfect than reality. We can always imagine something that would improve our condition.

One of the purposes of writing is to portray and implement change. Yet the changes we think are wise may not suit others. They may be happy with the world as it is, or fear that change will make things worse.

We can accept or challenge the status quo. Acceptance of the way things are is not necessarily passivity. It does not necessarily imply that we are content with whatever happens to us or are patiently willing to suffer any indignity. Acceptance of the status quo does not mean that a person has been indoctrinated or brainwashed, that he or she will mindlessly believe or uncritically endorse whatever is proposed. There are examined beliefs. Acceptance of imperfection can be an ethical and philosophic stance.

Dissatisfaction with the way things are is not necessarily radical or rebellious, not necessarily the result of overcriticalness and chronic discontent or a sign that we are spoiled, decadent, and self-indulgent. Trying to

126

change the status quo is not necessarily an attempt to seize power or to control what others do and say.

There are legitimate grievances. There have been legitimate (as well as illegitimate) revolutions in political, social, economic, aesthetic, and scientific thought. And consensual restrictions on behavior are the essence of society and culture.

Acceptance and change are related to questions of venue—to stylistic and rhetorical decisions about the place you choose to express your opinions. Accepting the way things are implies adapting to the forum or situation at hand, acknowledging the laws, procedures, and conventions of the moment and the audience's right to judge us. It is the style of working through channels, within theoretical paradigms, and within systems of belief. There is no attempt to change either the status quo or the forum in which one speaks.

Dissatisfaction with the status quo is reflected in attempts to change laws, procedures, and conventions; to educate, guide, or control other people; and to restructure society and the environment. It is the style of reform, revision, progress, and reassessment.

A style based on accepting the forum or the occasion as it is may be perceived as good or bad.

### ◀ ACCEPTANCE ▶

| Good Qualities | Bad Qualities |
| --- | --- |
| conservative | unimaginative |
| supportive | compliant |
| civic | bureaucratic |
| involved | self-sacrificing |
| appropriate | conventional |

A style that challenges the status quo or attempts to change the forum may also be perceived as good or bad.

### ◀ CHANGE ▶

| Good Qualities | Bad Qualities |
| --- | --- |
| visionary | radical |
| unceremonious | presumptuous |
| effective | inappropriate |
| immediate or authentic | manipulative |
| original | unconventional |

## *Where to Publish or Speak*

Publication involves more than sending off essays, stories, and poems to magazines. It is the process of choosing your venue, the place where you feel comfortable presenting your work and can hope for a fair hearing—whether that means finding a receptive audience for your essay or finding a judge and jury who will look favorably on your case.

The analogy between writing and speaking is especially important when considering occasion and forum. Where you speak or publish can have a dramatic effect on your style and reception. The manner of delivery suited to one forum may be inappropriate for another. The result assured by one form of publication may be denied elsewhere. If you present your arguments on placards in a public demonstration, you expect a different response than if you pursue your goals through private talks or legal action. Usually the placards emerge after private talks have failed.

The dimension of style at issue here is the interaction of discourse with the setting or scene—the relationship of speech to the circumstances that surround it. These circumstances include

- the physical characteristics of the place where the speech occurs or the manner in which the essay is presented
- the distance between author and audience
- the appearance, facial expression, stance, and gestures of the author and audience
- the time, date, and season
- the medium of expression used
- the general atmosphere or state of affairs at the time

In theory, at least, understanding the scene should enable a person to write or function more effectively.

The importance and complexity of the setting is often underestimated, especially in writing. We are at least more aware of the setting when we speak, and we can sense the effect of the room, the proximity of the audience, and the current state of affairs on our reception.

Nevertheless, we make many decisions about forum on the basis of intuition. We decide, for instance, to call a person on the phone instead of writing a letter; to express an opinion after class, in one-on-one conversation with the teacher, instead of during class discussion; or to speak in a public committee meeting instead of in a private office conversation. We talk about people behind their backs instead of face to face, or try to go over someone's head or outside the political process to get things done instead of going through channels.

We decide to write in poetry instead of prose, to distribute a formal report instead of writing a casual memo expressing our opinion, to send a letter to the editor instead of complaining to friends or developing a re-searched discussion of the issue, to post a cartoon on a filing cabinet instead of wearing a T-shirt imprinted with a viewpoint we endorse, to express our-selves in pictures rather than in words or in a story rather than through analysis or direct criticism.

## Accepting the Forum

Styles that accept the situation and forum adapt to the prevailing conditions. Adapting to the situation at hand means accepting the rules, conventions, and circumstances of the moment and the manner of discourse that has been offered to you. It means accepting the given "context" of the discus-sion—the social and institutional setting, the perspective, and the intellec-tual framework.

To adapt to the forum, you should do the following:

*1. Consider the Exigence.* Is there need for debate and action? Is there a clear crisis at hand? Does the audience perceive this crisis as real? Does the audience want to do anything about it?

These things can be surprisingly difficult to be sure of. Few crises are particularly obvious. Many are contrived or represent chronic and largely insoluble problems. What is a serious crisis to one person may look like busi-ness as usual to another.

Sometimes through confusion or ill will, people will ask you to address a particular crisis and then disappear when the debate becomes angry or heated, leaving you to suffer the consequences of raising the issue.

*2. Analyze the Power Structure of the Community.* The power struc-ture of the audience may influence the kinds of evidence you use, your as-sertiveness, and the possibility of success. If key people are not present, for example, you may be wasting your time. In an essay about airline safety, you might choose to address the Federal Aviation Administration rather than airline passengers—if the FAA appears to have greater control over the situ-ation.

*Note:* It is important to distinguish between the stated or institutional power structure of a community and the actual location of authority and influence. Apparent leaders are sometimes figureheads, and the real power lies elsewhere.

*3. Study the Rules of Order Pertinent to the Forum.* Rules of order are the manner in which decisions are made or consensus is reached. As with power structure, it is important to distinguish between the apparent and real. The stated procedures, often recorded in formal bylaws or parliamentary procedures, may differ widely from standard practices, which often include such unofficial channels of consensus building as gossip, rumors, ritual visits and dinners, closed-door lobbying, unannounced deals, and discussions in the hallway.

This advice applies to scientific and expository writing as well as to political discourse. In scientific writing the rules of order are defined by the scientific method. In expository writing the decision-making process is a diffuse pattern of persuasion, influence, and adherence.

*4. Study the Intellectual and Emotional Climate.* The forum is partially defined by the composition of the audience and the chemistry within it. Are people tired, upbeat, or bitter? Do they get along well or compete with each other? What do they have in common? How long have they known each other? What are the social relationships among them? And so on.

*5. Study the Value Structure of the Community.* The value structure of the audience is like unseen furniture in the room. It affects distance, formality, the forms of appeal, and the agenda of debate.

What do members of the group value most? What are their priorities? Are these pragmatic compromises or sincere goals? What is the audience willing to sacrifice? How much flexibility is there in the audience's beliefs? What do they value in you?

Even fragmented audiences have their own value structure. If you are writing travel brochures, for instance, the criteria by which tourists choose their destinations are part of the system of values inherent in the situation. Those who value active pursuits must be addressed differently from those who value leisure.

*6. Research the History of the Debate.* The history of the issue, audience, and institution is part of the context of discussion. Understanding this history is especially important if you are new to a community.

How has debate gotten to this point? What mistakes or conceptual errors have been made? What secrets are kept? How much effort and commitment has been expended on the matter? Have there been political battles or serious confrontations? What bargains were struck? What topics are taboo or tainted?

Styles that accept the context may make allusions to the history of a debate but seldom review the history in detail, assuming that the audience is already familiar with it.

*7. Study the Medium.* The nature of the medium being used must be explored. Telecommunication is different from the dramatic stage. Drama is different from normal conversation. Normal conversation is different from telephone conversation. It is not just a matter of differences in convention. The media themselves have different characteristics and constraints—the proximity, size, and visibility of the audience, the scope or dimension of the setting, the potential for interaction. Each medium must be scripted differently.

The same is true of written discourse. The "stage" for an anecdote told in a letter is not the same as the stage for a short story. The forum for research notes is not the same as the forum for an article in a scientific journal.

*8. Consider the Layout of the Room or Publication.* Adjust your presentation to suit the layout, appearance, and nature of the room in which you are speaking. Some of these adjustments are obvious: speaking louder if the room is large, for example, or darkening the room if you are using audiovisual aids.

Other adjustments are less obvious. A large window in the room can be a distraction to you and to the audience. Teachers know that a clock on the wall may get more attention than the lecture. The seating arrangement may or may not allow the audience to interact. To deal with distractions, you can either incorporate them into your delivery or increase your effort to hold the audience's attention. The arrangement of the audience can be exploited. If the seating facilitates interaction, then your presentation might be designed to include interaction.

More subtle still are problems of atmosphere. A room that is somewhat dark or depressing can so affect the audience's mood that any attempt to elevate spirits will seem incongruous. A room can be so confining and close that the audience subconsciously feels trapped and threatened, so imbued with tradition that the speaker feels inadequate and the topic seems trivial.

The same problems exist in the layout and design of written discourse. The venue may draw the wrong audience for your subject matter or style. Its reputation may enhance or subvert your effect. Its style and format may create either a desirable or distracting atmosphere or mood. Its character may create unwanted distance, intimacy, or tension. If the venue is a job application letter, for example, the forum itself may have the scent of urgency and supplication.

None of this is trivial. We tend to underestimate vastly the effects of layout and physical surroundings.

*9. Evaluate Your Appearance and Reputation.* Status, position, or authority, though technically part of your persona or stance, can function like a podium. They raise barriers between you and the audience. Your appearance and reputation can also affect the forum. A taller or more intimidating person may seem physically more distant. Attractiveness or oddness in one's appearance can create tension. A reputation for humor can create anticipation and alertness.

*10. Consider the Prospect of Resolution.* The prospect of success, resolution, or failure can change the forum. If there appear to be viable options for resolving a crisis or explaining a problem, the audience is more likely to be upbeat and tractable. If resources are limited, the audience is more likely to be defensive and hostile. If there appears to be little chance for success, the audience may be passive, bitter, and difficult to convince.

*11. Consider the Time and Season.* The time and season are part of the physical setting and include such seemingly irrelevant factors as the weather, temperature, and lighting. Audiences respond differently at different times of the day. The weather and lighting obviously affect our mood; they also affect our impression of a speaker.

The circumstances in which your audience will read an essay or report must also be considered. Will they see it first in private or at a meeting? In the morning or evening? On a holiday or weekday? During regular working hours or at a time when they would normally be at home?

*12. Study the Event or Assignment.* The occasion or assignment may determine the venue. A religious ceremony, for instance, directly defines the forum. Assigned research carries with it the mode of report, as well as the time and place for presenting your findings.

Is the event a regular or special meeting? A formal interview or dinner? An invited sales opportunity or an uninvited call? Is it related to a discovery you have made, an award or benefit you will announce, or an impending crisis? Is it a news report, a public hearing, or a celebration?

The nature of the event creates its own constraints on your style.

*13. Use Conventional Terminology and Development.* A well-defined forum may carry with it not only a conventional style but also a great deal of traditional phrasing, terminology, and even development. To a certain extent, you are actually expected to "boilerplate" this conventional development, to use standard phrasing for standard situations. Doing so preserves time-tested language and reinforces the culture. That is why, for instance, legal terminology is sometimes duplicated from one document to the next.

*14. Let the Audience Supply Part of the Development.* When the forum is an organization, the frame of reference may be very familiar to the audience. There may be no need to supply background information or build context for the discussion.

*15. Focus on the Particular Case.* Styles adapted to the forum may be more case specific, aimed at a particular incident or circumstance rather than at a general phenomenon. Once a venue or institution has been defined, it tends to focus on routine business rather than on philosophy.

## Changing the Forum

Styles that attempt to change the forum must supply their own context or setting. In physical terms, this means designing the forum to suit your own abilities and needs. In social terms, supplying the context means building or restructuring relationships between the author and audience. Intellectually it means creating a logical framework to supplant the conventional perspective. In rhetorical terms, supplying a context means creating a sense of place or "presence." It means portraying the rhetorical situation, so the audience can envision the circumstances that have led you to speak.

You can change the forum or context by doing the following:

*1. Describe the Setting.* Context may be created by including a description of the setting or scene of the action within the essay, often in the introduction.

*2. Tell the Story.* Manipulation of the forum or situation may be reflected in an emphasis on describing or narrating events. The author who wishes us to rethink a situation may do so by actually revisualizing the matter for us in the essay. This may be done at any point in the presentation:

- *In the introduction,* narrative may capture attention and create a sense of immediacy.
- *In the body of the essay,* a continuous narrative may serve to establish eyewitness credibility for the author and contribute to the support of the author's contentions.
- *Discontinuous narrative,* interspersed with commentary in the body of the essay, may provide continuity and a repeated "anchor" in fact for abstract discussion of the issues.
- *In the conclusion,* an account of what happened can provide an effective portrayal and summation of the case—with the author's interpretation of events built into the narration. At that point, the audience may be more receptive, influenced by the presentation of arguments that preceded the narrative.

*3. Recount or Explore the History of the Subject.* Readers perceive any historical survey as part of the context of a discussion. If they are not familiar with the subject, you may need to recount its history to establish its significance. If they are familiar with the subject, you may want to "rewrite" history, to reinterpret events to change the context.

*4. Create a Panoramic View of Vision of the Issue.* Any broad or all-encompassing perspective may provide a sense of context. You can achieve this effect by

- defining the boundaries of the discussion or subject
- viewing the issue from a distance
- imagining the outcome
- proposing sweeping changes or broad goals
- characterizing the endeavor in grand terms
- synthesizing complex information
- connecting the immediate subject to other events and ideas, creating a network of related information

*5. Reclassify the Subject.*   The way we categorize a subject is part of its context. If you impose a new or unfamiliar category on the topic, you have essentially changed the forum. In contemporary debate about abortion, for example, those against abortion changed the venue by classifying it as murder and as a question of infant rights. Doing so removed the argument from the forum of private conscience and placed it in the criminal courts. Those supporting abortion responded by arguing that the true issue was freedom of choice, attempting to return the debate to the venue of individual decisions and personal rights.

*6. Add a Level of Generalization.*   A sense of context may be created by generalizing about the subject. Instead of focusing only on the particular event, you discuss it in relation to a whole group of similar events or with reference to a widely applicable principle.

*7. Put Dialogue Into the Essay.*   Context may be created by including the author and other persons involved in the case as "characters" in the essay. There may be dialogue, description of peoples' appearance and behavior, description of their thoughts, and analysis of their intent and actions.

In academic writing, the characters and dialogue appear as the review of research, which recounts the general progress that has been made in resolving an issue.

The effect of either dramatic dialogue or the review of research is to incorporate a sense of debate into the discussion, representing more than one point of view in the essay.

*8. Choose or Frame a Symbolic Location.*   A symbolic location is a setting that has special meaning. It can be, for instance, a place where significant events occurred; a place with national, ritual, or psychological connotations; or a place that you invest with special significance.

Symbolic locations are commonly chosen for political speeches because they add historical and national dimension to partisan messages. It is as if the place itself endorses the candidate. Similarly, a movie director might choose symbolic locations for climactic events—as Hitchcock did—to indi-

cate the larger significance of the particular incidents. And marriage proposals are often made in places with romantic connotations—presumably to
heighten the effect and support the appeal.

*9. Describe a Crisis.*    Context may be created by demonstrating the
existence of a crisis, problem, or issue. If the author can convince the readers
that a problem exists or that the topic raised is in need of discussion, then
not only is the purpose of the essay established, but half of the argument is
won, as well.

*10. Frame a Dilemma.*    Context may be created by framing a dilemma
or confronting an issue. Like the review of research in academic writing, this
strategy often involves outlining or describing both sides of an argument or
the various theories on the matter that have been proposed. If the author can
show that others have debated the matter, then its place on the agenda of
discussion, its "right to be heard" or significance, is proven.

Among its other advantages, framing a dilemma demonstrates the author's knowledge of the subject. And it places the author's particular point of
view in the context of the wider debate or "meta-textual" discussion of the
subject.

*11. Make Associations.*    Context may be created by exploiting analogies within the realm of the audience's experience. If the readers are not
familiar with the specific matter you are describing, you can help them to
understand the subject better by comparing it to events or ideas they already know something about.

In so doing, you essentially "borrow" a preexisting frame of reference.
For example, if your audience does not know anything about the French
Revolution, you might rely on allusions to the American Revolution to ex-
plain at least some of the issues.

*12. Change the Layout.*    Context may be changed by altering physical
circumstances of the presentation. In speaking, this means changing the
physical layout of the room or one's distance from the audience. In writing,
the physical circumstances of the forum may be altered by changing the
appearance or layout of the presentation.

*13. Change Your Body Language.*    You can change the forum by changing your body language. Sitting down, stepping out from behind the podium,
walking out into the audience, pacing from one end of the room to the other,
and making sweeping gestures are all means of altering your relationship to
the audience and setting.

In writing, body language must be implied. It can be suggested, for example, through changes in distance, formality, tone, abstractness, assertiveness, metaphor, prosody, and the use of graphics.

*14. Change Roles.*   Context may be changed by redefining your relationship with the audience. Franklin D. Roosevelt did this in his "fireside chats"—radio addresses presented as if they were conversations from a sitting room. Instead of invoking the role of president or leader, he put himself in the role of an uncle or wise friend.

Redefining relationships is easier to do if you are in the superior position than if you are a subordinate. You can lower your guard and create intimacy more readily than you can force intimacy on someone above you in status or authority.

*15. Move to a Different Forum.*   There are two ways of changing the forum:

a. You can argue that the forum at hand does not have jurisdiction over your case. For example, if the matter is being addressed as a point of law, you can claim it is more properly a question of ethics, psychology, or taste—not subject to judicial review. If someone has criticized your work, you can argue that the person is not qualified to judge it.

In legal rhetoric, this tactic is called a change of venue. A lawyer might ask that the case be transferred to a different court because the client could not get a fair trial in the present locality, or because the case falls more appropriately within the jurisdiction of the other court.

Appeals to a higher court are also changes of forum.

b. You can change the forum by physically moving the audience to a different setting. Conducting a class outside, for example, is a change of forum. Likewise, it is a change of forum to draw someone out of a public place and into a private setting, or to schedule a business meeting at a restaurant.

*16. Change the Audience.*   You can manipulate the forum by changing the composition of the audience. In casual conversation, this might be done by inviting someone else into the conversation. In corporate affairs, one might change the audience by accumulating a large number of proxy votes (votes controlled by a spokesperson or by the board of directors) from stockholders not present at a meeting.

The composition of the audience can also be changed by

- restricting entry or inviting a select group
- offering inducements
- choosing a particular format of publication (posters or billboards, for example, reach a wider audience than a magazine about mechanical engineering)

- appealing to an audience not immediately present (for example, to future generations, to the common man or woman, or to history)

There are other means. The most difficult, perhaps, is to transform the audience at hand, to change the nature of the group itself. This transformation can be accomplished by reeducation, by fragmenting the group, by creating new alliances, by directly appealing for change, by slow social evolution, or by evoking some imaginary condition or circumstance ("Suppose you've just been robbed").

*17. Change the Value Structure.*   Context may be changed by claiming that a different set of conventions and values applies to the given case. If your opponent is arguing that the issue is just a matter of policy, you can redefine the situation as a matter of contractual agreement or human rights. If you can prove your point, you have essentially restructured the entire agenda for the debate.

*18. Define an Ideology.*   Context may be created or changed by establishing a coherent system of belief, an ideology or theory that supports and explains the specific actions and ideas you wish to promote.

*19. Redefine the Occasion.*   It is possible to change the essential function and scope of the occasion by revising its purpose, method, or focus. For example, you can change a business meeting into a group therapy session or turn a progress report into an attack on corporate policy.

## EXERCISE A

In the following venues, how should you adapt to the forum at hand?

1. Giving an oral report in a small seminar class
2. Asking a question in a large public hearing
3. Recording a message on someone's telephone answering machine
4. Conducting a study of park and recreation facilities commissioned by the city council
5. Writing a "for sale" ad for your fifteen-year-old Chevy convertible
6. Writing a chemistry lab report
7. Writing an essay on space stations for a science fiction magazine
8. Writing a letter complaining about road maintenance to the editor of the local newspaper

**9.** Writing a traditional sonnet (a highly conventional love poem)

**10.** Writing a television ad for cosmetics

## EXERCISE B

In the following venues, how might you build context or change the forum to your advantage?

**1.** Writing an essay about a summer job at a fast-food restaurant

**2.** Writing a report on television viewing habits among young adults

**3.** Lecturing in a large, echoing classroom with desks fixed in rows

**4.** Conducting business in an office in which your desk, which faces the door, is between you and the client

**5.** Conducting telephone sales of portrait photography sessions for new parents

**6.** Holding a business meeting at a busy, noisy restaurant

**7.** Completing a fill-in-the-blanks application form for a school or job

**8.** Writing a routine annual report on sales—which have been average, at best

**9.** Writing a traditional sonnet

**10.** Writing a television ad for cosmetics

### WHEN TO ACCEPT THE FORUM AS IT IS

You should consider accepting the forum

- when it is related to your role or responsibility
- when you are a subordinate
- when a crisis exists
- when the subject is routine
- in conversation or debate
- when communicating with experts

### WHEN TO CHANGE THE FORUM OR CONTEXT

You should consider building context or changing the forum when

- the audience is complacent
- the subject is distant or abstract
- the topic is assigned

- you need to establish your perspective or vision
- the audience is not familiar with the situation
- the forum does not suit your abilities or needs

## GAINS AND LOSSES

### ◀ ACCEPTING THE FORUM AS IT IS ▶

| Advantages | Disadvantages |
|---|---|
| Uses existing power structure | Accepts decisions of existing authority |
| Reinforces the community and its institutions | Requires ingratiation |
| Formal procedures offer safety and support | Requires knowledge of ceremonies and procedures |
| Provides built-in context and roles | Restricts author to fixed topics, styles, and roles |

## GAINS AND LOSSES

### ◀ CHANGING THE FORUM ▶

| Advantages | Disadvantages |
|---|---|
| Escapes application of existing rules and procedures | Attacks institutions and procedures |
| Preempts existing authority | Threatens comfort and complacency |
| Frees style and method, self-contextualizing | Loses the authority of conventions |
| Establishes new arena of expertise and new agenda | Challenges existing ideas and expertise |

## *Wider Implications*

At the most basic level of communication, the rhetorical situation, the forum, and the occasion for speaking are the same: there is some direct correspondence between the motive for writing, the opportunity to speak, and the place or venue. Someone steps on your toes; you tell the person to stop. You do not wait for a more convenient time or search for a better place to address the issue.

Likewise, if someone nets specimens of an endangered species of minnow, you might choose to ask immediately that the person return them to the stream. If you go to find a game warden, the fish will die. But in practice the gap between motive and discourse is frequently greater. The situation that calls for speaking, the occasion when we actually speak, and the forum may be considerably different. You might be called on three years after the incident to testify in a court of law. You might recall the incident years later when speaking with a friend.

### INSTITUTIONS

Our social, professional, and political institutions are by definition forums for speaking. Culture establishes conventional venues for doing business, distributing and compartmentalizing issues so similar problems are addressed in the same place and manner. To channel our efforts, we set up committees, think tanks, research groups, and boards of directors. Less formal but no less important are the social venues—the family, the personal relationship, the group, and the community.

Where you speak involves more than finding a publisher. Changing the setting involves more than moving the chairs around or stepping off the stage. Society is the ultimate forum.

### CAREERS

Your profession is the venue within which you choose to work. It has both concrete and abstract dimensions: the physical place where you conduct business and the wider community of people who share the same career and discuss the same topics. In the workplace, you solve problems. In the community of professionals, you discuss issues and develop consensus.

### IDEOLOGIES, THEORETICAL PARADIGMS, AND CONCEPTUAL FRAMEWORKS

A system of belief may be seen as an abstract forum. It provides a context for communication, an intellectual framework within which people (figuratively) gather and discuss their common interests.

### SOAPBOXES

We all have our private interests, our personal causes, affections, and passing fancies. For some of these, conventional forums exist—magazines for bird lovers, for instance, and associations for sportsmen and women. But we often find ourselves with an interest or passion and no ready place to speak our mind.

So we set up our soapbox and preach on the streets. In a sense, the essay form is a written soapbox. It is a place to editorialize and discuss, to rant and argue, to teach and entertain, to exhort and warn.

## Conclusion

We invent the forum. Whether it is an institution, an ideology, a soapbox, a novel, or a newspaper, the location or lectern from which we speak is a feature of our style. When we write, we not only adapt to the forum, we change it.

The places in which we speak are part of the message.

## ASSIGNMENT A: Analyzing the Forum

1. Consider a problem, objective, or topic usually addressed in a particular forum—in meetings, in public hearings, in classrooms, in private conversation, in one-on-one counseling sessions, in a salesroom or store, or in court, for example—or in a particular medium—like a brochure, ad, printed form, survey, documentary, interview, or lecture. Discuss the possible consequences of making some conscious change in the forum or medium, either changing the time and place or the audience or changing some aspect of the existing occasion.

2. Compare different forums in which similar topics are addressed (for example, a chemistry classroom and a history classroom, or a television talk show and a private argument). Analyze each forum and discuss the effects that each has on the resulting discourse.

3. Observe and analyze a ceremonial or public occasion, the layout for a particular kind of verbal exchange (like an automobile showroom, a party, or a boardroom for business meetings), or the setting depicted or implied in an ad, an essay, or television show. Discuss how the setting affects our response to the message.

## ASSIGNMENT B: Ceremonial Discourse

1. Choose a holiday, anniversary of a significant event, or formal occasion and write an "occasional" piece—a sketch, commentary, or encomium designed to renew memories, to evoke appropriate emotions, and to reinforce the social fabric.

2. Study and analyze a form of discourse used on some ritual occasion. Discuss its style, structure, conventions, uses, effect, and significance.

## ASSIGNMENT C:   Spectacle

1. Consider and analyze an occasion calling for display and pageantry. Discuss what makes an effective spectacle, including both the messages conveyed (in words and otherwise) and the various trappings and decorations. Describe the event as you might stage it, and tell what you would say.

2. Observe, describe, and analyze a spectacle (like a formal church wedding, a graduation ceremony, a trade show, an exhibition, or a half-time show at a bowl game). Discuss its social significance, its psychological impact, and its ritual meaning.

3. Use elements of display and ceremony to invest an everyday topic or simple event with greater significance and authority. Try to make the event worthy of such treatment, or else the effect will be ridiculous.

# 9

# Subjects: Commonplace and Significant

Look in thy heart and write.

—Sir Philip Sidney

You know . . . everybody is ignorant, only on different subjects.

—Will Rogers

It needs at least as much accomplishment to develop an empty theme as to sustain a weighty one.

—Montaigne

## Setting Agendas

Those who talk control not only the conversation, but also the attention and efforts of the community. They focus debate on the issues that seem important to them, to the exclusion of other people's interests. That is why the choice of topics is important. It sets the agenda for future action.

What you write about is who you are. If you habitually choose superficial and trivial subjects to talk about, you may be regarded as entertaining or easy to chat with but risk being perceived as shallow and irrelevant. If you habitually focus on personal accomplishments, you risk being perceived as an egotist. If you habitually discuss volatile political and legal issues, you may be seen as high-minded and serious. Or people may suspect that you associate with such causes to garner attention.

Essays about familiar topics and common knowledge may be perceived as good or bad.

### ◀ FAMILIAR TOPICS ▶

| Good Qualities | Bad Qualities |
| --- | --- |
| doctrinal | unoriginal |
| true | commonplace |
| egalitarian | condescending |
| accessible | folksy |
| observant | trivial |

Essays about significant topics may also be perceived as good or bad.

### ◀ SIGNIFICANT TOPICS ▶

| Good Qualities | Bad Qualities |
| --- | --- |
| intelligent | pretentious |
| original | overly ingenious |
| mature | stuffy |
| impressive | forced |
| serious or deep | self-righteous |

Writing reflects and changes the value structure of society. If everyone talks about reforestation, then trees are important. If no one does, they are not.

## *What to Write About*

In the romantic view, topics and ideas are found through inspiration, chance, and discovery. Hard work and calculation have little to do with it. But the question of what to write about is as much a matter of what you believe in, what you find interesting or significant, what you think your audience should know or accept as true, and who you are.

There is no such thing as a "bad" topic. What matters is what you *do* with the topic you choose. You can bore people with a murder mystery. And you can tell how to tie a shoelace and make it interesting.

Subjects can be relatively

| | | |
|---:|:---:|:---|
| significant | or | commonplace |
| newsworthy | or | routine |
| exceptional | or | ordinary |
| large | or | small |
| momentous | or | trivial |
| abstract | or | concrete or particular |
| of public interest | or | of personal interest |
| immediate or present | or | distant |
| exigent or urgent | or | inexigent (not pressing) |
| safe | or | dangerous/controversial |

In general, subjects are considered important if they meet one or more of the following criteria: (1) they involve catastrophic or unusual events; (2) they involve accidents or exceptional circumstances; (3) they affect many people; (4) they have extensive and serious (or beneficial) consequences; (5) they are associated with things we value highly; (6) they represent true discoveries; (7) they evince general principles or laws that help us understand, explain, or improve our condition; (8) they cover a wide scope in time, location, or application; (9) they are extremely evocative or symbolic.

But there may be clear and necessary distinctions between one kind of significance and another. A subject that is inherently important, like a death in the family, may not in fact be of public interest or even particularly newsworthy. An exceptional topic such as the outbreak of war is inherently significant, while the exceptional (out of the ordinary) topic of a science fiction fantasy may not be.

Urgent matters may involve routine and personal business, like filing an income tax return on April 15, or problems that face a nation, like a crisis in care for the elderly. To a person with an aging and ill parent, this crisis may be an immediate, concrete, and personal issue. To others in the audience it may be distant, abstract, and of public concern.

Commonplace subjects include routine or trivial events, daily rituals, and familiar objects, people, and places. They include familiar relationships, roles, and elements of culture—anything we generally overlook, expect, or take for granted.

The differences in the perceived importance of a topic can be important. The presentation of the subject must suit its nature or transcend its limitations.

## EXERCISE A

Discuss the nature of the following topics.

1. A recent earthquake in Armenia
2. The San Francisco earthquake of 1906
3. The likelihood of a major earthquake in California
4. Your parents' divorce (or any broken relationship)
5. Funding for the space program
6. Funding for welfare programs
7. Funding for military defense
8. The chair you are sitting in
9. The weather today
10. The shape of a detergent bottle
11. The president's height
12. Conservation
13. Fingernails
14. Anger
15. Car sales during the last three months

## *Originality and Common Knowledge*

There is a distinction, of course, between having a topic and having an idea. Chapters 10, 11, and 12 address more directly the question of what to say about the subject of conversation. But concepts, ideas, and perceptions can be commonplace or significant, as well. We make a distinction between common knowledge and original thinking.

Common knowledge includes any information, idea, belief, or way of doing things that many or most people are familiar with. But the fact that you or even your circle of acquaintances does not know something does not mean that it is not common knowledge. There are levels of "commonness."

What is considered common knowledge varies from audience to audience. Most people know at least that if you step on the brakes in a car, it slows down and stops. Fewer people know how disk brakes work, but among those who do, such knowledge is considered common. People who read *Road and Track* may be aware of new developments in braking systems. Automotive engineers may regard as common knowledge the physics and the mechanical stresses involved, information that would seem "new" to the rest of us.

Though people often welcome hearing "common" knowledge that is unfamiliar to them, they may be bored or bothered if you repeat things they already know. To offer common knowledge as advice is often seen as rude, even when it may be pertinent and useful. To repeat common knowledge as if it were some kind of discovery is more a sign of ignorance than insight. But recognizing common knowledge is one of the most difficult skills of topic selection and the formulation of ideas.

People are likely to be antagonized if you miscalculate common knowledge. To avoid problems, do the following:

*1. Study the Subject.* In terms of knowledge, originality means making a discovery. You cannot know what is "new," however, if you are not thoroughly informed about the subject. This applies to new perspectives, concepts, styles, and arguments, as well as to physical and scientific discoveries.

In matters of interpretation and judgment, it is all the more difficult to distinguish between original thinking and commonplace ideas. It requires a great deal of expertise and experience to know the difference.

*2. Find out What Your Audience Knows About the Subject.* Listen to your audience. Discuss the subject with people informally before you write about it. Read what others have to say about the subject. Try out your material in advance or note the audience's reaction as you speak.

*3. Be Suspicious of "Easy" Subjects.* When topics seem easy to write about, you may be focusing on preconceptions or common knowledge without realizing it, simply reporting conventional ideas rather than thinking for yourself.

The first idea that comes to mind is almost always a familiar one, something everyone knows and may not want to hear again. But it is difficult to conceive of the subject any differently. Common knowledge is so ingrained that we can imagine nothing else to say.

*4. Distinguish Between Different Levels of Expertise.* There are shades and gradations of expertise. Specialists within a field may consider commonplace ideas their own colleagues might regard as new information. And a wide range of understanding may exist within the population at large, with some people operating largely on misconceptions, some on opinion and preconception, and some on folklore or on ideas from popular culture. Still others may be fairly well informed, familiar with popularizations of technical and scientific ideas.

It is useful and even necessary to identify in your writing the level or levels of ideas you are dealing with. People need to know whether or not you are speaking to them.

## *Writing About Commonplace Subjects*

Commonplace subjects are not necessarily boring. There is an inherent appeal in the familiar and mundane. It makes us feel secure and comfortable. It reflects our culture, values, habits, and beliefs.

If you choose to write about a topic or idea familiar to most people, you might improve the effect if you do the following:

*1. Offer a Fresh Perspective.*   Change the point of view from which you examine the subject. See it through different eyes or from a less common perspective (see Chapter 12).

For a relatively trivial subject like "pencils," for example, you could start from the perspective of a student taking a multiple choice test. You could focus on personal experience, on learning script in elementary school, smudging the paper as you tried to stay within the dittoed lines. You could take the perspective of technical drawing or graphic art.

Or you could make changes in the intellectual perspective, discussing the subject in terms of historical development, social status (wood pencils versus mechanical pencils, for example), or the size and financial strength of the pencil industry.

*2. Focus on Reinforcing Beliefs.*   There is always need for reassessment and reinforcement of conventional wisdom. If your ideas are commonplace, emphasize the importance of remembering and understanding the significance of familiar beliefs. This is the strategy the media use on virtually every holiday, for instance. It is also the stock in trade of advice books and tracts.

*3. Acknowledge Standard Arguments and Revive Dogma.*   Even when the topic is of considerable significance, what is usually said about it may be commonplace and trite. Examples include the arguments often cited on both sides of debates over gun control, abortion, and the drinking age. To repeat these is more report or paraphrase than thinking.

If, after examining them at length, you feel that the standard arguments and ideas are valid, it may be wise to acknowledge the conventionality of your material, or to argue directly that it is more than dogma, to show in the essay that these ideas have real meaning and relevance. Otherwise there is a danger that your audience will simply stop listening, assuming that you are just repeating all-too-familiar jargon and cant.

*4. Argue the Significance of the Subject.*   One of the reasons to write is to call people's attention to things that are undervalued, ignored, or misunderstood, topics that the general public mistakenly thinks are trivial. For this reason, authors commonly will claim significance for their subjects and argue in support of them, trying to persuade us to change our evaluation.

Doing so can make a routine topic more important.

5. *Articulate Your Own Interest in the Subject.* It may help to include in the writing some sense of the topic's interest to you. This can be conveyed indirectly, by showing the subject through your own eyes, for instance, or by incorporating a degree of enthusiasm or emotion into the tone and word choice. Or you can directly assert and explain the interest of the subject.

6. *Express Your Own Sense of Discovery.* Your own sense of discovery can be substituted for actual discovery. Present the insight as a personal recognition. Don't assert that the discovery is absolutely new, just that it is new to you.

7. *Emphasize Emotions and Connotations.* Many commonplace objects, events, and ideas may have strong emotional attachments for us. They may have significant personal or human connotations. Focusing of these, rather than the subject itself, may make the writing more interesting.

8. *Dramatize and Depict the Subject.* Commonplace subjects seem more interesting when they are dramatized and depicted. Use first-person narrative and graphic description. Try to aim for a "recognition" response, the pleasure people take in seeing a good likeness. Include details and incidents we either overlook or do not normally acknowledge.

9. *Discover or Create Controversy.* Although the strategy is often abused, you can make a subject more significant by attaching it to or manufacturing a crisis or controversy. In fact, it is common practice to "discover" crises repeatedly—the crises in care for the elderly, in teenagers' drinking habits, in students' knowledge of geography' or math, for example. The problems are often real enough, but to characterize them as emergencies or impending disasters is sometimes inappropriate hype.

10. *Attach Your Topic to a Significant Issue.* Trivial topics may be made more significant by association with issues that seem inherently important. "Shoveling snow" becomes more significant if you connect it to back injuries, heart attacks, or personal injury lawsuits, for example.

But even these associations may become commonplace. To appear significant, it may be necessary to move further afield. If you can establish a believable connection between "shoveling snow" and topics like child abuse, self-deception, or the work ethic, the essay may seem more original.

11. *Include a Level of Abstraction or Generalization.* If you are dealing with a single incident or object that is of limited, local, or personal signifi-

cance, you can invest it with greater meaning by generalizing about the subject or by dealing with it on a higher level of abstraction.

For example, if the immediate subject is your rent, which has gone up, focus instead or in part on the general subject of rental costs. Instead of saying "I'm paying too much" say "People are being asked to pay too much."

Or discuss the topic in abstract terms. If the immediate subject is the cost of maintaining a rental property you own, focus instead on the issue of fair return on investments or a loss of respect for other people's property.

*12. Combine Several Subjects and Ideas.* The familiar can be made more interesting by adding other pertinent issues, concepts, or levels of development to the essay. Instead of simply focusing on how to change a tire, for instance, include discussion of how we learn the routine survival skills of modern life. Write about frustration and technology, about one's lack of foresight, about the cost and complications of owning a car.

Adding parameters or issues to the discussion makes it seem more erudite or difficult as well as more original. Instead of handling just one or two topics, the author keeps five or six ideas in the air at once. The more topics under discussion at the same time, the less likely it is that the audience will have thought of the subject in that way.

For instance, instead of simply arguing that "Skyscrapers are ugly" (two topics) or that "Skyscrapers make maximum use of a minimum of land" (perhaps three topics), one might claim that "The ugliest skyscrapers are those that obviously abuse the landscape, crassly squeezing as much rentable floor space as they can out of odd scraps of real estate" (all five topics together, plus two more by implication).

*13. Reclassify or Redivide the Subject.* Part of what is commonplace about a subject is the category of experience or conceptual context in which we routinely place it, or the way we normally divide it up. By reclassifying or recategorizing the topic, we can escape common knowledge and make an otherwise familiar topic more interesting.

If we are used to thinking of computer programming under the heading of engineering, the topic can be retreaded by shifting the context, as in "Computer programming has become a cottage industry" or "Computer programming has the same basic appeal as a crossword puzzle—with a touch of masochism thrown in."

If we usually think of supermarkets as modern conveniences, we might instead look at them as public pantries or entertainments, or as a reflection of a particular corporate image or a growing dependency on institutions and businesses. Instead of automatically dividing the population of movie actors into leading men and women and character actors, or stage, big screen, and little screen (TV) actors, or comedy, dramatic, and adventure actors, we might try different ways of grouping them, like "impressionistic and realistic" or "artists, craftspeople, and professionals."

14. *Reverse Relationships.*    Significance can also be heightened or discovered by reversing the usual relationships. If people usually associate ignorance with poverty, consider instead how ignorance is associated with wealth. If people usually think of owning a car as a necessity, look instead at how it is still a luxury for many.

15. *Constrast Your View With Common Knowledge.*    You can also build a sense of significance or originality for your views by contrasting them with common knowledge, misconceptions, and appearances—as in "Glass is not as solid as it looks," or "The public has a simplistic view of the stock market, thinking of it only in terms of profit and loss. The truth is that the stock market is. . . ." Beth Neman terms this the "although" clause—a turning point or transition common in introductions to essays (see Chapter 13).

16. *Acknowledge the Insignificance of the Subject.*    Sometimes the easiest and best thing to do is simply to acknowledge a lack of originality or the limited significance of the topic. Readers may find this disarming.

Remember, we are not all that adverse to common knowledge and commonplace subjects. In fact, we rather like them, as long as the author does not force them on us or make overly pretentious claims.

## EXERCISE B

Reclassify the following subjects. Begin with one or two standard characterizations, contexts, or divisions of the topic, and then try to come up with several new categorizations. This may be fairly difficult, even with practice. (Standard answers are indicated for the first few subjects.)

1. Voter turnout at elections      [apathy]
2. Participation in school activities      [school spirit]
3. Cars      [foreign and domestic; sports and family]
4. Fathers
5. Businesses
6. The traffic conditions in the area
7. Air travel
8. College football
9. The divorce rate
10. The family pet

## EXERCISE C

Write about one of the following commonplace subjects, trying to heighten or properly acknowledge and convey its significance.

1. Today's weather
2. Curtains and draperies
3. Paper plates
4. Your favorite sweater, shirt, blouse, etc.
5. Videocassette recorders (VCRs)
6. Mowing lawns
7. An annoying commercial on TV
8. Wristwatches
9. Lettuce
10. Knowing how to type
11. Lawyers
12. Numbers or fractions
13. Pizza delivery service
14. An outing, a day at the beach, a visit to a museum or zoo
15. Styrofoam or plastic

## *Writing About Significant Topics*

Significant topics can present their own problems. They are not automatically interesting or even intelligible to readers. They may seem to challenge beliefs. People may not want to hear about unpleasant conditions and imminent problems.

If you choose a subject that is inherently controversial, complex, emotional, and significant, you may want to do the following:

*1. Identify Your Point of View With Conventional Wisdom.* Associating a controversial point of view with an accepted principle or belief may make it more palatable. But be careful not to submerge your idea so deeply in the status quo that no one can see its significance.

*2. Avoid Prefabricated Development.* When the topic is of obvious importance, be especially watchful for "standard" arguments and opinions. These are often so widely cited and relied on that they become dogmatic. Simply repeating these standard arguments or opinions can make you look like an unthinking partisan, mindlessly repeating the party line.

*3. Understate Claims to Originality.* It may be wise to understate claims of significance and originality. Better to be accorded more credit than you claim than to be blamed for seeking too much credit.

If the audience prides itself on its knowledge of the subject, there may be good reason to characterize your own ideas, however original they may be, as common knowledge.

Disclaiming originality is also useful when readers think that their current practices are quite similar to what you propose, if they think they have tried your way of doing things before (and it didn't work), or if they might regard your idea as direct criticism.

Readers may accept your opinions more readily if they can credit themselves with prior knowledge. And the point may be won (if not the attention).

Of course, the opposite is often true in sales, advertising, and public relations, where louder and more insistent assertions are often rewarded. But even then, a certain caution is advisable. Claiming too much for a product or client verges on being unethical or outright illegal.

*4. Provide Detailed Evidence and Thorough Explanation.* Especially when you are claiming that your thesis or discovery is new and original, be prepared to support the contention in detail. Though the value or truth of a discovery may appear self-evident to you, audiences tend to be more suspicious, critical, and demanding when prevailing beliefs are challenged.

*5. Emphasize Key Issues or Key Words.* Significant topics are often more complex, less easily grasped. Readers may respond better if you simplify the issues (preferably without falsifying them), focusing on a few essential concepts, at least at first. Or highlight key terms that have useful connotations. Slogans and catch phrases can also be effective.

These are strategies of propaganda and slander, or course, but they have many ethical applications (for instance, in teaching, parenting, counseling, encouragement, and exhortation).

*6. Speak From a Position of Collective Authority.* On significant and original topics, it may be safer and more effective to speak as the representative of a group opinion, of consensus, or collective authority. When you say "I believe," you seem an isolated and perhaps eccentric voice. When you say "We believe," or even "I'm sure others would agree," it creates the impression that an organized opposition exists. When you say "Most experts agree," you become the disinterested reporter of considered truths.

*7. Distribute "Ownership" of the Idea.* You can diminish any threat to the status quo if you

- characterize the subject as one that many people have studied and contributed to an understanding of

- credit your own success to help or guidance from others
- ask for suggestions, additions, or refinements, thereby encouraging the reader to share "ownership" of the idea
- identify some other authority, preferably a widely respected one, as the ultimate source of your idea

*Note:* Usually it is wiser to avoid asking for criticism, since that invites the reader to see your work in a negative light.

*8. Distance Yourself From the Subject.*   Significant topics are often strongly tied to self-interest and personal beliefs. If you distance yourself from the subject, you may avoid being seen as self-serving.

Discuss the subject in general terms or in the abstract. Avoid reference to personal experience or self-interest. Avoid expressions of emotion. Make your stance as neutral and impersonal as possible. Do not put your personality into the presentation.

*9. Emphasize Personal Experience.*   The opposite strategy can also work. Instead of distancing yourself from the subject, treat it entirely as a matter of your individual experience. Avoid generalizing. Convey the impression that only the personal significance of the issue matters to you.

*10. Expect Competition.*   The fact that the subject is widely considered significant means that many people have a stake in the outcome, that others have likely thought long and deeply about the matter. There will be greater competition among speakers and greater knowledgeability in the audience.

*11. Show Respect for Accepted Views.*   Determine the generally accepted views of a subject—what most people think about it, what is widely felt to be true. Include some respectful discussion of these viewpoints in your essay.

*12. Describe Your Methodology or Process of Discovery.*   It can be useful to include in your essay some direct description of the process you went through to arrive at your present conclusions.

Another possibility is to think as you write, to discover—or appear to discover—new aspects of the subject in the course of the essay.

These strategies have the advantage of making your point of view look like a considered opinion, a reasoned judgment rather than a simple opinion or preconception.

*13. Do Not Rely on Inherent Interest.*   If your topic is of obvious or extreme significance, do not expect the gravity of the issue to sell your ideas. People might agree that improving civil rights is important, but they may do nothing about it. They might be fascinated by earthquakes but not by your report about an earthquake.

*14. Distinguish Between Evident and Invisible Crises.* Sometimes the importance of the subject is not obvious to the audience, as when potential danger is out of sight or still in the future, or when a discovery contradicts common knowledge or is counterintuitive. When this happens, authors may respond by arguing for the significance of the topic, perhaps in the case of an impending crisis with a note of warning or admonition in the style. Or with somewhat greater chance of success, they may accept the burden of proof and present an exhaustive survey of the evidence.

*15. Use a Serious or Measured Tone.* In keeping with the importance of the subject, significant topics usually call for a more dignified and measured tone. Informality may seem inappropriate or disrespectful, unless the author uses it as a means of self-depreciation. There is less likely to be humor, except perhaps to express fatalism or to reduce the tension of the moment.

Authors often use understatement or a flat, more reportative style, allowing the strength of the material to speak for itself. If there is an obvious crisis at hand, the essay is apt to be more deliberative in focus and manner, counseling a particular course of action.

*16. Take an Appropriate Stance.* Significant subjects often are related to continuing or recurrent problems for which defined roles have evolved ("army general," for instance). The author's stance should be adapted to the nature of the subject's significance and to the author's actual role in the situation.

A crisis might be written about from any or all of the following perspectives: by participants in the events; by eyewitnesses; by reporters, who sum up for us what happened; by commentators, who put the events in perspective and discuss their causes, consequences, and meanings; by moralists, who judge their virtue or worth; by scholars, who ask how or why such events happen and what general principles they evince; by technicians, who study how to fix the problem or avoid recurrence; and by administrators, who consider what is to be done next, how to allocate resources, and how to assess blame.

Each of these roles implies a different kind of essay, but it is not uncommon for the different perspectives to overlap within the same essay. One's involvement with the subject may, for example, include both participation and crisis management.

## WHEN TO WRITE ABOUT COMMONPLACE OR TOPICAL SUBJECTS

Commonplace subjects are the focus of much of our daily conversation and discussion. They are appropriate

- in informal situations
- when the audience is less informed
- when seeking to create human interest
- when evoking sentiment or common feeling
- when the audience would not welcome serious issues
- when you are not an expert
- when you wish to put people at ease
- when you want to encourage dialogue
- when writing introductions
- when you wish to evoke humor

## WHEN TO FOCUS ON SIGNIFICANT OR EXCEPTIONAL SUBJECTS

Although many situations imply their subject matter, the relationship between topic and situation is not necessarily fixed. One can choose to address trivial aspects of a momentous event, or to bring up totally irrelevant matter. Significant topics are appropriate, however,

- when the occasion is serious or ceremonial
- when the occasion is formal or professional
- in academic, scientific, and technical writing
- during a crisis
- in consulting and instruction
- in argument and persuasion

### GAINS AND LOSSES

#### ◀ COMMONPLACE TOPICS ▶

| Advantages | Disadvantages |
|---|---|
| Familiarity and acceptance | Easy to ignore or tune out |
| Reinforce status quo | Conventional interpretations may win out |
| Noncontroversial or not surprising | Low priority on social agenda |
| Put author and audience on the same footing | Lose benefit of status and distance |
| Require no special expertise or support | Confer no authority or expertise |
| Invite readers to see personal relevance | May not support weighty treatment or styles |

## GAINS AND LOSSES

### ◆ SIGNIFICANT TOPICS ▶

| Advantages | Disadvantages |
|---|---|
| Inherent interest | Inherent controversy and conventional development |
| Challenging and complex | Simplistic answers often preferred |
| Carry automatic authority and weight | May require extensive research and experience |
| Demand attention and a place on the agenda | Except in a crisis, need greater support |
| Justify speaking up | Require leadership and personal responsibility |
| Carry strong emotional appeal | May subvert audience's will and self-interest |
| May carry with them a standard role | May call for a heightened style |

## EXERCISE D

Analyze the attractions and difficulties of the following topics. What audiences might be interested in them? How would you make the topics seem more significant to other audiences? How much knowledge or research would it take to write effectively about them? What kind of research would be useful?

1. Men's neckties
2. The cost of a new house
3. The threat of nuclear destruction
4. The gradual destruction of tropical rainforests
5. World War II
6. Abortion
7. Paper cuts
8. The U.S. Postal Service
9. Jamaica
10. Limestone
11. A local nightclub
12. A popular song
13. Breakfast

14. Materialism or greed
15. A child you saw playing in a schoolyard this morning

## *Wider Implications*

In rhetorical theory, questions of topic and originality have been addressed under a number of headings. The issue has been variously considered as a matter of invention, self-expression, presumption or the burden of proof, and exigence, the need to speak.

### INVENTION AND THE CHOICE OF TOPICS

In terms of invention, the choice of topics involves

- recalling subjects, ideas, and experiences
- perceiving subjects that ought to be addressed
- making discoveries
- studying the subject from different perspectives
- rearranging or recombining information to form new subjects and ideas

These are skills of memory, imagination, observation, inference, and conceptualization.

### SELF-EXPRESSION

What you write about is also affected by who you are, by the need to express your identity, emotions, and beliefs. We write expressively to seek attention, appreciation, consolation, and understanding, to validate the self.

### PRESUMPTION

We tend not to write about things that are generally accepted as true or matters of fact. There is no need to. But when your ideas challenge or contradict the status quo, you are expected to defend them. These are questions of presumption.

The study of presumption is concerned with determining which side in a given dispute has the burden of proof—or in other words, which side must initiate the debate and work hardest to prove its case. In our own legal system, this matter is codified: the suspect is innocent until proven guilty (that is, the burden of proof is on the prosecuter).

In many other circumstances, the burden of proof is not so clearly defined. When there are several competing policy recommendations in a business, for instance, you might expect the burden of proof to rest on the least conservative suggestion. But if traditional practices are in disrepute or the business has suffered reversals, the burden of proof might fall instead on more conservative courses of action.

In scientific and technical fields, the ideal is that all theories should share the same burden of proof. No hypothesis should have an advantage because of familiarity, tradition, or emotional preference.

In practice, the burden of proof falls on theories that seem extreme, sensational, unnecessarily complex, or radical. These generally receive greater publicity and attention at the outset but thereafter are held to the highest standards of evidence and subjected to the closest scrutiny.

## EXIGENCE AND THE CHOICE OF TOPICS

Your topic may be determined by the circumstances. When a rhetorical situation exists—an event, crisis, or other circumstance so pressing that it compels an orator to speak—the topic is defined by the exigence.

## MOTIVATION AND THE CHOICE OF TOPICS

Exigence is related to the writer's motivation, his or her reason for writing. What you write about varies according to your purposes or aims. In addition to self-expression, these may include personal objectives or goals, a desire to please or help the audience, the search for knowledge, a need for solutions to problems, and so on. The purpose becomes the meaning or significance of the subject, the content of the essay.

From the perspective of motivation, what makes a "good topic to write about" is a clear and acceptable sense of purpose. To write about coffee for no reason at all would seem pointless and unjustified. It would be a bad topic. But if one's purpose is warning people about the effects of caffeine, or explaining the social and managerial impact of coffee breaks, then the subject becomes worthwhile.

## AUTHENTICITY AND THE CHOICE OF TOPICS

It is not enough simply to "have a purpose," however. One's motivation about the subject must be conveyed in the style. This reflection of purposefulness is related to the style's apparent sincerity or engagement with the subject, to the immediacy of the presentation and authenticity of the expressed ideas and emotions.

Topics appear worthwhile when we feel that the author has a genuine interest in the subject. Topics appear worthless when the style does not communicate the author's emotional, intellectual, and/or personal involvement with the subject, or when the involvement seems contrived.

## SIMPLE, RECEIVED, AND CONSIDERED OPINIONS

Our interpretation of an author's motivation and engagement is also connected to the difference between simple, received, and considered opinions; that is, between superficial generalizations, learned preconceptions, and concepts validated through speculation, criticism, observation, and experience.

Topics seem "better" when the author can convince us that the claims being made are not prejudices or uncritical judgments but intelligently considered opinions. Simple opinions may seem motivated but superficial. Received opinions seem to be motivated by prejudice rather than conscious thought. But considered opinions seem to be the result of extended interest in and study of the subject.

## COGNITIVE DISSONANCE AND THE CHOICE OF TOPICS

Because of the relationship between good subjects to write about and speculation or self-doubt, some teachers of rhetoric suggest that the most viable topics are associated with "cognitive dissonance"—the unsettled state of mind that occurs when our mental image of the world conflicts with the world we perceive, when our beliefs or opinions are apparently in need of revision to conform to the facts.

To take a simple example, "fast food is convenient" would be a bad topic because it simply confirms a preconception. But after sitting at a drive-through window for twenty minutes, one might seriously question the preconception and choose to write about how "fast food is not as convenient as it seems." The topic becomes better when you are confronting doubts and contradictions.

At a more sophisticated level, cognitive dissonance involves confronting serious questions of doubt, even to the extent of challenging one's own assumptions and beliefs.

## EXPERTISE, OPPORTUNITY, EVIDENCE, AND EXPECTATIONS

Choice of subject is also related to questions of expertise, *kairos*, logical validity and adequate support for assertions, and audience expectations.

We can only write about topics we perceive or can say something about. When we feel that little can be said about a subject, we tend to avoid it. We sidestep topics we do not understnad—sometimes pretending they do not exist.

Choosing not to speak about something is in its own way a decision about subject matter. To avoid speaking on a topic is to place limits on the agenda of debate, to limit the focus of the discussion.

The existing degree of consensus may affect your choice of topics. If almost everyone agrees about a particular subject, there is usually less need to discuss it and less interest in hearing about it. Conversely, when popular ideas and beliefs have been threatened, opposed, or challenged, there may be great opportunity for writing about them. People like to have their beliefs reinforced.

We often say the things we think people want us to say—and avoid topics that the audience might not approve of. When we do, the readers' attitudes and expectations are controlling our choice of topics.

We may avoid making claims that seem invalid or unsubstantiated. In academic and professional writing (and interpersonal communication), it is more ethical to do so. But speculative discourse and humor may require you to develop, if not to endorse, such claims.

## OPPORTUNITY AND THE CHOICE OF TOPICS

The choice of topic is affected by the author's personal interests, by his or her stake in the outcome of a debate, by the author's perceptiveness, and by sheer opportunity. If a reporter is in a restaurant when it is held up, circumstances have provided a possible story. If a scientist accidentally contaminates a bacterial culture with the right mold, opportunity may lead to the discovery of penicillin.

## IDENTITY AND THE CHOICE OF TOPICS

What you talk about tells a lot about who you are. It reflects your interests, concerns, attitudes, idiosyncracies, and emotional state. It tells others what you like, what you know, and what you value. From the subjects you choose to address, your motives, beliefs, and autobiography can be inferred.

## REPUTATION AND THE CHOICE OF TOPICS

Our estimation of people is partially based on their habitual choice of topics. People who talk about themselves, for instance, may appear to be egocentric. People who talk excessively about status, social events, and appearance may seem superficial.

Writing about one's past can seem nostalgic, bitter, pensive, world-weary, or excessively proud. Focusing on daily events and minor details may sound either trivial or observant, petty or meticulous, depending on how well the material is presented.

A person who can talk only about his or her work may seem self-absorbed and highly motivated or socially maladroit. Speaking continually about one's problems or worries may create the impression that the author is a complainer or neurotic, or suggest that he or she seeks or deserves the troubles being reported. Constant discussion of social problems may make the speaker seem altruistic and high-minded.

## INTEREST

Significance and interest are not the same thing. We may be bored by significant issues and fascinated by trivial and commonplace things. Frequent exposure to disasters and crimes may make them seem commonplace, trivializing events and hardening the emotions. Personal taste may lean toward baseball cards and rock collections, things familiar, rewarding, and easily explained.

Interest can be generated and maintained by effective presentation. If the subject is trivial, there may be a need to create interest. If the subject happens to be of major and obvious significance, the author needs to do it justice. If the subject has major significance that is not immediately apparent, the author has a certain responsibility to speak up in its behalf, to make others see its importance and meaning.

## INNOCENCE, ORIGINALITY, AND INTEREST

It is natural but a mistake to think that whatever seems new and fresh to us must also be new to our readers. We continually rediscover things that have long been known. Our comprehension of others is often so imperfect that what we have read or been told repeatedly may nevertheless seem like a true discovery when we recognize the principle for ourselves.

We have a tendency to think that whatever is interesting to us must of course be interesting to our audience. And so we offer our views without embroidery, making no effort to dress them up or sell them to others. We assume that readers will see the subject as we do, and we become upset or frustrated when they do not, though the fault is our own.

We tend to think that we are personally interesting because we are of interest to ourselves. And so we expect others to like us, listen to us, believe us, and admire our accomplishments no matter how tedious and self-important we become.

## *Conclusion*

We often feel that unique subjects sell themselves. If a person has discovered a new molecule, climbed Mount Everest, or somehow made history, it seems that he or she has an unfair advantage, a subject that requires no effort to make it interesting and original. But a truly boring writer can ruin a Mount Everest topic as easily as any other topic. Bad home movies of a trip to Tahiti are not necessarily any better than bad home movies of a trip to the shopping mall.

We see people whose lives we envy and we think they are interesting by nature, birth, occupation, or good fortune, not recognizing that the interest they excite is our own creation, no credit to them. Such people might be as dull or uninspiring as the rest of us.

No person, topic, or event is inherently fascinating or automatically guaranteed an audience. Interest comes and goes as tastes change, as new ideas become common knowledge, as the strange, surprising, and clever become by stages the familiar, the commonplace, and then the annoying, or as writers discover new ways to invest their subjects with meaning.

## ASSIGNMENT: Magnification and Diminution

1. Make a relatively insignificant event seem important, without losing a sense of proportion. Or willfully exaggerate its importance for comic effect.

2. Try to depreciate—at least temporarily—the significance of a relatively important event, current or historical, or a relatively significant object, belief, issue, or argument. Consider in advance the feelings of your audience, and decide whether you wish to avoid giving offense or whether the point merits engendering some displeasure.

3. Choose an event or moment that was important to you personally (but had little effect on or interest for anyone else) and try to make it seem important to others, without seeming self-centered or self-indulgent.

4. Start with a commonplace idea, perhaps a maxim, truism, or bit of common knowledge, and try to make it seem original and fresh while acknowledging your audience's familiarity with the subject.

5. Write about a very important and well-known event, idea, or person, reemphasizing the subject's significance without rehashing the same old arguments, stories, and points of view. You might try to emphasize a new perspective or a new interpretation of the available material.

# 10

# Interpretation and Representation

The life which is unexamined is not worth living.               —Plato

To interpret is to impoverish, to deplete the world—in order to set up a
shadow world of "meanings."                                —Susan Sontag

The imposition of meaning on life is the major end and primary condition of human existence                                    —Clifford Geertz

## Developing Ideas

Readers are jealous of information and ideas. They want to know what happened and what it means. Reports, descriptions, stories, and dramatizations
increase their range of perception, extend the limits of what the audience
can see and experience. Commentary and interpretation extend the scope
of understanding. They explain the significance and effect of what has happened, defining and characterizing an event, exploring its connotations and
essence, its causes and implications. They distill the meaning from the subject and infuse it with other ideas, amalgamating one event or idea with another.

These are constant occupations. We read, watch, listen to, and repeat
accounts of our experiences and observations. We interpret and reinterpret
their meaning.

But we are skeptical, as well. We may doubt someone else's version of
events, suspecting that the person may not be telling us all the facts or that
the story is skewed to the author's benefit. We distrust commentary that

seems to force a meaning on events or to read into them the author's pre-conceptions or beliefs. A credible interpretation must be substantiated by the facts.

Audiences may regard interpretation, regardless of its quality or appropriateness, as good or bad.

### ◆ INTERPRETATION ◆

| Good Qualities | Bad Qualities |
|---|---|
| substantive | subjective |
| explanatory | sophistic |
| wise | overanalytical |
| enhancement | detraction |

It does not seem to matter whether the interpretation is scientific or philosophical: the good and bad perceptions remain basically the same.

The response to representation, however, can vary widely depending on whether the aim of the depiction is more literary or scientific. These two aims are presented together in this chapter (as vivid or dramatic representation and as accurate representation, respectively), since both kinds of writing emphasize the portrayal of the subject, but the resulting styles are obviously quite different. For that reason, it is useful to separate the range of judgments applied to each.

Audiences may think that dramatic representation is good or bad.

### ◆ DRAMATIC REPRESENTATION ◆

| Good Qualities | Bad Qualities |
|---|---|
| entertaining | useless |
| true to life | contrived |
| immediate, authentic | manipulative |
| meaningful | oblique, circuitous |

Audiences may also regard accurate representation (as in documentaries, statistics, or reports) as good or bad.

### ◀ ACCURATE REPRESENTATION ▶

| Good Qualities | Bad Qualities |
| --- | --- |
| useful | pointless |
| informative | obvious |
| objective | unexamined |
| scientific | arid |

In practice, there is considerable crossover between the two kinds of representation. Popularized science may become more graphic and evocative. Documentaries may take a stance that is more literary than scientific. And dramatic representations may verge on the scientific and objective.

## What to Say

To understand a subject is to have some control over it. This control may be as simple as knowing what the subject looks like. It may be as complex as knowing the subject's composition, significance, or nature. These forms of understanding, inherent in representation and interpretation, are the fundamental content of an essay.

Control of a subject is implied in an ability to replicate it; to physically replace or duplicate it or to "show" it to others through description, artwork, formulas, or laws; to present the subject in a coherent, consistent, or encapsulated form. And control is implied in the ability to predict a subject's behavior or effects, to analyze its causes, and to articulate its connotations.

Human knowledge is a compilation. We rely on each other's experience and understanding, sharing ideas and information because we cannot expect by ourselves to know any subject completely.

## Meaning

How much meaning an author reads into the subject can vary widely. The extremes range from pure representation (if such a thing is possible) to pure interpretation, as diagramed in Figure 10.1. Pure representation is an attempt to be as realistic as possible without intruding authorial comment or imposing a perspective on the subject. Pure interpretation becomes an ideology or belief.

The distinction between the surface mode (representation or interpretation) and the semantic mode (report and meaning) is necessary because

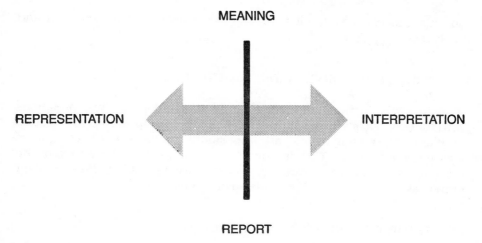

**Figure 10.1**

highly representative writing may convey more meaning than a clearly interpretive essay. And highly interpretive writing may become dramatic and vivid, as in the case of philosophic dialogues, for instance, or reflective writing.

Mythology and allegory tend toward the portrayal of meaning. An image or symbol may speak volumes (or remain silent). A novel may imply and evoke more (or less) understanding than a direct exposition of the subject. And interpretation can verge on paraphrase and report.

*A Caution:* The terms used here are inherently slippery. All discourse, whether overtly representative or not, makes some attempt at representation. One might say, for instance, that interpretive writing is a particular style of representation—using analysis rather than description to portray the subject. And discourse can hardly avoid conveying some degree of interpretation. Even a random list implies a selection process.

## The Nature of Interpretations

Forming an interpretation might be roughly equated with expressing an opinion, making a claim, developing a hypothesis, framing a model of how something is formed or how it works, offering a scenario or schedule of events, fixing a plan of action or solving a problem, arriving at a logical conclusion, or making an assertion. These are all part of the same phenomenon, the desire to explain things, to be able to identify what is there to be seen and how it affects us, to control it, to predict its behavior and consequences, and to file it away for future reference.

## THESIS STATEMENTS AND CHARACTERIZATIONS

Some distinctions are necessary. To equate forming interpretations with the process of arriving at thesis statements or propositions may lead to problems. Thesis statements and propositions are more precisely a part of logical demonstration. They isolate the point that is to be illustrated or the claim to be proven. In explanatory and interpretive writing, the equivalent form of assertion might best be called a characterization.

## THE IRREDUCIBILITY OF INTERPRETATION

It would be a mistake to think of single-sentence characterizations as the end product of interpretation. An interpretation is a complete "essay" or text, the entire assessment and reading of an event, person, or phenomenon. The characterization or interpretive thesis is just a means of emphasizing, characterizing, and framing the overall point of view.

## PERCEIVING THE ESSENCE OF THINGS

We interpret events, objects, character, and people's actions in much the same manner as we interpret discourse. A good reader will discern the central meaning of an essay or communication, will see through appearances, amibiguities, or indirections and find the essential significance of what has been said. A good observer performs a similar function, deciding what message should be read from the signs or symptoms, from the incidents experienced, or from the data received.

In this way interpretation makes reams of information more manageable and fills in the gaps where our information is sketchy. Through interpretation we are able to apprehend, understand, and recall the subject without having to keep the entire matter before our eyes. And we are able to communicate about objects and events not immediately visible or present.

## INTERPRETATION AS KNOWLEDGE

We continually interpret and reinterpret the world around us, and we use the process of interpretation to guide our actions. If there is sufficient evidence to support an interpretation or if it proves helpful in some way, we may come to regard it as "knowledge" or fact. If experience does not bear out our initial conclusions, we modify or adjust our views. This is essentially the same process as revising for accuracy in writing.

## THE PLURALITY OF INTERPRETATION

An interpretation is a partial truth, accurate insofar as the evidence supports it. Any subject is open to multiple interpretations. For instance, an earthquake might be variously interpreted as a major geologic event, as a human tragedy, as a conflict between humans and nature, as a test of building codes, as an economic crisis in the making, as a serious problem for health and emergency services, as a warning against complacency, and as a personal triumph over the odds.

The list of these characterizations could go on almost indefinitely, and each one could be supported by the facts. They are all potentially "true." Supporting any one of them does not necessarily deny the validity of the others. In fact, one might argue that the most complete understanding of the event—the earthquake—would be a composite of many interpretations.

## INTERPRETATION AS THOUGHT

Interpretive writing, then, is closely tied to the quality of thought that goes into it. Formulating a characterization or thesis statement for an interpretive essay is not a pointless exercise but the essence of thinking and comprehension—if it is done well. It is the same skill we use to size up a situation and respond to it, to intuit the character of people we deal with, to decide what ought to be done.

## *Interpreting the Subject*

Interpretive writing puts in the foreground the author's ideas, perceptions, or feelings about a subject, pushing the phenomenon or object itself off center stage. This displacement may be difficult to see, since even in fairly interpretive writing the author still appears to be talking about the subject.

But a biologist proposing a theory to explain the chemical basis of photosynthesis is in fact not writing directly about photosynthesis—the apparent topic. The existence and general nature of photosynthesis is considered common knowledge and as such is excluded from or at most summarized in the essay. The true focus of the discussion is the author's own explanation of how the process of photosynthesis is effected.

To write effective interpretation, do the following:

*1. Take a Speculative Stance.* An interpretive style is often more speculative, scientific, or philosophical in tone. The author's role in interpretive writing is that of commentator or scientific observer—someone with a responsibility not only to report the subject but also to explain it.

*2. Emphasize Abstractions and Generalizations.*    Interpretive writing is more likely to focus on the general case than the particular. This may even hold true when the writer discusses at length a specific object, event, or person. A highly interpretive discussion of a specific case often concludes or implies that general truths and principles can be inferred from the subject.

*3. Deemphasize Specific Incidents, People, and Objects.*    You can make your style more expository or interpretive by deemphasizing specific events, phenomena, people, or objects. Discuss general cases and trends, using particulars only in a supporting role.

*4. Make Your Meaning Explicit.*    Style becomes more interpretive or expository as the attempt to explain the significance of events, phenomena, or objects becomes more direct. Try to put in words exactly what you mean.

*5. Use Principles and Beliefs to Analyze the Subject.*    One form of interpretation arises from applying preexisting concepts to the immediate topic of discussion. This is a deductive approach to meaning. The author finds evidence in the subject to support and illustrate his or her beliefs, theories, or ideology.

*6. Draw Inferences From the Subject.*    A second form of interpretation is inductive. It creates meaning by studying the subject and drawing inferences from it. The author attempts to form a new ideology, theory, or paradigm based on observation of the subject.

*7. Characterize.*    Interpretations sum up and characterize experiences, observations, facts, and data. They define the essence of things, the dominant impression, the determining factor, the identifying trait, the central motive or tendency. It is a process of distillation, even caricature.

*8. Analyze.*    Interpretations analyze the features or components of the subject. They explain how things fit together, what they represent, where they come from, how they might be accomplished, how they affect us, and what their consequences might be. They suggest connections between different events, objects, and ideas.

*9. Paraphrase, Apply, and Refine Accepted Interpretations.*    It is not always necessary to form independent interpretations. Many subjects have standard and accepted meanings, part of the received wisdom of the culture. The ability to repeat and paraphrase these standard interpretations—

with real comprehension of their significance—may be all that is expected. It is a kind of scholarship.

Originality, in such cases, may consist of being able to apply, extend, alter, or challenge the standard interpretations.

*10. Use Metaphorical Thinking.* Interpretation is akin to metaphorical thinking; it requires you to conceive of the subject as something it is not. The following list (based on *A General Rhetoric* by Group Mu [Jacques Dubois, *et al.*], (Baltimore: Johns Hopkins UP, 1981), begins with synonymy (paraphrase or common knowledge) and becomes increasingly metaphorical:

| street | = | an established route for cars and trucks |
| street | = | the roads we follow from one place to another |
| street | = | an escape route during disasters |
| street | = | a barrier to pedestrian traffic |
| street | = | supply routes for cities |
| street | = | a means of communication |
| street | = | the arteries and veins of the community |
| street | = | a psychological escape route |
| street | = | a symbol of choice, the road not taken |
| street | = | trust |
| street | = | sagebrush |

The placement of individual items on the preceding list could be disputed, but what matters is the general trend from paraphrase or report to generalization to logical metaphor or association and finally to illogical association. Scientific or logical interpretation tends to appear toward the middle of the spectrum, poetic or personal interpretation toward the end.

*11. Diverge From Strict Paraphrase, Description, and Narration.* The metaphorical tendencies of interpretation suggest that something like an interpretation can be formed by warping paraphrase, description, and narrative in a systematic and intentional way. It becomes a rendering or personal reading of the subject.

*An Important Caution:* If you find yourself simply retelling a story, reporting events, or describing an author's ideas, then you are probably not developing an interpretation. An interpretation *can* be embodied in a deft narrative that reenvisions events or a paraphrase that purports to tell not so much what the author said as what he or she really meant, or the essential meaning of an essay, but this can be hard to do. Narrative and paraphrastic report tend to take over, suppressing interpretation despite all good intentions to the contrary.

In general, the closer your retelling is to description or narration, the less interpretive it becomes. The closer your paraphrase is to accepted definitions, the less original it becomes. Conversely, as your paraphrase diverges further from the established view of the subject, it will sound more original and seem more like a figure of speech—an image or metaphor.

If your interpretation diverges too far from the accepted definition of the subject, it is likely to be dismissed as no more than an analogy or myth, an eccentric and overly ingenious attempt to explain the facts. When the association becomes too tenuous or extreme, the audience may reject it out of hand as a sign of ignorance, self-indulgence, or irrationality.

*12. Develop Several Distinctly Different Interpretations.*   Don't stop at the first interpretation that comes to mind. Often it is either fiction or common knowledge. Develop several markedly different interpretations and decide which fits the facts best.

*13. Support Your Interpretations.*   Your reading of a subject is always open to question. Like any other assertion, an interpretation may need to be supported with evidence and argument. The more unusual, extreme, or surprising your interpretation, the more support it may require.

## *The Provinces of Interpretation*

It may be useful to differentiate between four different provinces of interpretation, namely

- natural phenomena
- human actions and behavior
- discourse
- technology

The substance of interpretation varies significantly from one province to another.

### NATURAL PHENOMENA

Largely the province of the natural sciences and, to some extent, philosophy, interpretation of natural phenomena tends to focus on (a) defining their nature or essence; (b) explaining their origin and development; (c) describing their behavior, environment, properties, or characteristics; (d) predicting of controlling their future behavior; (e) exploring their uses; and (f) explaining their emotional and intellectual significance.

## HUMAN ACTIONS AND BEHAVIOR

Interpretations of human actions and behavior are the substance of the social sciences, of business administration, and of the humanities in general.

Interpretation of human action tends to focus on (a) its motives, objectives, or intent; (b) influences on it or causes for it; (c) its immediate or potential consequences; (d) the emotions it evokes or incites; and (e) the attitudes or culture it reflects.

## DISCOURSE

Interpretation of discourse is more directly the province of literary criticism, linguistics, rhetoric, semiotics, philosophy, information design, and communication theory.

These interpretations may be especially complex, since they include interpretation of human actions and of natural phenomenon as well as interpretation of the text or essay itself. When we interpret discourse, we tend to focus on (a) its intent or objectives, (b) its overt message, (c) its covert or indirect messages, (d) what it means to the author, (e) what it means to us and to others in the audience, (f) its foundation in the author's experience and culture, (g) its relevance to our own experience, (h) its effects or consequences, (i) its implications in other areas of knowledge, (j) its applications to other cases, and (k) potential extensions of or extrapolations from the author's ideas.

## TECHNOLOGY

Interpretation of technology is the major concern of the various fields of engineering and design.

Interpretation in technological fields often focuses on (a) problem solving, (b) utility, (c) need, (d) causes and effects, (e) feasibility or practicality, (f) the exploitable properties of different materials and structures, (g) the inherent limitations or weaknessess of different materials and structures, (h) the various and potential applications of different materials and designs, (i) cost, (j) efficiency, and (k) alternative means of solving the same problem. (The technological fields are so inherently evaluative that it is almost impossible to separate questions of interpretation from questions of judgment in discussing them.)

## *The Nature of Representation*

Representation attempts to portray the subject in words, to show us people, events, places, and objects as they really are. A representational style can stress either vividness or accuracy—making the subject seem dramatic and immediate or offering a complete, clear-sighted, and even scientific description or portrayal. Representation shows us the character or nature of the subject. It focuses on the details and particulars, the individual case.

### DRAMATIC REPRESENTATION

Dramatic representation focuses on re-creating the subject, on depicting it, dramatizing it, or bringing it to life. It tries to make the audience experience or envision the event or object, to capture a sense of its entire, complex, and undivided nature.

### SCIENTIFIC REPRESENTATION

Scientific representation tells us what happened, without excessive embellishment or commentary. The emphasis is on giving a precise chronicle of occurrences rather than on re-creating events. The genre includes reports, academic history, objective journalism, and scientific accounts, as well as resumes, some biography, and many informal modes of narrative and anecdote.

### IMPRESSIONISTIC DESCRIPTION

Vivid description focuses on the connotations of the object being described or on the impression it makes on the observer. It tries to convey the appearance or essence of the object by showing what it looks like or by incorporating and evoking emotional responses.

As in dramatic representation of events, there may be some effort to re-create the object, to make it seem real and present.

### ACCURATE DESCRIPTION

Scientific description offers precise details, measurements, and characteristics. It may tell us the object's appearance, its composition, its location and surroundings, its orientation, and its properties or uses. The genre includes scientific description, technical reports and technical drawing, instructional writing, directions, statistics, case studies, and market analyses, among other forms of discourse.

### THE INFORMATIONAL CONTENT OF REPRESENTATION

Representational writing is not necessarily devoid of meaning. The author has a choice of either

- avoiding all commentary and interpretation
- conveying meaning indirectly
- evoking meaning
- offering commentary and discussion in a secondary role

The indirect and evoked content of representational writing may actually exceed the meaning conveyed by explicit interpretation.

Some styles also reject the validity of interpretation and analysis. They may take the stance that the only way to truly apprehend and "know" the subject is to see it whole, to experience it.

## *Representing the Subject*

It can be extremely difficult to convey in words a true sense of action, character, place, and relationship. We tend to underestimate the problems. The informal narrative and description of casual conversation is more complex than it seems—and often less effective than it is thought.

One can only begin to discuss the possibilities. In general, however, a representational style will do the following:

*1. Focus on the Subject.* Representational writing emphasizes the subject rather than its significance. The author's ideas or attitudes are expressed indirectly or are suppressed.

*2. Be Specific.* The particular case is most important in representation. It is important to observe the subject closely and report not only broad outlines and features, but also the characteristics peculiar to the individual event, person, object, or place.

*3. Use Graphic and Sensory Detail.* Representation tends to emphasize the perceptions. It provides concrete details, sensory impressions, and visual cues that might enable the audience mentally to reconstruct the subject.

*4. Focus on Specific Incidents.* Generalized accounts of events and experience are often ineffective, or at best just a framework for more detailed narrative. Re-creating a sense of what happened, whether in report or in dramatic representation, requires at least some focus on specific incidents.

*5. Create a Sequence of Events.* In simple narrative, the author creates a progression from one incident to the next, establishing a sequence. Though it may seem that these are "natural" or an inherent part of the events themselves, the narrative progression is often a conventional pattern imposed on the subject. For example, we conventionally might group a sequence of reversals, seeing them as bad luck or as a sign that fate is against us. Or an auto accident and subsequent recovery may be read together as a learning experience or a discovery of one's own fragility.

These patterns are really buried interpretations. More original sequences may be formed by grouping events differently and basing the narrative on more subtle meanings.

Rearranging chronology can have the same effect. Even then, readers usually expect some connection or pattern to emerge.

*6. Observe Events Closely.* Simple narrative implies that only one thing happens at a time and that incidents happen one after the other in a causal sequence. This is an extreme oversimplification of history and experience. Accurate and dramatic representation alike depend on closer observation, on more complex and sophisticated portrayal of events.

*7. Create an Image or Impression.* Representational writing may attempt to create an image or collective impression of the subject. While this may be accomplished through description and narrative alone, there may be considerable reliance on pictures, sketches, or filmed scenes and action to back up the author's verbal account. Much the same effect can be achieved through the use of imagery—through metaphors, characterizations, and allusions.

*8. Be Thorough.* One may also attempt to convey a collective impression by offering an exhaustive assemblage of data, trusting the audience to be able to reconstruct the subject from the details given. This strategy may be especially useful when addressing readers who are extremely knowledgeable on the topic; their expertise makes it easier for them to recognize significant patterns in the data. They can draw on their knowledge and experience of the subject to provide the outline, framework, or image that encompasses and explains the masses of detail.

A variation on this is to represent the subject through statistics and analysis, and ultimately through interpretation itself.

When accuracy is important for practical reasons—as in technical instructions or scientific report—then thoroughness in representation and report may be essential. To a certain extent, however, this sacrifices impact and vividness. The eye does not normally capture such intricate detail; our impressions of things focus on broad and distinguishing features.

Thoroughness does not necessarily make a story or sketch more true to life, however. When representation is meant to capture a mood or create an impression, excessive detail can obscure the broader features of the subject and excessive incident can confuse the narrative. If scientific accuracy is not at stake, it may be wiser to emphasize the more unique or significant aspects of the subject and omit or merely suggest the nuances.

9. *Avoid Excessive Abstraction and Explanation.* Representational writing, as a rule, uses fewer explicit abstractions and generalizations. It is less likely to amplify a subject through definition, self-paraphrase, classification, and division and more likely to develop the subject by adding further incidents, details, and perspectives (e.g., other eyewitness accounts of the same event).

10. *Convey Meaning Indirectly.* Representational styles often imply the meaning of events and objects. This effect may be accomplished by focusing on and emphasizing incidents and details that most clearly and exclusively reflect the desired interpretation, while simultaneously deemphasizing or excluding material that might lead readers to infer other meanings.

If the message is fairly overt and specific, the resulting story is an apologue or fable; if the events and setting embody moral or religious values, or, in some cases, psychological traits and social norms, we consider them to be allegorical.

When the message is more indirect, diffuse, or complex, the resulting text may seem more literary, more entertaining, and more true-to-life, as long as the author's worldview or state of mind remains relatively constant and the manner of presentation consistent and appropriate. Otherwise the text will seem incoherent, unfocused, or random. (Note that an incoherent state of mind, if it is represented in a consistent and appropriate manner, can produce a text we regard as "coherent" in expressing its own incoherence.)

## EXERCISE A

Combine and extend the following pairs of topics to form various interpretations. You can change the forms of the words to suit your meaning.

Which interpretations seem more original or interesting? Which seem more valid? Discuss differences in meaning.

1. Houses          Security
2. Houses          Luxuries

**3.** Houses   Sameness

**4.** Houses   Castles

**5.** Houses   Dreams realized or denied

**6.** Insults   Weapons

**7.** Insults   Insecurities

**8.** Insults   Entertainment

**9.** Insults   Self-image, self-esteem

**10.** Insults   Children

**11.** Drug abuse  Contemporary diseases

**12.** Drug abuse  Recreation

**13.** Drug abuse  Small business opportunities

**14.** Drug abuse  Prohibition

**15.** Drug abuse  Quality of life

**16.** Cars    Necessities of life

**17.** Cars    Personality

**18.** Cars    Freedom

**19.** Cars    Disintegration of small communities

**20.** Cars    Social life

## EXERCISE B

Combine each of the following sets of assertions into a single interpretation. You can change the forms and placement of words and add information where it seems necessary or useful, or reverse or qualify meanings where you disagree with a statement. *Variations:* Use as few sentences as possible, or as many.

**1.** The music has an unearthly quality.
   The music seems to reflect anger and despair.
   The lyrics are socially aware and idealistic.

**2.** Time flies.
   Time is anticipation.
   Life is becoming more unpredictable.
   Recent events have been earthshaking.

**3.** Phone calls are better than letters.
   We need to talk to each other.
   True friendship takes hard work.
   Compromise is the essence of understanding.

**4.** Things get broken.
   The more fragile it is, the more expensive.

We prefer the unbreakable.
Imperfection and decay are disturbing.
5. Science becomes the servant of industry.
Social responsibility is more necessary than ever.
Eagerness for technological advancements can be damaging. It is important to pursue knowledge for its own sake.

## EXERCISE C

Develop several different characterizations of each of the following subjects. Which seem most routine, accurate, or fair? Which are most striking or entertaining?

1. A well-known political figure
2. A television actor or movie star
3. A rock star or group
4. A relative's behavior or personality
5. A particular department store
6. A product
7. The current behavior of the stock market (or gasoline prices, or the costs of dating)
8. The weather
9. A fashion trend (or current fad, or cultural event)
10. An event recently in the news

## EXERCISE D

Describe each of the following subjects twice, the first time focusing on scientific accuracy and completeness, the second time on conveying an impression or graphic "picture" (perhaps incorporating emotions the subject evokes or its connotations). Discuss the differences in effect and usefulness.

1. A particular classroom
2. A tree
3. A person
4. An egg
5. Snow
6. A football
7. A street
8. A piece of notebook paper
9. A grocery store
10. A dog, cat, insect, bird, or another kind of animal

## EXERCISE E

Choose a personal experience or recent event and retell the story twice, once as a journalistic report and once as a dramatic representation. Compare and discuss the results.

### *WHEN TO USE REPRESENTATION*

Representational writing is appropriate

- when the audience wants to draw its own conclusions
- when an overview is needed
- when words fail you
- as evidence and support
- when you are unprepared or wish to be unspecific
- to entertain

### *WHEN TO USE INTERPRETATION*

Interpretation is the basis of understanding, appropriate whenever you are trying to define or comprehend the nature of the subject. More specifically, it is useful

- when the meaning is more important than the subject itself
- to try to predict or control a phenomenon
- in supporting a judgment
- in self-expression
- when the subject is unmanageable
- when the subject is trivial or commonplace
- when emphasis is needed
- to channel or focus attention

---

### GAINS AND LOSSES

---

#### ◀ REPRESENTATION ▶

| Advantages | Disadvantages |
|---|---|
| Lets audience form conclusions | Subject to misinterpretation |
| Provides a sense of the whole issue or subject | Not analytical, reducible, or "intellectual" |
| Authenticates or "makes real" a point of view | Less valid, since only one instance is presented |
| Humanizes abstract discussion | May become too personal or idiosyncratic |

---

## GAINS AND LOSSES

### ◀ INTERPRETATION ▶

| Advantages | Disadvantages |
|---|---|
| Reads events as author wishes them to be read | May prevent or subvert other interpretations |
| Defines the significance and character of things | Fixes and limits meaning, becomes prejudice |
| Offers prospect of making real discoveries | Must be supported and defended |
| Organizes, controls, and abstracts information | May fall short of adequately explaining the case |

## *Wider Implications*

Representation and interpretation correspond to two basic forms of apprehension: experiencing the world and thinking about it. We apprehend or "know" the world around us either through participation in events or through analysis of them. When we attempt to communicate our knowledge of the world to others, we naturally do so in ways that parallel our means of acquiring it: we try to duplicate the experience, to re-create it in stories, description, and report, or we try to sum it up, to characterize or explain its essential features, its abstract meaning, in essays, statistics, and logical argument.

### THE PRESENCE OF MEANING

Representation and interpretation reflect the absence or presence of explicit meanings in an author's rendering of the subject, the extent to which the writer tells us what the implications of the subject are, what its consequences will be or what its "true" nature or essential qualities are, how it relates to our own experience, and where we should place it in the context of other things we know.

### SHOWING AND TELLING

In relatively simple terms, this is the difference between showing the readers what happened and telling them, between depicting or reporting on something and summarizing or characterizing it. It is the difference between describing a subject to the audience, allowing readers to draw their own conclusions, and explaining or "selling" your own point of view.

### THE TRANSFER OF EXPERIENCE

Pure representation tries to transfer the whole experience or perception to the readers as if they were present on the occasion or saw the subject through the author's eyes. This can be extremely effective, but it can also be extremely difficult and time-consuming.

Taking representation to its logical extreme, a portrayal of the entire history of England, for instance, would require virtually endless narrative and description. To represent as "simple" a matter as a basketball game would require you to recount literally thousands of readily perceptible incidents and details in addition to the essential events of the game and the more obvious characteristics and features of the players, the action, and court.

And that is not even considering whether players' thoughts and emotions should be reported, whether the context of the game—league standings, long-term rivalries, individual attitudes toward the sport, and personality clashes—should be described, and whether it is relevant to include the most minute or trivial details—like the vibration of the rim on each shot, the amount of slippage between floor and shoe, the weight loss of players, the wrinkles in each uniform, and the changes in humidity as the event progresses. All of these things and other details are indisputably *there*, a part of what is happening. When should they be mentioned or excluded from the representation of the event?

### THE ESSENCE OF THINGS

If communication is to be at all useful, it must save us time—save us from having to relive the history of England to apprehend it, from having to watch patiently the entire process of discovery in order to understand a scientific hypothesis. Our information on any subject is always incomplete. We do not have on file every event of the last two days, much less of the Norman conquest. Our perception of the "whole experience" is limited and fragmentary. So how can we expect to portray it whole?

The alternative is to encapsulate or "label" the phenomenon, to develop an attitude toward it or a belief about it that helps us comprehend, categorize, and respond to the event. This attitude or belief constitutes our interpretation of the phenomenon, a characterization of the subject. It is an entire state of mind or attitude, encompassing not only the author's ideas but also the data that supports and explains them and the context or belief structure that influenced their creation. Each separate interpretation is like a separate essay, implying within itself the evidence that could be marshalled to support it.

### READING THE SUBJECT

In the widest sense, interpretation is the intellectual process through which we "read" the subject—the person, object, or sequence of events, the process or phenomenon. Interpretation may emphasize certain features at the expense of others. It sums up; it highlights a particular pattern or group of details; it adds a particular perspective, slant, or "spin" to our view of the subject, seeing the matter in terms of some principle, attitude, or shade of belief, or from some particular angle or focus to the exclusion or diminution of others. It may categorize, analyze, or define the subject, abstract certain features (removing them from the wider context or presenting them as the essence of the subject), infer things not seen but also part of the subject, or extrapolate beyond the available data.

### MEANINGLESSNESS AND MISREADING

In deciding whether to emphasize representation or interpretation, the problem is that neither approach by itself can give a complete picture of the subject. Pure representation and report, if such things were possible, would be devoid of significance. They would simply describe what is there, without omission and without explanation, with no attempt to filter out irrelevancies or trivia. There would be nothing to explain.

Pure interpretation, by contrast, quickly would lose sight of the subject under discussion, would see only what the author wanted to see or would focus on the author's feelings and opinions, with little reference to the subject that occasioned them. Personal interpretations, even when valid for the author proposing them, can be so idiosyncratic that they bear little resemblance to reality.

## *Conclusion*

Representation and interpretation are pointless without each other. Representational writing is never completely free of interpretation, since the simple act of choosing details to include or deciding what should be mentioned first implies an evaluation, conveys a message about what the author thinks is important or what is most essential or meaningful about the subject. By the same token, interpretive writing can never be completely free of representation, since interpretation must have an object or event to explain, and an interpretation must often be supported by comparison to the facts (that is, with the subject being interpreted).

Representation is dramatic and graphic. It does not, by itself, mean anything. It simply shows what happened or what was there. Interpretation is abstract and introspective, the basic art of thinking. It creates significance; it tells us how we should regard or respond to what happened or what was there. Representation shows us what is there; interpretation tells us what it means.

## ASSIGNMENT A:   Reports, Descriptions, and Sketches

1. Put yourself in a position where you must give an informative account and portrayal of something to people who have not seen it themselves—as in travel writing and newspaper reporting.

2. Write about a physical object, phenomenon, or relatively simple construct with the intent of enabling your audience to visualize, recognize, or copy it—as in architectural designs, real estate ads, instructions, "how-to" writing, and much scientific writing. Use pictures, sketches, and graphics, if necessary or useful, but do not rely on them to take the place of extensive report and commentary. Make sure that you adequately distinguish the object from similar objects that might be confused with it.

3. Write a sketch portraying the character, appearance, and ambiance of a town, area, community, or place.

4. Give a factual account and justification of your actions in some significant matter or some controversy. Tell what happened and why. Explain your role in the events, without self-aggrandization.

5. Recount accurately a series of local, national, or international events. Acknowledge whatever familiarity with the events your audience might have. Take the role of a historian, reminding us of our past or calling attention to events we might not have noticed while conveying some estimate of their consequences or meaning.

## ASSIGNMENT B:   Narratives and Re-Creations

1. Retell a familiar story, striving for vividness, immediacy, and dramatic effect. You might also wish to alter, reverse, or put a twist on some aspect of the story, like the setting the circumstances, relationships, or motives of the characters, the historical period, or even the ending.

2. Write an imaginative account of some conversation or confrontation between two historical figures, perhaps choosing a crucial historical mo-

ment or a time of reflection as the occasion. You may need to include actions or references to historical events.

3. Re-create for us a moment in your life that led to some recognition, new awareness, self-awareness, or change. Remember as you write that your audience was not present at these events, as you were, that the audience may have been through similar experiences (and therefore may not regard your experience as singular or special), that you may need to generate interest in the subject, and that it is usually not necessary to recount every detail, minor incident, and moment of time.

## ASSIGNMENT C:   Interpretation and Commentary

1. Write an extended commentary on some current event.

2. Discuss the effects and significance of some major technological change or scientific advancement of the present or past.

3. Offer your interpretation of a book, movie, or human interest story. Support and explain your impression of the subject's wider or underlying meaning, its interactions with culture, emotions, and the history of ideas, its effects, the themes it represents, and its essential nature. If you are familiar with other interpretations, you might wish to cite them and to show how yours is different, or how it refines, extends, or reinforces an existing viewpoint. Do not retell more of the story than is necessary to remind your audience of what happened or to support some part of your viewpoint.

4. Reassert the significance and meaning of some tradition or element of culture. Assume you are speaking to an audience that would appreciate having its sentiments, customs, conventions, and beliefs reinforced. Try to avoid excessive triteness or sentimentality. Consider admitting the conventionality of your message. And attempt to rediscover and re-evoke the deeper feelings and significance that has been lost in routine, repetition, cynicism, abuse, and distortion.

*Note:* This assignment is particularly difficult and dangerous for seasonal and emotional topics like family, Christmas, Mother's Day, marriage, love, the return of spring, and so on. Though there is a recurring call for occasional pieces on such subjects, and though there is great psychological need to refresh the values these subjects represent, it is extremely difficult both to escape repeating truisms about them and to avoid sounding mushy or adolescent—hence the continuing popularity of a few literary works that have managed the trick, like *A Christmas Carol, How the Grinch Stole Christmas,* and *It's a Wonderful Life.* Of course, there is also a market for truisms and mush.

# 11

# Invention, Experience, and Education

A little learning is a dangerous thing; Drink deep, or taste not the Pierian spring.　　　　　　　　　　　　　　　　　　　—ALEXANDER POPE

To write well, one must know something well.　　　　—STEPHEN TCHUDI

Knowledge is of two kinds. We know a subject ourselves, or we know where we can find information upon it.　　　　　　—SAMUEL JOHNSON

There is not less wit nor less invention in applying rightly a thought one finds in a book, than in being the first author of that thought.
　　　　　　　　　　　　　　　　　　　　　　　　—PIERRE BAYLE

## Insight and Erudition

We seek out people who seem to know the answers—teachers to instruct us, consultants to advise us, critics to appraise worth, actuaries to appraise risk, prophets and sages to enlighten us, authorities to support our contentions, and guides to show us the way. Expertise is a valuable commodity.

A style that demonstrates knowledge commands attention and respect. We may recognize as learned people who have received extended formal education, are widely read, have traveled extensively or speak several languages, have engaged in methodical observation and study of a subject, or have considerable and varied experience. People with practical wisdom in the form of technical skills, sophistication, and familiarity with common knowledge may also be credited with great authority.

But scholarship and sagacity can be annoying. We tire of aphorisms and standard answers and grow suspicious of experts. Errors in judgment,

186

accidents, and repeated modifications of theory make us lose confidence in government, technology, and science. We become skeptical about, even hostile to, intellectual, philosophical, and academic viewpoints. Book learning doesn't seem practical or real.

We regard erudite styles as good or bad.

### ◀ ERUDITION ▶

| Good Qualities | Bad Qualities |
| --- | --- |
| learned | well schooled |
| authoritative | dogmatic |
| mature | uninspired |
| traditional | unoriginal |

When the audience is disenchanted with experts, the writer who claims to be an independent thinker may be more welcome. We are attracted to inventiveness and intuition, to prophets, rebels, and pioneers. The authority they offer may be no more than common sense, a return to simple answers and easy solutions. Or it may reflect true insight, originality, and awareness.

An emphasis on invention and insight can be as "objective" in its own way as any other form of expertise. In fact, empiricism and scientific experimentation are closer in philosophy to inventiveness than to scholarship. A style based on insight and personal authority may appear as good or bad.

### ◀ INSIGHT ▶

| Good Qualities | Bad Qualities |
| --- | --- |
| visionary | unschooled |
| creative | disrespectful |
| insightful | subjective |
| enthusiastic | undisciplined |

Obviously, there is considerable overlap between styles based on invention and styles based on education. It takes a combination of learning and insight to arrive at and express conclusions.

## The Need for a Fund of Ideas

The "texture" and effect of the writing changes as you change the sources of material, even when the message stays essentially the same. If you use personal anecdotes to illustrate a point, the writing seems more informal and has more immediacy than if you cite what experts studying the subject have said. If you rely on familiar maxims, truisms, and principles to support the same idea, the effect is more parental or avuncular, more "down home" and folksy; it conjures up images of backporch philosophy and machine shop know-how, of lessons learned from long experience and the school of hard knocks.

Reporting what someone else has observed or experienced sounds less pretentious than if you present the thought as your own perception—and you can always disown it if attacked. Discussing your own observations of a single instance or incident seems more humane and tangible—but less valid—than recording and interpreting statistics from a thousand cases.

It is not just the source of information that matters. The quantity or diversity of material can also make a difference in the complexion of style. Styles are seen as spare or copious, monotonous or varied, reserved or effusive, even superficial or learned in part because of the sheer amount and diversity of information used.

An author able to draw on many different sources of information may appear more scholarly than one who draws on just a few, though the message offered may be no different. An author who can tie together diverse or seemingly disparate subjects may seem more clever. Authors who lard their prose with detail, with frequent allusions, or with multiple quotes may create an impression of solidity and truth not warranted by actual evidence.

It is useful, then, to develop both inventiveness and a fund of ideas and to cultivate the ability to combine and recombine different sources of information coherently. Ideas come from many sources, among them

- experience
- upbringing
- observation
- discussion
- introspection
- imagination
- formal and informal invention or inquiry
- formal and informal reasoning
- memory and methods of recall
- culture
- reading, media, and library research
- formal and informal surveys or questioning
- experimentation
- education
- apprenticeship in a profession

## *The Nature of Research*

Research serves two functions: it is a process of validation and a process of discovery. It seeks, through reading and observation, to prove or support a hypothesis or to learn more about the subject.

### CONSIDERED OPINIONS

Writing based on research is essentially a way of showing the audience that the author has thought long and deeply about the subject. It suggests that the author has explored and critically examined his or her beliefs and perceptions, testing them against other viewpoints and refining them accordingly.

Researched writing thereby elevates the trustworthiness, if not always the validity, of an author's contentions. Educated, supported, and considered opinions carry more weight than unexamined beliefs. They are not necessarily more persuasive, since people sometimes prefer assertive and simplistic opinions. But considered opinions have greater claim to authority.

### SELF-EDUCATION

Research is a process of self-education. Through reading and observation, the author learns more about a subject, trying out different ways of understanding the subject and different ways of predicting its behavior.

This is quite the reverse of prescriptive education, in which students are told what subjects to study, what to think, and what to do. Research-centered education, at its best, is self-motivated and self-directed. The "students" become part of the community of scholars. They seek authorities out of personal interest in the subject and out of respect for knowledge and experience, as well as for other points of view.

Scholars are not taught; they study and engage in discussion. They listen and respond. They inquire and seek answers, not just from others but also from themselves.

### INTERNALIZED DIALOGUE

Writing based on research usually reflects an internalized dialogue about the subject. The author includes other points of view in the essay and responds to them, almost as if he or she were "talking" to other authorities about the subject.

The author shows how his or her ideas fit into the meta-text, the wider discussion of the subject ongoing within a profession or culture. Other people's theories are represented, examined, and explored in relation to the author's viewpoint. And "transitions" or connections are established between the author's ideas and theirs.

### DRAWING ON MEMORY

Research is a dimension of memory. It draws on the author's recollection of what he or she has read and heard, whether that is recorded in notes or simply remembered. And it goes beyond personal memory. Research consults the collective memory of the society, as preserved in libraries, culture, and oral traditions.

## *Becoming, and Appearing to Be, Better Informed*

Becoming better informed and sounding informed are two different things. Being knowledgeable may be personally satisfying. It may help you feel that you understand and can cope with the world around you. But there is no public benefit in being knowledgeable unless you reflect it in your style and demonstrate it in your actions.

To research a subject, you should do the following:

*1. Read Widely.* Time permitting, you should read widely about a subject, not limiting yourself to sources that clearly support your own point of view or take similar perspectives. The reading ought, to some extent, precede your focusing on a topic. Wide reading is, like a liberal arts education, a means of exploring the possibilities and discovering your interests.

You might start in a general area of interest and read or survey articles and books that address the subject in many different ways. If the subject is warfare, for example, it would be a mistake to limit yourself just to war movies or even television documentaries. For that matter, it could be a mistake to limit yourself to reading the work of military historians, important though such authors might be to deepening your understanding of the subject. The perspective of a particular field is a liability as well as a strength. It restricts the scope of inquiry.

On the subject of warfare, you might extend your research to include such diverse sources as

- first-person accounts
- discussions of the psychological effects of war
- sociological studies of peaceful and warring societies
- government documents concerning the military

- legislative debates that took place during a war
- newspaper accounts of a war, perhaps from different countries
- philosophical and psychological theories of conflict, aggression, and struggle
- novels about wars or people caught in the midst of wars
- poetry that responds to the experience of war
- paintings and sculpture of military scenes and characters
- advertisements for weapons
- studies in political science
- discussions of statemanship and diplomacy
- accounts of economic causes and effects of war
- discussions of nationalism, class, radicalism, and oppression

This list is by no means complete.

*2. Challenge Yourself.* You should at least attempt to read sources that are difficult for you to comprehend. If you only consult sources that are easily understood or contain familiar ideas, then you are probably just reviewing material you already know, perhaps even reinforcing preconceptions and prejudices.

Challenging yourself extends to the point of attempting to understand points of view that seem alien, unpleasant, controversial, ridiculous, or extreme. After study, you might still reject such ideas or judge them harshly. But you do so with better reason.

*3. Paraphrase Your Sources.* The first obligation of research is not to be critical but to be accepting, to learn another person's ideas as completely as possible. This means apprenticing oneself to one's reading and suspending disbelief.

Attempt to paraphrase your sources. Try to get to the point where you can accurately explain another person's ideas in your own words. Your style will appear more learned if you include such paraphrase and explanation in your writing—with proper attribution of the ideas to their actual author, of course.

Since paraphrase is never completely accurate, you should be cautious about claiming to recount another person's point of view, at least until you are very sure of your own authority on the subject. To be safe you might qualify your paraphrase, saying something like "Sontag appears to be saying that. . . ."

*4. Apply and Test Learned Concepts.* Once you understand a concept, you should try to apply and extend it, to see how it "fits" or explains a particular case. If you are dealing with a theory of management, for instance, you might try out the theory in your own organization or analyze an organization in terms of the theory.

An economic theory like the law of supply and demand might be applied to the sale of real estate in the local market. The idea that students learn best what they discover for themselves might be applied to teaching a mathematical operation.

Concepts are generalizations. They claim to define what is usually or characteristically true of a subject. In applying a concept, you show how well it operates in practice, how good it is at predicting outcomes, or how well it describes a specific instance. Your style will appear better informed if you are able to apply concepts routinely.

*5. Read Critically.* While there is an obligation to listen to one's sources with respect and understanding, there is also a need for questioning and incredulity. Uncritical acceptance of everything you read leads to a reputation for gullibility rather than expertise.

To a certain extent, we regard styles as more informed or learned when the author is critical of other points of view. Judging others implies that you have both the authority and right to do so. Criticism implies that you could do better yourself. But superficial criticism is all too easy, no more than a matter of expressing reservations, acting superior, or finding fault.

Maintaining critical distance in research is a more rigorous occupation. It includes open-mindedness and self-doubt as well as close examination of your sources, constantly accepting and questioning their validity. It requires understanding of refutation, methodology and structure, and all forms of evidence and support. Criticizing sources in this fashion will make your style appear more reasoned and scholarly.

*6. Read Selectively.* Often we do not have the time to explore a subject in a leisurely fashion, or need only to confirm suspicions or find support. Though these motives may not result in the purest or most thorough research, they represent common necessity.

On such occasions, you may be able to focus or shorten the research process by doing the following:

- *Consulting encyclopedias.* Though sometimes scorned, general and special-topic encyclopedias can be useful sources for background knowledge of a subject. If all you need are broad outlines and accepted facts, the encyclopedia may be sufficient. But often encyclopedias offer information of limited complexity and depth. They do not usually give a sense of scholarly controversies or current debate.
- *Consulting popularized discussions of technical subjects.* You can acquire some knowledge of technical subjects through the medium of articles that "popularize" them, explaining technical concepts or discoveries in language accessible to the nonexpert.

- ***Consulting college-level textbooks.*** Textbooks designed for higher education are often more current and complex than encyclopedias. They have the advantage of being written for nonexperts, and they usually suggest the range of continuing discussion about a subject in addition to portraying the conventional wisdom. Landmark books and classic studies in the field may be identified and summarized.

- ***Consulting review articles.*** Review articles are essays that give an overview of research on a particular issue or subject. They are used to assess and consolidate all that experts have said about the matter over an extended period of time.

  A typical review article will sum up many different articles and books about a subject, noting which are of special interest and which are of limited value. It will define trends and characterize the accumulated body of research.

  Review articles should not be used as a substitute for reading the research itself. They are limited by the author's ability to paraphrase accurately and to interpret what he or she has read. Even the best review article can be misleading to some degree, undervaluing some ideas and misrepresenting others. But review articles can provide a broad understanding of the pertinent issues and can guide further study of the subject. Ideally, you should read the work referred to in the review article and form your own opinion of its significance.

  Unfortunately, review articles are not always easy to find. They may not be designated as such and may appear at widely irregular intervals in a given field.

- ***Consulting "background" chapters or sections in scholarly works.*** Many scholarly works include sections or chapters that either review the history of research on the subject or survey current research. These may serve many of the same purposes as review articles and are relatively common.

  The difference is that the author usually spends far more time on his or her own idea. The review of research may be sketchy and may tend to favor precedents that support the author's point of view.

- ***Consulting bibliographic essays.*** In some fields, bibliographic essays are routinely published. These are extended commentaries on research done during a prescribed period of time, perhaps in the previous year or decade.

- ***Consulting classic articles and books.*** It is always useful to consult research regarded by the experts in a field as classic, definitive, or groundbreaking. Rather than relying on secondhand accounts of such work, you should read it yourself.

  Take special note of research that is frequently cited or often alluded to. You can assume that it is influential, respected, or at least controversial.

- ***Consulting current articles and books.*** Recent essays and books about a subject may, if read with care, give you an immediate understanding of current issues in a field. Seldom is an article published in a contemporary journal that does not address a present controversy or significant discovery.

  When material is more than three or four years old, it may already be considered out of date. In many scientific fields, theories may come and go far more quickly. If you rely on highly current material, however, you should be all the more cautious and critical. New theories and perspectives may not be readily accepted and may yet be disproven.

- *Consulting bibliographies.* Most fields sponsor their own bibliographies. These are lists of pertinent articles and books recently published. Some include brief comments, or annotations, that describe the contents of the articles or books listed. Bibliographies may appear as separate publications, as books or periodicals devoted solely to cataloguing current research. Or they may appear as regularly printed features of scholarly journals.

*7. Discuss the Subject With Different Audiences.* It is often important to do more than just read. You should seek out opportunities to discuss the subject with various audiences, with different experts, as well as with informed laypersons and interested parties.

When you are researching a particular author's point of view, this discussion may take the form of an interview. But more often we discuss subjects on an informal basis, and in so doing we learn what other people think about the issues and how they respond to our ideas.

A further benefit of dialogue is that it greatly extends the scope of one's research. On any subject, there is so much written that no one could possibly read it all. Through conversation we may quickly learn what articles and books our colleagues have found interesting and gain an initial impression of their contents. We can share our resources.

This aspect of research is so important that many professions organize the process, scheduling conferences, conventions, seminars, and panel discussions. They form institutes, think tanks, and research groups. These formal occasions mirror the underlying, less formal support network and system of alliances that is the foundation of the professional community.

*8. Synthesize Different Points of View.* Informed writing, it was suggested earlier, is essentially a dialogue within an essay, a complex discussion of the author's point of view in relation to what others have said, or might say, about the subject. A research paper is a collection of voices, an implied debate.

Researched writing typically combines or synthesizes different points of view, presenting alternate theories, similar ideas, or divergent opinions and explaining how they fit together. The basic methods for combining ideas are as follows:

- *Testimony:* using multiple sources that agree with you as testimony to support your views.
- *Convergence and Divergence:* focusing on areas of agreement or disagreement among the sources, places where their perspectives or theories overlap or diverge.
- *Subsuming Parts Into the Whole:* focusing on a larger category, concept, or framework of ideas within which the various sources all fit.

- **Accumulation:** adding the sources together to give what purports to be a complete or "whole" picture of the subject.

- **Division of the Whole:** viewing the sources as "pieces of a pie" or subdivisions of the whole, sometimes with the author filling in an area of discussion not covered by the sources.

- **The Common Denominator:** focusing on a single term, idea, or common denominator that cuts across all the sources. Sometimes the author will claim that this common denominator is the central, essential, or key issue, though it may not be presented as such in the sources. Sometimes the author will claim that this common denominator reflects a small or hidden truth.

- **Pursuing Tangents:** focusing on a tangential idea, a topic that is not directly discussed in the sources but touches on all of them.

- **Criticism:** weighing the validity of the various sources, rejecting whatever is false and assembling from the process a purportedly more correct version of the truth, or rejecting a number of invalid ideas and supporting the single source or sources that appear to give the best answers.

- **The History of Ideas:** focusing on the development and sequence of ideas, tracing historical connections or lines of influence and emphasizing the progression from one source to the next.

- **Perspectives:** presenting various sources as different perspectives on the same subject, perhaps seeing it psychologically, economically, and philosophically, for instance.

- **Dialectic:** focusing on contradictory or antithetical ideas and attempting to show how both are simultaneously true, or how some higher truth emerges from embracing contraries.

*9. Emphasize Deductive Reasoning.*   Your writing will appear more informed if you work deductively, reaching conclusions based on widely accepted principles or standard theories. Doing so demonstrates that you know the accepted truths and that you support them.

*10. Attach Your Idea to Some Learned Controversy or Debate.*   Your writing may appear more informed if you place your own ideas within the context of a wider controversy or debate, identifying two sides to an issue or outlining various points of view on the subject you are about to address. This implies not only wide reading but also that you are party to high-level academic or scientific discussion.

*11. Suggest Long or Wide Acquaintance With the Subject.*   Informed styles may imply, claim, or demonstrate a lengthy acquaintance with the subject. Expertise is associated with age and experience. Anything that establishes such credentials will suggest authority.

In informal writing, such experience may be represented in narrative form, as autobiography or anecdote. More formal research implies lengthy experience in the scope of the study, the research methodology, the reported passage of time, and a process of extended speculation, reconsideration, and ultimate resolution.

Wide familiarity with the subject may be indicated by many devices, among them an ability to see the subject from many angles and perspectives or to draw on the whole range of topics associated with it in the research.

*12. Distance Yourself From the Subject.*   An informed stance may be implied in the author's role. The author might take the role of a spokesperson for the status quo, reporting on what experts in the field consider common knowledge. Or the author might take the stance of objective generalization, discussing "what happens" in general or "what's there" in general, as if the author were simply a neutral observer or spectator who had watched the phenomenon from a distance.

This stance often uses the passive voice—"Three levels of occupation were found"—and the past tense—"Nationalism has had its greatest influence on warfare in modern times"—or the historical present—"George Eliot says that. . . ." The spectator stance may itself imply that the author speaks for a group of people, or at least that anyone watching from the same perspective would have seen and reported the same thing. Any suggestion of personal opinion is thereby suppressed or camouflaged.

*13. Avoid Expressiveness and Extreme Claims.*   Informed writing tends to be unemotional and measured. It does not make extreme claims or focus on the author's feelings. We associate a learned style with dispassion and reason, with cautious assertions and mature reflection. Extreme claims and inflexibility seem to us signs of radical youth or hardened old age, rather than scholarship.

Of course, a learned style is contentious in its own way.

*14. Use Technical Terminology.*   Correct use of technical terms is essential to an informed style. Whether you are speaking to an audience of laypeople or to an audience of professionals, you have to demonstrate that you can use the language an expert uses to describe the subject. To a certain extent, this means that jargon, often proscribed by teachers of writing, is absolutely necessary in writing that has any pretensions to scholarship.

Definition is often a characteristic mode of thinking in the intellectual style, since much knowledge is embodied in accepted and refined meanings—the terms, concepts, and categorizations of any field.

*15. Review Pertinent Research.*   The review of research, mentioned earlier as a source of ideas about a topic, is also a means of demonstrating your knowledge, of establishing your credentials as a scholar and your right to be heard. It implies wide acquaintance with the subject. A style looks more informed if the author, however briefly or at length, describes the history of research on the matter, using formal documentation methods when appropriate.

The importance of the review of research can scarcely be overstated. The learned audience is often unwilling to credit or even listen to opinions offered by those who have not studied the subject at a length commensurate to its own level of authority. Scholarly readers tend to discount or ignore authors who do not reflect in their writing familiarity with the pertinent research. Failure to cite a well-known article on a subject can be fatal.

*16. Use Quotes, Citations, Testimony, and Allusions.* A style may also appear informed if the author quotes other people, even when they are not necessarily experts, or uses the words of others as testimony in support of his or her point of view. In informal writing, especially, allusions to well-known ideas and authors may sometimes take the place of a scholarly review of research.

## *Informal Documentation*

Informed writers draw on many sources of information. If they choose to reflect this debt in their style, they may decide to use formal or informal systems of documentation. We will examine informal documentation first.

The most basic skill of documentation is to identify within the essay the sources of your material. In conversation, people do this routinely. They say "A friend of mine saw," "I know for a fact," "In my opinion," or "I heard a rumor that. . . ." Such "attributions" are essentially verbal footnotes. They tag or label the kind of information you are about to present.

There are perhaps ten basic kinds of information:

1. Personal observation
2. Personal experience
3. Accumulated observation and experience, and impressions
4. Other people's reported observations, experiences, and opinions
5. Your own conclusions or generalizations
6. Commonly held beliefs or common perceptions
7. The observations and conclusions of a single expert
8. The observations and conclusions of a group of experts
9. The consensus among experts
10. An impersonal indicator or sign, an instructive event

Informal attributions are usually variations on these possibilities, whether or not a particular author's name happens to be mentioned. When the information comes from the author's own resources, the attribution may be optional.

The following examples illustrate each type of information.

**Personal observation**

I don't see many people buying stationery for personal correspondence. They buy greeting cards instead.

**Personal experience**

I wrote no more than ten personal letters all last year.

**Accumulated experience and observation, and impressions**

It seems to me that the written word has become less personal and spontaneous.

**Reported observation, experience, and opinion**

A close friend of mine says he can't tell for sure if his own brother can write. They always "correspond" by telephone.

**Conclusions or generalizations**

Writing has become a product, something to buy and sell.

**Commonly held beliefs, common perceptions**

Many people think of writing as a dying art.

**One expert's conclusions**

One noted commentator suggests that we have become dependent on a whole new class of professional writers, people who write for us, who script our thoughts and lives.

**The conclusions of a group of experts**

Researchers at a midwestern university report that writing skill is actually more important to prospective employers than it used to be.

**The consensus among experts**

Most experts agree that modern technology has radically changed our relationship to the written word.

**Impersonal indicators or signs**

Declining scores on national tests of verbal ability suggest that students do not consider linguistic skill important.

# EXERCISE A

Rewrite the following sentences so they include reference to the source of information indicated in brackets.

1. Traffic in Los Angeles is awful.  [Common belief]
2. High school does a better job than you might think of preparing you for college.  [Conclusion of a group of experts]
3. The vice president should be given more responsibility.  [Impression from accumulated experience]
4. Expressing anger makes you feel better.  [Personal experience *and* expert consensus]
5. The economy is getting worse.  [Reported opinion]
6. The economy is getting worse.  [Group of experts]
7. The United States still has not come to terms with the Vietnam war.  [Impersonal sign]
8. Self-reliance is a sign of maturity.  [Personal observation]
9. Self-reliance is a sign of maturity.  [Common belief]
10. Self-reliance is a sign of maturity.  [Single expert's conclusion]
11. Airline safety is suspect.  [Impersonal indicator or sign]
12. I've noticed a lot of airplane accidents in the news recently.  [Conclusion or generalization]
13. Many of the homeless are mentally ill.  [Impression from accumulated experience]
14. Smoking can be injurious to your health.  [Single expert's conclusion]
15. Last week four trees were cut down on Hartman Green.  [Reported observation]

## *Characterizing Sources*

Attribution includes not only the ability to identify your sources of information but also to characterize them, to provide some brief estimate of their worth or a passing comment on their significance. These characterizations convey a sense of how the various sources of material fit together. They tell us how to value or react to a particular idea or piece of information.

Characterizations are especially obvious in journalism, where reporters commonly use tag lines like "Sources close to the president report that" or "A high official in the administration says that" to describe sources they have not been given permission to name. But the device is useful and necessary even in formal research papers where confidentiality is hardly an issue.

Some of the typical approaches to characterization include the following:

### Identifying the author by status, position, or profession

**a.** Hamilton Smith, a lawyer in the firm of Hart, Schaffner, and Marx, observed that . . .

**b.** Dr. Susan Escobar, senior physician at St. Joseph's Hospital, has concluded that . . .

**c.** A research team at the University of Chicago recently announced that . . .

### Assessing the authority of the author

**a.** Noted scholar and critic Jean Willis avers that . . .

**b.** A man of principle, Proxmire was forced to attack . . .

**c.** A principal architect of this theory, Stephen Jay Gould, suggests that . . .

### Assessing the worth of the research or idea

**a.** An influential study conducted at Stanford demonstrated that . . .

**b.** The author reaches the less-than-earthshaking conclusion that . . .

**c.** In a meticulously documented experiment, it was learned that . . .

### Referring to the situation

**a.** Never to be outdone, Roger Ebert answered that . . .

**b.** Faced with new and conflicting evidence, the team of geologists revised its hypothesis, concluding that . . .

**c.** A last-minute compromise has been reached. Both parties agree to . . .

### Referring to the chronology or history of research

**a.** A later development was the theory that . . .

**b.** Freudenthal and Misawa independently suggested that the principle be enlarged to include . . .

**c.** The first step in this direction was taken by Kumar and Smith in their now classic study of . . .

## Formal Documentation

In more formal discourse, attribution is all the more necessary, both as a courtesy to other scholars, who may wish to consult an author's sources, and to help prove the point. But it is often neglected. In attempting to seem objective and impersonal, writers omit any reference to themselves and to other people. The sources of their information become unclear as a result.

Formal documentation includes bibliographic references and footnoting, specifying in a prescribed manner whatever information readers might need to locate your sources themselves. The essential data usually consists of the following items:

1. author's name
2. title of the article or book
3. name of the journal or book in which an individual article appeared
4. city in which the book was published
5. publisher
6. date of publication
7. beginning and ending page numbers of an article in a journal or a chapter in a book
8. page numbers where specific quotes and data can be found

There are many variations in documentation styles and formats. Different fields present bibliographic information in different ways. The system of documentation described here is called the Modern Language Association style, or the MLA style for short. Other major styles of documentation are the American Psychological Association (APA) style, commonly used in the social sciences, and the American Chemical Society (ACS) style, used in some of the physical sciences and technical fields.

### WORKS CITED: MLA STYLE

In the MLA style, works that are mentioned in the article are listed in a *Works Cited* section at the end of the essay, arranged alphabetically by the author's last name and presented as follows:

**For a book**

> Anderson, Rebecca. <u>Selfishness in the American Novel.</u> Englewood Cliffs: Prentice, 1990.

**For an article in a journal**

> Anderson, Rebecca. "Selfishness in the American Novel." <u>Studies in the Novel</u> 6 (1990): 130–49.

*Note:* The journal entry includes the volume number of the periodical (6) as well as the year in which the article was published (1990) and the pages on which the essay appears (130–49).

### IN-TEXT CITATION

MLA style relies on parenthetical notes within the text to refer the reader to the proper entry in the *Works Cited* section. The in-text citation includes only enough information for the reader to tell which article or book is referred to and what page or pages a particular quote appears on, if material is directly quoted, as follows:

**Parenthetical Reference: MLA Style**

. . . (Anderson, "Selfishness" 132)

This is nearly the fullest possible form of parenthetical reference in the MLA style. It includes the author's last name, the first key word from the title (in quotes for an article, underlined or in italics for a book), and the number of the page or pages on which the given quote appears. Usually less information is needed, and the citation is reduced accordingly. If the author is identified in the sentence and there is no direct quote, and only one work by the author is listed in the *Works Cited* section, then no parenthetical reference is required.

In the following examples, note how the parenthetical reference gradually disappears as less and less information is needed to locate the source in the *Works Cited* list:

**One of two or more articles by an author not named in the sentence, plus a quote**

One author finally arrives at the conclusion that "There is no such thing as a selfish hero" (Anderson, "Selfishness" 132).

**Two or more articles by an author identified in the sentence plus a quote**

Anderson claims that "There is no such thing as a selfish hero" ("Selfishness" 132).

**Two or more articles by different authors not named in the sentence, without any quotes**

A number of recent studies suggest that modern heroism is flawed by self-interest and greed (Anderson; Carver and Kostecka; Weinsheimer).

**An author and article named in the sentence, plus a quote**

In "Selfishness in the American Novel," Rebecca Anderson concludes that "There is no such thing as a selfish hero" (132).

**Only one article by an author not named in the sentence, no quote included**

Many contemporary novels portray self-interested and even greedy characters, but these people are seldom represented as role models or heroes (Anderson).

**Only one article by the author named in the sentence, plus a direct quote**

Anderson ultimately concludes that "There is no such thing as a selfish hero" (132).

**Only one article by an author named in the sentence, no direct quote**

Anderson, in particular, suggests that selfishness precludes heroism.

In each case, the reader should be able to turn to the Works Cited section and locate a complete bibliographic citation for the specific work. There should be no possibility of confusing it with other articles by the same author, other articles by an author with the same last name, or other articles on the same subject. The important thing is to give precisely as much information as is necessary, and no more than is needed.

## EXERCISE B

Write a single paragraph that incorporates at least four of the following maxims or quotes:

The squeaky wheel gets the grease.
Children should be seen and not heard.
Faint heart ne'er won fair lady (or man).
Silence is golden.
Actions speak louder than words.
Talk is cheap.
Listen to what I do, not what I say.
Those who can, do. Those who can't, teach.
Experience is the best teacher.
The pen is mightier than the sword.

Analyze the paragraph you have written. Determine how the different perspectives were synthesized. Note the use of attributions and characterizations. Distinguish your own point of view from that of your sources.

## *The Nature of Invention*

The opposite of research and education is to rely on your own resources, to be able to create ideas independently and to draw on material from your own experience and imagination. These skills are as important and necessary as scholarship and reading. Invention is the art of thinking for oneself.

## THE ART OF THINKING

Although it is tempting to believe that thought is a purely natural behavior, instinctive, innate, or unteachable, thinking is as much an art as a capacity. Intelligence might be constrained by nature, but the skills and habits of reflection can be cultivated and refined.

## FORMING OPINIONS

Thinking is not the same thing as "having" an opinion. It involves forming, testing, and refining your own opinions, continually studying and reassessing what you know and believe about a subject.

We like to think that one opinion is as good as the next, but merely to have an opinion is nothing. Opinions are cheap. By this reasoning, the opinion of a dog counts as much as a person's: if the dog leaves a room because a movie on television is annoying, then the animal's "viewpoint" is as credible and important as yours, or a movie critic's, or the consensus of opinion from millions of viewers over twenty years.

## INVENTION AND THE VALUE OF PERSONAL OPINION

Equally dangerous, in its way, is the assumption that thinking is reserved for the privileged few, that no one can think well or be right unless he or she follows some rigorous method of discovery or reasoning, unless he or she has the "proper" training and education. We too-readily equate thinking with "logic" or with rationality, with scholarship or a university education. The dog may be right about the television show. The emperor may have no clothes.

## PERSONAL OPINION AND PERSONAL AUTHORITY

Writing based on invention tends to emphasize the author's personal opinion and individual authority. It emphasizes experience and thought rather than abstraction and scholarship. Received ideas are replaced by personal discoveries and, for better or worse, personal rediscoveries.

## PERSONAL AUTHORITY VERSUS INFORMAL EDUCATION

Writing based on invention and experience is often confused with informal writing or with folk knowledge. But the fact is that informal writing may draw extensively on education and research. And authors who make no claim to formal education or wide reading may nevertheless be writing from sources and a kind of scholarship, citing proverbs, folk wisdom, and extended, though unscientific, study.

## Being Inventive

We measure the inventiveness of style by its copiousness, spontaneity, self-reliance, and wit, the impression that the author has an active and fertile imagination and draws material from his or her own resources. The two primary bases of an inventive style are introspection and experience.

### WRITING FROM INTROSPECTION

If your ideas and material seem to come from reflection and thought rather than reading, your style will appear less "learned" and more inventive. To write effectively from introspection, the following strategies can be helpful:

*1. Rely on Inferences.*   Making inferences is the process of combining, selecting, and filling in information to form or complete a pattern, to arrive at an interpretation or meaning. If someone walks into the room dripping wet, we "infer" that it is raining outside, or perhaps that someone has dumped a pail of water on him or her. We provide from our experience and past observation the frame of reference that completes or "explains" the phenomenon.

If we find small frogs in the mouth of a larger frog, we may infer that they are being eaten. This interpretation, based on a knowledge of the habits of amphibians and the usual purposes of the mouth, esophagus, and stomach, may be confirmed or disproven by further observation. Other inferences and interpretations of the data may prove more accurate.

Perhaps the animal is protecting its young, as some alligators do, by carrying them in its mouth. In the case of a recently discovered and rare species of frog, the explanation proved to be that the young were actually gestated in a part of the frog's stomach and "born" by exiting from the mouth.

Skill in forming and supporting inferences is a means of arriving at or creating meaning. An ability to find more than one explanation for appearances, to be able to imagine multiple ways to complete or connect data, can lead to greater originality and depth in writing and thinking.

*2. Pursue Associations or Think Laterally.*   Thinking rationally about a subject can restrict the imagination. The act of focusing one's thoughts can make it more difficult to come up with new ideas. It excludes rather than extends the range of speculation. It limits opportunities for cross-fertilization, for combining ideas and information from different sources and perspectives.

Various formal and informal methods of thinking are used to escape such restrictions on discovery and invention.

**Free Association.**   In brainstorming or free association, the author randomly puts down on paper anything and everything that comes to mind, whether or not it seems in any way connected with the main issue. The advantage of this is that it can encourage new or surprising combinations of ideas, can help the author bypass preconceptions and common knowledge.

**Lateral Thinking.**   New ideas can be generated by pursuing tangents, by digressing from the main topic to side issues or by working "sideways." Instead of focusing on a linear progression of ideas, lateral thinking looks at the wider phenomenon, at all that is related to or associated with the subject. It looks for and explores unusual connections between ideas.

**Speculative Thinking.**   Speculation is both a rhetorical stance and a habit of mind. It requires continual questioning of one's own assumptions and a continual search for new and better answers. The process of speculation may be purposely digressive, as well, following reason and inclination outward from the initial topic toward increasing distant issues. It never rests.

**Right-brained Thinking.**   Psychologists generally distinguish between left-brained thinking, which is analytical, and right-brained thinking, which is more intuitive, metaphorical, and graphic. The terms derive from the fact that the two sides of the human brain appear to work in these different ways.

Analytic thinking tends to lock a person into a particular focus on a subject and thereby limit creative associations. Invention can be encouraged, many experts say, by using right-brained strategies for examining the subject, thinking in terms of images, models, and metaphors, for instance, even sketching out the connections between ideas in graphic or pictoral form.

**Meditation.**   Meditation has long been used in religious ceremony and the search for enlightenment. Some people have also found meditation useful as a more secular means of exploring and coming to terms with a subject. Meditation is not, however, to be taken (or undertaken) lightly. In its ceremonial uses, it is considered a spiritual exercise, a labor. Mastery of the subject through meditation, or any other invention device, for that matter, requires extended practice, attention, and effort. A person should not expect immediate results.

One traditional meditation exercise has three parts:

- **Composition.** In the first phase of meditation, one exhaustively studies, observes, and describes the subject, attempting to build or reconstruct a thorough mental image of it. Composition makes the subject immediate or "present" in the mind.
- **Analysis.** The second stage of meditation is careful and repeated analysis, attempting to develop and deepen one's understanding of the subject through intense inquiry, reasoning, criticism, and interpretation. Analysis verifies one's reconstruction of the subject and explores its form, nature, and implications.
- **Colloquy.** After composing and analyzing the subject or situation, one progresses to a level of transcendent or elevated interaction with it, mentally immersing oneself in the scene, empathizing with the subject, and engaging in an internal dialogue with it.

Like research, the process of meditation is closely parallel to the process of education or self-education. The quality of the results depends in great measure on the quality of the effort put into it.

**Incubation and Relying on the Subconscious.** Research in psychology and rhetoric alike has indicated that the subconscious mind plays an important role in invention. Given time and sufficient stimulus from conscious thought, the subconscious will eventually, as if by inspiration, suggest to us ideas or solutions.

This does not mean that one can hope to come up with good ideas with no effort at all. The necessary precursors of inspiration are extended study, a degree of intellectual frustration or cognitive dissonance, and a period of "incubation," where the issue or subject is set aside for the moment while the mind rests or turns to other matters.

How this works is not entirely clear. But it appears that after one has tried at length to solve a problem through analytic, focused, or intense thinking, the subconscious mind starts operating behind the scenes, searching for ways to relieve the cognitive stress. The subconscious is apparently more fluid and associative than focused thought, which tends to stay in existing channels or to conceive of the subject in terms of preset categories and frames of reference. Under the right conditions, the subconscious recombines and rearranges ideas, working outside and beyond strict definitions and precise logic. The eventual result may be a true discovery or a creative resolution to a problem.

*3. Explore the Subject Using Rhetorical Modes.* Material about a subject can be generated through various methods of formal and informal analysis. One of the most familiar of these is the system of rhetorical modes. These are fairly universal categories of development or patterns of thinking. Whatever the subject, it can be studied and explained through the rhetorical modes of

- narration [telling stories]
- exemplification [giving examples]
- description [showing physical characteristics]
- comparison [showing likenesses and dissimilarities]
- classification [grouping or categorizing]
- division [analyzing structure or parts]
- process analysis [analyzing sequences or stages]
- causal analysis [analyzing causes and effects]
- definition [analyzing meaning or connotations]
- evaluation [assessing worth]

In actual writing, these modes usually appear in combination and may be used repeatedly. An author may offer several successive comparisons or definitions. The same paragraph may divide, describe, and interpret a subject.

*4. Rely on Inquiry or Questioning.* Invention can be almost like a self-contained interview, a process of exploring the subject by asking oneself questions. Like an interview, the result depends partially on the quality of the questions asked and partially on the openness and depth of the responses.

At a fairly rudimentary level, formal inquiry is implied in the journalistic formula, the questions "Who? What? Where? When? and How?" used by reporters to make sure that all of the most essential facts of a case have been collected. But productive inquiry may depend on being able to ask tougher or more insightful questions, to recognize in advance which query or line of reasoning might lead to productive development. If you ask stupid questions, you cannot blame the person interviewed for giving you stupid answers.

Questions tend to focus on

- facts or the present situation
- motives, influences, or the past
- outcomes or the future
- beliefs, concepts, or policy
- attitudes, feelings, or emotions
- style, manner, or performance
- circumstance or context
- worth or value
- meanings, secrets, subtexts, or hidden agendas

**Convergent and Divergent Questioning.** Educators point out that questions may be convergent or divergent. Convergent questions are focused. They try to pry out or uncover specific and predicted answers, to confirm hypotheses or test knowledge of the status quo.

Divergent questions are open-ended. The interviewer or instructor does not know what answer he or she wants, or multiple answers are possible. Divergent questioning opens the floor to different points of view and unexpected interpretations. The questioner sacrifices control of the agenda of conversation in the hope of finding out things he or she might not have thought to ask about.

**Tagmemic Inquiry.**   The "tagmemic grid" of Young, Becker, and Pike, explained at length in *Rhetoric: Discovery and Change* (1970), is a formula for observation based, like the rhetorical modes, on differences in the manner in which we look at a subject. The authors suggest that the mind tends to perceive objects in a limited number of ways, as a

- *Particle:* a single and whole entity
- *Wave:* an ongoing process or pattern of motion
- *Field:* a category, array, habitat, or range

Furthermore, the particle, wave, or field may be discussed in terms of

- *Contrast:* its difference from or likeness to other things
- *Variation:* its different manifestations or its variability (the extent to which it changes or takes different forms, or the extent to which it can change and still be perceived as "the same thing")
- *Distribution:* the locations in which and/or frequency with which it can be found

This need not be intimidating. In some ways, the tagmemic system restates some of the familiar rhetorical modes—comparison and classification, for instance—from a slightly more scientific perspective.

Tagmemic inquiry can be particularly useful for technological and scientific definition. For example, the tagmemic categories might aid one in developing a complete description of a new species of animal or mineral or a new astronomical phenomenon: what it looks like, how it acts or is formed, what context it is found in or what categories of knowledge it seems to fit, how it differs from related phenomena, how many shapes of forms it can take, and how frequent it is or how it tends to be distributed in a region—densely, in groups, in isolated units, and so on.

## WRITING FROM EXPERIENCE

Your writing will seem more inventive if you rely more on experience than reading as a source of information and ideas. To make writing from experience more effective, however, you need to do the following:

**1. *Trust Your Own Perceptions.*** If you regularly rely on invention, you must come to believe in the validity and worth of your own perceptions and ideas. To a certain extent, this means speaking up in spite of the limitations of your understanding, recognizing that the person next to you is probably no better informed than you are.

Trusting your own perceptions means being properly assertive, not apologizing for yourself or doubting your personal authority to speak. It means defending your feelings, opinions, and impressions, even when others disagree or when the weight of educated opinion is against you.

**2. *Emphasize Inductive Proof.*** When you are forced to rely on your own resources, the best way to establish a sense of personal authority is to build a case inductively, multiplying the number of examples you present, the number of incidents from personal experience you draw on, and the amount of observed data you report. Sufficient first-person and empirical evidence can eventually overcome even the most imposing arguments based on research and traditional wisdom.

**3. *Generalize From Experience.*** The more you are able to generalize, to characterize groups of similar experiences or observations, the greater the force or impact personal authority can have. It begins to look and sound more and more like expertise.

It is just personal experience talking when you say "Steve told me that he and Susan disagreed a lot about. . . ." It becomes reflection or thought when you generalize, saying "Most of the couples I know seem to argue about. . . ." And it becomes true authority when you are eventually able to report that "In most (or three fourths, or 75%) of the families observed, the primary cause of dissension was. . . ."

**4. *See Yourself as a Representative Case.*** Many people are incapacitated by their own sense of uniqueness. They assume that their experience is somehow different from everyone else's, that they are atypical of the human race—weirder, more stupid, more boring, or more unsightly.

Or they are shyly unwilling to speak for others, to pretend that they know what others have been through or what others are thinking. In either case, the result is that they become trapped within their own personal world, within first-person address and private opinion, able to say "I like sports cars because they make me look like something I'm not" but unable to generalize that "We like cars that have the personality we lack."

**5. *Regard the Experience as Unique.*** The opposite danger is to see nothing at all unique in your own experiences and perceptions. If you always regard your experiences as typical or routine, you may not recognize either the interest inherent in them or their true nature.

People who have worked in fast-food restaurants may regard the experience as nothing special to write about, but to those who have not worked in fast-food restaurants, they not only seem like experts, they *are* experts. Their first-person accounts may be at least as interesting and enlightening as a formal survey of three hundred restaurant employees.

6. *Avoid Reducing Experience to Simple Meanings.* A danger in writing from experience is the tendency to tack a moral onto every story, to stop analyzing personal experience after finding in it an explicit and usually oversimplified thesis or message. Often the correlation is not very good; the story may illustrate something, but generally not the proposition imposed on it. An accident caused by your own reckless driving may "mean" far more than "Drinking and driving don't mix" or "Better safe than sorry."

The better option, frequently counseled by writing teachers, is to find the message within the story and within yourself rather than forcing the experience to fit an exterior meaning.

7. *Associate Your Experiences With Human Universals.* We are also more likely to credit personal authority when it evokes connotations of universal human experience, when the author perceives symbolic and archetypal significance in his or her material. Through allusions, key words, metaphors, and complex associations an everyday event, place, object, or person can be invested with deeper meanings, with psychological, ritual, and emotional connotations that elevate and transform it.

A casual dinner might be invested with connotations of communion. A business lunch might become a ceremonial last meal. Entering an office party might be, at some less-than-explicit level, like crossing the threshold into another world where morality and the social order are momentarily suspended.

These connotations are not frivolous or irrelevant. Nonrational though they might be, they reflect real and culturally significant responses to experience. It may not be rational to perceive strangers as evil or illness as a sign of guilt, but associations like these are part of us and part of the meaning of events.

## EXERCISE C

The following subjects might normally require knowledge drawn from research and education. How might you manage to write about them using material derived primarily from invention and personal authority?

Develop information about the subjects by using a number of different invention devices and finding parallels in your personal experience. Then choose one subject and write a short essay about it, avoiding the use of learned concepts where possible, or expressing learned ideas in the form of personal knowledge.

Do not be afraid to make mistakes, but express your assertions with reasonable caution and qualification. Identify personal definitions, personal opinions, speculation, and guesswork as such.

1. The Kennedy administration
2. The psychological effects of reaching retirement age (if you haven't yet)
3. What it is like to be disabled or handicapped
4. Japanese foreign policy
5. Impressionist or abstract painting
6. Corporate ethics: how large businesses treat their employees, management, suppliers, consumers, and competitors; how they develop, seek, and protect technology; and how they manufacture, promote, and distribute their products
7. The effect of wave action on beaches
8. The price of gold
9. The nature of parallel lines, or the shortest distance between two points
10. The nature of tragedy or comedy

## WHEN TO RELY ON EDUCATION

Content that emphasizes knowledge, scholarship, and derivative information is appropriate

- when report is expected
- in interviews
- in reviews
- when you are already an expert
- when the audience is unfamiliar with the subject
- when the application of concepts is called for
- when your audience doubts you
- when your audience holds contrary views
- when proof is based on principles and precedents
- when your own experience is limited

## WHEN TO RELY ON INVENTION

It is appropriate or effective to rely on invention

- when writing about personal experience
- in expressive writing
- when you lack expertise
- when the situation is informal

- when time is short
- when you want to escape common knowledge

## GAINS AND LOSSES

### ◀ RELYING ON EDUCATION ▶

| Advantages | Disadvantages |
| --- | --- |
| Difficult to attack | May become inflexible |
| Displaces responsibility to one's sources | Limits credit coming to the individual |
| Makes author a spokesperson for discipline or vocation | Distances the author from the audience |
| Inherent credibility in topics others have discussed | Limits opportunities for speaking |
| Appears more weighty and substantial | Requires extensive study and research |

## GAINS AND LOSSES

### ◀ RELYING ON INVENTION ▶

| Advantages | Disadvantages |
| --- | --- |
| Little extended research needed | Limits one's perspective on the subject |
| Increases extemporaneity | Higher risk of error or infelicity |
| Makes author independent of other authorities | Requires continual effort to sustain credibility |
| Lowers barriers of education and expertise | Lacks formal status and authority |
| More opportunities for discovery | Easily attacked and refuted |

## *Wider Implications*

The distinctions between knowledge based on education, experience, and invention are not artificial, or at least not entirely so. We routinely evaluate the authority of others on this basis. The person who has studied the subject at school or through reading we consider a scholar. We associate hands-on experience with practical wisdom; it makes a person a technician, practitioner, or master of the subject. Invention makes the philosopher, visionary, theoretician, and wit.

Desirable though it might be to combine all three forms of expertise in the same person, it is rare that an author will have had the time, willpower, and opportunity to acquire such depth and dimension. And even when learning, experience, and imagination are present in one person, it is stylistically difficult to represent and convey such complex authority.

### SOPHISTS, POLITICIANS, AND PHILOSOPHERS

In classical rhetoric, the dilemma over invention and education was often illustrated through the example of politics. The question was whether the speaker would benefit more from having held political office, from philosophical study of politics, or from invention and sophistry, or sometimes whether one should devote oneself first to practical experience, to formal education, or to the study of rhetoric.

The politician would argue that one could not speak effectively without having had experience. The philosopher would argue that education should be prerequisite either to holding office or to speaking effectively about political matters. And the sophist would claim that skill in speaking and invention could make both experience and education unnecessary.

Beneath these false dilemmas lie real and continuing questions:

- whether knowledge exists apart from words
- whether one learns best by rote or by discovery
- whether knowledge is a body of information or a kind of know-how
- what relationship there might be between theory and practice
- how knowledge can best be demonstrated or proven
- whether learning precedes writing, or whether writing (or "textualizing") is the essence of learning

### WRITING AND KNOWING

Many contemporary scholars have argued either that writing is an act of discovery or that discovery is a form of composition. They suggest that the process of composing one's thoughts or forming a theory is the same as the process of composing a text or essay. The implication is that writing *is* knowing and that one does not truly "know" a subject until one can perform it.

### KNOWLEDGE AS AN ART

If one accepts the equation between writing and knowing, the consequences are great. It suggests that expertise is not contained in education, or in experience, or even in perception and thought, that knowledge is instead an art, a way of structuring and conveying ideas. The best thinking, by this definition, is embodied in the most attractive and convincing presentation of the issues.

Some might argue that this opens the door to sophistry: any viewpoint can be made to look "true" if it is cleverly presented; and any theory, idea, or belief can be proven to be a contrivance, a manipulation of the facts. But the specter of sophistry is a red herring. Artistic knowledge is not necessarily deceptive. An effective "performance" is not only attractive but well informed, ethical, and credible.

### TRUE AND FALSE SCHOLARSHIP

The role of revising and transmitting accepted wisdom is an important one, crucial to the conveyance and continuance of culture. Research that actively refines, tests, and enlivens knowledge is always needed.

This is true scholarship. It continually reaffirms, questions, and amplifies accepted theories and beliefs, working within the standard paradigm or framework of ideas to study, support, and, where necessary, change the status quo. Intellectual culture requires constant renewal and debate.

False scholarship is intellectual stagnation. It perpetuates half-truths and defeats progress. Learning becomes a credential or dogmatic creed. Researchers become intellectual bureaucrats, the mindless gatekeepers of arcane knowledge.

### TRUE AND FALSE INVENTION

Creative and independent thinking is always necessary. It challenges, tests, and refines accepted beliefs and finds new directions for research. Invention enables us to speak despite the incompleteness and imperfection of our understanding. In the form of wit it amuses us. In imagination it inspires.

Invention misused is a substitute for discipline, authority, and learning, a sham. Through plausible lies and the appearance of truth, it misleads us.

### THE INTERDEPENDENCE OF EDUCATION AND INVENTION

It's true enough that some people get by on wit and some on study. But in the wider endeavor—the perpetuation and increase of human understanding—both have their place. When erudition and imagination are combined in the same style, we respect it all the more.

The writer we admire most, or the ideal speaker, is neither scholar alone, treasuring the lore and learning of past generations, nor the creative thinker who scorns received ideas, concerned only with the coherence and integrity of his or her own thoughts.

Essays by nature are combinations of old and new, combinations of learning—in the form of principles, facts, assumptions, premises, and theories—and personal interpretation. Education provides both background and support for the author's own contentions.

## Conclusion

The underlying meaning can be the same no matter what the source of information. Truth emerges from practice as well as from theory, from imagination as well as from books. Each form of authority deserves its own measure of respect. Ultimately, how one acquires information is not so important as having it and making good use of what one has.

## ASSIGNMENT A: Drawing on Education and Research

1. Teach a fairly advanced concept or theory to an audience largely unfamiliar with it. Do not assume that the audience is interested in the subject or motivated to learn about it. Your role (like an actual teacher's) is to both inculcate the message and to convey a sense of its importance, utility, and fascination.

2. Choose a concept you encountered in your reading or a lecture and either use it to analyze and explain a specific case or apply it to a related phenomenon.

## ASSIGNMENT B: Drawing on Memory

1. Write for an audience that is suspicious of academic, technical, and intellectual perspectives. Try to discuss a subject you have studied in the classroom without directly drawing on books and education. Substitute real-life experiences, common knowledge, and colloquial language for the technical information, philosophical speculations, and theories.

2. Address an audience with which you have common experiences and a common perspective (generally speaking, this might apply to people in your own age group or people who entered an organization at the same time that you did). Reflect on shared memories and their significance to you and your peers.

## ASSIGNMENT C:  Invention

1. Assume you have been asked to discuss a subject you are relatively unacquainted with. Take some time to study, analyze, and review the topic. Then try to write intelligently about it, without seeming to be talking nonsense. You might, as a precaution, wish to confess some ignorance of the subject as you begin.

2. Use imagination to reconstruct what might have happened in some distant and inaccessible setting or what some situation unfamiliar to you might be like.

# 12

# Observation, Focus, Perspective, and Criticism

[Criticism is] a disinterested endeavor to learn and propagate the best that is known and thought in the world. —Matthew Arnold

Essays are aggressive even if the mind from which they come is fair, humane and, when it is to the point, disinterested —Elizabeth Hardwick

Genius . . . means little more than the faculty of perceiving in an unhabitual way. —William James

Liberation is a praxis: the action and reflection of men upon their world in order to transform it. —Paulo Freire

## *Discernment and Discrimination*

We consider people observant when they call our attention to things we consider interesting or important. It might be

- something we find enlightening or useful
- something that is potentially dangerous or in need of review
- something that evokes memories or emotion
- something we regret having overlooked
- something that has, through familiarity, lost its true significance

- something we have noticed ourselves, but not understood
- an observation we would like confirmed
- something we could not see by ourselves

It does not impress us when people are sponges, soaking up data indiscriminately, absorbed by anything they see.

Selectiveness can be as attractive in style as discernment. We admire the ability to appraise and assess the true (or present) worth of things. Uncritical people can be annoying and expensive. They consider every incident, example, or detail to be equally valuable, telling us *everything* about their trip to Florida, their high school reunion, or their hernia, showing neither discretion nor judgment. They would have us pay as much for an Avon bottle as for Tiffany glass.

Regardless of its quality, a style based on observation may be perceived as good or bad.

### ◀ OBSERVATION ▶

| Good Qualities | Bad Qualities |
| --- | --- |
| speculative | unsystemmatic |
| perceptive | unfocused, diffuse |
| descriptive | pointless |
| objective | lacking in vision |

A style based on criticism or selection may also be considered good or bad.

### ◀ CRITICISM ▶

| Good Qualities | Bad Qualities |
| --- | --- |
| forceful | opinionated |
| discriminating | judgmental |
| principled | self-righteous |
| self-assured | prejudiced |

## Collecting Information

Style varies in relation to how you perceive the subject and what information you consider significant or pertinent—worth "collecting" and reporting. Considerations include

- the scope or focus of your study
- the orientation or perspective from which you examine the case (including methodology, ideology, and equipment)
- your involvement with or emotional distance from the subject
- the attitudes or values that shape your perceptions

There are other constraints on the ultimate content of an essay—rhetorical effectiveness, a desire for accuracy, the conventions of a genre, and the preferences of the audience, for example—but focus, perspective, involvement, and values are the most important influences on the author's apprehension of the subject.

**Scope and Focus.**   Scope and focus determine how wide or narrow the field of study will be, whether it will encompass many instances or few, an extended time span or a matter of seconds, a micron or a panorama.

**Perspectives.**   Perspectives are the angles, contexts, perceptual tools, and intellectual structures we use to reveal other "sides" of the subject— its components, its history, its structure, its chemistry, its behavior, its relationship to other phenomena, and its appearance to other people or cultures.

**Involvement and Distance.**   Involvement is the author's relative separation from or participation in the subject, whether emotionally or experientially.

**Values.**   Values are the criteria on which judgments are based and data is selected. In evaluation, they are preemptively applied to the subject. In observation, they serve (for better or worse) to edit perception, filtering out details that seem unimportant or irrelevant.

## The Nature of Observation

People often think that observation comes naturally, that it is no more than a matter of looking at things or absorbing information. But observation is an art in itself, a focused or heightened version of perception. Observation is the art of seeing the subject clearly and completely, without unconsciously filtering out, ignoring, or suppressing data. It is a talent for finding new ways to view the subject and for recognizing their significance.

The quality and nature of observation is affected by the writer's worldview or ideology, by the writer's vision and perceptual acuity (or lack of it), and by the perspective or stance a writer takes with respect to the subject. These are largely questions of focus—the manner in which we restrict, alter, or enlarge the field of perception.

### THE RANGE OF PERCEPTION

Observation may vary in terms of the length of time involved, the breadth or narrowness of coverage, and the number or kinds of ideas and parameters that will be considered. In scientific experiment, for instance, only one or two factors are permitted to vary (hence the term *variables* to describe them). Everything else is held constant, so if the predicted effect occurs, one can be fairly confident that the variables produced it.

You can change the effect of an essay by changing the focus. You can make an essay longer by adding perspectives or different focuses to the development.

Some of the many possible views of a subject include the following:

## CHANGES IN FOCUS

1. Short-term and long-term views of it
2. Close-up and distant views
3. In cross-section, slice of life
4. Inside and exterior views
5. From different angles
6. From an aerial or panoramic perspective
7. Cropped or partial views, interrupted views
8. Before and after, then and now, repeated instances
9. At reduced or accelerated speeds

## SURVEYS OF PROCESS, FORM, AND STRUCTURE

10. In terms of its utility or application
11. In terms of its general appearance or conformation
12. In terms of its composition, structure, or component parts
13. In terms of its formation, development, or design

## CHANGES IN PERSPECTIVE

14. Through the eyes or accounts of different witnesses or participants
15. From a personal perspective
16. As seen by different age groups

17. As seen by different social groups
18. As seen by different professions
19. As seen in terms of different roles
20. As seen by different countries or regions
21. From a historical perspective
22. From a psychological perspective
23. From a sociological perspective
24. From a political perspective
25. From a legal perspective
26. In aesthetic terms
27. In ethical, moral, or religious terms

## SUBJECTIVE VIEWS

28. In terms of ideal forms, as it ought to be
29. As seen in emotional terms (e.g., as one fears it to be, wishes it to be, or as distorted by anger)
30. As changed, displaced, or reshaped by imagination and association, as it might be

## EXAMINATION THROUGH METHODS AND DEVICES

31. Through microscopic or telescopic observation
32. Through different sensing devices (e.g., radiotelescopes in astronomy, inclinometers in geology, X-rays and thermometers in medicine)
33. Under the influence of different factors (e.g, pressure, electricity, stress, impact, or heat for metals, or unemployment, dual careers, alcoholism, sibling rivalry, depression, success, or choice of housing for the family unit, a social phenomenon)
34. Placing the subject in a wider category or a succession of categories
35. Placing the subject in its context (e.g., its social, environmental, or physical setting)

## SELECTIVE AND INCLUSIVE VIEWS

36. Emphasizing one feature or quality over all others (foregrounding it or caricaturing it)
37. Abstracting one or more features or qualities of the subject from the whole, omitting or suppressing all other information
38. In terms of a particular ideology, theory, or conceptual framework

Changing perspective is an invention device for writing based on observation. Each new perspective provides additional information about the subject.

## EXERCISE A

Describe each of the following subjects from several different perspectives.

1. The Vietnam war
2. The loss of the space shuttle Challenger
3. A volcano or geyser
4. Thanksgiving Day
5. The sport of baseball
6. A wedding or divorce
7. A grasshopper or locust
8. Sunglasses
9. A cassette tape recording
10. An angry or emotional outburst
11. Sand
12. A city
13. Broken glass
14. A closed door
15. Smoke

## *Writing From Observation*

The underlying elements of an essay based on observation usually include the following:

- A review of accepted interpretations of the subject
- A perspective or "position" from which the subject is being observed
- A plan or method for conducting observation—perhaps expressed as a narrative account of the observation process or perhaps as a formal methodology
- Some restriction or definition of the scope and extent of the observation
- An account of what was observed—in narrative and/or statistical summary
- An interpretation of the findings—this being perhaps a revision or refinement of established views or a new explanation of the phenomenon
- A comparative and critical review of the author's interpretation and previous views on the subject

Not all of these may directly and explicitly appear in an observation-based essay. Nor will they necessarily appear in the order given here.

### OBSERVATION AND THE SCIENTIFIC METHOD

There is a necessary relationship between the elements of observational writing and the methods of empirical research. Any research methodology is by definition a structured form of perception. Observation therefore includes in its scope the structural, imaginative, and organizational skill it takes to plan one's perceptions—constructing experiments, surveys, and case studies so the information one seeks is highlighted, so one can increase the validity of the results by reducing the influence of competing variables.

The scientific method (the sequence of observation, hypothesis, experimentation, and replication of results) combines elements of observation and proof. It is intended to channel the process of perception to increase the validity of findings.

### INFORMAL AND PHILOSOPHICAL OBSERVATION

The same processes occur in more informal observation and in philosophical writing based on observation. An author writing an interpretive account of his or her experiences with nature, for instance, might indirectly portray a perspective, presenting himself or herself as a person naive about the degree of conflict and struggle in the natural world. The author might identify the locale observed and characterize his or her interaction with it, perhaps admitting the limitations of his or her knowledge, interest, and insight.

There would probably be some narrative account of natural struggles the author observed, and casual allusions to classic discussions of conflict, like Darwin's, Marx's, and Machiavelli's, might appear in describing the outcome. The author's own personal interpretation of the significance of the events observed might be contrasted with the naive view of nature he or she started out with.

### FORMAL AND INFORMAL OBSERVATION

The primary differences between informal and scientific observation are not differences in underlying structure. They are instead differences in the directness or indirectness of the style, the perspective taken and audience addressed, the formality and scope of the observation process, the kinds and quantity of evidence cited, and the intellectual framework used.

## *Being Observant*

A reputation for perceptiveness depends on developing the habits associated with being observant and emphasizing perceptions in your style. You can make your style appear more observant or perceptive by applying some of the following suggestions:

*1. Avoid Making Judgments.* Styles based on observation make few value judgments. What matters is not whether the object is good or bad, moral or immoral, useful or useless, pleasing or unpleasant, accurate or inaccurate, but rather what it actually is. Observation is largely descriptive and reportative, interpreting and explaining findings but not assessing their general worth.

Judgments made in observational writing are usually limited to (a) the quality of the data and methodology, and (b) the scientific or intellectual significance of the data. These are often understated, qualified, or expressed in a highly distanced or objective style.

*2. Take a Spectator's Role.* The author's role is usually that of a student, scholar, or scientist rather than that of a participant or critic. The participant intervenes in the event, changing the outcome in accord with his or her values and beliefs. The critic "revises" the event in terms of how it should have happened or could have been different.

The spectator, by contrast, seeks to be revised by the event, to test his or her preconceptions and theories against reality and to change them accordingly. The scientist may shape the context of events or the context of observation, but the focus, once events are underway, is on watching inquisitively, without involvement.

*Note:* The distinction between spectator and participant roles is adapted from the work of James Britton in *Language and Learning* (Harmondsworth, England: Penguin, 1970).

*3. Study the Subject Without Preconceptions.* However you eventually intend to address the topic, observe the subject initially without preconceptions. Do not assume that you already know everything there is to know about the issue. Do not assume that your previous experience with similar subjects is necessarily applicable to the specific topic at hand.

*4. Examine the Subject Repeatedly and at Length.* A cursory inspection of the subject is not sufficient. Nor, for that matter, is a moderately close examination. First impressions usually reveal no more than the obvious. You should examine the subject repeatedly and at length, keeping track of your observations and adding to them.

You might want to imply or recount the extent of the observations in your writing.

*5. Describe or Depict the Subject.*   Spend time describing or portraying the object being studied, even if you and your audience are already quite familiar with it. Styles appear more perceptive when they show the author's familiarity with the details of the object or event, thereby verifying that the author is an eyewitness and hopefully demonstrating that he or she can see things that we cannot.

*6. Change Focus, Perspective, and Context.*   Try to observe the subject from new angles and perspectives, in the context of different frames of reference than you have previously applied to it. For example, if you have always thought of amusement parks in terms of entertainment, look at them instead in economic terms, in psychological terms, in moral or ethical terms, or as alternate realities—as places where the laws of nature and society are momentarily suspended.

View the subject in a historical perspective. Approach it on a highly focused basis—an individual encounter or case, for example. Or try to get behind the scenes.

## The Nature of Criticism

Evaluative writing is characterized by a focus on faults or virtues of the object under review. Since judgment strongly implies the presence of the author—a person forming an opinion—criticism is more likely to include both the author's persona in the essay and an obvious tone of voice. There is more likely to be emotional appeal and emotional response, though these may be veiled, suppressed, or artfully rationalized.

### VALUES OR CRITERIA

Essential to evaluation is the presence of criteria for judgment, a system of values, rules, laws, standards, principles, and ideals against which the subject is measured. On the basis of these criteria, a hierarchy or rating scale may be established, ranking similar objects as increasingly better or worse than each other.

Criteria for judgment vary from field to field, subject to subject, and culture to culture. No complete list is possible, but the following selection is perhaps at least somewhat indicative. We judge the worth of other people, of events, of places and objects, and of ideas or artistic representations in terms of positive and negative values like the following:

| | | |
|---|---|---|
| accuracy | appropriateness | perceptiveness |
| morality or immorality | authority | truth |
| altruism | innocence | strength |
| attractiveness | quietness | flexibility |
| rarity | variety | technical advancement |
| security | complexity | speed |
| interest | sophistication | impact |
| efficiency | openness | danger |
| memorableness | endurance | weakness |
| depth | capacity | completeness |
| originality | closeness to an ideal | vision or design |
| wit | closeness to an expectation | propriety |
| naturalness | effectiveness | newness |
| precision | usefulness | freshness |
| toughness | refinement | smoothness |
| currency | stability | brevity |
| evocativeness | validity | maturity |
| clarity | cost | humanity |
| excitement | familiarity | privacy |
| power | legality | honesty |
| incoherence | cleverness | courage |
| integrity | | |

This list is far from complete. Such a list can hardly begin to account for all the various standards we use for judgment, much less to show their applications.

Values are inevitably situational. They are dependent on the subject and often peculiar to it. It is regarded as a positive good for a lawn, for instance, to be green. But the criterion of "greenness" does not apply to evaluating engine performance in a car or the quality of an opera. Even seemingly inclusive standards vary to suit the topic. Although a standard like "lushness" can be used to judge both the lawn and the opera, and all three objects might be considered aesthetically pleasing, the criteria in question do not mean quite the same thing in their different applications.

## *Writing Criticism*

The most basic elements of a critical essay are as follows:

- The object to be evaluated
- The general case—the category to which the object belongs
- The ideal case—the type that the object represents

- The values or criteria by which the object is judged

When the object being evaluated is a literary or artistic performance, or a theory or hypothesis, criticism also includes an important fifth element:

- The object or events represented or explained

Much criticism is further complicated by such related considerations as

- How the object appears to the audience
- What the person intended or meant to produce
- What perspective or set of beliefs the writer uses as a frame of reference

Consider the following two examples. First, suppose you have been asked to write a report recommending which computer your firm should purchase. In making a choice, you would not only examine the object but also compare it to other computers, in general, and to the ideal computer for your needs. You would rate the different products available on the basis of a number of standards. These standards might include such criteria as speed of operation, reliability, capacity, availability of software, appearance, technological advancement, and cost, among others. The more criteria you apply to the decision, the better informed it might appear to be.

The final report might reflect this process of evaluation in any number of ways. You might start with a direct discussion of the problem at hand, followed in turn by a list of the criteria that seemed appropriate and a comparative review of the computers examined. Or you might begin with your recommendation, then describe the alternatives (and their drawbacks) one at a time, indirectly incorporating criteria into the discussion in the form of value judgments. Another possibility would be to describe the ideal machine for your company or office, and then to show (in essay form and/or on a chart) how well each of the computers reviewed matches up to the ideal.

Second, you have been asked to review a book. The finished review might include a capsule description of the author's ideas, subject, or themes, a comparison of his or her portrayal of events to the thing supposedly represented, and an extended judgment based on various criteria (in this case probably including such values as accuracy, completeness, coherence of vision, and the like).

If the book is literary, you might also consider the many complex criteria used to assess whether a work of art is aesthetically pleasing, emotionally satisfying, perceptive, well written, and well conceived. It would also be appropriate to compare the work to others of its type or to the general principles or ideals such works are based on. You might encompass the entire review in the wider perspective of a particular literary theory or ideology—for instance, assessing the book in terms of its folkloric substrata, its feminist relevance, or its conceptual form and structure.

If the book presents a theory or hypothesis, you might include in the finished review some discussion of alternative viewpoints. The criteria used might include measures of the quality of the research or data, the utility of the concept, the adequacy of the theory (how well it explains and predicts behavior and events), and so on.

### COMMON FAULTS IN CRITICAL WRITING

The following are common problems in writing criticism:

1. Simply reporting events or ideas—without offering any extended judgment
2. Content that does not support the judgment stated at the outset
3. Reliance on a too-limited or inappropriate set of criteria
4. Overemphasis on trivial or less important criteria at the expense of those more relevant
5. Forgetting to measure the theory or performance against the thing it intends to explain or portray

## *Showing Good Judgment*

A reputation for good judgment depends on more than being critical, in the usual sense. We do not admire people who find fault with everything. Readers may perceive good judgment in your style if you do the following:

*1. Consciously Examine Your Own Values.* Spend time specifically thinking or writing about the criteria or values that apply to the subject. Ask yourself which are most valid and appropriate and what other values might also be pertinent.

*2. Question Your Own Judgments.* Continually question your previous evaluations. This does not mean that you have to change them. It simply means that you should keep examining and testing the worth of your conclusions, refining and revising them as necessary.

*3. Base Judgments on Relevant Criteria.* The intrinsic worth of something is based on the properties it exhibits, not on the properties we wish it possessed. You should at least attempt to understand a subject on its own merits, on what it attempts to be, before you begin to judge it on the basis of what you would like it to be or what you think in general of similar objects or ideas.

A building you criticize for its inefficiency may have been designed primarily for aesthetic appeal, purposely sacrificing a degree of practicality. A person you force to be deferential can hardly be criticized for a lack of assertiveness. A plant cannot be faulted for having thorns. The problem for the writer is to seek out and understand the internal logic of things, the values on which they are based and contrived.

*4. Allow for Changes in Taste.*   Tastes change and vary. The fact that people liked something yesterday does not mean they should still like it today. In fact, they may have tired of the subject.

*5. Leave Room for Other People's Values and Preferences.*   Taste is democratic. The fact that you personally like or dislike something does not mean that everyone else must share your appreciation or distaste. The fact that many people like or dislike something does not mean that you must share their opinion, but it does suggest that this consensus judgment deserves some respect.

*6. Consider the Context or Situation.*   Value judgments are very situational. Something worthless in one context may be precious in another. A procedure that does not work in one case should not automatically be abandoned.

Applying the same set of criteria to every situation is restrictive and dangerous.

*7. Be Gracious in Expressing Criticism.*   Criticism can be very offensive. If you must criticize, it is usually wiser to avoid directly assaulting your audience or directly attacking things the audience values. There are many ways of doing this.

**Put the Audience on Your Side.**   One of the classic dodges in evaluation is to include the audience on your own side of the issue, to frame the criticism in terms of "our" views or what "we" think, as opposed to a specified or unspecified third party. You are able then to criticize "them" without seeming to criticize your readers.

**Suggest That the Thing Criticized Is an Exception.**   Another common device is to identify the object criticized as an exception to the rule. If your audience generally likes sports cars, say that "Unlike most sports cars, the 3900 is neither fun to drive nor pleasing in appearance." Or to be even safer, "The 3900 we drove didn't live up to our expectations. But the company says some assembly-line adjustments have been made in both the performance and sheet metal since our prototype was built."

**Give the Audience Credit for Anticipating the Criticism.** Writers can sometimes avoid giving offense by assuming that the audience has already considered the criticism proposed, though this strategy takes considerable finesse and insight. It may require the writer to go so far as to imagine why the alternative might have been proposed and discarded, as in "Increasing the size of the orchestra must have been too costly."

**Criticize Your Own Criticism.** The effect of good judgment may be enhanced by actually criticizing your own criticism: "Of course, one option would be to use more temporary workers and fewer payroll employees. But that could decrease morale and efficiency."

8. *Acknowledge Worth in the Thing Criticized.* A similar and frequently effective ploy is to acknowledge a degree of truth in the idea criticized. Usually the writer's stance is that the idea attacked was not carried far enough, was based on good intentions, or was well conceived but based on the wrong notions or incomplete data.

For example, a movie critic might say, "The director apparently felt that the additional special effects would make the film more believable. And she was right. But the special effects also distract us from the relationship between the characters, which in this story should take center stage."

9. *Qualify Your Criticisms.* Criticism can be softened by qualification and speculativeness in the writer's style. Somehow it hurts less to say "Perhaps the problem is that . . ." or "Sometimes the evidence seems less conclusive than it might be."

## EXERCISE B

List three or more criteria that apply to each of the following subjects. Then choose one of the topics, focus on a particular example, and develop a short criticism or appreciation that discusses at least the three most important values.

**1.** A photograph from a family album
**2.** A friend
**3.** An employer
**4.** An employee

**5.** A job

**6.** A television set

**7.** A pen

**8.** A house or apartment

**9.** An adventure movie

**10.** A computer

**11.** A supermarket

**12.** A convenience store

**13.** A small corner grocery store, part of the neighborhood for years

**14.** A leader

**15.** An actor


## WHEN TO APPEAR OBSERVANT

Writing based on observation has an inherent cautiousness and diplomacy. It does not force one's own system of values on the subject or audience. It presumes that the evidence will speak for itself.

A style based on observation is generally appropriate

- in scientific, professional, and technical writing
- when documentation and proof are expected
- when the subject is new to you
- when the subject is highly emotional
- when the subject is taken for granted
- when present understanding of the subject seems inadequate


## WHEN TO BE CRITICAL

We use criticism to redirect or revise the behavior of other people, to guide them away from potential dangers, and to lead them toward experiences and ideas that seemed useful or enjoyable.

Criticism is appropriate

- when correction or redirection seems necessary
- when praise is merited
- when a warning is called for
- in decision making and deliberation
- when discussing proposed beliefs, theories, and laws

## GAINS AND LOSSES

### ◀ OBSERVATION ▶

**Advantages**

Focuses and controls attention

Opens eyes and extends scope of the senses

Provides secure and inexorable support

Can effectively attack and supplant expertise

Makes the subject the common property of all

**Disadvantages**

Omits information

Challenges misperceptions

Requires time, discipline, and clear-sightedness

Can be misleading; your eyes may deceive you

Provides an overwhelming amount of information

## GAINS AND LOSSES

### ◀ CRITICISM ▶

**Advantages**

Provides self-conferred status

Implies long experience

Puts opposition on the defensive

Filters out unwanted data

Directs actions and choices

**Disadvantages**

Seems condescending or self-important

May become self-righteous or dogmatic

Opens floor to return criticism

May exclude important data

Hurts and demeans those criticized

## *Wider Implications*

Observation and evaluation are opposite ways of seeing a subject. Observation attempts to look at the subject without preconceptions, to see what is really there. Criticism and appreciation look at the subject in terms of abstract standards, criteria, or values—comparing it to what ought to be there.

The choice between criticism and observation is at its heart a choice between ideology and empiricism, between traditional values or beliefs and ideas arrived at through direct study of the object. On one side are the lessons of history and culture. On the other are the insight, experience, and uniqueness of the individual.

### OBSERVATION WITHOUT EVALUATION

Although some people pride themselves on total objectivity and the avoidance of judgment, "pure" observation is an impossibility. It would require a person to look at a subject without referring to anything previously learned, without responding emotionally, without overlooking anything, and without drawing conclusions during the observation.

One can, however, attempt to describe the subject with as little intrusion of opinion or judgment as possible. Description may be needed to make a record of the subject, to ensure that all possible data about it is recovered and preserved.

But apart from documenting the phenomenon, plain observation can become a pointless venture. Looking for the sake of looking gives you a clutter of details but no ideas. It can become purely experiential, an animal or mystical response to the subject, either meaningless or without meaning that can be expressed in words.

### EVALUATION WITHOUT OBSERVATION

Evaluation focuses not so much on the subject itself as on how well the subject conforms to certain standards. It moves the center of attention from outside to inside, away from the exterior event, object, or topic of discussion and toward the author's values, judgments, or attitudes.

Pure criticism becomes dogmatic. It works from a set of rules, criteria, or principles that have, so to speak, taken on a life of their own, becoming a static ideology or prescriptive code divorced from reality and common practice, no longer subjected to revision or refinement. Dogma has ceased to truly observe or consider the subject at all. It tells us what we should see rather than what is really there.

### THE RELATIONSHIP BETWEEN OBSERVATION AND IDEOLOGY

Research in various fields suggests that a continual process of assessment and reassessment takes place in the mind. Values and beliefs are constantly measured against the evidence our senses and experience provide. When the evidence strongly contradicts our preconceptions, we seek to reestablish equilibrium, to make the evidence and ideology conform to each other.

**Cognitive Dissonance.** In *A Theory of Cognitive Dissonance* (1957), Leon Festinger describes how people develop a general conception or image of the world around them and constantly monitor the correlations between this worldview and the actual events and experiences of life. As long as reality and the worldview are relatively congruent, a person feels more or less content and satisfied. But stress emerges when the person recognizes that reality and the worldview are significantly different. There is a sense of disharmony or dissonance.

In response to this stress, a person might (1) "rewrite" his or her worldview to fit the facts, (2) attempt to change reality to fit the worldview (e.g., by passing laws or making various physical changes in the environment), or (3) in some way protect or reinforce the worldview, perhaps by suppressing the dissonant facts, by rationalizing them, or by retreating to a situation or social group that supports the desired interpretation of reality.

**Scientific Revolutions.** In *The Structure of Scientific Revolutions* (1962), Thomas S. Kuhn suggests that scientific knowledge evolves through similar periods of refinement and change. According to Kuhn, when a theory or concept is generally accepted, it is used as a framework for observation and experimentation. The theory is continually applied, extended, and tested. But during this process of application and testing, miscellaneous or anomalous facts begin to appear—data that does not fit neatly into the conceptual framework. Like the dissonance in Festinger's psychology, these anomalies conflict with the prevailing mindset. Eventually enough anomalies emerge to force a complete reevaluation of scientific thought, a scientific revolution.

**Criticism and Revision.** In a way, both Festinger and Kuhn are describing what in rhetoric and composition theory would be called revision processes—the ability to compare the text one has written with the subject described, the meaning intended, and the effect desired and to refine or rethink the idea and delivery to improve the correlations.

Whether described in psychological, scientific, or rhetorical terms, this ability requires both effective criticism and perceptive observation. The two are interwoven parts of the same thought process. Criticism relies on observation to verify its judgments. And observations relies on criticism to determine which details support, and which confute, a particular thesis, theory, or worldview.

## OBSERVATION AS LISTENING OR OPEN-MINDEDNESS

To observe well is to see without preconceptions. An emphasis on observation suggests that the author is neither judgmental nor biased, that he or she is still in the process of gathering information. The case isn't closed yet. Observation is associated, therefore, with open-mindedness, with listening, studying the situation, and reserving judgment.

### OBSERVATION AS VISION OR TRANSFORMATION

But observation is not simply a matter of clear-sightedness or "seeing what is there." At some level, the highly observant person sees things that others do not, sees the subject in new ways, or transforms our perceptions of it. There is an element of imagination and discovery, even prescience, in this.

### CRITICISM AS CEREMONIAL DISCOURSE

To criticize is to invoke praise or blame, to perceive the virtues or faults of the subject. Therefore, criticism is related to the epideictic or ceremonial discourse of classical rhetoric. Its function is to magnify or diminish, to elevate the reputation or worth of the thing praised or to lower our estimate of its value.

### CRITICISM AS DELIBERATIVE DISCOURSE

But criticism is also part of deliberative discourse, one of the means through which we arrive at decisions or determine the best course of action. It helps us choose among competing programs, candidates, and policies in business and government. It guides decisions we make about how to spend our time, where to spend it, and with whom.

## *Conclusion*

Good writing relies on both perceptiveness and criticism. You have to observe the object without preconceptions but not uncritically. You have to apply standards and assess the worth of an object without overlooking the qualities and features that make it unique.

## ASSIGNMENT A:    Appreciations and Criticisms, Praise and Blame

1. Write an extended disparagement of someone or something.

2. Write an extended compliment, an appreciation of someone's work, influence, or personality.

3. Take the role of a consumer advocate. Review a particular product or group of products. Refer to a product's reputation where appropriate, but offer an independent assessment. You do not need to imitate the style or format of consumer magazine articles. And you do not necessarily need to limit yourself to a narrow and practical perspective. The essay could use the specific subject as a springboard for addressing a more abstract social, historical, economic, or political issue.

4. Take the role of social critic. Identify, call attention to, and deplore some fault or shortcoming in people's behavior, in an organization, or in some social service.

5. Observe and review some human creation or construction in three ways, in terms of what you prefer or value in the object, in terms of its designer's values or goals, and in terms of the purpose or purposes it was intended to fulfill.

## ASSIGNMENT B:  Ideals, Best and Worst Cases, Utopias and Dystopias

1. Describe and discuss the characteristics that make someone ideal for a particular role—as leader, teacher, student, parent, or lawyer, for example. You might wish to contrast the ideal with the typical or with worst cases.

2. Portray and review one of the worst examples of something you can recall encountering.

3. In a situation where there are several possible courses of action, review and discuss the possible outcomes to determine which course of action might be best.

4. Imagine and describe what would be the ideal or worst state of affairs in some institution, organization, or group—a utopia or dystopia. You could explain how this condition might be achieved or avoided, and indicate why it is better or worse than the way things are now.

## ASSIGNMENT C: Observation and Perspectives

1. Observe a subject from some unusual angle or perspective, and directly or indirectly contrast this view of it with how people usually see the subject.

2. Observe some emerging political or social problem, an unsettled state of affairs, or an anticipated series of events. Write about what you ex-

pect to or hope will happen and/or what ought to happen. You might refer to parallel events or circumstances in the past.

3. Look at a subject or event through someone else's eyes, or contrast how you saw it when you were younger with how you perceive it now.

## ASSIGNMENT D: Predictions and Visions

1. Predict and explain what will happen to a particular person, group, company, team, or phenomenon in the next few months or years.

2. Envision simpler, better, or more interesting times, perhaps a pastoral, heroic, or golden age. Either represent what things would be like, or discuss the subject on a more abstract basis, analyzing the appeal and validity of such dreams. You might reminisce about some period of your life or call our attention to some historical period. Or you might create a completely imaginary vision—in narrative or expository form.

# 13

# Introductions and Conclusions

The first sentence can't be written until the final sentence is written.

—JOYCE CAROL OATES

Begin at the beginning . . . and go on till you come to the end: then stop.

—LEWIS CARROLL

If a man will begin with certainties, he shall end in doubts; but if he will be content to begin with doubts he shall end in certainties.

—FRANCIS BACON

## Making Entrances and Exits

We feel uncomfortable when topics are thrown at us, when issues are raised without preface, explanation, or justification. The abruptness is unsettling. It keeps us off balance. People who put us at ease are less threatening.

We appreciate speakers who are able to draw others into the conversation and leave no one out, who adroitly fit their ideas into the flow of discussion without attempting to dominate it. Comprehension is easier when the connections are clear, when the person speaking makes an effective transition from what has previously been said and the subject he or she wants to discuss.

Likewise, we envy people who are able to wrap things up effectively, to deliver a punch line or surprise ending when necessary, to gracefully invite further discussion, or to extract themselves from tedious conversations and difficult situations.

These are skills associated with introductions and conclusions, called the "framing devices" of discourse because they outline or frame the perimeters of discussion. Essay frames are generally either informational or rhetorical.

Informational frames build a logical or ideological context, using a wider concept, belief, or generalization to delimit and shape the body of the essay. They emphasize a one-sided, monologic presentation of the case. Rhetorical frames are more dialogic. They connect the content of the essay to the surrounding debate and attempt to influence the audience's attitudes, emotions, and beliefs.

Informational frames may be quite useful and adroit, providing a comprehensive and uncompromised look at the author's viewpoint. They are perceived as good or bad.

### ◀ INFORMATIONAL FRAMES ▶

| Good Qualities | Bad Qualities |
| --- | --- |
| efficient | mechanical |
| straightforward | impolite |
| confident | arrogant |
| convincing | one-sided |

Rhetorical framing devices may sacrifice objectivity and distance for the sake of effect. They are also considered to be good or bad.

### ◀ RHETORICAL FRAMES ▶

| Good Qualities | Bad Qualities |
| --- | --- |
| ingratiating | manipulative |
| attentive | unassertive |
| open, communicative | glib |
| diplomatic | evasive |

## Historical Approaches

Informational and rhetorical framing devices have much different histories. The informational model of the essay can be traced back at least to the Renaissance and the development of scientific and empirical reasoning. The rhetorical model, which dates back to classical times, owes its nature to public disputation and debate.

## CLASSICAL RHETORIC

In classical rhetoric, the introduction was referred to as the prologue, proem, or exordium, and the conclusion was called the epilogue or peroration. Because classical rhetoric focused largely on oral and persuasive discourse, advice about introductions and conclusions emphasized preparing, convincing, and appealing to a visible and present audience, usually a jury or legislature.

Generally an introduction was expected to

- put the audience in an appropriate frame of mind
- ingratiate the speaker with the audience
- create favor or goodwill for the cause and, in forensic discourse, the client
- indicate the aim or theme of the speech

The recommended elements of a conclusion were usually

- graceful reiteration of the aim, major arguments, or theme
- emotional appeal designed to leave the audience in a favorable state of mind
- magnification of the positive aspects of the case and diminution of its less-than-attractive features

The conclusion might also include magnification of weaknesses in the opposition's case and diminution of its strengths.

There were differences of opinion about the necessity for introductions and conclusions. Aristotle felt that the only truly essential features of a speech were the statement of the case and the proof. He saw introductions and conclusions as useful but not absolutely necessary. But in general the exordium and peroration were considered to be normal and accepted parts of an oration.

Although it was common to counsel an ingratiating style in the exordium and an impassioned style in the peroration (when a ringing statement of the case might be used to best effect), many alternatives to this pattern were acknowledged since the nature of the situation and cause might require other strategems.

## THE POST-RENAISSANCE

From the Renaissance onward, there has been a growing tendency to discuss introductions and conclusions as if essays were a means of either transmitting information or presenting a formal proof rather than a vehicle for persuasion. The sources of this change are complex. It was initiated in part by the work of Peter Ramus, who in the sixteenth century appropriated the arts of invention and arrangement from rhetoric and assigned them to logic. It is related to the emergence of empiricism and modern science, and perhaps, as Walter Ong suggests, to our increasing dependency on the written word after the development of the printing press.

In the informational model of discourse, introductions primarily serve to identify the nature and use of the ensuing data or to attach the author's thesis to a wider topic or generalization. The conclusion becomes largely extraneous. Once the requested or intended information has been presented, nothing more needs to be said.

In an essay based on logical demonstration and proof, the end of the essay becomes a logical conclusion or an interpretation of findings. Closure is defined by completing the proof, by showing that which was to be demonstrated. Introductions set forth the question being answered or problem being solved.

### THE CONTEMPORARY VIEW

Even while theorists and teachers were counseling an informational and logical approach to introductions and conclusions, everyday practice continued to follow a more rhetorical model of discourse. The need to be polite and ingratiating, to deal with people's emotions, attitudes, and occasional lack of knowledge, is simply too great to be ignored. The need to express oneself and one's feelings is too compelling, and the result too effective, to be omitted from either writing or speaking.

Introductions and conclusions are more than mechanical strategies for beginning and ending an essay, more than superficial or *pro forma* additions to the "real" content of a speech or report. An introduction does more than attract the reader's attention, announce the topic, and outline the essay's content. Conclusions are not just summaries of what has been said.

Framing devices are essential parts of discourse, integral to effective communication, as important as the internal or supporting development. They shape the context of debate.

## *Creating Informational Frames*

Informational frames are designed to be efficient. They present the material with as little context and background as possible. They often assume that the reader is interested in the subject already, prepared to make an effort to understand the essay, if necessary, and willing to forgive a lack of grace or tact for the sake of the argument and proof.

## INTRODUCTIONS IN THE INFORMATIONAL STYLE

Framing devices appear more informational when they do the following:

*1. Focus Exclusively on the Subject.*   Informational frames tend to ignore audience, emotion, author, and circumstance, to focus primarily on the subject. They are reportative, concerned simply with presenting content or presenting the author's point of view to the exclusion of other perspectives.

*2. Describe a Problem to be Solved.*   Informational frames often set up a straightforward problem-and-solution or question-and-answer presentation. The introduction may do no more than describe the problem, and the body of the essay is devoted to discussing or evaluating alternative solutions.

*3. Describe a Theory or Thesis That Will Be Tested or Applied.*   A thesis-and-support structure is also common in informational frames. The introduction states a direct "thesis," a point to be demonstrated, and the body of the essay provides the necessary illustration, evidence, argument, and proof.

This format is not just pertinent to argumentative writing. It is the basic pattern of writing about scientific and technical research. An experiment, for instance, tests or applies a concept to see if there is valid and sufficient evidence to support it.

*4. Describe the Theoretical Context or the Relevant Principle.*   An informational frame may review a generally accepted theory that fits the case or a relevant principle. The body of the essay may then simply narrate or report the facts, assuming that the connections are clear. Or it may make some attempt to explain the connection between the theoretical context and the specific case.

*5. Start at a General Level and Move Toward the Specific Case.*   Informational frames locate the author's thesis or claim within a larger category of ideas. They may

- state a generalization that applies to the specific case
- describe or discuss the general class to which the specific case belongs
- encompass the author's thesis or claim in a wider issue
- characterize the problem or question, discussing the general species of problem or question of which the specific case is an instance

*6. Carefully Limit and Define the Scope of the Discussion.*   Informational writing is often highly focused. It deals with one specific, even narrow problem and nothing else. The parameters of the discussion are generally stated in the introduction. There may be a clearcut statement of direction, telling exactly what material will be covered in the ensuing essay and the order in which it will be presented.

There may be an enumeration of the topics that will be considered, the issues considered relevant, or the variables to be observed and tested. These are invariably few.

Because logical demonstration and proof are concerned with validity, they tend to limit and carefully monitor the variables of the discussion or study. Information defined as irrelevant is carefully, and sometimes explicitly, excluded.

*7. Define the Standards for Proof.*  Subject-based frames carefully define the boundaries of the debate or the standards of proof. There is usually an implicit or explicit equation involved: "if this and that are proven, then my point is carried." Or "to prove my point I need to demonstrate this and that." It is a goal-oriented, logical, or problem-solving approach.

*8. Define Terms.*  In the interest of efficiency and to make sure that the message is transmitted accurately, informational styles often define the most important terms early in the essay. Sometimes this is the first thing in the introduction, especially when the term defined also represents a general concept under discussion. Or there may be a passage at the end of the introduction that reviews and specifies the meaning of particular terminology important to the author's point.

*9. Use an Objective or Reportative Stance.*  The tone of informational frames is often objective, reportative, and distant (uninvolved and dispassionate). The author poses as a spectator of the events or research described.

*10. Use a Monologic Approach.*  Informational frames often portray the issue as a closed system, with no room for debate. This can be accomplished in many ways.

- The material can be presented as fact. Journalism takes this approach, but the device is by no means limited to the reporting of concrete data. Virtually any form of information can be styled a fact.
- The material can be portrayed as accepted truth, as in many textbooks and classroom lectures and in recitations of a party line.
- The author can take an all-or-nothing view of the subject or present the subject as an either–or option—usually with one choice portrayed as ideal or the other option portrayed as a potential disaster.
- The agenda can be reduced to such a level that only a yes-or-no, positive-or-negative result is obtained. This is the practice used in much scientific and

technical writing. It is, of course, inherent in scientific experimentation and well-designed statistical surveys. But it can also be used in more strictly expository or persuasive writing.

- The definition of "truth" may be based on an unquestioned axiom, principle, maxim, or premise or on a standard theory or accepted theoretical paradigm in the field. This provides a floor or framework for a seemingly irrefutable case: if the premises or principles are accepted and go unchallenged, then the author's conclusions usually seem inevitable and logical.

*11. Demonstrate the Significance of Your Subject.*   Although informational styles assume that the audience values the subject, there still may be some need to establish the significance of the author's point of view. In the most strictly informational introduction, this might be accomplished by listing benefits and advantages, costs and dangers, or directly illustrating the worth or utility of the idea.

### CONCLUSIONS IN THE INFORMATIONAL STYLE

The endings of essays appear more informational when they do the following:

*1. Omit or Truncate the Conclusion.*   Often there will be little or no conclusion to the essay or report. Once the promised material has been covered, the essay ends or offers only a rudimentary ending.

*2. Briefly Reiterate the Hypothesis and Proof.*   Informational conclusions are likely to confirm the proof or ensure that the message has been transmitted by restating it at the end of the essay. They summarize the hypothesis and the main points of the argument and perhaps explain that the intended proof has been accomplished.

This practice is more appropriate in extended and complex discourse than in short essays. When the essay is short, a summarizing conclusion is more offensive than useful. It suggests that the reader cannot remember what you have just said.

*3. Arrive at a Logical Conclusion.*   An author's conclusions about a subject have no necessary relationship to the conclusion of an essay. The word is being used in a very different sense. But in writing based on conveying information or proving a point, the two may coincide.

Scientific and technical writing commonly end a report with a "Conclusions" section or a section titled "Discussion." In either case, the closing of the essay becomes the place where the author focuses on what has been learned from the study, what he or she infers or concludes from the findings.

The same strategy, without the formal headings, may also be used in any essay based on discovery or induction.

## Creating Rhetorical Frames

Rhetorical frames are audience based. They assume that the subject is open to debate. They begin and end with some acknowledgment of the audience's existence, its point of view, its knowledge of the subject, and its attitudes and beliefs.

### INTRODUCTIONS IN THE RHETORICAL STYLE

Framing devices appear more rhetorical when they do the following:

*1. Make Some Transition From Silence to Speech.*   When striking up a conversation, people do not normally start right in. There is a period of polite adjustment, a gradual easing into speech. It may include irrelevancies, like talk about the occasion, family, work, noncontroversial events, or the weather. Or it may be more focused, more pertinent to the business at hand but still not aggressive in jumping right to the point.

In essay writing, the introduction often serves this purpose. It makes us more comfortable about "conversing" with the author, more ready to accept that he or she has broken the silence and made a demand on our attention. It may do so by starting (as in casual talk) with seemingly irrelevant or unfocused discussion, by referring to current events or familiar ideas that eventually will prove pertinent, and by telling a story, among other things.

Rhetorical introductions also ease the transition from the diffuse thinking of normal discussion to the concentrated thought of an extended essay.

*2. Acknowledge and Define the Audience.*   Rhetorical frames may directly address the audience or indirectly acknowledge its presence. There may be obvious reference to the authority and position of the audience, as when a lawyer defers to the jury or judge. Or an essay may establish a role for the audience when no clearcut role exists, perhaps casting the readers as critics (letting them join you in ridiculing something) or as neutral observers, responsible employees, injured parties, or informed coequals.

A rhetorical introduction may show respect for the audience, making concessions or qualifying the author's point of view. Or it may be forceful and adversarial, debating or defending a point of view with passion and intensity.

*3. Channel the Readers' Attention.*   Rhetorical introductions channel the audience's perception not so much by setting agendas, focusing the discussion, defining terms, or enumerating the points to be covered as by building or framing a perspective, by showing the audience the subject from a certain angle, in light of a particular set of values, or in terms of a particular field of study or a specific conceptual framework.

*4. Make Connections to Ongoing Discussion.*   Rhetorical introductions provide transitions between the author's point of view and the wider dialogue, discussion, or academic debate. They establish the relationship between the author's single voice and what might be termed the "meta-text," the collective and often disconnected conversation that encircles a subject.

This connection can be suggested in various ways, including

- formal reviews of research
- reference to accepted or competing views of a subject
- actual reported dialogue or incidents
- quoting a number of experts on the subject
- internal dialogue or speculation (the author mentally "talking through" several points of view)
- looking at the subject from various perspectives
- raising a series of questions

These devices create a sense of dialogue at the beginning of an essay. They make it seem like several people are talking at once, that the writer is acting as spokesperson for other opinions (the reader's point of view among them) before speaking his or her own mind.

*5. Supply Context.*   Rhetorical frames sometimes evoke or explain the immediate context of the essay or report, the rhetorical situation or circumstances that led to the essay or report being written.

*6. Set the Scene.*   At the beginning of an essay, it is often valuable to establish the background of or set the scene for discussion. This may involve identifying or describing places, people, and events. It may involve recounting the history behind a particular incident or issue or the action and discussion that immediately preceded it.

*7. Build Common Ground.*   Introductions often seek and define areas of agreement or common ground between the author and audience.

*8. Educate.*   Introductions may gracefully instruct the less-informed members of an audience, building a common level of understanding among a diverse group of readers, a common frame of reference or a common starting point in discussion of the issue.

*9. Introduce the Author.*    The introduction may directly or indirectly establish the character and perspective of the author, conveying his or her attitudes, emotions, personality or role, and frame of reference.

*10. Imply or Assert Authority.*    Introductions directly or, more often, indirectly establish the authority of the author. They suggest the author's credentials and his or her sources of information.

*11. Express Emotion or Show Involvement.*    The tone or style is more often emotional or "involved," with the author showing or evoking some degree of feeling. This may be quite subdued or impassioned, depending on the subject, occasion, and circumstances. Particularly when persuasion is intended, the introduction and conclusion may use speech and diction unlike conventional prose—more heightened or lowered, more intimate and revealing or abstract and philosophical, more poetic or more plain.

*12. Set a Tone for the Discussion.*    Part of the framework of an essay is the tone of the discussion. This might be established by setting the agenda or establishing the "attitude" of the dialogue, whether the approach to the subject is businesslike, bitterly critical, humorously critical, accepting and humane, objective and distant, and so on.

*13. Provide Various Forms of Access to Your Idea.*    Rhetorical frames may provide different avenues or "on-ramps" into the discussion. They try to offer various ways to approach the issue so readers with different perspectives, vocabularies, and interests will see how the ensuing essay addresses them.

Access may be improved by giving several different (and brief) examples, by paraphrasing your major point in several different ways, by beginning with quotes that represent a number of different sources and perspectives, and by indicating the relevance of the issue to different audiences, as well as by other means mentioned hereafter.

*14. Characterize Your Point of View.*    It is of course still important in a rhetorical introduction to tell the reader what you are going to be talking about. This is usually not accomplished through a formal thesis statement or logical proposition, however. The "theme" may be expressed more as a stance or point of view than a formal and direct assertion.

The author may characterize his or her position. Or the introduction may offer an initial focus or starting point for the ensuing discussion.

*15. Establish Significance.*    Like informational styles, rhetorical frames may establish the significance of the issue by showing benefits and costs.

They may also directly argue the importance of the author's claim or attempt to establish the relevance of the author's experience and ideas to that of the audience. Other important means of establishing significance are the following:

**The "Although Clause".** In *Teaching Students to Write* (1980), Beth Neman demonstrates that introductions frequently incorporate what she calls an "although clause." In this strategy, the author states one point of view and then takes exception to it in the process of expressing his or her own opinion or theory.

Essentially, any although clause says that "although it might appear that X is Y, in fact the truth is that X is Z." This effectively makes the author's point of view sound more original and important. It strongly suggests that the author's idea is better, newer, and more expert than the position he or she contradicts.

**Depicting a Crisis.** Introductions may portray an obvious or unseen crisis that makes it imperative to discuss the subject at hand.

**Creating a Need.** Introductions may envision circumstances so inviting that the audience feels compelled to read further.

*16. Create Interest.* Rhetorical frames work to create interest in the subject. Part of this may be accomplished through establishing significance and referring to context, but interest may also be generated by the attractiveness of the author's point of view, persona, and delivery, by establishing connections to the audience's interests and self-interests and by wit and imagination.

Interest is not just a matter of entertainment. It includes the ability to impress an audience with the quality of one's thinking, scholarship, or decision making.

*17. Render the Audience Receptive.* Rhetorical introductions not only accommodate the audience but also attempt to put it in a frame of mind that is favorable to your point of view.

You may do so in part through ethical appeal, through establishing your expertise or trustworthiness, for example, since we are more ready to accept the arguments of a person we respect. Implied or expressed self-depreciation, altruism, enthusiasm, strength, and maturity may be effective, as might various emotional appeals—creating sympathy, appealing to self-interest, appealing to beliefs, desires, or fears, appealing to community, and appealing to good nature (for instance, through humor).

### CONCLUSIONS IN THE RHETORICAL STYLE

The endings of essays appear more rhetorical when they use some of the following devices, many of which are discussed by Catherine A. Curtis in her dissertation, "A Study of Conclusions in Expository Prose: Professional Writers versus Textbook Conventions" (Columbus, OH: Ohio State U, 1985):

*1. Invite Dialogue.*    Rhetorical conclusions invite further discussion. They reestablish dialogue after extended discussion of your own point of view.

Reopening the floor to wider or additional debate may be accomplished through various means, including asking for or raising questions, inviting or offering criticism of what you have said, suggesting the need for additional discussion or research, and so on.

*2. Qualify or Increase Your Assertiveness.*    Rhetorical conclusions often raise or lower the level of assertiveness. If the bulk of the essay was forceful, the end may be more moderate in tone. If the essay has been cautious and methodical, the conclusion may look back on the evidence, the foundation so carefully laid, and arrive at an unqualified conclusion.

Qualification may include finishing with an exception to the rule, depreciating or undercutting your assertions, and admitting the limitations of your perspective or methodology. In addition to the normal methods of raising the level of assertiveness, increased force may be signaled in the conclusion by such means as direct claims of significance, showing the uses and applications of the concept, and assembling testimony that supports your point.

*3. Establish a Theoretical Context.*    If you have been talking largely on your own authority or from your own observations and experience, the conclusion may locate your comments in some wider intellectual context that explains or supports them.

This practice essentially places your perspective under the protection of an accepted theory, practice, viewpoint, or conceptual framework, showing that you are not radical or idiosyncratic, that you are not speaking on just your own authority, and that you are not attempting unilaterally to supplant other points of view. It suggests that you are just one of many people who would say the same thing.

*4. Reassess the Issue.*    A rhetorical conclusion is more likely to reinterpret the issue in light of the preceding discussion, offering not so much a new point of view as an extension or refinement of the essay's initial perspective. This is a very common and important device but one that must be used cautiously, since reinterpretations that diverge too far from the original viewpoint may be perceived as contradictions or digressions.

*5. Provide an Overview.*    Rhetorical framing may offer in the conclusion a panoramic look back at the ground that has been covered, characterizing it or describing its essence. This may be suggested in phrases like "Looking back, I see" or "The wide variation in test results appears now to be" or "What this all adds up to is" or "The gist of it was. . . ." The author may characterize his or her perspective or findings, as in "I have tried to be a sympathetic observer" or "The evidence is strong."

*6. Give a Formal Summation.*    Rhetorical conclusions usually do not summarize. Instead they may offer a compressed, heightened, and even emotional review of the situation, a formal summation. This may not, and for the most part does not, cover all the arguments presented. It picks and chooses, highlighting some points and ignoring others. The idea is to give the strongest possible overview of your position, to leave a lasting impression in the reader's mind.

The summation can serve other purposes, especially in spoken discourse. It may be the time to amplify a detail that did not get enough attention in the rest of a speech, trial, curriculum, or essay. It may be a chance to revise and clarify an earlier comment or to change the whole tenor of the discussion. In legal debate, the summation may be one's only opportunity to attack last-minute arguments and to expose weaknesses in the opposition's case, which during the summation is seen in entirety for the first time.

Summation is, like summary, more appropriate for extended and complex discourse than for short essays. But a heightened review of one or two arguments might be useful even in a short work.

*7. Allude to the Body of the Essay.*    More common than summation in essays is the practice of alluding in the conclusion to one's previous comments. A few references to the preceding discussion or a gathering together of key words from the body of the essay can be more than sufficient to call the discussion to mind and serves to draw the whole essay together. The conclusion may also continue and collect motifs or themes from the rest of the essay.

When unobtrusively incorporated into the rest of the conclusion, such devices achieve the purposes of summary without a tedious effect, and they still leave space for other concluding remarks.

*8. Change Perspective or Stance.*    Rhetorical conclusions often include a perspective or form of development that is significantly different from that in the rest of the essay. This may be a shift

- *to a different rhetorical mode*—for example, a switch from extended classification and exemplification to causal analysis, or a switch from narrative and process analysis to description or definition
- *in the author's relationship to the audience*—for example, changing from offering information to giving advice
- *in attitude or tone*—for example, changing from objectivity to self-consciousness, from humor to serious discussion, or from acceptance to questioning
- *in the source or kind of development*—for example, changing from a reliance on empirical data to interpretation, from report to review, or from personal experience to research or testimony
- *in perspective*—for example, from political to psychological dimensions of the subject, from general to personal views, from scientific description to a discussion of practical effects, or from a personal to a historical perspective

*9. Make an Impassioned Statement or Appeal.*  When the essay has been concerned with exhortation and persuasion, its conclusion may include a request for action, an appeal for justice, or a call for change. It may attempt to incite the audience to act. This may occur apart from any attempt at summation.

In other forms of discourse, the heightened and emotional tone may be less obvious, though still present. Expressive essays may end with a moment of quiet exhilaration or despair. Intellectual writing may conclude in an indirect appeal for support and consensus.

*10. Leave the Audience in a Favorable State of Mind.*  Rhetorical conclusions may attempt to put the audience in a favorable state of mind, but not always a pleasant one.

This may involve appeals to emotion; evocation of attitudes or beliefs; outright and indirect threats or intimidation; appeals to good nature, morality, or justice; attempts to make the author or his or her point of view appear attractive; appeals to self-interest; criticism of or aspersions cast on competing views and authors; and claims of disinterest and objectivity. It can be as useful to make an audience feel disturbed, upset, and angry with you as to make it feel pleased and complacent.

*11. Return to Your Starting Point.*  Especially in literary essays and when a note of reflection or wit is desired, it can be effective to circle back in the conclusion, to return to the place, point, question, or part of the story you began with.

*12. Show Courtesy.*  The conclusion may delicately or indirectly apologize for having taken so much of the audience's time, or in some other way thank or reward the readers for their attention and interest.

# EXERCISE A

Write two different introductions for an essay on one of the following topics. The first should emphasize information and proof. The second should emphasize addressing an audience. Compare the results, and discuss the advantages and disadvantages of each.

You may write on either side of the stated issue and rephrase the topic to suit the form of introduction.

1. Military spending should be [increased, decreased, maintained at its present level].
2. Prime farmland is disappearing at an alarming rate. [to city dwellers]
3. Everyone should learn how to cook.
4. A surprising amount of the news is really disguised advertising. Public relations people make sure their clients' products, causes, organizations, and accomplishments get air time.
5. Some [children, adults, people] are too serious for their own good.
6. There is no true wilderness left.
7. Someday whole libraries will consist of nothing more than computer files.
8. The better part of valor is discretion.
9. Good breeding consists of concealing how much we think of ourselves and how little we think of the other person.
10. Tapwater is more pure than people think.

# EXERCISE B

Three short essays are outlined. Choose one of them and write two alternative conclusions for it. The first conclusion should emphasize conveying information or completing a proof. The second should emphasize addressing an audience.

Compare the results, and discuss the advantages and disadvantages of each.

1. I remember having sidewalks wherever I went.
   They don't make sidewalks anymore.
   New housing developments omit them.
   People walk on the grass or on the street.
   Children tricycle and skateboard on the street.
   You need a smooth surface for some things.
   But sidewalks are a luxury.
   Conclusion

**2.** Some people rank schools according to the skill of their athletic teams.
Being well known is valuable.
A familiar school name can draw students.
A familiar product's brand name can be worth a fortune.
A familiar face and family name can win votes.
Conclusion

**3.** Heavy machinery gives us tremendous power.
We can literally change the face of the earth.
We can make artificial mountains and valleys.
Not all change, however, is progress.
Not all progress is change.
Conclusion

## *Framing Devices and the Composing Process*

Introductions and conclusions are notoriously hard to write. Introductions, especially, can be frustrating. They require an author to introduce something that has not been written yet, that he or she may not yet understand. How can you acquaint the reader with what is coming when you do not know what you are going to say?

Conclusions are difficult because at that point both author and reader are often mentally exhausted. It seems to a writer that the case must surely be clear by then. It may be hard to imagine what else could be said about the subject. One may be so deeply engaged in and committed to the perspective of the essay that it is nearly impossible to draw back and offer a wider viewpoint or to reintroduce an element of dialogue.

When writing introductions and conclusions, do the following:

*1. Avoid Trying to Say Everything at Once.* Sometimes introductions fail when we try to cover everything at once, forgetting that language is linear. Topics have to be strung together, one after another. Thoughts are more three dimensional and simultaneous. To fit them into writing, it may be necessary to be patient, to save some ideas for later in the essay.

*2. Don't Confuse Writing Introductions With Starting to Write.* Sometimes we are defeated by the sheer number of decisions that have to be made while "starting up"—decisions about how to approach the topic, where to start, what to say, what stance to take, and so on. Since these choices are often being made at the same time you begin to write an essay, they are easily confused with the process of writing an introduction.

This is a problem if you settle for an introduction that was written before all the various questions have been resolved or if you show too much of the decision-making process in the writing itself. But you can use it to your advantage. For example, you might do the following:

**Write Multiple Introductions.**   Some people routinely write introduction after introduction as a means of coming to terms with the rhetorical situation. You can review each attempt and consider how well or ill it matches your impression of the subject, the audience, and your own position or role.

**Begin With Speculation.**   Writing in a more inductive manner can help you bypass the difficulties of starting an essay. Raising a series of questions or intentionally exploring various approaches to the subject can, for example, serve as reasonably effective introductions as long as you eventually arrive at and express some clearcut point of view. Speculation that leads nowhere is irritating.

**Use a Working Introduction.**   People commonly use working introductions as a means of writing their way into a subject. They use a tentative "frame" and continue on to draft the rest of the essay. Then they go back to the beginning, drop the working introduction, and write a beginning that more nearly matches what they have said.

**Write the Introduction Last.**   A similar strategy is to write the first draft of the essay without any formal opening, and then, when you know essentially what you are going to say, write the introduction.

**Use the Conclusion as the Introduction.**   It is quite common to find that the end of your first draft provides a good starting point for the next one. This happens because in the process of writing the draft you discover what you believe and who you are with respect to the subject. By the time you finish, you arrive at a logical and emotional resolution of the issue, a state of mind more appropriate for an effective introduction.

*3. Don't Confuse Finishing a Draft With Writing the Conclusion.* Writers often complete a draft of an essay and feel like they are done. The sense of satisfaction that comes from completing the task is mistaken for creating closure in the subject and evoking a sense of closure in the audience. Instead, you need to do the following:

**Resolve the Discussion.**   Effective conclusions may make us feel that the subject has been closed, that there is nothing more to be said, at least for now. This does not mean answering every question that might be raised or covering the entire subject. It means wrapping things up, synthesizing the various arguments that have been presented, and reintegrating our knowledge of the subject.

Readers feel a sense of intellectual resolution when they are confident that the given answers conform to the facts, that the subject has been adequately explained, that the problem has been resolved, and that the point of view you represent either fits into their understanding of the subject or convincingly replaces it.

**Open the Discussion.** It may also be effective as a conclusion to open the discussion, to set the audience thinking and talking, to raise questions, or to leave the issue unresolved. To do this, however, you must have first demonstrated in the essay that the issue is not closed, that further exploration and ongoing debate is necessary.

Opening discussion is much like what a teacher does when trying to get people to talk in class. It may require challenging beliefs, attacking preconceptions, and creating cognitive dissonance. It may require that you find a level of discussion at which there is still controversy (that is, a matter open to interpretation and dispute).

**Provide Emotional Closure.** Effective endings may create a sense of emotional closure, positive or negative. Positive closure is the feeling that things are under control, that everything is as it should be, that justice will be done, that our hopes and expectations have been realized. Negative closure suggests that our worst fears will come true.

**Create Social Closure.** We also feel a sense of closure when it seems that either social harmony or consensus has been reestablished. Stories, essays, meetings, and negotiations alike may come to an end when some agreement or understanding is reached, when the group (or the community portrayed in a story or essay) has been reintegrated, or when people feel they have been brought closer together, whether by tragedy, hard labor, or a common enemy or by a common goal, aspiration, and dream.

*4. Avoid Routine Endings.* The attraction of conventional endings can be great. There is a standard moral to every story, a standard answer for every question, and a standard sentiment for every occasion. These may be useful when you are forced to think on your feet, but they seldom are effective conclusions for polished writing.

*5. Avoid Disconnected Framing Devices.* A frequent problem in writing both introductions and conclusions is having no clear relationship between the body of the essay and its framing devices. Stories, reviews of research, or extended reports are sandwiched between seemingly irrelevant beginnings and endings, ones that discuss a concept not directly addressed in the internal development.

This is both a coherence problem and a misunderstanding of the relationship between generalizations and support. The writer believes that the audience sees or will make the connections between the conceptual framework and the evidence or incidents presented. But these connections cannot be assumed. They are part of the necessary content and meaning of an essay. One cannot simply list the evidence after stating the idea. One must explain how the evidence supports and clarifies the concept.

*6. Create Proportion Between Framing Devices and the Text.*   Teachers and textbooks often give the impression that the introduction and conclusion are each a paragraph long, and only a paragraph long. This advice is based on the usual brevity of student assignments rather than the nature of framing devices. In a two- or three-page essay, introductions and conclusions longer than a paragraph might often be inappropriate or out of proportion.

However, in most discourse, accomplishing the necessary objectives of introducing and concluding a discussion may take much longer. The length can vary dramatically, depending on your purpose and situation. You could have a conclusion that takes up a third of the essay, if the circumstances warrant it (for example, when the conclusion involves a discussion of your findings). But an introduction of this length would usually seem too slow in arriving at the central issue. Readers still expect that the body or development will take up the major portion of an essay.

## WHEN TO USE INFORMATIONAL FRAMES

Informational frames are appropriate

- when focusing exclusively on the subject
- when the support is largely empirical
- when efficiency is important
- when accuracy is important
- when teaching or giving instructions
- in formal demonstration and proof

## WHEN TO USE RHETORICAL FRAMES

Rhetorical and dialogic frames are useful or appropriate

- in negotiation
- in counseling

- when being courteous or discourteous
- in persuasion
- in expressive discourse
- when the author is compromised by self-interest

## GAINS AND LOSSES

### ◀ INFORMATIONAL FRAMES ▶

| Advantages | Disadvantages |
|---|---|
| Conceal self-interest | Limit persuasive appeal |
| Make issues seem more factual | More inaccessible |
| Ritualize and depersonalize the discussion | Limit stylistic choices |
| Limit agenda of debate | May be too topical or arcane |
| Anticipate no response | May not anticipate refutation |
| Imply expertise | Require real scholarship or understanding |

## GAINS AND LOSSES

### ◀ RHETORICAL FRAMES ▶

| Advantages | Disadvantages |
|---|---|
| Can use emotional and ethical appeal | May invite argument |
| More occasion to educate the audience | More occasion to offend |
| Provide social dimension and context | Tie outcome to social influences |
| Allow inclusion of diverse material | Audience may become impatient |
| Better chances of comprehension | Less mystery and authority |
| More purposeful | Suggest self-interest |

## *Wider Implications*

Framing is not limited to essays. It is part of the structure of meetings, ceremonies, spectacles, and social events, as well as of discourse. It may be part of the structure of organizations, journals, and forums for speech.

People who organize events may consciously arrange the activities to provide an inviting opening and satisfying sense of closure. Ceremonies may open with a prayer or invocation and close with a benediction. Framing accounts for opening acts at concerts, opening monologues on talk shows, and for the fireworks show that closes the amusement park at night. Coffee and doughnuts before a meeting are part of the exordium. Bowl games are the peroration of the football season.

Architecture, travel, and scenery may be arranged to provide similar effects. A place of business may separate the reception area and payment counter. There may be a side exit for speakers and administrators to leave the meetingplace. Formal landscaping may begin with an enticing prospect and close with an archway, bridge, or panoramic view of the whole garden. A golf course may purposely begin with an elevated tee overlooking the course and end with an inviting view of the clubhouse. Rollercoasters start with an ominious climb and end with a jolting series of fast turns.

## THE ARTIFICIALITY OF FRAMING DEVICES

Knowing where to start and stop is more difficult than it might seem at first glance. Every incident leads to another. Every topic is intertwined in our thoughts with other topics and ideas.

If the immediate subject is an auto accident, the essay could start at the moment of impact, after the crash, in the hospital, or at the moment the drivers perceived the danger. The essay or story could start at the moment the drivers started their cars for that trip, or with incidents that led up to the accident, whether an hour before or years previous to the event. The essay could start years later, focusing on the aftermath and emotional damage. It could start with another accident you had witnessed, with the first recorded automobile crash in history, with an experience in a driver's training course, or with a stunt-car crash in a movie.

The essay could also stop at any of these moments. It could stop at the second of impact; at the end, years later, of a lawsuit based on the accident, with the ultimate effect that the damages awarded had on the parties to the lawsuit; or with a lawyer citing the case, a generation later, as a legal precedent. It could start with the first time you bought a car.

The intellectual starting point and conclusion are no more obvious than the chronological beginning and ending of the narrative. The essay could start or end with a discussion of driver education, with a description of the cars involved or the engineering they represent, with comments on human frailty or the inevitability of mishaps, with an acknowledgment that increased mechanization brings increased dangers, or with a description of the author's emotional response to the event. It could begin or conclude with the serious issues involved or could focus on ironies and morbid humor.

There is no fixed starting or stopping point in chronology or thought. Where you begin depends on what you want to accomplish, what you value, and what you believe.

## *Conclusion*

Ultimately essays are both ideological and social. They express ideas, which must be connected to a wider intellectual context. And they address people, who must be drawn into the essay and prepared for what they will read. Introductions serve both functions.

The same is true of conclusions. They provide at the same time logical closure and emotional resolution.

### ASSIGNMENT: Introductions and Leave-Takings

1. Introduce people to a subject or place with which they seem largely unfamiliar.

2. Write a passage introducing people to a person they do not know or know relatively little about.

3. Write an imaginary farewell of sorts: a graduation address, a retirement speech, a farewell to someone leaving public life or to a public figure recently deceased, a closing address for a conference or meeting, a ceremonial leave-taking (as in a benediction). This need not force you to pose as someone you are not. You might want, for instance, to write as yourself and speculate about what you would say in such circumstances. Or you might write as yourself and present what you think ought to be said on such occasions. Do not feel you have to limit yourself to just the narrow occasion or specific business of taking leave. This may be an opportunity to address a wide variety of related topics.

4. Try to wrap up and close discussion of a complex issue, tying together loose ends, cutting through complexities, characterizing what others have said, and/or suggesting some mutually acceptable solution to a problem.

# 14

# Development: Amplification and Compression

Brevity is the soul of wit.

—William Shakespeare

Let anyone speak long enough, he will get believers.

—Robert Louis Stevenson

## *How Long to Hold Forth*

We like people to get to the point, to say things in as few words as possible. It seems more honest and direct. People who fill up every second of the conversation often seem garrulous and self-centered. At the same time, we are offended by bluntness and impatient with those who refuse to explain themselves. We deplore carelessness and oversimplification, but we prefer to spend as little time as possible on comprehension.

If it is well written, a concise style avoids the impression of rudeness and has considerable impact. It may be aphoristic and assertive, achieving almost the force of law. Ideally, conciseness should reflect not simple opinion or unstudied arrogance, but true understanding of the subject. Even at its best, however, writing that is brief and compressed may be perceived as good or bad.

261

### ◆ COMPRESSED WRITING ◆

| Good Qualities | Bad Qualities |
| --- | --- |
| straightforward | abrupt |
| conclusive | unsupported |
| vivid | oversimplified |
| reserved | ignorant |

An expansive style should arise from a genuine desire to be thorough and clear, from respect for the complexity of the issues rather than from a need to be seen and heard. Yet even at its best, writing that is amplified and thorough may appear good or bad.

### ◆ AMPLIFIED WRITING ◆

| Good Qualities | Bad Qualities |
| --- | --- |
| comprehensive | neurotic, verbose |
| well researched | derivative |
| complex | unfocused |
| weighty | contrived |

To speak at length may imply that you have a low regard for your audience's intelligence or powers of comprehension. But it may also reflect intellectual courage, a willingness to speak your mind and risk censure, and a gracious effort to please, to avoid uncomfortable gaps in the discussion.

## Audience and Explanation

Development encompasses evidence and logic. But the development of an essay is distinct from the amount of support or argument it contains. A long essay can provide little or no evidence. A short one may provide all the evidence that is necessary or appropriate for the situation.

There can be much in an essay besides support. For example, an essay may include a great deal of concealed repetition and restatement, meant to clarify or emphasize the author's message. It may include analysis, illustration, description, interpretation, and criticism.

Part of an essay's content may be social rather than substantive, designed to heighten relevance and immediacy, to establish the role and character of the author and audience, to identify the source or nature of the information presented, to describe the situation or setting, to establish the context of the discussion, and to fill in background information.

The intent of development is to explain the subject adequately and effectively, to be informative without seeming to condescend, to teach without pedantry. If this can be done in few words, it may be as much a compliment to the audience's powers of understanding as the result of any great skill in the author.

## The Nature and Uses of Emphasis

Compression and amplification alike depend for effect on the skills of emphasis and deemphasis, also known as magnification and diminution or intensifying and downplaying. Emphasis is the ability to draw attention to something, deemphasis the ability to divert or minimize attention. Through these skills, one highlights or backgrounds information, making sure that the relative importance of various points is obvious and their relationships to each other are distinct.

Emphasis is used to

- establish the importance or significance of main ideas
- show the relative importance of different material
- maintain coherence in the essay
- create impact or memorability
- create the impression of a spoken presentation

It is related both to assertiveness and focus. Proper emphasis makes reading easier and leaves less room for misunderstanding.

## Means of Creating Emphasis

Some of the primary means of creating emphasis are discussed next.

### VISUAL AND ORTHOGRAPHIC DEVICES

The simplest forms of positive emphasis are visual or orthographic. Adding a picture or graph can call attention to a particular concept or perspective. Making a clear break in the text—a paragraph division or a section partition—can place the ensuing thought at the forefront of the reader's mind. Adding titles, subtitles, and underlining at crucial points, or using different typefaces, capitalization, and enlarged print, can make a stronger visual impression.

### PLACEMENT OF MATERIAL

It is common advice, for the same reason, to put your most important arguments or data at the beginning or end of sentences, paragraphs, sections, or the overall development of an essay. Material buried in the middle of a longer passage can easily be overlooked.

### REPETITION FOR EMPHASIS

Emphasis can be achieved by judicious repetition, by intentional reiteration of key words or phrases. Commercial advertising commonly makes use of this device, repeating brand names, business addresses, and catch phrases as many times as possible until they stick in the audience's memory, like it or not. The same method can be used in explication and argument to highlight opinions we especially value or evidence that is especially telling.

### RESTATEMENT FOR EMPHASIS

The effect of emphasis that arises from paraphrase or restatement is slightly different. Expressing the same thought over again in several different ways, varying the words and sentence structure, the style and manner, may settle or fix the meaning better in the reader's mind. Straight repetition can result in memorization without comprehension or persuasion; self-paraphrase aims more for understanding and appreciation.

### EMPHASIS THROUGH VOLUME, PACE, GESTURE, AND STANCE

In oral discourse, emphasis can be heightened by increasing or decreasing the volume or pace of speech and by any number of devices related to posture, attitude, and gesture, as well as tone. Some of the same effects can be achieved in written discourse by varying syntax and diction and by establishing a persona for the author that evokes an image or impression of voice and stance.

### ASSERTIVENESS AND EMPHASIS

Obviously, increased or decreased assertiveness, qualification, or force in making one's claims will have the same effect. The stronger and less qualified the assertion, the "louder" it seems. When writers state some ideas with more force than others, we tend to assume that the unqualified comments are somehow more important than those expressed more quietly. This may not always be the case. Authors may be cautious in discussing ideas they feel are important or original, while at the same time making strong assertions about common knowledge. Readers proceeding on the assumption that strong statements are important statements may get the wrong impression from such writing.

### SELECTION AND FOCUS AS A MEANS OF CREATING EMPHASIS

Emphasis can be created by selection or focus, as well. Leaving a particular detail, point, concept, or opinion out of an essay is a fairly effective, if sometimes unscrupulous, means of suppressing it, decreasing the attention it receives. Including a particular detail or argument gives it prominence over other details and arguments omitted. Selecting certain features or aspects of a subject can emphasize a particular dimension or view of it, downplaying or deemphasizing others—in much the same way that a caricature artist may exaggerate one feature of a person's face or one interpretation of a person's character and minimize another.

### CLAIMING ATTENTION FOR THE SUBJECT

Characterizing an idea is a direct and explicit means of providing emphasis. Any time a point is called "crucial" or "minor," the audience is likely to accept without much question the valuation that has been placed on it. Similarly, to characterize an assertion as "my personal opinion" not only lessens the force of the claim but also tends to reduce the emphasis on it.

Transitional comments that label forthcoming material as examples, evidence, or background data and support serve to deemphasize it, to subordinate it to the preceding claim or thesis it defends.

## *Amplifying and Explaining*

Amplification is the art of elaborating on and explicating ideas. It instructs by paraphrasing and illustrating, by restating a concept in familiar terms or in the context of familiar examples. It explains the significance of ideas and explores their nuances and implications.

This section discusses and illustrates various ways to make an essay longer without seeming to be repetitive or tedious.

*1. Restate Ideas Gracefully.* Repetition and self-paraphrase appear frequently in amplified writing. There may be restatement within sentences, in the form of appositives, or extended restatement in several consecutive sentences. When author is striving to clarify his or her point, to define an idea as clearly as possible, whole paragraphs may be composed of little more than extended reiteration of a central message.

Restatements may vary the words, the meaning, and the syntax of the basic idea, as follows:

## VARIATIONS IN DICTION AND MEANING

### Direct paraphrase

Children should be seen and not heard.
When visible, they should be silent.

### Explanatory paraphrase (digressive or "slant" paraphrase, elaboration)

Children should be seen and not heard.
They should be taught to listen.

### Qualified paraphrase

Children should be seen and not heard.
They should be encouraged to play and to express themselves, but not at the expense of our sanity and hearing.

### Characterization

Children should be seen and not heard.
Squelching expression is a hallmark of the traditional parenting style.

### Negation

Children should be seen and not heard.
They should not be noisy or obnoxious. One should not have to hide them.

### Restatement in terms of a particular case

Children should be seen and not heard.
My nephew thinks adults should listen to him.

### Restatement in terms of a general case

Children should be seen and not heard.
The neophyte should listen and learn.

### Restatement from another perspective

Children should be seen and not heard.
When youth control the forum, they control the agenda. It is a question of power.

### Intensification

Children should be seen and not heard.
No self-expression of any sort should be permitted.

### Ironic paraphrase

Children should be seen and not heard.
Gag them I say. Then send them to a writing class.

### Antithetical paraphrase

Children should be seen and not heard.
But youth must be served.

## VARIATIONS IN SYNTAX

### Parallel paraphrase (paraphrasing the entire topical sequence)

Children should be seen and not heard.
They should be visible but silent.

### Divided paraphrase (paraphrasing one topic at a time)

Children should be seen and not heard.
They should be conspicuous in our lives and hearts. But children should be inconspicuous in our social gatherings and conversations.

### Inverted paraphrase (paraphrasing topics in inverse order)

Children should be seen and not heard.
They should know when to be quiet. A well-mannered child is a joy to behold.

### Accumulated paraphrase (paraphrasing repeatedly)

Children should be seen and not heard.
They can be placated but not pandered to, admired but not worshipped, given affection but not absolute rule. There is a fine line between loving and catering to a child.

## *EXTENDED AMPLIFICATION*

Assembled into a paragraph or short essay, an extended amplification might sound like this:

> Children should be seen and not heard.
> Rather than speaking in company,
> they should be silent.
> Rather than controlling the conversation,
> becoming the center of attention,
> forcing everyone to admire them,
> however obnoxious their behavior,
> they should be peripheral.
> They should listen to their parents, at least occasionally,
> and not always expect to be listened to themselves.
> Not everything a child says is worth hearing,
> however cute it might be.
> Children are, after all, unsophisticated and greedy about attention.
> If they find a ready and appreciative audience, they will monopolize its time.
> If the audience resists, they raise the volume.

*A Word of Caution:* Taken to an extreme, of course, this kind of elaborateness in restatement becomes an obvious and annoying affectation. But within limits it is extremely useful for explaining and developing ideas.

2. *Be Thorough and Precise.*   An amplified style puts more emphasis on accuracy, completeness, and understanding, on making sure that the audience not only hears but comprehends the message—in all its complexity and detail.

In scientific and philosophical writing, this interest in accuracy appears in the form of extremely precise description and definition, greater attention to individual characteristics and specifics, more of an effort to describe or represent the subject carefully and completely.

In educational writing and popularizations, the same focus on accuracy is transformed into explanation and illustration, into careful explication of one's meaning.

3. *Emphasize Connections, Transitions, and Relationships.*   When authors are amplifying or explaining a subject, they often spend more time discussing the connections between their point of view and others, between the point being made and related concepts drawn from research or from invention and observation. There is a tendency in explanatory discourse to include in the development as many associations and interrelationships of

ideas and as many perspectives on the subject as possible, as many ways of seeing it or as many complexities within a single interpretation as can be discovered.

*4. Use Complex and Extended Sentences.* An amplified style will typically have longer sentences, with multiple embedded clauses and more frequent use of modifying phrases, adjectives, and adverbs. These all serve to make the description more accurate, more specific, and more thorough. Complex sentence structure helps express and embody the connections between ideas.

*5. Subdivide or Analyze Concepts.* A style appears more full or amplified when the author divides and redivides the topic, developing each part of the primary issue at length. If the topic were "acting," an elaborated style might divide the issue as follows:

ACTING
  *as an art*
    based on talent
    based on learning
    based on inspiration
  *as a craft*
    based on family traditions
    based on culture
    based on theater traditions
  *as a science*
    based on theory
    based on practice
    based on demands of the medium

One of the side benefits of such division is a degree of inherent structure. Even if the essay is not physically organized according to the divisions, the basic form of the material may show through.

Dividing the material also emphasizes the separate subtopics or distinctions. The effect is to combine the virtues of compression and expansion, breaking up the longer text into more manageable and concise pieces.

*6. Make Fine Distinctions.* An amplified style tends to make fine distinctions between related concepts and to regard these as important. If the topic were "celebrity," for instance, an amplified style might explore the difference between

    deserved and undeserved celebrity
    celebrity and fame

celebrity and notoriety
celebrity and respect
celebrity and self-promotion
celebrities and public servants
celebrity and dignity

An amplified essay might be based on just one of these distinctions, discussed at length, or on many such comparisons.

*7. Qualify Assertions and Include Other Points of View.*    Amplification also tends to be more diffuse, to offer many points of view on the subject. There may be careful modification, qualification, and hedging of one's claims. Expansion softens or moderates one's opinions. As we explore a subject at length, we begin to see how little we know about it and to recognize the validity of other perspectives.

The emphatic or broad generalizations of compression are made possible by taking a more panoramic stance and by ignoring contradictory data or abstracting evidence from the mass of conflicting details available. An amplified style may incorporate more of these contradictions into the writing and therefore may often be forced to qualify or limit its generalizations.

But amplification is not necessarily unemphatic. The extensive repetition, division of the subject, and self-paraphrase that characterize explaining and amplifying can make the presentation all the more dramatic and immediate.

## EXERCISE A

Use various strategies of amplification to explain and elaborate on the following concise maxims and quotations.

**1.** A fool and his [her] money are soon parted.

**2.** Don't count your chickens before they're hatched.

**3.** A stitch in time saves nine.

**4.** The eggs do not teach the hen.    —Russian proverb

**5.** Handsome is as handsome does.

**6.** Man [woman] cannot live without self-control.    —Isaac Bashevis Singer

**7.** Solitude sometimes is best society.    —John Milton

**8.** Great men [women] are not always wise.    —Job 32:9

**9.** If a house be divided against itself, that house cannot stand.
—Mark 3:25

**10.** Thou seest the mountains and thou deemest them affixed; they are as fleeting as the clouds.    —The *Koran* 27:88

## *How to Be Concise*

Compression depends on the author's ability to sum up or abstract from experience and observation. At its worst, it is the result of inexperience, arrogance, ignorance, reductiveness, and a lack of insight. When you know little, or when the subject seems plain and simple, compression comes naturally. At its best, compression represents an ability to control and make sense of complex material.

To make an essay shorter without sacrificing effect, do the following:

*1. Make the Presentation More Dense.*   Compressed styles have little patience with the audience or with opposing points of view. They force the audience to do more of the work in communication. They are more dense and less varied. Ideas may be strung together one on top of the other, with little effort to entertain or please, little interest in softening the blow or easing the transmission of information. Efficiency is sometimes more important than effectiveness.

*2. Omit Tangential Information.*   Compression can be achieved by leaving out background, precedents, and associations. Any tangential information must be considered irrelevant. Any material not directly useful or pertinent to the immediate goal of the essay must be omitted.

*3. Generalize.*   A compressed style may avoid discussing particular cases, focusing on generalities instead of nuances and shades of meaning. If you regard the difference between things as important, then the development is almost necessarily extended and amplified. Conciseness privileges the sameness of things.

*4. Avoid Giving Details and Providing Support.*   There are likely to be few details given in a compressed style. Support is often limited to one or two arguments or principles regarded almost as religious precepts (e.g., freedom, common sense, fair play, fair pay, etc.). This device of standing on principle is common in propaganda, public opinion campaigns, tough negotiating stances, and dogmatic reasoning.

*5. Be Highly Assertive.*   Increasing the assertiveness with which claims are expressed can compensate for a lack of development. Compressed styles tend to be more forceful in expression. Hypotheses and opinions may be stated in the most extreme, oversimplified, or unqualified terms.

Qualification implies that there are nuances, exceptions to the rule, or shades of opinion. None of these can readily be explored in a concise fashion. So the preferred mode is strong generalization, even to the point of exaggerating the validity of one's claims, of not admitting the possibility of other interpretations, judgments, or viewpoints.

This is, in a way, a posture designed to defend against the weaknesses of compression. It fends off criticism and retort by implying that none is possible. It compensates for a lack of evidence by an increase in arrogance or assurance. We tend to assume that anyone who would state something so forcibly must have sufficient evidence to confirm the view, even when it is not forthcoming.

*6. Stand on Your Own Authority and Opinion.*   Compression may be increased by invoking your status, authority, stance, or reputation. Insisting that the audience take your word for it allows you to avoid offering explanation and support.

The style of compression puts more of a premium on personal opinion and perception. It tends to rely on and imply the superior authority of the common man or woman, exalting the individual point of view over collective and expert opinion.

*7. Cite Authorities as Testimony.*   While the compressed style puts a premium on personal authority, it is subject to attacks based on personal authority—your opinion against mine. To overcome this, authors may cite one or two authorities, mentioning them as if their opinions or research were nearly irrefutable evidence—as in "Millen and Hobbs reported some time ago the danger of. . . ."

Testimony or citations of research can replace evidence, extended discussion of the issues, and description of the subject.

*8. Claim Consensus.*   The author may also rely on a claimed consensus or collective authority, as in a statement like "Current research supports the view that intellectual maturation continues far beyond the age of nineteen or twenty." The cited opinions are meant to sweep away the arguments of anyone speaking from personal opinion alone, anyone who cannot offer equal and opposite testimony or who cannot find some way to criticize or attack the testimony being used.

*9. State Your Ideas as Maxims and Principles.*   The greatest conciseness is embodied in single-sentence aphorisms and principles. If they are well written, these seem almost true by nature. They sound like common knowledge, axioms, or universal laws. They make amplification and proof less necessary, because truisms do not normally require explanation. Even highly original or strange perceptions, when phrased in this manner, may seem incontrovertible and obvious, things everyone believes already.

*10. Rely on Common Knowledge and Context.*   Common knowledge or a shared context can provide additional development not included in the text. If you leave out or refer to information familiar to your audience, like current events or the present situation, the writing need not be as long. Conversation routinely does this, since people often talk about shared experiences or things that are immediately visible. For the same reason, business memos tend to be concise and sketchy.

*11. Use Allusions and Imagery.* Imagery or allusions can actually evoke development not actually included in the writing. In the compressed style, this can compensate for a lack of evidence and explanation. Topical references and highly graphic metaphors and similes can take the place of further development, creating as they do a picture or image of an event in the reader's mind that helps support or illustrate the assertion being made.

For the same reason, compressed styles are often combined with the use of pictures, graphs, visual demonstrations, diagrams, and charts. These graphic devices supplement or substitute for evidence and explanation in the essay itself.

*12. Use Simple, Direct Sentences.* The simplification of the subject is often reflected in short sentences and straightforward, uncomplicated syntax. There are likely to be fewer instances of subordination (the embedding of one clause or sentence inside another) and fewer phrases per sentence. Subordinations and phrases are used to express the interrelationships and connections of ideas and of things: such complexity of thought is not common in the concise style.

*13. Suggest Depth With Paradoxes and Ironies.* If the author seeks, nevertheless, to create an impression of complexity, he or she may do so in the compressed style by stating the message as a paradox, dilemma, irony, or contradiction in terms. This note of contradiction or irony implies a level of distance or intellectual maturity from the subject, since the ability to recognize any dilemma or doublebind suggests that the author is master of both sides of the argument, in control of two perspectives rather than limited to his or her own.

*14. Assume That the Audience Agrees With You.* The compressed style frequently aims at an audience of like-thinking people. It preaches to the converted, assumes that readers already share the author's viewpoint—or should—and will welcome hearing it. Sometimes authors use the compressed style when addressing people who reportedly disagree with them; this may indicate that they are actually basing their style more on the so-called home audience, that they are writing to be overheard by their friends and compatriots rather than to persuade anyone.

*15. Take a Panoramic Perspective.* Concise styles often give an overview of the subject, take a panoramic or sweeping point of view. This perspective enables the author to sum up long stretches of time and large amounts of diverse information.

The same device may be used to improve the effect of highly amplified writing. You can make the meaning clearer by including graphic, concise overviews or brief, compressed characterizations of your ideas and support at intervals throughout an extended essay.

*16. Repeat Key Words and Phrases.* In brief or concise writing, there is a tendency to express the concept in memorable terms, using heightened diction, poetic devices, key words, catch phrases, and slogans.

Even in amplified writing, compression may be suggested by the use of such motifs and formulaic phrases. Repeating key words and catch phrases can emphasize the main points in expanded discourse, making thoroughness and complexity more readily intelligible.

## EXERCISE B

Take an article or book chapter that you find interesting but relatively complex (it should be at least ten pages long) and try to sum it up in one or two paragraphs. Do not quote. Paraphrase the ideas.

Then compare your summary, or abstract, with the original. Is the summary accurate? Does it completely represent the author's ideas? What did you leave out? What does the original essay gain from being longer?

### WHEN TO AMPLIFY OR EXPLAIN

An amplified style is particularly useful

- when the audience is largely uninformed about the subject
- when the audience sees the subject from a different perspective
- when the audience is diverse
- when speaking rather than writing
- when the subject is complex
- when you are seen as inexperienced or lacking in authority
- when you wish to emphasize or inculcate a point

### WHEN TO BE BRIEF

Compression is useful

- when time is short
- in summations, reviews, and overviews

- in casual conversation
- when popularizing a subject
- when the subject is common knowledge
- when you wish to be memorable or dramatic

---

## GAINS AND LOSSES

---

### ◀ AMPLIFICATION ▶

| Advantages | Disadvantages |
|---|---|
| More expansive and generous in discussing the subject | Explanatory posture is more passive or ingratiating |
| Increases understanding | May condescend |
| Gives the author more time on stage | Takes time the audience may not be willing to give |
| May close out other speakers | May create animosity |

---

## GAINS AND LOSSES

---

### ◀ COMPRESSION ▶

| Advantages | Disadvantages |
|---|---|
| Reduces contact with the audience | Less time for ingratiation |
| Increases depth, focus, and density | Forces readers to decipher the meaning |
| Adds emphasis | Lacks explanatory power |
| Sounds more conclusive | Relies more on assertion |

---

## EXERCISE C

Read the following passages, all with the same basic message, and discuss the differences in effect that different kinds of compression and amplification can have.

**1.** Still waters run deep.

**2.** His bark is worse than his bite.

**3.** He's all talk and no show.

**4.** Quiet, complex people are potentially dangerous.

**5.** Watch out for the quiet ones.

**6.** People who are quiet and reserved may be regarded as more complex in character and thought than those who speak freely.

**7.** People who make a lot of noise are no threat. When you are looking for a place to cross a stream, water that is rippled and noisy is probably safe. Even if it is murky, you know it must be shallow. The surface of deep and dangerous water, on the other hand, is often quiet and calm.

**8.** Still waters run deep. Smooth and inviting though they might seem, they hide pools that will swallow you up and currents that can sweep you away. They conceal their nature and intent. Beneath a calm surface lie dangerous possibilities.

**9.** One of the patriarchal biases of popular culture is the excessive worth it attaches to silence. The culture trains boys to become as men "strong, silent types" with little to say for themselves or to others. They learn that "still waters run deep," that talking at any length is useless—a sign of weakness and effeminacy.

   Men do not talk or listen; they act. They do not communicate ideas or express their feelings. They live inside themselves and keep their own counsel, equating silence with wisdom, taciturnity with intelligence, reserve with maturity and strength.

**10.** It's not fashionable anymore to keep quiet, to suck it up or play it down, to be philosophical about losses and diffident about gains. To get ahead you've got to brag and complain, call attention to good fortune and whine like crazy when anything goes wrong. The rules of the game are simple: setbacks are someone else's fault; success is entirely of your own making.

   Everyone has a press agent and a lawyer. If the ref's call goes against a team—and offers even the slightest opportunity for dispute—twenty football players converge on the scene, each yelling as loud as the next. If your car hits a curb, you file a lawsuit. "It wasn't built right." "It's too high." "The lane is too narrow." "It was crazy to put a curb there in the first place." The world has to be safe for bad drivers. The story must have a happy ending.

   One of my neighbors, Eliot Wertham, seems nearly the last of a dying breed. He's "strong and silent" in the classic mold—a bit on the shy side but solid as they come. If you're out in the yard he'll walk over and say hello. Not "hi" or "hey there." Then he'll fold his arms, put his back to the sun, and stand there, comfortably, unembarrassed by gaps in the conversation. If you're sharpening the lawn mower blades or trimming the hedges, he doesn't offer advice unless asked. He minds his own business.

   He knows intuitively that conversation isn't as important as community, as being there. It's a throwback, I suppose, to the front porch era, the times when folks would sit out on the stoop together listening to cicadas, watching dragonflies zip by, and smelling the summer heat, humidity, and dust rise from the street.

We're more vocal now. Self-dramatization is the norm. People splash their personalities around like red paint, vandalizing the composure and privacy of others, our peace and quiet. The louder a message is, the better. It's not enough to believe in something or enjoy a song. The belief and the song must be worn on T-shirts, posted on walls, played in CD stereo at thirty decibels, or jingled incessantly from a wind chime. Everyone must see and hear.

There's a kind of insecurity and aggression in this. We need reassurance that what we like is likable enough. And we're not really sure about that until enough people agree with our T-shirts and bumper stickers. People who disagree are useful, too. Invariably we can see in them "the enemy," the bad guys who hate our music, kill puppies and kittens, and deprive us of handguns—or the bad guys who hate our music, keep pit bull terriers, and hand out guns to criminals, toddlers, and other riff-raff. We validate our own tastes and attitudes by forcing them on others.

Reticence is considered a crime.

## Wider Implications

Compression and amplification are inherent in the nature of the essay and the nature of interpretation, since the processes of forming and presenting an opinion must inevitably heighten the importance of some material and diminish the significance of the rest. Essays, by nature, distinguish relevant from irrelevant detail; impose principles, values, or assumptions on the subject; and cast some information and ideas in the role of evidence or support.

The main points are developed at length. Anything perceived as evidence is subordinated to the larger issues, subsumed in the amplification and proof. Minor points are delivered in more compressed form.

### PROPORTION IN DEVELOPMENT

The question of development is partially an issue of balance or proportion, the relationship between the number of words expended on a given idea or fact and its importance or significance relative to the main topic, the rest of the essay, or the circumstances at hand. Increasing the proportion of time spent discussing an idea also increases its perceived importance in relation to everything else the author says or does not say.

Readers can be all too unsophisticated about the weight assigned to different parts of the message: despite all your protestations about what is most and least important, readers tend to perceive as most important the issue you spend the most time on. They may subconsciously translate the proportions of an essay into a value structure and come away remembering the values rather than the message.

A report that spends too much time on possible drawbacks of a plan or proposal, or that overdramatizes a "worst case" scenario, may subvert its own recommendations. Children whose parents spend five hours a week talking about hunting and fishing and two minutes a week stressing the importance of a good education are likely to infer that hunting and fishing are much more important than intellectual pursuits. Readers told briefly that a dancer or actor's performance was superb and told at length that his or her costume was dreadful are likely to reach the conclusion that the performance was not all that good or that the poor quality of the costume somehow affected or seriously detracted from the quality of the dancing and acting.

### BALANCE AND VARIETY

Although even or balanced development may seem attractive, giving the same weight and attention to each successive argument may not reflect their relative worth. A pleasing symmetry may be gained at the expense of accuracy.

Balance may also lead us to overlook the variations in compression and expansion that may exist within equally weighted sections of the discussion. While the *appearance* of balance can be created and maintained, no writer can give equal time to every idea expressed, every detail mentioned. Some data must be glossed over, some principles must be alluded to and not explained, and some premises must remain assumptions. Not every example, instance, or argument can be explored completely and presented thoroughly.

Balanced development is just one of many possibilities.

### THE COMPRESSION/EXPANSION INTERRELATIONSHIP

The pattern of development in an essay expands and contracts. Some material is presented in compressed form; other material is presented at length. The primary divisions of the topic are commonly presented in *both* compressed and expanded form—as contracted and compressed thesis statements and topic sentences, collective assertions that provide an overview of the subject, and as support or explanation, the amplified discussion of the claims being made.

In simpler terms, this means that the essay tends to contract, expand, and contract again in a continuous cycle. Authors vary the amount of time spent on the different dimensions of the topic, discussing one point at length and in depth and the next just superficially, in a few words. A side comment, readily accepted premise, or reference to common knowledge may be introduced, developed, and dropped, all in the course of a sentence or two, while the main subtopics of the issue under discussion may be developed over several paragraphs, pages, or even chapters.

## MEANING AND DEVELOPMENT

Length does not necessarily correspond to meaning or to the amount of information conveyed. A good example of this is the use of statistics. Saying "87 percent of all homes have television sets" conveys considerably more information than saying "Bob has a television set in his home," though the number of words in each message is basically the same. It is possible to write at length and say little, or to write briefly and say a lot.

## THE READER'S ROLE IN DEVELOPMENT

A complete understanding of development must consider the role the reader plays in developing an essay. The knowledge an audience brings to the reading process is often relied on to fill in or flesh out sketchy development—as when we assume a person's familiarity with a current event, and instead of recounting it in detail we simply move on to a discussion of the issues it raises. Readers are frequently called on in this manner to draw on common knowledge or to supply their own background information. Or an author may evoke reader participation with imagery, passing references, and topical allusions.

Changes that occur in the audience as it reads can also affect the shape or extent of development. Perelman and Tyteca note that in the course of reading an essay, the audience becomes increasingly more familiar with the subject, more "educated" in a sense, and therefore may need less and less explanation or evidence on each successive point (*The New Rhetoric:* 495–502). The nature and expertise of the audience changes as the discussion progresses.

## DEPTH AND DEVELOPMENT

The appearance of depth, or of shallowness, in an essay is a product of a combination of factors, notably the quality or maturity of thought, the relative denseness of the development, the choice of topics, the author's values, and the proportion of development spent on various topics.

Extensive and well-supported interpretation or analysis suggests depth. But good ideas or perceptions are not enough. The thinking must be sustained and concentrated. Rapid lateral movement from one perception or association to another can seem flighty, insubstantial. To be weighty, the style must be layered, with one level of analysis embedded within another.

Highly compressed styles, as evident in maxims, some poetry, and much academic prose, tend to appear deeper than amplified writing, even when the ideas are essentially the same. If an essay is too easy to understand or decode, it may seem less impressive than an essay written in a dense style. Conversely (or perversely), a relatively thin or unoriginal subject can be made to appear more impressive if the style is obscure.

One's discourse may also seem deeper when most of the development addresses issues of some importance and the tone is at least moderately serious. An author who focuses too much attention on strictly personal interests or on humor may seem superficial.

Likewise, an apparent lack of proportion or perspective can make an author seem shallow: placing as much value on the outcome of a baseball game as on the outcome of a diplomatic mission; weighing the life and welfare of a pet above the condition of impoverished people; perceiving a slow-moving vehicle on the freeway as a personal affront, a serious insult to one's pride or an infringement on one's rights. Discourse seems shallow when the author's sense of values is skewed.

### THE SITUATIONAL NATURE OF DEVELOPMENT

There is no simple way to predict the amount or variety of development a particular situation might call for. When an audience is especially familiar with the subject, one might think that less explanation would be needed. But extended development might nevertheless be welcomed, confirming the beliefs and perceptions of the readers and avoiding the appearance of oversimplification or of disregard for the subject. By the same token, although careful amplification can make difficult material more accessible, it can also seem condescending and tedious.

### THE OBLIGATION TO SPEAK AT LENGTH

Unless someone speaks or writes for a significant amount of time, we don't feel like we are getting our money's worth. If we pay for an expert, we want to see enough data, thinking, and verbiage to justify the expense.

Of course, there's more to it than that. Zen wisdom is sought after and appreciated, too.

Speaking at length is in part a moral and intellectual responsibility. One has an obligation to record and transmit information, to express one's beliefs, to discover and teach.

THE OBLIGATION TO BE BRIEF

Extended discourse takes up time. It keeps us from listening to or reading the work of others. And it is difficult to grasp and hold in the mind. Consequently writers are under some obligation to be brief, to confine their comments to a limited or conventional scope. These limits are commonly observed, understood, and even legislated in various forums.

## Conclusion

Accomplished writers manage to combine the virtues of conciseness and amplification. They make brief passages of writing appear positively spacious—conveying a sense of extended support, detailed explanation, and legitimate authority. And the accomplished writer can make lengthy essays easier to read, apprehend, and remember, using the devices of compression and emphasis to highlight significant information and to maintain interest.

## ASSIGNMENT A: Amplification as Entertainment, Explanation, and Speculation

1. Amplify at some modest length a truism, concept, exclamation, judgment, or other assertion. Your goal might be reemphasis, clarification, or sheer wit. The amplification might also be attached to some purpose like insult, ceremony, praise, or courtship ("let me count the ways"), or even inculcation of a scientific principle (like survival of the fittest).

2. Start making assertions about something, and continually paraphrase, qualify, and explicate what you are saying as you proceed. Think of it as explaining to yourself what you think and what you mean. Allow yourself to digress gradually as other associations and questions arise.

*Note:* Unless you are particularly good at making transitions, this may not result in writing that would be regarded as finished or fit for public consumption. But it may, like freewriting, result in interesting ideas and connections.

3. Use amplification to clarify a difficult concept or to reveal the complexities of a concept that seems simple.

## ASSIGNMENT B: Compression as Focus

1. Identify and discuss a complex or emotion-charged subject, first attempting to include as many nuances, contradictions, and points of view as

possible, and then trying in the final draft to compress the issue by (a) defining what the central issues are, (b) dividing the question into its constituent parts, (c) categorizing the material, and/or (d) summing it up in a thesis, a generalization, a maxim, a slogan, or a catch phrase of some sort.

2. Identify a pattern of similar personal experiences or historical events, a social or environmental problem that is widely evident, or a group of parallel examples of something. Instead of describing all of the available instances, use a single, extended example as a representative case. Or use some simple form of statistics, like a series of percentages or a pie chart, to characterize and compress your data.

## ASSIGNMENT C:   Laws, Principles, Commands, and Instructions

1. Propose, explain, and defend a law to regulate, or a principle governing, a certain kind of behavior. This may be a serious or humorous proposal.

2. Focus on an ethical dilemma, a situation where people are torn between two or more competing values. Study, reflect on, and explain the authority and application of each precept or value, and then attempt to chart a clear course through the dilemma.

3. Put yourself in a role where you have to give orders, telling people (in writing) what to do or what they ought to do in certain circumstances. Choose a subject that takes considerable explanation. Think of yourself as something like an expert talking to the uninitiated, a supervisor talking to employees, or a parent talking to children. Consider as you write how much you want to include of the reasoning behind the orders, how likely the audience is to follow your direction readily, and how comfortable you are giving orders.

4. Find written instructions for some procedure, game, or craft. Cite these, showing how the process should *really* be done or what other steps, emotions, peripheral knowledge, know-how, and skills are not included in the standard instructions.

# 15

# Support: Reasoning and Persuasion

Life is the art of drawing sufficient conclusions from insufficient premises.
—SAMUEL BUTLER

"Contrariwise," continued Tweedledee, "if it was so, it might be; and if it were so, it would be; but as it isn't, it ain't. That's logic." —LEWIS CARROLL

Logicians sometimes prove too much by an argument. —HENRY FIELDING

## Telling the Truth

Discussion of support is ultimately concerned with what it takes to confirm the truth, not just in the sense of proof or verification but in the wider sense of establishing an idea or judgment as part of the history and beliefs of the community. The means to this end can vary. Truth may be established by reasoning (including both scientific discourse and logical argument) or by persuasion.

Reasoning operates on the assumption that the truth speaks for itself, that sufficient explanation, evidence, and analysis will in and of itself convince the reader. It assumes that the absolute truth can, in fact, be determined. Reasoning emphasizes evidence, issues, logic, analysis, ideas, methodology, and principles or laws. It relies on demonstration and proof.

When support is based primarily on reasoning and evidence, it may be perceived as good or bad.

### ◀ REASONING ▶

| Good Qualities | Bad Qualities |
|---|---|
| intellectual | unemotional |
| rational | argumentative |
| valid | rationalized |
| scientific | inhumane |

Persuasion, on the other hand, assumes that people are often illogical and emotional, that even the best evidence may not convince them unless the author's point of view is directly advocated, emphasized, and inculcated. It assumes that the truth is often difficult, if not impossible, to determine and that knowledge consists of partial, tentative, and probable truths about which disagreement is not only possible but necessary.

Persuasion emphasizes beliefs, images, scenarios, models, identification, attitudes, claims to vision and insight, and the attraction of community goals and ideals. It attempts to make an impression on the reader. Persuasion is more political and social than reasoning, measuring success by consequences rather than by accuracy.

When support is based more directly on persuasion and making an impression, it may be perceived as good or bad.

### ◀ PERSUASION ▶

| Good Qualities | Bad Qualities |
|---|---|
| farsighted | impractical |
| personable | shallow |
| decisive | impulsive |
| compelling | demagogic |

These extremes are familiar to us in political campaigning, where candidates are often described as running on issues or running on image. The same basic difference in approach is also suggested by the popular distinction between argument that relies on facts and arguments based on style.

Such terms, however, imply more faith in facts than they deserve and too much prejudice against vision, which many would agree plays a major role in the processes of leadership, conceptualization, and decision making. The options might better be called logic-based and persuasion-based support, analytic and holistic support, or proof and proselytism. One attempts to establish truth, the other to convince the audience. The important thing to remember is that neither approach is inherently better or worse than the other. Neither is necessarily more "true" or convincing.

The same case can often be presented in either way—as reasoning or as persuasion. All that is changed is the style. Arguments and exhortation can be turned into explanation and analysis. Reason and evidence can be turned into emotional and ethical appeals.

## Being Credible

The distinction between reasoning and persuasion dates back to classical rhetoric. Formal demonstration or reasoning was reserved for matters susceptible to absolute proof, for questions of fact, of philosophy, and of science. Persuasion was considered different because it dealt not in natural facts or philosophical truths but in probabilities, in issues open to interpretation and debate. Probabilities were not seen as subject to formal proof. The best one could hope for was a sense of conviction or belief rather than certainty.

In contemporary rhetoric the two styles of support are still recognized as separate, but their provinces overlap considerably. It is recognized that support for either probable or absolute assertions may require both exhortation and sufficient evidence.

The ultimate goal of reasoning and persuasion alike is to be credible, to convince people of the rightness of one's views. A speaker is not credible who assembles all the necessary information but cannot make us see or feel its importance. Support must be presented in a convincing manner. Nor is the speaker credible who offers us grand assertions and ideals without any substance. Persuasion must be legitimized by reason and fact.

We believe people who appear to be reasonable, who examine the issues and data impartially according to an established or justified methodology and arrive at significant and appropriate conclusions sustained by the evidence. We admire solid, meticulous research and thought, clear understanding and application of accepted principles and laws, and patient explication. Creative arguments and fine distinctions are welcome but suspicious, acceptable only insofar as they bear close examination.

And yet, suspicions aside, we need more than charts and graphs, statistics and data, logic and restraint. We truly appreciate wit, kindness, and charm. We are influenced by power and by strength of personality. And we may be inspired and converted by the sheer attractiveness of a speaker's vision of truth, by a speaker's portrayal of the way things are or ought to be. We are persuaded as much by the sound, the impression, and presence of the author as by the evidence.

## *The Forms of Appeal*

Aristotle suggested that there are three principal means of persuading an audience:

- Logical appeal
- Ethical appeal
- Emotional appeal

### LOGICAL APPEALS

Arguments based on logic attempt to affect or change the audience's opinions by appealing to its sense of reason. This includes logical proof and demonstration, of course. But any attempt to create conviction based on truth, a sense of what's right and proper, or the appearance of truth may be considered logical appeal.

In addition to logic and evidence, we regard as reasonable appeals to common sense and intuition; appeals to preconception and culture; appeals to laws, principles, precedents, and values; and appeals to psychological rationality itself, among other things. These do not "prove" your point, as such, but can make your position more convincing.

### ETHICAL APPEALS

Ethical appeals include any form of influence—positive or negative—that is based on the character, reputation, and perceived expertise of the author. These patterns of influence are extremely complex. The appearance of knowledgeability might, for instance, be variously derived from a display of scholarship; from age, status, or an imposing demeanor; from a mature style; from assertiveness or intimidation; from reference to tradition; or from personal involvement with the subject. We may even regard an author as more knowledgeable if he or she disclaims any certain knowledge of the subject.

The same mixed response is apparent in all other aspects of ethical appeal (or style). We may be attracted to an author's strength and authority but may also shy away from it. We may be persuaded by physical beauty or an appropriate demeanor or become suspicious of it, regarding plainness and dishevellment as somehow more sincere or believable.

Likewise, enthusiasm and sentiment may seem engaging or repellent. A touch of immorality may seem pragmatic, forceful, and attractive. Or it may seem sleazy, unprincipled, and superficial. Morality may be dismissed as prissy self-righteousness or admired as strength of character. An avuncular or fatherly stance may inspire confidence or disgust. Much depends on the circumstances and presentation.

### EMOTIONAL APPEALS

Emotional appeals attempt to put the audience in a frame of mind or an emotional state that sways, conditions, or reinforces its judgment. This may include evoking strong emotion—like fear, anger, despair, prejudice, patriotism, or sympathy. It may include attempts to moderate or change the tone of the occasion.

The emotional state of readers may be changed by introducing humor and relieving tension. Their attitude toward the subject may be changed by heightening or lowering the significance or seriousness of the offense (calling it the "moral equivalent of war," for example, or characterizing a crime as an honest mistake or harmless prank).

The audience may be mollified if you offer concessions. It may look at the case differently if you redefine the occasion in any number of ways—for instance, by physically changing the setting, by increasing or decreasing the formality of the presentation, by altering the level of ceremony used, or by changing the degree of discussion and debate allowed. The audience's responses may be altered if you change the role it occupies with respect to the subject (if, for instance, you put the audience more in the role of parent than judge, or appeal to its sense of humanity).

Less obviously, but no less important, emotional appeal may include the negation of emotion—appeals based on objectivity, distance, dispassion, and abstract thinking. If your evidence is strong, or if strong emotions have clouded the issue, you probably would want to place your audience in an objective and rational frame of mind.

## Being Reasonable

Your claims may appear to be better supported if you create a formal demonstration of their validity. But logic is not always sufficient to make a style appear well reasoned and well supported. Being reasonable is as much a stance as a matter of evidence and proof. We recognize as reasonable people who

- are consistent without being narrowminded
- avoid extreme positions on issues
- avoid extreme styles and behavior
- defer judgment

- consult authority
- consider humanity as well as principle
- listen to and sometimes accommodate other points of view
- avoid intense emotional involvement in the issue
- make assertions that conform to the evidence
- support their assertions
- question or test their assertions
- change their point of view to fit new evidence

Wide divergence from these standards is regarded as evidence of being unreasonable, if not irrational.

The nature of proof itself is quite complex. The ensuing discussion will review five methods for building and attacking arguments: (1) traditional logic, (2) Toulmin logic, (3) Aristotelian and Rogerian styles of argument, (4) practical argumentation, and (5) refutation.

### TRADITIONAL LOGIC

Traditional logic is as much an invention device and methodology as a means of constructing support. It regularizes and defines two processes, induction and deduction, through which people discover ideas or arrive at conclusions. In addition, traditional logic sets standards for distinguishing between the many conclusions people, given the same evidence, might reach. It allows us to determine which conclusions are more valid and trustworthy.

**Induction.** Induction is the process of generalizing from specific cases. The process of induction begins with direct observation and the accumulation of data about a subject. On the basis of this information, the author draws a conclusion—interpreting the general meaning or significance of what has been observed. This conclusion is valid to the extent that (1) the evidence supports it, (2) the conclusion does not over- or underexplain the facts (this is called adequacy), (3) the evidence reliably reflects the subject being studied, and (4) there are not better conclusions available—ones that are more probable or that leave fewer details unexplained.

Support based on induction works on the principle that if something is true in one case, it might be true in others. Inductive support becomes stronger as the quantity of evidence collected from a specific case increases or as the number of cases observed increases. To cement the proof further, any exceptions to the rule must be explained away—as the result of aberrations or of other influences. Taken to an extreme, induction assumes that if something is true in many cases, it must be true in all cases.

**Deduction.** Deductive reasoning argues from premises to conclusions. On the basis of things already known (the premises), it infers new information or applies a general rule to a particular case.

If you know that the people who live in Jones Tower are graduate students, and Alice tells you she lives in Jones Tower, you might reasonably conclude that Alice is a graduate student. This conclusion is valid as long as the premises are true and reliable or apply to all cases. If only graduate students and all graduate students live in Jones Tower, your conclusion is more secure than if some who live there are graduate students or honors students can live there, too.

Formal deduction is expressed in a three-part structure known as a syllogism, as follows:

MAJOR PREMISE: Raising corn requires a great deal of water.
MINOR PREMISE: Corn is a major crop in this area.
CONCLUSION: Annual rainfall totals here must be fairly high.

This conclusion might be valid unless (1) local farmers preferred not to make a profit, (2) the farmers irrigated their crops, (3) the water table was very high, as in a river bottom, or (4) a dry-land variety of corn had been developed. The hazard of deductive reasoning is that unexamined or uncritically accepted premises may lead to false conclusions, as follows:

MAJOR PREMISE: Only birds and reptiles lay eggs.
MINOR PREMISE: The platypus lays eggs.
CONCLUSION: The platypus must be either a bird or reptile.

Support based on deduction relies on classifications or categories, on something akin to what a mathematician would call set theory. If you assert that "Alice is a graduate student" (as in the earlier example), your proof relies on being able to demonstrate that she evinces certain characteristics that are exclusive to and representative of graduate students as a group. You have placed her in the category of graduate students.

The same process is used in less formal deduction. The informal assertion that motorcycles are dangerous locates the nature and characteristics of motorcycles in general within the category of things that are dangerous. Support for this claim relies on your being able to show that riding a motorcycle fits the definition of things more dangerous to human life than is necessary or proper.

**Thesis Statements and Propositions.** Deductive argument often centers around a thesis statement, hypothesis, or formal proposition. This assertion represents the point to be proven or the conclusion to be supported in the ensuing essay. The thesis statement focuses and directs the proof.

Logicians make a distinction between real (or arguable) propositions and apparent propositions (as in statements of fact or matters of taste). Technically speaking, the claim that motorcycles are dangerous is not entirely arguable. To the extent that it is similar to saying that hand grenades are dangerous, no one would dispute it.

But in informal argument we frequently use less assertive or precise claims to represent or take the place of our actual meaning. This is an acceptable practice as long as author and audience are intuitively aware of the "real" proposition being argued. The arguable proposition underlying a "motorcycles are dangerous" essay might be something like "Motorcycles are inherently unsafe" or "People should not be allowed to ride motorcycles" or "Many people who buy motorcycles do not really understand the risks they are taking when they ride them."

### TOULMIN LOGIC

The philosopher Stephen Toulmin, in *The Uses of Argument* (1958) and in *An Introduction to Reasoning* (1979), written with Richard Rieke and Allan Janik, has proposed an alternative way of viewing the reasoning process. He suggests that all logic—whatever the subject or perspective—has the same underlying structure. These basic elements of reasoning, according to Toulmin, are as follows:

| | | |
|---|---|---|
| 1. | The claim: | a proposition, opinion, theory, or contention |
| 2. | Grounds or data: | information drawn from the specific case that supports the claim |
| 3. | Warrants: | laws, principles, or premises that apply to the case |
| 4. | Backing: | precedents or historical cases that led to the establishment of the warrant in the first place |
| 5. | Modal qualifiers: | the degree of confidence with which the claim is asserted to be true |
| 6. | Rebuttals: | anomalies and contradictions that must be either explained away or excluded from consideration for the claim to be true |

Toulmin logic differs from traditional logic in a number of significant ways. First, it combines induction and deduction instead of seeing them as separate ways of thinking. Second, it incorporates the evidence or support for a conclusion into the reasoning process. In effect, Toulmin logic focuses on the total thesis-and-support structure (and interrelationships within it) rather than on separate and constituent parts of reasoning.

Third, Toulmin logic makes the process of qualifying assertions more important. Qualifiers become in Toulmin's system essential characterizations of the validity and reliability of the evidence and method. This allows more room within the study of logic for assertions that are probable, doubtful, or open to question. In traditional logic, any qualifications that are made may be seen as flaws in reasoning or hedges against contradiction.

Fourth, Toulmin logic suggests a useful connection between refutation in public debate and the processes through which we revise theories, concepts, attitudes, and worldviews. Explaining anomalous data and answering competing theories is seen as much the same thing as responding to an adversary's counterarguments or "deconstructing" his or her viewpoint. Rhetorical refutation may, in this light, be considered not separate and distinct from logical proof but an inevitable part of the way in which we establish conviction and certainty about a subject. This effectively synthesizes rhetorical support and logical proof.

Traditional logic is, to some extent, based on a belief in absolute and mathematical standards of proof. It is appropriate to apply it wherever such a stance is possible or desirable. Toulmin logic, by contrast, seems better adapted to relativistic, pluralistic, and phenomenological thinking.

One of the special virtues of Toulmin logic is its ability to explain how multiple and even contradictory assertions about the same evidence can *all* be "logical." The key to this explanation lies in the fact that if the warrant applied to a case is changed, then in a very real sense the "truth" changes.

For example, the claim that someone has stolen your car is defensible as long as the warrant applied is the legal definition of theft. But if the warrant applied is "might makes right," then the car may, in fact, logically be said to "belong" to your adversary, if he or she is more powerful than you are. Other warrants that would change the truth substantially are "Possession is nine-tenths of the law" and "To each according to his or her need." This example is offered not to defend the practice of theft but to show how theft may be defended.

The relativism of Toulmin logic also explains the basis of much human antagonism and misunderstanding. People who strongly believe in the warrants they choose may regard themselves as entirely logical—and their enemies as irrational—not even conceiving of the possibility that their opposition might have reasonable warrants of its own.

In such misapprehension of logic lies its potential tyranny. We tend to form dogmatic and insular belief structures. Within these belief structures—which might also be called ideologies or paradigms—we regard ourselves as totally correct in our thinking. We feel justified, therefore, in forcing others to act in accord with our wishes. And people all too often submit to this—

because as long as you accept the warrant being used, the argument is unassailable. People accept what seems like "reason" because they do not see how to challenge its warrants, how to deconstruct an ideology and construct in its place a counterlogic that is equally valid and supportable.

## EXERCISE A

Using Toulmin logic, develop the complete structure of an argument for one of the following cases. List as many grounds and as much backing as you can think of. Try substituting different warrants and varying the level of qualification. What is the effect?

1. Proving the claim that a particular car is substandard
2. Proving the claim that current television shows are better than people admit
3. Proving the claim that power tends to corrupt the people who have it
4. Proving the claim that someone copied from a song you wrote
5. Proving the claim that a new local high school, and the corresponding tax increase, is unnecessary

### ARISTOTELIAN AND ROGERIAN STYLES OF ARGUMENT

Some contemporary theorists, notably Maxine Hairston in "Using Carl Rogers' Communication Theories in the Composition Classroom," (*Rhetoric Review* 1 [September 1982]: 50–55), make a distinction between monologic and dialogic argumentation—often called Aristotelian and Rogerian after the classical rhetorician, Aristotle, and the modern psychologist, Carl Rogers. These styles of argument were discussed in Chapter 6 as matters of audience awareness. It may be useful to review them here as they pertain to support.

The Aristotelian style is not so much aimed at persuading the person who disagrees with you as at overwhelming that person. Often the true audience is not even the one who disagrees—the opposition—but a real or implied third party, an impartial jury or group of onlookers.

The author using an Aristotelian style is likely to build a one-sided or monologic case. The Aristotelian approach may pile up arguments and evidence. It may directly or indirectly ridicule the opposition. It tries to close off communication, to end the debate by creating an unassailable argument or by silencing the adversary. It tends to polarize and politicize the debate, to push people into opposing camps. The emphasis is on winning. Truth or justice is seen in black-and-white terms, where only one side can be right.

A Rogerian approach is more dialogic, more interested in hearing out the opposition and trying to understand its point of view. The basic assumption is that *both* sides in a dispute can have good reasons for believing as they do.

In Rogerian argument, the author tries first to listen to and understand the opposition's point of view, actually attempting to paraphrase what the other person says to confirm that it has been understood. Typically, you might ask the audience to verify or correct your paraphrase—to make absolutely sure that communication has taken place. A Rogerian stance tries to keep people talking and negotiating, to engender dialogue rather than stop it. It may be content with partial solutions and compromises, may see understanding and mutual respect rather than winning as the goal. It is not less assertive, however. A Rogerian approach may require more effort or patience, but it is not necessarily weak in forwarding the author's views. It may, in fact, be more effective in achieving lasting and productive results.

The essential features of each style are compared in the following table.

| **Aristotelian** | **Rogerian** |
| --- | --- |
| argumentative | persuasive |
| jury-directed | opposition-directed |
| monologic | dialogic |
| adversarial, confrontational | communal, nonconfrontational |
| piles up evidence | listens and explains |
| closes off communication | keeps communication going |
| sees the opposition as misguided or ignorant | shows respect for the opposition |
| emphasizes winning | emphasizes understanding |
| recognizes only one truth | allows pluralistic truths |

The Rogerian stance is less confrontational; it seems more likely to result in compromise and understanding. But it would be a mistake to assume that all disputes are best resolved by the Rogerian approach. A Rogerian style may fail if it is perceived as weak or manipulative. And it may be an inappropriate stance when the opposition remains adversarial, when the focus is clearly on winning, and when an audience other than the opponent is addressed.

# EXERCISE B

Develop both an Aristotelian and a Rogerian stance for one of the following situations. Discuss the audience's likely response to each.

**1.** Returning a faulty small appliance to a store and asking for a refund

**2.** Complaining to city hall about the quality of city services in your neighborhood

**3.** Explaining to a friend why you think he or she should dress more professionally

**4.** Telling an employee to limit personal calls on company time

**5.** Talking to an outdoor sports group about why snowmobiles and/or all-terrain vehicles should not be allowed in national parks; or talking to a conservation group about why such vehicles should be allowed in national parks

## PRACTICAL ARGUMENTATION

Much of the support for our contentions comes less from formal logic than from practical argumentation. We assemble reasons why the audience should accept our recommendations or views. These may take many forms.

*1. Arguing From Reality.* Arguments can be based on reality—on "the way things are." These are essentially arguments from fact, nature, observation, or example, including the entire range from simple opinion and impression to carefully designed experimentation and statistical analysis.

Determining what is "real," of course, can be difficult. Appeals to reality are effective as long as the facts relied on are generally accepted as true or appear to be patently obvious. If the reality appealed to is counterintuitive, the author may be obligated to demonstrate that what seems to be true is not, before offering his or her alternative. If the reality appealed to is unknown or outside the realm of normal observation, the author may be able to make his or her point by simply describing the phenomenon in question—since no one else can claim to be a witness to it. Or the author may support his or her personal observation with statistics and experimental controls on the observing process—essentially arguing that what he or she has discovered is indeed a fact.

*2. Arguing From Beliefs or Values.* Arguments can be based on the beliefs or values of your audience—on what your readers accept as important, right, and true. Such appeals are likely to be more effective than those based on beliefs with which your readers are unfamiliar or beliefs and principles they see as connected with your own self-interest.

*3. Arguing From Fears or Hopes.* Arguments can be based on the audience's fears or hopes. Essentially, the author claims that his or her program will fulfill hopes or avert dangers, or that the opposition's ideas will lead to disaster. For better or worse, such appeals often have greater impact than arguments based on truth, pragmatism, or rectitude.

*4. Arguing From Ideals or Ideal Cases.* Arguments can be based on ideals or ideal cases—on the way things "ought to be." However, these are often surprisingly ineffective. The author may appear to be criticizing the audience, may seem to have a "holier-than-thou" attitude. And readers can easily discredit such arguments by seeing the author as an impractical idealist.

Arguments from ideals are more safe and useful when the author is siding with the status quo, when the author is considered an elder statesperson, or when there is general and real agreement that change is needed.

*5. Arguing From Contracts, Promises, or Expectations.* Arguments can be based on the way things "were supposed to be done"—on the correlation or lack of correlation between the conditions of a promise, agreement, treaty, bargain, or contract and the performance or result of the agreement.

*6. Arguing From Personal Prerogative.* Arguments can be based on "the way I/we want things to be done." This is essentially an argument from authority or assertion. It embodies a claim to privilege, worth, or correctness, a demand on the time, property, and credulity of the audience. The author may make no pretence of being reasonable.

While this might seem laughable in the abstract or offensive in a child, in actual fact it is the method by which prescriptive leadership and many social relationships operate. It is the point at which many bargaining and negotiating processes begin. And it is the vehicle through which the normal operation of society is conducted.

Argument from authority assumes that the speaker has a certain right to determine policies, procedures, and price. It asks the reader to defer to the speaker's superior power, rank, and knowledge. The essential message is that "I know how things should be done. Do as I say, believe what I say, give me what I ask for." The argument may rest on an implied or actual threat rather than on questions of truth, rectitude, ideals, or law.

If the audience acknowledges in advance the superior wisdom of the speaker, then there is no need for persuasion. The interchange becomes almost a teacher/student or expert/child transaction, and the style becomes more expository and reportative than persuasive.

*7. Arguing From History or From Standard Practices.* Arguments can be based on standard practice or history—on the way things have always been done. This includes not only appeals to personal experience but also to precedents and to correlative situations. Such arguments imply the weight and force of the status quo—standard practices being conventional or socially accepted. They also embody an appeal to fact, since things that happened in the past can be taken as examples of the way things really are. But historical arguments are susceptible to attack when standard practice has been obviously ineffective.

Other ways to attack the historical argument include arguing that what ought to be done (arguing from ideals) should take precedence over what has commonly been done; arguing that the standard practices have become excessively bureaucratic, self-serving, or dogmatic; and arguing that change is important in and of itself. Not much confidence should be placed in these criticisms, however, since they presume that people want to improve the way things are done, that bureaucrats do not like or benefit from bureaucracy and dogma, and that people are receptive to change.

A common turn on the historical argument is to claim that a policy or recommendation under consideration has been tried before and it did not work. Unattractive though it may be, this is almost a "can't lose" stance. It places the audience in the unpleasant position of having either to dispute historical fact (usually concerning events that the audience did not witness) or to directly criticize the speaker, claiming that he or she botched the previous attempt to implement the policy.

*8. Arguing From Results or From the Future State of Affairs.* Arguments can be based on the way things will be. Usually this strategy involves claiming that benefits, improvements, or some other favorable outcome will result from following your recommendation, or claiming that disaster will result if the opposition's course of action is adopted.

If the claimed benefits or losses are itemized, then the style will appear to be reasoned and analytic. However, if the author describes an improved or degenerated state of affairs, portraying the future, the style will be more visionary and holistic in effect.

*9. Arguing From Crises.* Arguments can be based on the existence of a crisis, real or contrived. This strategy is designed to preempt actual debate or consideration of alternatives. If the crisis seems real enough, readers will often accede to demands placed on them or follow a course of action that they would normally find unpleasant.

*10. Arguing From Utility.* Arguments can be based on claims of practicality, cost, or necessity. Like argument from crisis, the claim of practicality, cost-effectiveness, or necessity may serve to shut off other debate. If only limited resources are available, then options that require greater resources are effectively precluded. If it can be proven (or if the audience will accept without proof) that something needs to be done or is a requirement, then debate about the matter is forestalled.

*11. Arguing From Personal Rights or Privileges.* Arguments can be based on claims of individual and personal rights or privileges. If you can establish that there is a right to beach access, for instance, then claims to ownership of the beach may be debated.

*12. Arguing From Public Advantage.* Arguments can be based on claims of social or community advantage—usually to the detriment of personal privilege.

*13. Arguing From Relative Advantage.* Arguments can be based on comparative advantage—weighing one set of values against another in assessing potential gains and losses.

*14. Arguing From Laws, Principles, and Ideology.* Arguments can be based on principles, axioms, creeds, rules, laws, preconceptions, dogma, theory, or ideology. To the extent that laws and systems of belief embody conventional values, it is of course necessary to measure and judge decisions, actions, and ideas against such standards. We may argue that a particular course of action is prescribed by law or that it is not lawful, moral, or fair.

*Note:* Arguments based on law can be abused. Inhumanely applied, such appeals may reflect an essentially closed, tyrannical, and monologic point of view: the reasoning is that we must do something because the rule says so. Arguments from ideology are also an intrinsic part of prejudice and misreading of events: the reasoning is that because we believe this or that to be true, any evidence to the contrary must be an exception to the rule; we misperceive events, appearances, statements, and behavior to suit our preconceptions.

Arguments based on theory or ideology can be attacked in the same manner as arguments based on ideals. They can be discredited if you can assemble enough counterexamples or anomalies to prove them untrue or inadequate to explain the phenomenon or case in question. They can be challenged by competing interpretations of the phenomenon they purport to explain.

## EXERCISE C

Develop at least five practical arguments for or against one of the following positions. Discuss the effectiveness and originality of the arguments listed. Which seem most reductive? Which allow for complexities in the situation?

**1.** There should be free public access to beaches and waterfront land.
**2.** Guns should be registered.
**3.** Eighteen-year-olds should not be allowed to vote.
**4.** Parents should be held legally responsible for their children's actions.
**5.** Everyone should learn a foreign language in school.

### REFUTATION

Refutation is the art of attacking and disproving another person's reasoning. Though technically an adversarial device, a means of overcoming an opponent in debate, refutation can also be seen as a means of testing and validating arguments, a form of criticism. This is how refutation operates in both traditional logic and Toulmin logic.

On a more practical level, refutation may be accomplished through the following strategies:

**1. Challenging the Facts of the Case.**   It is often possible to question whether the facts of the case are exactly as represented by the opposition. If the speaker claims that a particular car was present at the scene of the crime, you might argue that many similar cars exist.

**2. Challenging the Definition of the Case.**   The characterization of an issue is often open to question. On the topic of abortion, for instance, what one side calls murder the other side calls freedom of choice. In a court case, a claim of self-defense might be the reply to a charge of assault.

**3. Questioning or Reassessing the Seriousness of the Case.**   The degree of seriousness of an offense or the significance of an idea is usually open to some interpretation. Attack the opponent's assertiveness or his or her evaluation of the subject, saying that the idea is less or more significant or the offense is less or more serious than claimed.

**4. Questioning the Venue or "Jury."**   You can usually challenge the competence or right of the audience at hand to decide the case. This may involve questioning the composition, authority, or objectivity of the judges or claiming that the decision should be made elsewhere, in a higher court, in a different context, by the public, by history, and so on. If the issue has been covered by the media, you can complain that you have been prejudged by the press. If it has not been covered by the media, you can claim that you have not had a public hearing.

**5. Attacking Assumptions.**   You can often effect refutation by challenging the assumptions or warrants on which an argument is based. This often requires the ability to identify and express hidden premises of the opponent's argument or to imagine other warrants that might apply to the case.

**6. Measuring the Opposition's Case Against an Ideal.**   You can always criticize something by measuring it against an ideal. Describe all that the thing should or could be, at its very best, and complain that the particular case does not measure up to the (impossible) standard.

**7. Faulting the Speaker for Omissions and for Antithetical Virtues.** You can always blame the speaker for what he or she does not do. It is possible to find fault with whatever choice an author makes in style or content by asserting that the opposite approach would have been better, or should at least have been considered. Some form of refutation can invariably be found in this strategy, since (as this book has demonstrated) stylistic choice is based on a series of antithetical values.

So if authors choose to emphasize empirical proof, one can blame them for not being philosophical enough (and vice versa). If they choose to focus on a particular case, one can criticize it as an unreliable example; if they focus on statistics or on generalizations about many cases, one can criticize their findings for not properly taking into account the important differences that exist between particular instances.

Similarly, authors who try to simplify an issue are often accused of being reductive (whether the charge is fair or not). Likewise, authors who try to discuss the complexities of a subject can be blamed for oversophistication or excessive ingenuity. If your opponent says the case is simple, you argue that it is far more complex than he or she admits. If your opponent says the case is very complex, you argue that the matter is really quite simple.

An author who is pragmatic can be faulted for his or her lack of vision. If the style is personal, it can be compared unfavorably to a more distant style. If the style is distant and formal, one can wish it had a more personal touch. If it is assertive, it can be called arrogant. If it is polite and deferential, the style can be called weak.

8. *Faulting the Speaker's Stance on the Issue.*   The same rather reprehensible strategy can be used in criticizing the substance of an author's ideas, since knowledge and opinion also commonly take a dialectical shape, with two or more equally defensible sides to an issue. Consequently, an argument based on personal freedom can be attacked as advocating license (the ironic or negative form of freedom) or by arguing that some individual freedom must be sacrificed for the public good, or that we need to provide more guidance or exert more self-control (control and community being the values antithetical to freedom and self-expression).

Likewise, arguments based on financial gain can be blamed for a lack of altruism, and those based on self-sacrifice can be faulted for not considering the potential profits (or for concealing a profit motive). Arguments based on progress can be answered with arguments based on conservation. Arguments based on efficiency can be answered with arguments based on humanity (and also the reverse).

9. *Exaggerating the Speaker's Position.*   More cynical still are the devices of characterizing the adversary's position on an issue as far more extreme than it really is, blaming him or her for one's own faults (what a psychologist might call "reflection"), and totally misrepresenting the opponent's stand. These might more properly be called outright lies than forms of refutation, but their effect, nevertheless, is to discredit or undercut the opposition.

*Note:* The last three of these strategies (7, 8, and 9) are quite common in politics, propaganda, and interpersonal communication, in part because they are (unfortunately) so effective—almost impossible to answer.

Misrepresentations are often more dramatic, and therefore more memorable, than the respondent's own point of view. They also put the respondent in a defensive posture; anything he or she says seems like an excuse or rationalization. Worse still, the energy and time wasted in denial cannot be spent on making one's own case. And attempting to attack the lie directly may actually help spread it. The assertion being denied leaves its impression on the mind.

In public debate, anger and counterattack might be the best reactions—but circumstances vary. The other alternatives are absorbing the punishment (and perhaps earning some sympathy), trying to wait it out (figuring that the lies will eventually collapse of their own weight or that the person's attacks will moderate), and overtly calling attention to the strategy being used.

*10. Questioning the Validity or Application of Laws and Principles.* Arguments based on law, rule, or preconception can be questioned on several grounds. One is the familiar argument that the spirit of the law should take precedence over the letter of the law. Appeals can be made to higher laws. The law in question can be attacked and discredited—perhaps as reflecting an outdated ethic or a code based on an incomplete understanding or perception of truth. You can claim that the law in question does not apply to your particular case. Or you can argue that the situation and circumstances either mitigate the offense or justify breaking the law (the Declaration of Independence justifies revolution on the basis of higher laws, attacks on present law, and the nature of the situation).

## Being Persuasive

Persuasion may include extensive reasoning and evidence, but it also calls on many nonlogical forms of support. These are not necessarily fallacious, sophistic, or purely emotional. Describing some kinds of support as nonlogical merely asserts that they do not constitute formal or scientific proof. They may, however, appear quite reasonable and convincing when the aim of discourse is persuasion.

Nonlogical support is even necessary. In many instances, the available evidence is incomplete. Or there may be several courses of action that are equally reasonable. On such occasions, we base our judgments not only on the evidence but also on less tangible factors—the attractiveness or familiarity of one choice over the other, the extent to which the group or community agrees with us, the character of the author and his or her sources, the appearance of simplicity, common sense, or morality, and the relative danger or cost.

These are not just elements of ethical and emotional appeal as defined by Aristotle. They reflect the importance of credibility, consensus, self-image and public image, and acceptance or community in discourse—the extent to which we are influenced to choose one person as our leader or prophet over another, one product to buy instead of another that does the same things and is equally well made, one group of people to associate with and one way of thinking to follow. While these mechanisms of support may be nonlogical in the strictest sense, they need not be unreasonable.

To make your style more persuasive, you might use the following strategies:

*1. Rely on Examples.* Examples can be substituted for statistically valid proof. While they do represent a limited degree of logical evidence, the intent is more to underscore, explain, or emphasize a point rather than prove it.

*2. Cite Testimony.* Testimony cites or directly quotes experts, respected citizens, or wits (who may occasionally be respected citizens, as well) who support your point of view. This is somewhat different from citing witnesses (whose observations may constitute real evidence or proof); from citing secondhand accounts, unattributed public opinion, and other forms of hearsay (which are more closely related to rumor); and from citing expert analysis of the facts of the case (which may provide logical corroboration of your claim).

Testimony more strictly is a means of appealing to our sense of community and consensus—our preference for the opinion of the group over the opinion of the isolated individual and our tendency to "jump on the bandwagon." If it seems that many people—or certain important people—support a particular point of view, we are more likely to agree with it. Unpopular opinions are lonely ones. And everyone wants to be on the winning side.

This reliance on testimony can be a perfectly reasonable approach, especially in matters where taste or public opinion is the final arbiter of the case. It becomes less rational when applied to matters of policy, truth, and morality, where mob rule and propaganda can do the most damage. But it still has some place in academic debate, since arriving at a consensus about a subject is part of the scholarly process of discovery.

*3. Rely on Maxims, Truisms, and Conventional Wisdom.* Maxims or truisms operate in much the same fashion. We cite them not only as logical premises but also as reinforcement for our assertions. They represent the testimony of culture, tradition, and preconception—the folk wisdom of the ages. Use of maxims is something of a colloquial strategy in rhetoric, and it can be dangerous. Maxims may either be respected as collective and consensual truth or scorned as prejudices or commonplaces.

*4. Stand on Your Reputation or Authority.* Reputation and authority are of course elements of ethical appeal. By claiming authority, you can reduce the need for explicit reasoning or extensive evidence.

The mechanism is not entirely irrational. Given a choice between two positions equally well supported and defended, we are likely to choose the one championed by an author who seems more experienced, wiser, better known, more widely respected, more mature, or more authoritative (though not necessarily more powerful or strong).

This preference is based on the reasonable basis that such an author's opinions should carry more weight. There are all-too-frequent exceptions to this rule, but the credence granted to reputation is quite natural, nevertheless.

*5. Rely on Associations.* Associations are topics connected with your point in a tangential or nonlogical way. They may reflect connotations of your subject or attitudes present in your audience. They may reflect casual regroupings or combinations of ideas, facts, and events not normally perceived as belonging in the same category.

The subject of justice might, for instance, be associated in the mind with topics like patriotism, courage, labor unions, and education and with objects like a traffic sign, the Bill of Rights, a social security check, a robe, and so on. These things do not comprise or explain justice, but they may be of significant and reasonable service in supporting your claims. Misused or abused, they become false agendas (supplanting the real issues) and inappropriate emotional appeals.

*6. Cite Analogies.* An analogy is a parallel case—usually simpler and more generally known—that helps explain and support the subject in question. The process of electrical conduction, for instance, might be likened to water flowing in a stream. A truly useful analogy illuminates the subject, makes it accessible and believable in much the same way as does a narrative.

*7. Use Representation in Place of Arguments.* Representation and other graphic devices can be used in place of or in support of arguments based on the future, on ideals, on reality, and on fact.

Representation is the mirror image of reasoning. To put the case before the audience "as it is happening" can have greater effect and immediacy than itemizing in detail the points of logic and law that apply to the situation. Literature is more persuasive than science.

The effect of graphic representation depends partially on its ability to make the subject seem like a part of the audience's direct personal experience, to make readers feel like they, too, are witnesses to the crime or observers present during a scientific discovery. It makes them the accomplices of the speaker.

Some of the possibilities include the following:

**Narrative Support.** Narrative or storytelling functions as support when the story makes the author's point of view seem more real and valid, more authentic. It can reify an otherwise abstract argument, thereby rendering the case more solid and convincing.

**Imagery as Support.** Metaphors are nonlogical comparisons, asserted not so much to explain the subject as to expand it or make it graphic. A metaphor basically proposes that A is like B or that A is B, even though the equation is not technically true. The claim that "My love is like a red, red rose" may emphasize, reify, and "support" the author's feelings and thereby further his suit, but it does not deal in facts or in logical evidence.

The metaphor may also be used to stand for or take the place of more complex and logical support. Saying that "A terrible beauty is born" implies dilemmas and consequences that the author does not elucidate. The saying "A stitch in time saves nine" metaphorically represents a whole pattern of events and behavior. As we imagine the many circumstances that fit the image, we essentially are collecting evidence that supports the contention being made.

Appropriate images may also create emotional involvement in the audience. The issue can be cast in a favorable light by metaphorical association with a pleasant or affecting subject. And obviously it may serve as well to associate unpleasant images and impressions with the arguments of the opposition.

**Connotations and Key Words as Support.** Greater impact and the impression of substance may be gained by choosing and repeating a few key words that have strong connotations for your audience, that imply the whole agenda they want or you offer. Typical of these would be the repeated use of the word *jobs* in a political campaign aimed at a depressed blue-collar economy, or the word *engineering* in an auto commercial.

This device is similar to what Kenneth Burke in *A Rhetoric of Motives* (1969) calls "god terms"—words like *freedom, democracy,* and *family* that are used to denote an entire philosophy or way of life.

Such words and phrases not only save one the time of explaining all they imply, but they also can be especially memorable and quite effective as rallying cries. For that reason, writers, political movements, and special interest groups often develop a memorable catch phrase or acronym that sums up and represents their point of view.

**Scenarios as Support.** Scenarios are imagined outcomes—narrative, descriptive, and analytic accounts of what might, could, or should happen if a particular decision is made. They attempt to predict the future, either reasoning from causes to effects, projecting from current trends, or basing the prognosis on parallel events. Authors often provide "best-case" and "worst-case" scenarios, claiming to represent the best and worst that can occur in response to an action, or other multiple views of what will occur.

Scenarios have several effects. They appear to provide concrete evidence or examples, when in fact they do not. They may have the inspiriting effect of narrative, as well, making the subject take on new life and meaning. Done well, scenarios prevent the audience from focusing on or recognizing other possible outcomes, thereby controlling the agenda of discussion. Because they frequently correspond to our wishes and fears, they may offer the attractiveness of wish fulfillment and the exhilaration of near disaster. And they may also benefit from the appearance of vision or imagination in the author.

**Ideal Cases and Ironies as Support.** Ideals and ironies, discussed in Chapter 12 as elements of criticism, also contribute to nonlogical support. They reflect our values and attitudes in an unanalyzed or unreduced form. The "ideal city," for example, is a kind of best-case scenario, combining and heightening all that we appreciate or wish for in the places we have lived. In like manner, an ironic view of child rearing might show a parent figure teaching children how to steal. An ironic view of bureaucracy might show it to be not merely frustrating and impersonal but malevolent. Ironies give us a perverse or distorted view of the subject, interpreting it in light of the author's attitudes or feelings.

Both ideals and ironies convey the impression of support, combining an implied argument with the effect or impact of example. They have many of the same virtues as scenarios and require less direct justification. But they also are less able to sustain direct criticism, since they may be dismissed as warped, emotional, or idealistic views.

*8. Create Identification.* Identification includes the processes of creating empathy between the author and audience, of generating a feeling of attachment, adherence, or participation between the audience and subject, or of forming and evoking a sense of community within the audience. Kenneth Burke perceives this as the central talent of persuasion, as an art of courtship or ingratiation (not unlike Plato's conception that rhetoric is the art of enchanting the soul).

Authors who ingratiate themselves with the audience seem more like colleagues or compatriots. We recognize them as citizens of our community, group, or culture and accept their views as our own. We identify with them.

Conversely, an author may benefit from being idolized, from appearing so attractive, talented, effective, or charismatic that parts of the audience suspend judgment, either admiring the author or imagining themselves to be like him or her.

*9. Create an Attractive Scene or Setting.* Another mechanism for persuading through identification is to romanticize the setting or culture associated with your point of view. People identify with surroundings and the community as well as with individuals. This strategy is a common device in advertising.

A romanticized setting depicts a state of affairs so appealing and attractive that the audience wishes to be a part of it or immodestly perceives itself that way. The attractive setting need not be an ideal; a pleasant, somewhat pastoral sense of normalcy is more likely to evoke the recognition response that identification depends on.

*10. Appeal to an Existing Sense of Community.* Evoking a sense of community can be an easy and disreputable substitute for reasoning. If the audience already has a strong sense of identity—as reflected in its patriotism, national pride, traditions, and culture—then an author can feed off this chauvinism by selecting topics, words, and attitudes that the audience associates with itself and its beliefs. The result, however, may be little better than demagoguery or jingoism. Done more discreetly, the effect is that of proper sentiment, justifiable anger, reasonable or conservative values, and "right thinking."

*11. Create a Sense of Community.* If no real sense of community exists, if the situation is ill defined or chaotic, or if the audience is fragmented and disverse, the task of inspiring a sense of togetherness and teamwork can be daunting. And even if you do manage to accomplish the feat, it may be taken for granted. The advantages, however, are great, since people who identify with each other will work together more effectively, with less internal competition.

Traditional approaches to creating community include the following:

**Community Based on a Perceived Crisis.** One of the most common means of building community can also be the least attractive: the practice of creating a sense of urgency or, much the same thing, proclaiming that an emergency exists. The presence of crisis, a perceived enemy, or an open war tends to bring people together, to force them to focus on common interests or survival and to suspend active judgment.

This is all well and good if the crisis is real, but unprincipled (or simply neurotic) people sometimes benefit by perceiving crises where there are none. Under the guise of martial law, the unprincipled person can halt normal and free debate of the issues. And actions may be taken that the audience would not, under other circumstances, agree to. The crisis is used to supplant justification or support.

**Community Based on an Appealing Goal.** More attractive is the process of defining a specific and appealing goal for the community. By focusing the audience's attention on a common task or objective, the author diminishes friction and creates a fund of shared experience that brings the group together. This seems an intuitively obvious and simple method, but it is quite difficult to convince people to commit time and effort to any goal when the benefits are not immediate and clear. The problem lies in overcoming inertia, doubt, and complacency. The familiarity, if not always the comfort, of the status quo is difficult to argue with.

**Community Based on Common Culture and Experience.** A sense of community can also be engendered by education, by teaching the audience a common tradition, culture, skill, knowledge, or set of beliefs. People who share ideas and technologies may perceive each other as friends and coworkers, whether the endeavor is the pursuit of knowledge or practice of a craft. People who share beliefs may recognize each other as partners in the faith.

A related device is to forge a common experience where little existed before, even if it means contriving a shared adventure or outing. People cast together and forced to rely on one another often come away feeling that they have more in common than just the event itself.

**Community Based on Good Humor and Acceptance.** Community can be inspired by entertainment, acceptance, and good humor. This may take the form of friendly teasing, clowning, and self-depreciation. It may include simple respect for and accommodation of differences of opinion. It may be furthered by social gatherings and celebrations.

Some of these effects are temporary or ephemeral, but a consistently accepting and good-humored approach can ease differences within a fragmented audience and hence lead to resolution and compromise.

## EXERCISE D

Develop a persuasive case for one of the following situations. Emphasize impression and identification rather than argument and support.

1. Selling a new soft drink
2. A campaign for a political candidate (real or imagined)
3. Not leaving pets alone in parked cars, even with the windows partially opened

4. Allowing students more (or less) freedom of choice in the selection of courses at school

5. Banning or limiting the use of fertilizers on lawns

6. Increasing aid to disadvantaged children

7. Increasing tax breaks for businesses

8. Raising or lowering the maximum speed limit

9. Buying American (or foreign) cars

10. Increasing attention to math and science skills

## WHEN TO BE REASONABLE

Styles that emphasize reasoning attempt to accumulate and present a strong array of arguments, counterarguments or refutations, supporting facts and examples, background information, principles, and corroborative interpretations. They may address the issues squarely and attempt, through the collective weight of evidence and support, to prove that the claim being made is true or that the recommendation being offered is preferable to others.

Reasoning attempts to represent the author's point of view—and to convince the audience to agree with it—in an analytical, linear, and cumulative fashion. It portrays the subject by taking it apart and showing us the pieces one at a time—by explaining how things fit together, what they mean, and why they are desirable.

Reasoning is appropriate

- in academic and scientific discourse
- when the audience will listen to reason
- in report
- when supporting an established viewpoint
- when you carry the burden of proof
- when working through channels
- when speaking from authority

## WHEN TO BE PERSUASIVE

Styles that emphasize identification or making an impression or are more holistic and phenomenological; that is, they attempt to represent and convey a sense of the whole subject, the whole experience, an entire point of view or perspective—*without* analyzing it, without breaking it down into constituent parts, separate arguments and issues, or subcategories and subtopics.

Such styles seek to engender adherence, identification, sympathy, and aspiration, almost a desire for the programs and ideas of the author. Used against the opposition, they seek to create distaste, to isolate and ostracize opposing authors and ideas, to separate or put distance distance between them and the audience.

Persuasion is appropriate

- when questioning beliefs or policies
- when the issue is identity or community
- when taking an adversarial stance
- when time is short
- when forced to work outside of normal operating channels
- in democratic leadership styles

## GAINS AND LOSSES

### ◀ REASONING ▶

| Advantages | Disadvantages |
|---|---|
| Detailed and thorough impressiveness | May lose perspective |
| May control an audience that cannot challenge it | May be tyrannical and inhumane |
| Suggests fairness | May only appear true |
| Appeals to learned audiences | May seem weak to an unlearned audience |
| Sense of finality | Lacks emotional impact |

## GAINS AND LOSSES

### ◀ PERSUASION ▶

| Advantages | Disadvantages |
|---|---|
| Emotional impact | May seem unreasonable |
| More adherence | More opposition |
| Greater stylistic range | More dependent on performance |
| Leadership connotations | Ties author to positions being advocated |
| Less attention to detail | Less certitude |

## *Wider Implications*

What makes an essay or theory convincing is not as obvious as it might seem. In some cases, the style alone is accepted as if it were proof: an author's assertiveness may be taken as evidence that his or her claims are true, on the theory that anyone so sure of himself or herself must know what he or she is talking about. An author's reputation or status can likewise reduce the need for evidence.

Familiarity matters, as well: even persons regarded as know-nothings and fools are often listened to and believed when they are well known to the audience. They are usually granted more credit than either newcomers to the group or total outsiders, however much these newcomers may know or however much evidence the outsiders adduce to support their contentions.

### THE INSUFFICIENCY OF EVIDENCE

What seems like airtight evidence may be discounted for other reasons: it may be perceived as sandbagging or rationalization, for instance. It may be dismissed as smug and condescending or resented as tyrannical, self-serving interpretation of the facts. The most patently obvious claims may be attacked despite the evidence, in part because the readers are jealous of the author's discovery, in part because they resent what seems like advice or preaching. The truth is unwelcome when it appears to preempt our own ideas. We would much rather think we made the discovery ourselves.

### EVIDENCE AND VERISIMILITUDE

In the abstract, however, all logical evidence or proof is based on the principle of verisimilitude—the degree to which a claim is shown to fit the facts, predict what will happen, or adequately explain the phenomenon. Verisimilitude is the property of being true to life or accurate. It may be sought either through analysis of the subject, as in scientific descriptions and generalizations, or through representation, as in artistic portrayals and imaginative characterizations.

This standard of proof is a fairly commonsensical notion at heart—demanding only that the depiction of reality should correspond to what is there to be seen, that any theory should be demonstrably accurate. Unfortunately, this is easier said than done. Reality is too complex to be described completely. Something is always left out. There are, more often than not, wide differences of opinion about the facts of a given case, and even when the basic facts are agreed on, multiple interpretations of their meaning are usually possible.

## EXAGGERATION AS SUPPORT

Some representations and theories appear true even when they are not—indeed, they may appear more true *because* they exaggerate, heighten, or alter the facts. We often prefer to see the world as we would like it to be, or fear it to be, rather than as it is. And some theories that are entirely defensible seem patently false, clumsy, or absurd—because they are counterintuitive, because they challenge the evidence of our senses, because they do not fit our expectations or wishes, or because they contradict accepted beliefs.

## SUPPORT AS REPRESENTATION

Both support based on reasoning and support based on vision are attempts to achieve the appearance of truth. Logical and analytic discussion attempts to understand the subject, present a case, and prove a claim by taking the issue apart, by subdividing it. Visionary and holistic argument attempts to apprehend and present the subject in entirety, to prove its point by graphically representing the phenomenon, outcome, conceptual framework, or belief in question.

## APPROPRIATENESS IN SUPPORT

How much evidence is required, and what kinds of evidence are acceptable, is often determined by the situation for which you are writing. In friendly discussion, much evidence may be taken on faith. Arguments may be less fully developed. But the conventions of reasoning change with the circumstances. Science, for instance, requires statistically valid and replicable proof based on observation and experiment.

In a court of law, the evidence pertinent to a case is very narrowly defined: much that the general public would regard as relevant is usually inadmissible—like the previous conviction record of a drug dealer. The standards of proof applied in legal decisions are that any claims must conform to established principle and precedent (or when precedent fails, to the spirit of the law), must be supported with factual evidence and valid logic, and must be established beyond all reasonable doubt—though what constitutes reasonableness is basically left to individual conscience and culture to decide.

## THE MEASURE OF PERSUASION

Persuasiveness is a much different matter. When support is based on persuasion rather than proof, the standard of success is not accuracy but effectiveness—whether in fact you accomplish your objectives, influence decisions, change people's minds, or get people to do what you want.

### REASONING AS AN ELEMENT OF PERSUASION

Logical proof does not disappear when persuasion is the aim, though the standards of evidence may change to a degree. Scientific proof requires a statistically valid sampling—evidence drawn from enough different cases to ensure that one's generalizations do, in fact, represent the general nature of the subject. If you only study one or two cases, there is always the danger that the instances chosen might be aberrant or atypical.

Persuasion is not necessarily subject to the same constraints. When the aim is effect rather than accuracy, authors may choose to rely on a single, telling example instead of on statistically valid proof. If statistics are used, they may be inserted more for their sense of authority and impregnability than for the sake of accuracy. Authors seeking to persuade may purposely omit evidence that does not directly support or that contradicts their contentions. They may heighten or diminish the significance of particular facts or events.

### PARTIAL OR IMPLIED EVIDENCE IN PERSUASION

Scientific or logical proof also requires an author to represent his or her reasoning completely. This means that, insofar as it is possible, one's assumptions and theoretical framework must be discussed, one's methodology described, one's data displayed for all to see, and one's reasoning—from premises to conclusions—explicitly presented.

Persuasion is seldom so thorough. Methodology is largely irrelevant in persuasive discourse. It does not matter how the conclusions were reached or how the data was collected. What matters is defending and emphasizing their significance. Persuasive discourse tends to use graphic and sketchy information rather than detailed accounts. It may substitute personality for ideology, implying rather than stating a theoretical framework. Its assumptions are often unexpressed. Persuasion tends to rely on readers to supply part of the reasoning themselves—to almost unconsciously fill in the logic from their store of experiences, observations, and preconceptions.

## *Conclusion*

Building a case and making an impression are often different means to the same end. Both seek to portray the subject. Both seek to change people's minds. Both seek to increase the credibility or authority of the author.

They are not mutually exclusive, either. Patient and methodical attention to building a case and providing evidence creates its own kind of useful impression. We may identify with the author's scholarship and attention to detail and feel all the more respect for the point of view that emerges from the evidence amassed—the image or vision we infer from the data and reasoning. By the same token, support based on making an impression may embody valid and accurate observation. The holistic viewpoint may reveal aspects of the subject that would be lost or devalued in the process of analysis.

Reasoning and identification are in some ways interdeterminate. Effective writing requires both. It needs both proof and persuasion, both evidence and vision, both content and form, both data and a conceptual framework. It requires the ability to explain and support a theory rationally and the ability to imagine and shape a theory or point of view in the first place.

When reasoning or persuasion are wisely and constructively used, their benefits are quite the same. Both are means of creating consensus, forming beliefs, and testing or refining our store of knowledge. They represent fundamental processes through which people manage to work together, agree with each other, make decisions, trade ideas or property, and form relationships.

Recourse to demonstration and debate allows us to measure one opinion against another, to examine the merits of competing theories, proposals, or claims, and thereby to make intelligent choices about what to believe, what to do, and how to interpret what we see and experience. Without them, one opinion would seem as good as the next.

## ASSIGNMENT A:   Peacemaking, Intercession, and Confrontation

1. Put yourself in the position of addressing people on both sides of an intellectual, political, or ethical dispute. Your role is to try to bring them to some degree of mutual understanding or to a compromise, if not to a rapprochement. Anticipate making little headway. Be content with small victories.

2. Identify two ideas or concepts that are diametrically opposed (for instance, the effects of nature and nurture on education), discuss the two extreme positions, and argue for some compromise view.

3. Writing primarily for people who have not yet taken sides on some issue, stand up to and argue against a point of view that has swept away, inhibited, or intimidated most opposition. Be prepared to attack and refute arguments that appear to the opposition to be eminently reasonable, morally correct, and perfectly true. Or consider making a counterattack based on identification and "courtship" rather than on reasoning and argument.

4. Debate with yourself the validity of your point of view on a subject. Discuss the sources of your opinions and the evidence on which they are based. Identify weaknesses in your argument and consider how you might answer objections people might raise.

5. For the purposes of argument only (without actually committing yourself to the view), take an extreme position on a subject and discuss what arguments, evidence, and benefits support it. Conclude by discussing what this extreme position teaches us, why it is either all too true or why it is untrue or untenable, and what a more moderate and practical point of view might be.

## ASSIGNMENT B:   Negotiation

1. Put yourself in the role of mediator between two or more adversaries in some practical, legal, or business matter, trying to explain to the various parties what each side wants and why and attempting to facilitate their reaching an agreement.

2. Write up and explain a hypothetical contract, deal, offer, proposal, settlement, or treaty (imaginary, historical, or in the context of a straightforward essay suggesting how some problem might be resolved). Assume that both parties involved are interested in pursuing self-interest at some expense to the other. But recognize that both sides must get something out of the deal for it to turn into a good working relationship.

## ASSIGNMENT C:   Advocacy, Promotion, and Proselytism

1. Select an existing product, region, point of view, or institution and extol its merits, using emotional, ethical, and logical appeals, attacks on the competition (where appropriate or effective), refutation of any negatives about the subject that might occur to people, identification, and image building. Create a role for yourself that justifies and explains your speaking on the subject.

2. Analyze an existing ad campaign, promotion, or public image (of an institution, celebrity, political figure, business, or product). Review its merits and weaknesses. Develop, describe, and propose an alternative, explaining why your version should replace, refine, or supplement the existing campaign or public image.

3. Take the role of an advocate or partisan, explaining and attempting to spread a point of view, a lifestyle, or an attitude and belief. See yourself as something of a cheerleader, promoting and building enthusiasm for the subject.

## ASSIGNMENT D:   Accusation and Defense

1. Defend someone's reputation against a charge, complaint, or characterization you perceive as unfair. Or focus on an institution, organization, business, social group, or point of view that is similarly stigmatized.

2. Charge someone with unfairness, lack of vision, or a similar offense. Or level the charge against an institution, organization, business, social group, or point of view. Be prepared to support your charge in a thorough and ethical manner. Name calling and mud slinging are too easy, too misleading, and too destructive.

## ASSIGNMENT E:   Excuse and Justification

Excuse or attempt to justify some action commonly thought blameworthy, wrongheaded, or foolish—your own or someone else's actions, or a current or historical event.

### ANALYSIS

SUBJECTS: Any offense might call for excuse or justification—from something trivial, like being late for a meeting or forgetting to acknowledge a birthday, to a serious international blunder or even a criminal offense. Justifying what is perceived as a notorious offense may seem original.

AUTHOR: This puts you in the position of being an apologist, identifying yourself with a cause your audience has already judged harshly. In the case of your own minor offenses, you may be seen as weak or afraid of punishment. In extreme and public cases, you may be seen as either immoral or something of a traitor. Defending the indefensible is often required in law, politics, statecraft, and sales.

Your hope might be to cast yourself as a defender of the underdog or as the white knight riding in to correct an injustice. Not altogether ethical but common is the practice of emphasizing positive aspects of the situation to the exclusion of negative features. When the offense is real and great and not subject to much reinterpretation, your role might be that of a historian, trying to develop in the audience a more complete understanding of the subject or to focus its attention on issues other than moral indignation.

AUDIENCE: The audience is likely to have a fixed opinion on the subject. In its eyes, there is no excuse for the behavior being defended. In many cases, the blameworthy action is associated with strong emotions in the audience. Some moral code has been broken or some personal injury has been suffered. In the case of foolish actions, the audience generally feels superior.

The audience is likely to rely on fairly static and simplified interpretations of historical incidents. It is likely to be surprised or shocked that someone would even attempt to defend the action in question.

OCCASION AND SITUATION: Excuse and justification are, of course, frequently used at the very moment the offense is discovered, as when a child tries to shift blame for a broken window away from himself or herself.

Writers often choose to discuss historical events on the anniversaries of such incidents or when a parallel current event brings them to mind. The desire to correct an injustice or misperception, however, is sufficient reason for writing in this vein. Apology (in the classical sense of a justification, rather than an asking for forgiveness) is often used by people who have been the subject of some controversy and use their writing to explain and defend their actions.

SUPPORT AND PERSUASION: Common arguments used to support excuses include claiming that a more important or prior commitment caused the lapse, shifting blame to a subordinate or superior, blaming one's sources of information, blaming an accident on circumstances beyond one's control, claiming a misunderstanding occurred, claiming ignorance or inability, and claiming good intent. Less common is the ploy of accepting or acknowledging blame. Saying nothing at all, publicly refusing to comment, or refusing to confirm or deny a charge can be reasonable and effective options as well. The hope is to appear to be above petty judgments and gossip.

To justify an action, one needs to prove that it was, after all, the right thing to do in spite of evidence and opinion to the contrary. This may force the writer to refute the accepted judgment. It may entail showing that the action was a success on terms other than those typically applied to it, or that the action, while not the moral thing to do, was at least explicable on pragmatic or emotional grounds. Justification might also be found in long-term consequences, in personal rather than public satisfaction, and in intangible results.

The most direct form of justification, however, would be to reassess all the losses and gains, all the consequences and results, all the virtues and errors that are usually cited in reference to the event, and to find that the good outweighs the bad. In the absence of new information, this may be accomplished by minimizing some dire consequences commonly held dear and by magnifying benefits, a procedure that need not be sophistic. It is possible to argue rightfully for a reapportionment of blame.

Common forms of persuasion in apology include humanizing oneself or the perpetrator; retelling the story in dramatic form, making the appropriate characters more sympathetic and the events more readily excusable; attacking those who assessed blame in the first place (attacking their motives or information, for instance); and shifting the status or perspective of the debate—from morality to historical truth, for instance, or from injuries suffered to more abstract consequences, like economic effects or public opinion.

# 16

# Organization: Formal and Organic

Digressions, incontestably, are the sunshine;—they are the life, the soul of reading;—take them out of this book for instance,—you might as well take the book along with them.                    —LAURENCE STERNE

Every discourse ought to be a living creature, having a body of its own and a head and feet; there should be a middle, beginning, and end, adapted to one another and to the whole.                    —PLATO

## Managing People and Ideas

Organization is a question of management and design. Its goals are (1) to establish relationships between ideas, (2) to present information in an accessible and attractive pattern or sequence, and (3) to create an effect on the audience. Good organization in an essay inspires confidence and security. It makes us feel that the speaker is decisive and in control, that the author knows where he or she is going.

But while it is attractive to look organized, there are also times when a degree of uncertainty, if not disorder, is pleasing. It introduces an element of surprise and danger, suggests flexibility and a willingness to take chances, a touch of randomness, a disregard for method and law. Being organized can mean being predictable.

The choice, however, is not so much between order and disorder as it is between methodical and dramatic presentation, between mechanical and organic form.

Methodical organization is evident in structure based on categories, lists, formats, and preannounced patterns of development. It may also result from presenting information in a sequence based on logical demonstration and proof, research design, or straightforward chronology. It may be perceived as good or bad.

### ◀ METHODICAL ORGANIZATION ▶

| Good Qualities | Bad Qualities |
| --- | --- |
| efficient | mechanical |
| controlled | routine |
| clear | barren |
| practical | commonplace |

Dramatic organization is more concerned with creating an effect or cumulative result than with outlining and transmitting data. It makes the essay an emotional or intellectual experience, a discovery, event, or revelation.

The appearance of structure may arise from the internal shape of the author's ideas and beliefs, from a coherent personality or perspective, from the desired effect on the reader, or from the untidy patterns of discovery and speculation (as opposed to the rigid sequences of designed research, formal logic, and prescribed decision-making procedures).

If it is handled well, dramatic form should not seem incoherent (though it may purposely meander or be intentionally disconnected when the occasion warrants it). But even at its best, dramatic form may be judged harshly by some though well-received by others. It may be considered good or bad.

### ◀ DRAMATIC ORGANIZATION ▶

| Good Qualities | Bad Qualities |
| --- | --- |
| intuitive | digressive |
| imaginative | undisciplined |
| surprising | unplanned |
| spontaneous | unprepared |

## *Finding Direction*

Organization is often thought of as a fairly simple or obvious matter, no more than a process of sorting ideas into appropriate categories or following some preset pattern. Such conceptions of arrangement are based on a desire for efficiency and economy in expression—on getting the job done with as little effort as possible—and on a highly simplified view of ideas and information, the notion that thoughts can be readily summed up in words, and that data, once acquired, is easy to transmit. One need only be clear and straightforward about it. Unfortunately, this is easier said than done. The process of structuring and communicating ideas is as complex as the process of arriving at them.

Organization in discourse is more than just a filing system. The arrangement of an essay is part of its content. It tells how your thoughts fit together, and it reflects the complexity and depth of your viewpoint. It is a means of dramatizing and portraying information and concepts, of educating and persuading an audience, of establishing a relationship between the author and reader, of creating an intellectual context or framework, a network of ideas. It reflects or represents the conceptual organization of the author's mind.

## Being Methodical

Organization appears methodical when it seems to follow a preset plan, when the author exerts control over the material. The arrangement of an essay may appear more methodical if you do the following:

*1. Use a Thesis Statement to Announce Your Focus.* Mechanically structured arrangement is more likely to use the traditional thesis statement—to sum up the main ideas or point of the essay in the introduction. In one or more sentences it explicitly states the proposition to be discussed or debated (for example, "Motorcycles are dangerous").

A simple thesis statement has two parts: a topic and a controlling idea (Joseph Gallo and Henry Rink, *Shaping College Writing*, 4th ed. San Diego: Harcourt, 1985). The topic is the immediate focus of the discussion; the controlling idea expresses an evaluation or interpretation of the topic. It is useful to recognize in this the operation of basic "set" theory. The thesis statement in its simplest form represents the overlap of two categories or sets of information—in this case, all things pertaining to motorcycles and all things pertaining to danger.

*2. Formally Announce Your Direction or Plan of Organization.* Mechanical structure also commonly includes in the introduction (usually at the end of the introduction) a clearcut statement of direction. This is a plain and unequivocal agenda for the essay, telling exactly what will follow and in what order.

Typically, the statement of direction will directly or indirectly list the subtopics, issues, or points of support the reader can expect to see discussed at length in the body of the essay (e.g., "The sources of the danger are the motorcycle's inherent instability, its lack of protection for the rider, and its relative invisibility on the road").

In classical rhetoric, the "division" of the issue was a separate section of the oration, placed immediately after the prologue or exordium and the narration of the facts of the case and before the confirmation or proof. Essentially, the function of this section was to establish what the orator felt were the major elements of the case or issues to be addressed. In modern legal debate, this element of the oration survives as an enumeration of that which must be proven to establish guilt. A section that divides the question may also be useful in long essays.

*3. Use Topic Sentences.*    Mechanical organization often further emphasizes the pattern of development by placing a topic sentence near the beginning of each section or paragraph in the body of the essay. These topic sentences are usually subdivisions of the thesis statement. In their most obvious form, they even restate the basic elements of the thesis (e.g., "Motorcycles are dangerous because they are unstable"; "Motorcycles are dangerous because they provide no protection for the rider"; and "Motorcycles are also dangerous because they are difficult for others to see"). Discussion ensues after each of these points to explain or prove the individual contentions.

*4. Stay on the Subject.*    Highly structured arrangement puts far greater emphasis on unity and continuity. What is referred to as "staying on the same topic"—that is, excluding side issues and details that do not clearly and obviously pertain to the basic premise—will make the essay seem more mechanical in form.

Explained in terms of the thesis statement, this means that nothing will be included in the essay that does not pertain to both parts of the thesis—to the topic and the controlling idea. If the thesis establishes a conjunction between the set of things pertaining to motorcycles and the set of things pertaining to danger, then subjects like "fun" or "merchandising" would seem (at least at first glance) to be excluded from the essay, since they do not clearly fit in both categories at once.

*5. Distribute Your Material in Separate Paragraphs and Sections.*    Paragraphs and sections of essays are both features of the development of an essay and elements of structure. Well-defined paragraphs can at least make the material look like it has been sorted and distributed into clearly distinct places, even if there is little progression from paragraph to paragraph or little sense in the division.

More effective paragraphing establishes separate and progressive levels or locations in the discussion, points at which the audience can explore and comprehend a manageable part of the topic before moving on to the next idea. Paragraphs and sections seem designed to deal with the limitations of human memory and cognition. For that reason, they are usually of a length that the anticipated audience can reasonably be expected to hold in its mind at once.

*6. Classify, Divide, or Enumerate the Material.*   Mechanical structure is likely to emphasize classification, division, and enumeration as patterns of development. Classification collects the data in separate, parallel groups (e.g., car buyers with incomes below $15,000, with incomes between $15,000 and $30,000, with incomes between $30,000 and $45,000, and so on).

Division takes a unified whole apart, revealing its components (e.g., the body has various internal systems, namely the muscular, circulatory, reproductive, skeletal, and digestive systems). Enumeration lists parallel or miscellaneous information (e.g., "The decline in the stock market appears to have been caused by three factors. The first of these was . . .").

*7. Use Obvious or Conventional Formats.*   Mechanical structure in style may be reflected in obvious or "outlined" formats, often divided into sections based on conventions, methodology, or procedural requirements. Here are a few examples:

**Scientific/Technical Report Form**

Introduction (including the author's hypothesis)
Review of research
Research design and procedures, description of site
Findings
Discussion or implications
Conclusion

**Classical Oration**

| | |
|---|---|
| Exordium | or introduction |
| Narration | of the situation or crime |
| Division | of the question |
| Confirmation | or proof |
| Refutation | of opposing arguments |
| Peroration | or summation |

**Proposal Format**

Abstract or overview
Recommendation

Alternatives (a comparative review)
Rationale or objectives
Best- and worst-case scenarios
Procedures, cost analysis, or implementation

**Letter of Application Format**

Formal request for consideration
Review of one's qualifications or special talents
Review of one's pertinent experience
Review of one's education
Formal close

There are many possible variations on such formats. The order of specific sections may be changed. Some material may be omitted or combined. Other issues may be included as necessary.

Specific audiences, organizations, journals, and disciplines often develop their own formats. You should consult these conventions before you write.

*8. Use Headings and Formal Manuscript Divisions.* Headings, subheadings, titles for chapters, and tables of contents can emphasize existing organization and help to clarify structure in material you don't quite have control of yet.

## EXERCISE A

Brainstorm ideas on one or more of the following topics, and then organize the resulting material in categories and subcategories, excluding information that doesn't fit and adding new ideas where needed.

Finally, write a short essay that presents the categorized material in a methodical fashion.

1. Things people consider funny
2. Things people consider private
3. Plants people cultivate
4. Things that use electricity
5. Forms of music
6. The modern necessities
7. Studying for exams
8. Government services and responsibilities
9. Political candidates
10. Parents

**11.** Sources of stress

**12.** Sources of conflict

**13.** Admirable and/or lucrative occupations

**14.** Road hazards

**15.** Kinds of books

## *Being Dramatic*

The structure of an essay appears more dramatic when the organization seems to develop before our eyes, when the material seems to control the author's thoughts or when the direction of the essay seems to exert some control over the emotions and thoughts of the audience.

The arrangement of an essay appears more organic and dramatic when you do the following:

*1. Follow the Pattern of Discovery.*   Organic arrangement tends to follow the pattern of discovery, to mimic or represent the writer's thought processes as he or she explores the subject. It may, therefore, include direct references to the thinking process, in the form of phrases like "It occurs to me" or "From this evidence I conclude that. . . ."

The essay may suggest that the thinking and writing are happening at the same time or may report on a discovery process in the past tense. It may present the thinking in chronological order or in stages of development. It is somewhat more likely than methodical form to include the normal digressions, false starts, and emotional reactions of thought than to "clean up" the mental processes, representing them in tidy, logical form.

*2. Incorporate New Ideas: Change Direction.*   Because of the emphasis on discovery, one common feature of organic arrangement is the gradual or sudden incorporation of new material, as if the author had just changed his or her mind, just discovered a new idea, or just recognized another implication of the topic.

*3. Speculate About the Subject.*   Organic form is often more speculative in stance and content. The author views the subject not as a fixed body of knowledge to be reported on but as an area to be explored, a matter to be discussed and examined. The author is likely to question or doubt existing truths and may offer his or her own conclusions as tentative.

*4. Avoid Conventional Formats and Classifications.*   Organic form, by definition, is an ad hoc plan of arrangement—designed for the particular occasion only. To impose any exterior convention on the essay automatically makes it more mechanical, less responsive to the moment at hand.

*5. Refer to the Specific Context.*   Because it is more case specific, organic structure may rely heavily on factors inherent in the rhetorical situation—responding to the interests and proclivities of the audience, the accidents of the moment (like a baby's cry from the back of the room), words used by the opposition, and the strengths of the immediately available evidence and appeals.

The author may incorporate into the essay an account of circumstances surrounding the thinking process—either irrelevant events or experiences that contributed to the formation of his or her conclusions.

*6. Follow Narrative Patterns.*   Organization can be based on patterns of experience. The natural sequence of events can provide a ready-made order for the presentation of material. The danger is that simple narrative— one event after another, with no differentiation between trivial and significant incidents—is all too easy to write and to slip into, and not necessarily very interesting. More sophisticated narrative can be extremely difficult to manage.

Some of the possible variations in narrative form include

- omitting or summarizing insignificant events and periods of time
- presenting events out of sequence
- having characters within the account report on some events while other incidents are actually depicted
- portraying simultaneous events, either interweaving them or presenting them in a sequence
- presenting parallel events or experiences
- juxtaposing events that inform each other
- offering several perspectives on the events depicted (as they appeared then and seem now, as they appear to different characters in the account, as they seem to the author and how they are interpreted by cited experts, and so on)
- making the author a participant in the events portrayed
- making the author an observer outside of the action
- including in the account some portrayal of the emotions and thoughts of the characters
- showing readers the action through the eyes or thoughts of one or more of the characters
- interweaving commentary and narrative
- describing the events in terms of some wider frame of reference or shaping the events to reflect some message or create an effect

Even highly abstract material may be presented in narrative form if you focus on the chronological order of your thoughts or your research.

*7. Find Structure in the Material.*   Organic form does not impose structure on the subject; it attempts to perceive and follow the form inherent in the material.

Structure inherent in the subject is most apparent in a sequence of events. But material may exhibit other natural patterns, as well. Information may be grouped by location or distribution, for example, or in perceptual order, from the larger outlines to the constituent details.

Less apparent are spatial and cognitive patterns that seem to underlie ideas and events and may even contradict the surface structure of the essay. Some of the possibilities include the following:

**Spatial Relationships Between Ideas.**   Organization based on patterns of thought and perception may include an almost spatial orientation of one topic to another—as if they were arrayed on a chart or screen, graphed in two or three dimensions, or presented as a model or apparatus. This spatial relationship may not be explicitly discussed in the essay, or it may be described in detail and even depicted.

**Conceptual Frameworks.**   The author's conceptual framework can control and give shape to complex development. Apparent unity of vision or purpose, for example, creates the impression that there is some underlying order to the discussion. A theory that explains the facts gives order to them, subordinating one detail to another, showing us how they fit together and what they mean.

When readers feel that the author has a coherent and comprehensive view of the subject, they are more likely to forgive momentary lapses in direction and clarity. The intellectual organization carries and informs the delivery.

**Perceptual Frameworks.**   Part of the seemingly inherent order of a subject comes from the way we habitually see it or the perspective from which we view it. This perceptual framework organizes, fills out, focuses, selects details, and regularizes the information we apprehend and report. Creating or drawing on a perceptual framework can not only give form to the material but enable the reader to supply some of the development.

The Grand Canyon looks different if seen from the perspective of education than if seen in terms of business and marketing. The structure of the discipline, its manner of looking at subjects, organizes both your perceptions and your presentation. If we hear a loud noise outside, we instantly search for a frame of reference that "explains" the event so we know how to react to it. If the frame that comes to mind is "explosion" or "crime," we react differently than if the frame of reference we impose on the scene is "airplane" or "the Fourth of July."

The mind is so good at regularizing experience that it attempts either to exclude from or synthesize into the framework any incongruous details. A handgun on a teacher's classroom desk might be interpreted, after a moment of confusion, as a weapon taken away from a juvenile delinquent. It would not as readily be seen as part of a physics experiment or a lesson on slow-motion photography. The same handgun lying on a stage in a school auditorium is more immediately interpreted as a prop in a school play than as a juvenile delinquent's weapon.

Since the frame of reference is education, the tendency for author and reader alike is to perceive and assign a meaning that fits the context and their expectations.

**Universal or Archetypal Patterns.**   There are subconscious or cultural patterns to be found in events, human experience, thought, and relationships—patterns that may be used in turn to shape our actions and discourse.

Some of these archetypes or universals are familiar to us from folklore, fantasy, and science fiction, like evil stepmothers and stepfathers, fairy godmothers, mad scientists, evil magicians, knights in shining armor, and mystical quests. Some are more directly a part of the human condition, like the tendency to see others in black-and-white terms, as good or bad, friend or enemy, with no middle ground, or the tendency to compete with others.

When paperwork and bureaucracy defeat us, we feel like we are "getting the runaround." When decisions are not made in our favor, we feel like "the authorities" are biased or "the system" is against us. We identify with underdogs. We associate a strong sense of closure and security with the family unit, kinship group, and tribe and hence with any small organization we belong to. We may perceive any nurturing, older man as a father figure or mentor. We may perceive any stranger to the community as a threat.

These reactions are so much a part of us that we do not necessarily recognize them for what they are: ways of "reading" and therefore organizing experience, essential structures of human thought.

Illogical though they may be, archetypes have high credibility, strong emotional connotations and deep significance for people. If you are able, through allusions or indirection, to build such patterns into your material, they may greatly increase its impact and make it seem more dramatically and organically structured.

Archetypes are not necessarily true, however. It is important to avoid simply reading into the material and events a conventional interpretation that misrepresents them.

*8. Organize Your Thoughts Around a Strong Persona.* A very strong, exaggerated, or stylized persona can provide a sense of structure. The consistent voice gives some unity and continuity to the presentation.

If the character of the author is evident enough, it can even hold together material that otherwise would seem disorganized or random. This is a common feature of comedy, but it works in other kinds of writing, as well.

*9. Use Recurrent Words and Phrases to Create Continuity.* A sense of structure can be evoked by almost poetic repetition, the recurrent use of key words and catch phrases, as in leitmotifs, rhymes, litanies, and refrains. Less formal repetition, when used in prose, may help establish some tangible, if not logical, connection between different aspects of the subject.

*10. Create Parallels.* Parelleling events, ideas, and data can provide a sense of organization. Some of this parallelism is inherent in categorization and division, but it is also possible to use grammatical, associative, and metaphorical parallels for structure.

**Grammatical Parallels.** These express ideas as a parallel series, each as the same part of speech or in the same syntactic form. For example, in writing about college students on spring break, you could talk about parties, romances, and youthful mistakes (all plural nouns) in sequence. Or you could discuss Congressional debate on a tax reform bill in terms of in-fighting, upstaging, and back-stabbing (all nominalized verbs).

Grammatical parallels focus your attention on just one dimension of the subject and group your material accordingly. The resulting series may not be logical, but it may nonetheless be effective.

**Associative Parallels.** These suggest a nonlogical equivalence between objects and ideas that are only partly similar. So, for instance, you could parallel General Patton, a particular calculus teacher, an artist, and a football player, showing how all possess a certain ruthlessness, drive, creativity, and disregard for the medium in which they work. Or in writing about trust, you could parallel discussions of air travel, banks, and neighbors.

**Metaphorical Parallels.** These assert an equivalence between subjects that are not at all related, using properties of one to explain the other. Saying "My love is nothing like the sun" or "My love is like a red, red rose" creates an inherent order, an inherent cognitive and perceptual connection between the things compared.

In prose, metaphorical parallels might be exploited to show how people perceive the stock market variously as a form of legalized gambling, as the epitome of capitalism, as a symbol of moral decline, as an adult playground, and so on. A metaphorical comparison between the condition of a person's backyard and his or her state of mind might help illustrate the nature of the subconscious or the connection between public image and private identity.

**11. Find a Common Denominator That Ties Material Together.**    Focusing on a single person, object, phenomenon, or idea can hold together diverse content and make it seem organized. There is still some continuity to the presentation if you follow one person through a number of experiences, place a single character in a number of different contexts, or interview one individual about a wide range of subjects.

A single object or event can serve as the common denominator, as well. For example, you could use the Vietnam War as the unifying element in a discussion of American values, education, industry, and laws in the 1960s, perhaps including vignettes from the lives of several public figures and common people. You could focus on a specific kind of weapon to connect a wide-ranging commentary on drugs, crime, private tragedy, and poverty.

Structure and continuity may also arise from focusing on an idea that touches on all of the various topics being addressed. The concept of self-reliance might, for instance, be referred to repeatedly throughout an otherwise disjointed account of various job successes and failures. Or the concept of ownership might be used to unify an essay that covers such otherwise unrelated subjects as the vandalism of churches, the space race, brand names, public cursing, and right-of-way while driving. (Instead of paralleling the subjects, the author would treat them as clearly different and use the concept like a key word to suggest continuity in the discussion.)

**12. Follow Changes in Perspective.**    Movement or direction in the essay may be created by pointedly shifting from one perspective to another. This strategy divides the various ways of looking at the subject, the viewpoints that might be taken. The subject might be seen from a historical perspective in the early passages of an essay, for instance, and later from political, psychological, theological, and personal perspectives in turn.

The different perspectives may also be more directly visual and descriptive, as when an author begins with a panoramic view and then focuses in on a series of details, perhaps moving from right to left, top to bottom, around the perimeter, or following some other pattern in scanning the scene.

**13. Displace One Point of View With Another.**    The appearance of direction in development may be created by beginning with one view of the subject, denying its validity, and immediately replacing it with another perspective that you suggest is more true. Often the two perspectives are diametrically opposed and fairly conventional. Some of the more common of these progressions include moving from

- before to after
- misconceptions to truth
- overt to covert meanings or stated to hidden meanings
- appearance to reality
- analysis to essence
- exterior to interior
- common knowledge to specialized knowledge
- short term to long term
- simple to complex

The movement can also be reversed. (*Note:* These patterns are related to the "although clause" discussed in Chapter 13 as a method for introducing a subject and increasing the apparent significance of your ideas.)

*14. Address Different Members of the Audience.* Movement can be created by addressing different parts of the audience in turn (as John F. Kennedy did in his Inaugural Address). This strategy divides the audience rather than the subject to create a sense of organization.

*15. Base Structure on the Audience's Knowledge of the Subject.* Organization can be based on the writer's perception of the audience's expertise. If the writer feels that the audience is relatively inexpert or uninformed, then there is a certain social and structural obligation to supply background information or explain basic concepts to the readers before moving on to more advanced or complex ideas. The author might step back even further and begin the discussion on common ground—with material the audience already knows.

Although this implies an obvious pattern—moving from common ground to basic concepts to advanced concepts—the essay does not necessarily have to follow that sequence. It is quite possible for an author to start with an advanced concept, for instance, and to follow with a discussion of the basic concepts that support it or the common knowledge to which it is related.

If the audience is well informed on the subject, the pattern of organization may change accordingly. The author might choose to begin by demonstrating his or her own expertise or by discussing an issue, then review various theories or viewpoints on the matter, and finally attempt to resolve the issue or to redefine the problem. The structure of the essay, in this case, would move from accepted knowledge to theories already under consideration in the field to the introduction of a tentative or proposed theory.

16. *Base Structure on the Audience's Attitudes.* Organization is partially based on the audience's attitudes or state of mind. If the audience appears indifferent, prejudiced, or hostile, for instance, one of the principles that guides the presentation is the need to render the audience more receptive to you and your point of view. Different material will be required and a different pattern of development than if you were simply laying out the evidence.

17. *Base Structure on the Relative Worth or Strength of Ideas.* Organization can be based in part on value judgments or beliefs. It is common advice, for instance, to determine the order or arguments according to their relative importance or strength. Arguments can be arranged from weakest to strongest or strongest to weakest. Another option is to put one of your best points first and to save another strong argument for the end of the essay, thereby hoping to avoid making a bad first impression or seeming to trail off anticlimactically.

Other hierarchical patterns can be constructed on the basis of any value or criteria. Besides the relative strength of arguments, the possibilities include relative utility, attractiveness, scope or size, speed, acceptability, newness, age, cost, and so on. Events or ideas can be arranged in terms of increasing or decreasing emotionalism. Ideas can be grouped according to their scope or range of application, objects according to their familiarity or distribution. The options are endless.

Even if the material is not actually presented in the hierarchical sequence, the audience may recognize the inherent value structure and therefore perceive your presentation as organized.

18. *Structure the Presentation to Create an Effect.* The author's purpose, objective, or intended effect may also guide the organization of the essay.

If the objective is to influence government policy, the order of presentation might be based on demonstrating the benefits that would result from pursuing a particular plan of action. If the objective is to entertain an audience by commenting on government policy, the order of presentation would be dramatically different.

## EXERCISE B

The same subjects used in Exercise A are listed here. This time, instead of brainstorming ideas and categorizing the material, start with a page or so of freewriting, or with a page of writing about a relevant personal opinion or an emotional response to the issue. Then try to generate a series of at least ten questions about the topic chosen.

Finally, write a short essay that explores and presents the issue in a dramatic or discovery-based manner.

1. Things people consider funny
2. Things people consider private
3. Plants people cultivate
4. Things that use electricity
5. Forms of music
6. The modern necessities
7. Studying for exams
8. Government services and responsibilities
9. Political candidates
10. Parents
11. Sources of stress
12. Sources of conflict
13. Admirable and/or lucrative occupations
14. Road hazards
15. Kinds of books

## Organization and the Composing Process

Organizing too soon can make it more difficult to write well and to think creatively. Organizing too late can make your research aimless and unproductive, your writing chaotic. As you explore a topic and begin to write, the following strategies may be useful:

*1. Outline the Material.* Teachers often advise students to arrange the material in a formal outline before actually beginning to write. Formal outlines are based on classifying or on dividing and subdividing the subject.

This should be done with caution, however. While some people work comfortably with formal outlines, others find that heavy advance planning of the essay's structure detracts from the quality of their writing and thinking. The problem is that outlining cannot precede thinking. If you don't have a concept or opinion to present, the outline will just be a filing system, a catalogue of things you already know.

If you already have a strong interpretation of the subject, the classification process may actually suppress or conceal it. Many complex ideas cannot be adequately represented by categorizations.

*2. Plan Ahead.*   Instead of outlines, many writers use informal lists or plans to record and keep track of what they intend to say. Usually this list is fairly tentative, a "working plan" that can be added to, changed, or abandoned as the needs of the essay dictate or the author's thoughts on the subject evolve.

People often come up with new ideas and more original perspectives on a topic as they write. If you commit to a rigid plan early and never allow any new material into the preconceived framework, your best thinking may never make it into print.

*3. Seek Alternative Patterns of Development.*   Don't assume that the first plan you think of is the only one. Write out several radically different plans for presenting the material and weigh the respective advantages of each.

*4. Organize After Drafting.*   To avoid the limiting effect of early organization, some authors write early drafts without advance planning, exerting only minimal control over the direction of the essay. Then, after they have discovered what they want to say about the subject, they rewrite to improve the focus and structure of the work.

Sometimes formal outlining and conventional formats are particularly useful at this stage in the composing process. After the basic message has been developed and explored, methodical arrangement can be imposed on the material without sacrificing originality and effect.

*5. Compress After Drafting ("Nutshelling").*   It can also be useful to try to abstract or sum up an essay after a rough draft has been written. As you compress the ideas into a single paragraph, you are forced to articulate the transitions and relationships between ideas. The result is a clearer sense of the internal or logical structure of your overall point of view. When you revise the larger essay, this coherence can be clarified and exploited to provide direction for the entire work.

## *Topical Progression*

One aspect of arrangement, the introduction of new information into an essay, is perhaps best described in terms of topical progression. This approach to organization is derived from the research of the Prague School of linguistics. It has been applied to larger questions of revision and structure by Stephen Witte in "Topical Structure and Revision" (*College Composition and Communication* 34 [Oct. 1983]), and to paragraphing by Robin Bell Markels in *A New Perspective on Cohesion in Expository Paragraphs* (1984).

The basic premise of topical progression is that discourse continually moves from old information to new information, gradually incorporating additional ideas into the discussion. Coherence and organization are created by connecting new topics to ideas previously mentioned in an essay.

On the sentence level, this is reflected in interlocking patterns of topics. If topics A and B are introduced in the first sentence, then to appear coherent the next sentence must include either A or B as one of its elements. If it is mentioned early in the next sentence, the sequence may seem more immediately and obviously coherent than if it is mentioned late. By this definition, the following patterns could be coherent:

| | |
|---|---|
| AB—AC | Motorcycles are dangerous. They should be banned. |
| AB—BC | Motorcycles are dangerous. But danger is part of life. |
| AB—ABC | Motorcycles are dangerous. They are unsafe but fun to ride. |
| AB—BAC | Motorcycles are dangerous. But the dangers they present are less serious than they seem. |
| AB—CA | Motorcycles are dangerous. People like them anyway. |
| AB—CB | Motorcycles are dangerous. People like danger. |
| AB—CAB | Motorcycles are dangerous. Statistics show that motorcycle riders are more likely to be seriously injured in accidents. |
| AB—CBAD | Motorcycles are dangerous. Technology creates such attractive methods of unintentional suicide as this and dares us to abstain. |

If the second sentence does not include a topic from the first, its chances of appearing coherent are lessened considerably. Hence,

| | |
|---|---|
| AB—CD | Motorcycles are dangerous. Technology is changing the face of the earth. |

does not seem coherent, though it can be made coherent if a sufficient topical connection between the two sentences is provided, as in: "Motorcycles are dangerous to the environment. Such simple technology can change the face of the earth" (ABC—ADC).

## CONTINUITY AS A HALLMARK OF METHODICAL STRUCTURE

In highly structured writing, there is a heavy emphasis on continuity almost to the exclusion of any progression, any introduction of new information into the development.

For example, in a hypothetical essay supporting the thesis that motorcycles are dangerous, methodical development might sound like this:

**Thesis Statement/Introduction**

Motorcycles are dangerous.

**Topic Sentence/Paragraph 2**

Motorcycles are dangerous because they can be difficult to control.

**Topic Sentence/Paragraph 3**

Motorcycles are dangerous because they offer no protection for the rider.

**Topic Sentence/Paragraph 4**

Motorcycles are dangerous because they are difficult for other drivers to see.

In purely schematic form, the underlying pattern of the essay looks like this:

A—B
A—B—C
A—B—D
A—B—E

If you consider that topics C, D, and E are really subdivisions of topic B (kinds of danger), the heavy emphasis on continuity is even more obvious:

A—B
A—B—$B_1$
A—B—$B_2$
A—B—$B_3$

## PROGRESSION AS A HALLMARK OF ORGANIC FORM

In dramatic and organic structure, the emphasis is on progression, on introducing new material into the discussion. Some continuity is maintained for the sake of coherence, but it is not as visible or complete. Topics may not be carried over from one paragraph to the next, or may be dropped for a number of paragraphs before they are reintroduced.

For example,

### Thesis Statement/Introduction

Motorcycles are dangerous.

### Topic Sentence/Paragraph 2

But people like danger.

### Topic Sentence/Paragraph 3

We associate danger with freedom and adventure.

### Topic Sentence/Paragraph 4

Whole industries—like amusement parks, river rafting, and horror movies—are based on the promotion and sale of "safe" danger.

### Topic Sentence/Paragraph 5

People who buy motorcycles know they are dangerous—that they are unstable, offer little protection for the rider, and are difficult for other drivers to see. In a way, that is the very reason why they buy them. They are not just buying transportation; they are buying a ticket on a rollercoaster, a ride in a hot air balloon. They are buying adventure and freedom.

In a somewhat simplified schematic form, the organization of this essay might be represented as

A—B
C—B
B—D
E—F—B
C—A—B [$B_1$—$B_2$—$B_3$] [C—A] [C—G] [C—E] [C—D]

The essay still appears organized, because in each ensuing paragraph at least one term is carried forward from the preceding paragraph. There is a sense of continuity.

But the essay also appears to have more movement or direction than in a mechanical structure, because additional terms are gradually added to the discussion and, to a lesser degree, because the place of the repeated term in each paragraph is sometimes varied. There is a sense of progression to the discussion.

Organic form, in this model, leaves more to the reader to infer or remember. Topics may be dropped for a time and then reintroduced later. The audience is often expected to fill out part of the development on its own, to carry in mind a term or topic that has been momentarily removed from center stage, and fit it into the ongoing discussion.

The example given represents only one of the many possible forms or patterns for topical progression. A skillful author might be able to handle more than just two or three terms in a paragraph, or might not need to continue one central topic through all successive paragraphs. Topics could conceivably be dropped entirely from the discussion and never reintroduced. In extreme cases, an author might even start a new section or paragraph with topics seemingly unconnected to the previous discussion, and then establish continuity by artfully working the development back towards issues previously introduced.

## EXERCISE C

Choose one of the following assertions and develop it in two ways, one emphasizing continuity and one emphasizing progression. Use either a series of topic sentences (as in the discussion of topical progression), or actually write out the discussion. You may take an opposing position, if you wish.

1. Nobody likes a loudmouth.
2. Technology has changed our culture.
3. Sometimes it is good to forget.
4. We tend to overestimate our abilities.
5. Cop shows on TV are too violent.
6. Family is more important than friends.
7. More students should major in mathematics. (Or: More people should study the physical sciences.)
8. Breaking up is hard to do.
9. Noise is a form of pollution.
10. Few of us really understand how public policy is formed.

## WHEN TO USE METHODICAL ARRANGEMENT

Methodical form is appropriate

- when the facts are clear and convincing
- in formal situations
- in highly conventional discourse

- when efficiency and accuracy are the objectives
- in organizational writing
- in public speaking
- in instructional writing
- in particularly long essays and in monographs

## WHEN TO USE DRAMATIC FORM

Dramatic form is appropriate

- in informal writing
- in expressive writing
- when writing from experience
- in speculative discourse
- in impassioned persuasion

---

### GAINS AND LOSSES

#### ◆ METHOD ◆

| Advantages | Disadvantages |
|---|---|
| Efficiency | May not adequately express your meaning |
| Relative safety | Lesser opportunities for great successes |
| Predictability | Limits creativity and surprise |
| Fits expectations and conventions | Loses readers' attention |

---

### GAINS AND LOSSES

#### ◆ DRAMATIC STRUCTURE ◆

| Advantages | Disadvantages |
|---|---|
| Inherent emphasis, even suspense | More difficult to construct |
| Incorporates experiential element into essay form | Harder to follow and appreciate |
| Greater force and immediacy | Elicits more subjective responses |
| More expressive and evocative | Focuses attention on form rather than the message |

## EXERCISE D

Choose one or more of the following lists of words and write a passage that ties them together in some coherent fashion. If possible, avoid using narrative. Or try one list with narrative and another without. You can change the forms of the words.

Analyze the resulting organization. Where does the sense of order or direction come from?

**1.** blue, quandaries, broken, newspaper, charity, yardsales
**2.** coffee, sure, soda, desperation, compromise, memories, see
**3.** confidence, react, video game, anger, freeway, reflection
**4.** soap, different, persuasion, enjoy, older, evening, torn
**5.** shove, blur, shade, impress, buy, hope, allow

## *Wider Implications*

Organization in writing reflects the organization of life. We create structure to create security, to gain control, to make things more predictable and familiar. To ensure continuity and to allow for orderly and inevitable change, we design political systems and social rituals.

We are uncomfortable—in discourse as in life—if things change too rapidly. We are bored if they do not change enough. So effective arrangement reassures the audience that the author is staying on the same subject. And it surprises and entertains readers by gracefully (or forcibly) incorporating new ideas or topics into the discussion. Effective structure finds some balance between the desire for continuity and for progression.

### BELIEFS AND DOUBTS

Methodical and dramatic form reflect radically different habits of mind. A methodical style seems conservative and centripetal. It supports and extends the status quo, working within the proposed idea or theory. Organic form is more speculative and centrifugal. It works outward from the central concept to wider and wider frames of reference, not rejecting it or contradicting it so much as saying "If this is so, then what does it lead to? What else does that imply?"

### ARRANGEMENT AND STYLE

It is important to avoid certain natural but inaccurate inferences about the attractiveness of method and dramatic form. There is a tendency to conclude that all methodical structure must be uncreative or plain and that all dramatic arrangement must be clever and imaginative.

This is far from true. A sonnet may be highly structured and methodical but also creative. It may combine method and dramatic effect. There may be cleverness in the way it uses the traditional form. And an advertisement meant to produce dramatic tension and discovery may fail miserably, falling into annoying formulas or obvious manipulation.

### ARRANGEMENT AND DEVELOPMENT

For the most part, organization is not static. It is based on the pattern of development or sequence of ideas in an essay, and is better described in words that imply movement, like direction, flow, or progression, than in words that suggest a fixed layout, architectural structure, or design. An essay is a performance or process, not a display.

### ARRANGEMENT AND COHERENCE

There is also some connection between sentence coherence or cohesion and the overall structure of ideas in an essay. Topical progression, especially in methodical structure, makes this quite obvious. If you extract the thesis statement and topic sentences from an essay and assemble them into a single paragraph, they often read as a perfectly logical and coherent sequence of ideas.

The relationship between syntax and organization may not be as readily apparent in dramatic form, since the subtopics or changes in direction may be less explicit. But it is still important.

### ARRANGEMENT AND CONTENT

Organization may actually be part of the content of your essay, part of the message itself, rather than simply a means of conveying content. The arrangement of ideas may reflect the author's value structure, the relationship between one idea and another, or the perspective and theoretical structure of a field or profession.

### ARRANGEMENT AND SUPPORT

Effective organization is also persuasive. It provides a credible, forceful, controlled, and seemingly comprehensive view of the subject. If we feel an author is disorganized, we are less likely to believe him or her. A lack of organization may be perceived as a lack of certainty or expertise, however good the logic and support may be.

### ARRANGEMENT AND UNDERSTANDING

Structure facilitates and reflects true understanding of the subject. It aids the transfer of information from one person to the next. It represents a degree of control over the subject that goes beyond passive comprehension. Arrangement is an active process, an ability to organize one's thoughts and settle issues, to give order to the daily chaos of perceptions, emotions, experiences, and conflicting beliefs.

## *Conclusion*

Methodical and dramatic form are more complementary than mutually exclusive. A systematic display of information allow readers to remember, visualize, and consult your ideas more readily. Categories, divisions, and lists are spatial devices. Dramatic form is more experiential, relying on movement, sequence, and the patterns of discovery to sweep the reader along. Most writing uses elements of both methodical and dramatic structure.

## ASSIGNMENT A:   Categories, Partitions, and Processes

1. Collect as many comments, ideas, and facts about a subject as you can, the more diverse the better. Then categorize the information you have acquired, putting explanatory or clever headings and subheadings on each set of ideas.

Search out and establish a reason for writing about this subject, even if it is only to claim that people have a confused or fairly random understanding of it, or to describe common knowledge, review attitudes, or analyze public opinion.

Present the relevant information in some sequence or order, explaining your system as you go along.

2. Take notes on the kinds of commercials run at a particular time of the day or on a particular program. Categorize and analyze these. You might also consider trying to reconstruct a profile or portrait of the audience these ads are aimed at. How do the advertisers perceive the audience?

Or do a similar study of the topics addressed on daytime talk shows, or the kinds of jokes used by a particular comedian, or the kinds of programs on television in prime time, or the kinds of articles in a particular magazine, or the kinds of junk mail you receive.

3. Pick a category of newsworthy events, like droughts, scientific discoveries, celebrity divorces, mass murders, recessions, volcanic eruptions, terrorist attacks, factory closings, political scandals, plane crashes, teacher strikes, environmental activism, and so on. Recall and write down whatever you can remember about the subject. Think about (and write down) how you feel about the subject. Study the subject in files of back newspapers, using newspaper indexes to find relevant stories. Write a collective review of a number of incidents, focusing on how they affect us, what we can learn from them, what has happened since (in our attitudes or in the affected areas), and so on.

## ASSIGNMENT B:   Systems and Synergies

1. Conceive of an institution, group, belief, concept, or organization as if it were an organism, a mechanism, or an inseparable whole. Discuss it as if it were a character or agent in historical or current events.

2. Portray an organization, a community, a phenomenon, an event, or a series of events as a system or network, a structure of tensional and interrelated forces or influences. Resist the temptation to divide the subject into categories, stages, or parts. Instead discuss it as if it were an environment, panorama, locale, stage, or medium within which people operated.

3. Discuss an abstract idea—like faith, responsibility, courage, intelligence, wit, or sloth—as if it were an agency or tool, a means of accomplishing something.

4. Discuss a currently popular idea, fashion, mannerism, affectation, action, or matter of taste as if it were part of a larger trend or phenomenon, an ongoing process or an abstract field of ideas and attitudes.

# 17

# Style: Apparent and Concealed

I see but one rule: to be clear. If I am not clear, all my world crumbles to nothing.
—STENDHAL

Approximate language [is] the language of poetry and eloquence, thrown out at a vast object of our consciousness not fully apprehended by it, but extending infinitely beyond it.
—MATTHEW ARNOLD

## The Plain Truth

It has long been commonplace to think of rhetoric as a cosmetic or dishonest art, a process of gilding lilies and justifying deceit. People have always preferred to believe that the unvarnished truth would speak for itself and have always suspected that too much varnish concealed a lie. The question is whether truth needs adornment.

Classical philosophers felt that reasoning and formal speculation were more honest and valid ways of arriving at truth than was rhetoric, which in their eyes simply persuaded people to accept a belief, irrespective of its validity. Logicians traditionally have emphasized the place of logical proof and critical thinking in discovering and certifying truth. Modern science has held that truth can be established only by trained observation, close analysis, sufficient data, and carefully designed experimentation. Arguments and effusion are beside the point.

But it is impossible to avoid being rhetorical. Even the most scientific and objective discourse still attempts to prove a point. The absence of metaphors and obvious appeals to emotion does not mean that rhetoric is not present. It merely means that a specific kind of rhetoric is being used, with

341

its own standards of proof, its own preferred style, and its own varieties of ethical and emotional appeal (the appeal to objectivity and dispassionate reason, for example). Scientific writing is artful and eloquent in its own way. Even the attempt to be *non*rhetorical is itself a sophisticated rhetorical stance, as Paolo Valesio demonstrates in *Novantiqua: Rhetorics as a Contemporary Theory* (1980). Truth is independent of style.

The choice is not whether to be objective or deceptive, logical or rhetorical, plain or poetic. The choice is whether to call attention to your style or to conceal it. Whatever the quality of the writing, a conspicuous style may be considered good or bad.

### ◀ CONSPICUOUS STYLE ▶

| Good Qualities | Bad Qualities |
|---|---|
| witty | flamboyant, effete |
| courtly | contrived |
| attractive | attention seeking |
| sophisticated | pretentious |

Inconspicuous styles may also be regarded as good or bad.

### ◀ INCONSPICUOUS STYLE ▶

| Good Qualities | Bad Qualities |
|---|---|
| straightforward | uncultured |
| businesslike | passionless |
| sincere, honest | artless |
| unpretentious | mundane |

## *Attractiveness*

We admire an artful style. The person who expresses ideas in a compelling or graceful manner stands out from the crowd. When the message is not original or unique, memorable lines may lend it significance and interest. When the subject is deep or the situation grave, a dramatic style can enlighten, renew our understanding or resolve, and stir us to action.

We also appreciate artlessness. It seems innocent, guileless, uncomplicated, and friendly. Fine words and high sentiments subordinate us; they invite adherence and admiration. A transparent style, by contrast, is pleasant and unpresuming.

Artlessness does not mean graceless or clumsy. It means being able to speak without apparent contrivance or affectation. Artfulness does not mean flamboyance or excessive refinement. It means speaking with obvious attention to the sound, shape, and effect of the language. The goal in either case is to be attractive.

## *The Elements of Style*

Style is based on many factors: on your personality and status, your expertise and sources of material, your values and your habits of thinking. It is based on your relationship to the audience and your familiarity with the community and forum in which you are speaking. It is based on your motives for writing, on the nature of the topic, and on the nature of the situation that has led you to speak.

It is also affected by your use of language, which changes in respect to the audience, occasion, subject, stance, and situation. Linguistic elements of style include the following:

### THE LEVELS OF STYLE

Classical rhetoric suggests three major divisions of styles: the elevated or high style, the middle style, and the plain or low style (with no value judgment implied by the word *low*).

The elevated style is more impassioned and stylized, more likely to use unusual words and highly patterned syntax. The low style is straightforward and undramatic, using familiar words and the syntax of everyday speech. The middle style is perceived not as a weak compromise between the extremes but as a respected and intelligent balance in one's delivery, neither unexceptionally plain nor ostentatiously extravagant in manner.

### PRIVATE AND PUBLIC LANGUAGE

People speak differently in private than in public. Private discourse is less guarded, more expressive and personal. It deals in opinions and antagonisms, friendships and affiliations. There is more emphasis on emotions and attitudes, less on evidence and proof. Public language is more visible, more deliberative, more professional, more substantive, and more considered. What you say is considered permanent. People regard it as policy or fixed belief.

### INFORMAL AND FORMAL LANGUAGE

Language may be formal or informal, depending on the occasion. Formality is expected in planned meetings, public hearings, ceremonial events, standard reports, and professional publications. Usually the intent is more serious or the significance more far reaching. The discourse is more likely to be conventional, the language defined by tradition, practice, and a clearly defined intent. Formal occasions can be public or private.

Informal occasions are casual, unplanned, and unstructured. The content of discussion is more trivial and personal. The style is likely to be unaffected and spontaneous, without much coherence or direction.

### INTIMATE AND DISTANT LANGUAGE

The relationship between author and audience is said to be intimate when they are long-term friends. People who are on intimate terms usually share confidences and ignore most conventions and roles. They may discuss beliefs and doubts as well as personal matters. A private vocabulary and style may develop, with personal jokes and extremely topical allusions.

Style becomes increasingly distant as the separation between author and audience is increased. This separation may be implied by physical distance, as when speakers place a podium or desk between themselves and the audience, or speak from a stage, or stand and pace while the audience sits. Or it may be implied by differences in status, role, or expertise between author and audience. As distance increases, the sense of kinship or community decreases. The writing and style become more impersonal.

### DIRECT AND INDIRECT LANGUAGE

Language can be direct or indirect. The stated meaning and actual meaning may be essentially the same. Or there may be various shades and degrees of difference between what is said and what is meant.

**Direct Expression.**   A direct presentation of the subject explicitly states the author's meaning and intent, without metaphor, camouflage, or misrepresentation. It puts the crucial events, objects, and ideas on center stage. Directness may reflect

- honesty
- accuracy
- bluntness or rudeness
- reductiveness
- a lack of sophistication

**Indirect Expression.**   Indirect language tries to convey a message or achieve some result, without actually stating it in so many words. It may be an attempt to be more tactful, more artful, more complex, or more evasive.

Indirection focuses on subjects other than the intended meaning. It may

- use description or narrative to illustrate the message without actually stating it
- be ambiguous or unclear, purposely or not
- have multiple meanings or layers of meaning
- convey both a literal message and one or more subtexts (for example, a veiled criticism, attitude, or assertion of authority)
- be ironic (the stated message is the opposite of the intended meaning)

Indirect expression may go so far as to conceal the author's intent, to focus on a false or overt subject and objective to achieve the covert aim or to advance a covert message. This behavior, if it is a systematic part of a person's style, is called Machiavellianism. Intentional or not, the practice evolves and prospers because concealing motives makes it difficult for others to argue with the perpetrator. They may not realize what is happening or may waste their time arguing about an issue that is little more than a smokescreen.

## INVOLVED AND DISPASSIONATE LANGUAGE

One's style can suggest personal motivation and direct involvement with the subject, or it can seem dispassionate. The terms *subjectivity* and *objectivity* which might be used here, are somewhat imprecise and have been greatly abused. Being subjective has become a synonym for bias. And anyone who agrees with us is considered objective.

The issue is really whether the author is passionate about the subject or stands to benefit from the outcome. It is a question of the distance between the author and the subject, of self-interest and altruism, of emotional attachment as opposed to disinterested study.

Involvement may also be evoked or discouraged in the audience.

**Involved Styles.**   Involved language appears more authentic and engaged, more sincere or immediate. It may emphasize emotions, personal experiences, and particular instances. There may be a sense of excitement and discovery when the writing is explanatory or reportative. In persuasion, the style may focus on injustice, injury, and hurt feelings. The author's claims are likely to be more extreme and assertive.

**Dispassionate Styles.**   Increasing the apparent separation between the author and the subject creates an impression of distance. In academic, professional, and scientific writing, as well as elsewhere, distance or disinterestedness is frequently implied by increasing the abstractness, generality, or public scope of the message. This effectively puts the author and audience on equal terms, with both sides presented as disinterested observers of a neutral, depoliticized phenomenon.

**Relevance.** Immediacy for readers is the degree to which the message is relevant, impinging on their personal experience. Authors can make their presentation more immediate by evoking emotion, by demonstrating the effects the subject has on the audience, by graphically portraying the subject, and by fostering identification with the topic or point of view they represent. The diction becomes more emphatic, more emotionally charged, and more laden with connotations.

**Disinterest and Altruism.** Creating distance between readers and the subject may be accomplished by the same devices used to suggest distance between the author and the subject. Writers also commonly displace events and ideas, moving them to another context, place, or point in time where they seem less immediately threatening or critical. One reason for increasing the distance from the issue is that a disinterested audience will be more neutral and less inclined to pursue its own self-interest to your disadvantage.

## EMPHASIS, NEUTRALITY, AND DEEMPHASIS IN LANGUAGE

Emphasis has already been discussed in relation to amplification and development (in Chapter 14). Emphatic styles incorporate gesture, repetition, amplification, titles and underlining, emotional appeal, parallel structure, pauses, metaphor, changes in pace, symbolic locations or carefully staged and constructed settings, references to charts, pictures, or other graphic devices (like writing on blackboards), and modulations of voice to underscore the author's meaning. These heighten or call attention to certain portions of the text, often at the expense of other parts of the subject.

An unemphatic or neutral style presents all information as if it were of equal importance. Absent are emotions, gestures, metaphorical flourishes, modulations in assertiveness, dramatic repetition, and any other device that might heighten effect or call attention to a particular part of the essay or speech.

Language can also deemphasize. It can omit, qualify, undercut, and minimize the importance of a subject. It can subordinate one topic to another or treat it as an afterthought. Comparisons, characterizations, and word choice may suggest that a subject is trivial or unworthy of notice.

## COHERENCE AND DIGRESSION

Syntax can be coherent or disconnected. A highly coherent style emphasizes continuity from one statement to the next, establishing clear and logical relationships between different ideas and information. A disconnected style emphasizes progression, moving rapidly from one idea to the next, often with minimal transition. Taken to an extreme, the disconnected style may become random, incoherent, or digressive. The relationship between successive ideas may not be readily apparent.

## COLLOQUIAL, POPULAR, AND TECHNICAL LANGUAGE

Degrees of expertise are also reflected in language. A colloquial style addresses a subject using the patterns of daily speech on a fairly intimate and inexpert level, using idiomatic expressions, slang, and the syntax and intonations of spoken language.

A popular or casual style reflects somewhat greater distance, formality, and knowledgeability. It is more clearly a "written" style, with fuller syntax and less reliance on tone, idiom, and the patterns of dialogue and conversation. There is little effort to present the author as a person with arcane technical, scholarly, or professional knowledge, though experts frequently use the popular style to make highly technical information more accessible to the general public.

A technical style presents the author as an authority on the subject and assumes that the audience is composed of other experts. Usually the diction is highly specialized or precise, consisting in part of terminology or jargon that is peculiar to the profession or field—words used mostly by experts or familiar words used with closely defined and particular meanings. Because a high level of background knowledge is presumed to exist in the readers, a technical style often seems dense and cryptic.

## CURRENT, PROVINCIAL, AND ARCHAIC DICTION

Language varies from place to place and changes over the course of time. Diction is said to be current and proper when the words chosen reflect standard usage for the situation at hand. The style does not use words that have gone out of fashion or fallen into disuse. It does not use words that are drawn from other circumstances, words that are used in other places but not familiar to the audience being addressed, or words that are borrowed from other disciplines or fields of endeavor.

Diction is said to be archaic when the vocabulary is old-fashioned or no longer in style. It is said to be provincial when the terms are common in a particular locality or discourse community but not in general use.

## DENOTATIONS AND CONNOTATIONS

Words are said to be connotative when they convey a range of attitudes and meanings beyond the direct application of the word to an event, person, object, place, or idea.

The denotation of a word is the thing it refers to, apart from any interpretation or judgment the author may wish to imply. While all words are supposed to denote something, there are some with fewer connotations attached. They convey fewer value judgments than other terms that might be used and so can lead to a style that seems more objective or descriptive.

## LITERAL AND FIGURATIVE LANGUAGE

Language can be literal or figurative. Literal diction reflects an effort to be accurate and thorough, to use words that analyze and describe the subject rather than words that offer an impression or portrayal of it. There is usually a one-to-one relationship between words and the things they denote. The style is more linear and less graphic.

Figurative language creates images or impressions. It uses words in unusual patterns, circumstances, or combinations in an attempt to increase the amount of information they convey. The style is more graphic.

Rather than attempting to describe a subject in detail, a metaphorical style attempts to create a mental picture, an emotional reaction, or an intellectual panorama that gives the audience an intuitive understanding of the point being made. It is the difference between saying "Still waters run deep" (a metaphor) and saying "People who are generally quiet and unemotional are often more thoughtful, complex, and considerate than those who speak constantly and indiscriminately" (an attempt at literal description).

## SPECIFIC DETAILS AND GENERALIZATIONS

Language can be specific or general. Specific details are discrete features of the object being described. Diction becomes increasingly more specific as it makes the time, place, event, and subject being observed seem more particular and special, more unique, and as it focuses on features of the object that distinguish it from similar and related objects. Hence, to say that someone lives "in a red house down the street" is less specific than saying "He lives in a red brick split-level at the corner of Anderson Street and Osage Avenue."

Generalizations sum up or characterize details, properties, and tendencies common to a number of related instances or objects. To say that "This rock I picked up is exceptionally light" is to describe a specific and concrete feature of that particular chunk of stone. To say that "Pumice, a kind of volcanic ash, is usually light in weight" is to define properties and features common to a whole species of rock. It is a generalization.

## CONCRETE DETAILS AND ABSTRACTIONS

Details are said to be concrete when they refer to specific physical and sensory properties of the subject described, such as its weight, color, texture, temperature, scent, sound, shape, and composition.

A style becomes increasingly abstract as it moves further away from actual events and objects, as it focuses more exclusively on general properties or principles, on concepts and theories, and on statistics.

## CUMULATIVE, PERIODIC, AND BALANCED SENTENCES

Sentences can be cumulative, periodic, or balanced. Style is said to be more cumulative or "loose" in syntax when it typically begins each sentence with an independent clause—either subject and verb or a subject-verb-object—and develops or modifies the idea by adding other phrases and clauses to the end of this base.

Style becomes increasingly more periodic in syntax as the author more frequently interrupts or inverts the syntax of the base sentence. Any displacement of the standard pattern or "period" of the sentence—its normal cycle from subject to verb to object—holds the reader (and comprehension of the message) in suspense. In a cumulative sentence, we have the basic elements of the sentence in hand from the outset, and we can see immediately where each new phrase or clause fits in. But in a periodic sentence, we are forced to wait. We cannot completely integrate the information given until all parts of the base sentence have been stated.

This is a cumulative sentence: "I planted an oak tree in the backyard last May, anticipating the fall color it would provide months later." A more periodic version of the same sentence would be, "Anticipating the fall color it would provide months later, I planted an oak tree in the backyard last May." And it is even more periodic to say, "In my backyard last May, anticipating the fall color it would provide months later, an oak tree I planted."

Style becomes increasingly more balanced in syntax as the author more frequently uses repeated, parallel, or highly patterned sentence structure, particularly when phrases, clauses, and sentences of the same length and shape are paired. It is balanced to say "It was the best of times, it was the worst of times." It is less balanced to say "It seemed like the best of times. But I know there were serious problems with it."

## *Concealing Style*

An inconspicuous style goes unnoticed. The words and sentences do not call attention to themselves. Because it seems almost as if one can read "through" the words directly to the meaning, this manner of writing is sometimes referred to as a transparent style.

The following strategies will make your style appear more transparent:

*1. Avoid Uncommon Diction or Syntax.* An inconspicuous style uses familiar language and sentence structure, avoiding unusual and complex syntax or strange and technical words unless the occasion clearly requires them. Nothing that might slow or distract the reader is included.

*2. Defer to the Content.* Meaning is preeminent in a transparent style. What you say is, at least ostensibly, more important than how it is said. The message should be clear and not excessively difficult to decipher. Writing that is hard to understand is more often a sign of a mannered style than a concealed one.

*3. Defer to Conventions.* Delivery may appear "styleless" when it follows the conventions of the situation without actually calling excessive attention to them. If the reference to conventions is too heavyhanded or if they are too rigidly followed, the style may be perceived as a parody or as a forced and inexpert imitation of a conventional style.

*4. Be Appropriate.* Since inappropriate speech and behavior is instantly noticeable, an inconspicuous style carefully observes the properties of the moment. It is not rude, annoying, outrageous, or offensive.

This does not mean that the transparent style is inherently moral, however. It tries to fit in, without going to excess. If the occasion involves ill-mannered behavior, a concealed style is usually neither unpleasantly prim nor unpleasantly obnoxious. It is politic.

*5. Defer to Expectations.* A transparent style does not usually deal in surprises, ironies, strange plot twists, or twisted arguments. It defers to the readers' expectations, sounding the way the audience assumes it will and saying not so much what they want to hear as what they have been well prepared to hear.

*6. Be Plain and Direct.* A concealed style may emphasize "plain" language or plainspokenness. This can mean many things, but mostly we associate plainness with the language of everyday speech and plainspokenness with a kind of rough sincerity and bluntness.

Either becomes an affectation if carried to an extreme, however. And people whose position or education removes them from the commonplace may seem to be condescending to us if they try to speak our language, if they seem to be lowering themselves to our level.

*7. Avoid Extremes.*   A transparent style usually does not indulge extremes, excluding strange or uncommon patterns of syntax, exceptionally graphic description, startling comparisons and metaphors, or unusual and eccentric opinions. It is likely to be rather middle-of-the-road in all respects, and even understated.

*8. Avoid Eccentricities.*   A concealed style avoids quirks or idiosyncratic habits of expression. The writer suppresses any tendency to repeat favorite phrases, words, or patterns of syntax, any obvious pattern of presentation, or any particular kind of material (like repeated use of statistics or quotes).

*9. Avoid Obvious Repetition.*   A transparent style does not use obvious repetition. This means avoiding not only repeated words and phrases but also repeated sounds and proper names, heavy parallelism, and the like.

If repetition seems unavoidable, as it often is, an inconspicuous style hides it by varying the delivery in some fashion, either changing the words used, changing the perspective, or changing the order in which things are said.

*Note:* Coherence and unity often *require* that the same words be repeated. Even so, the conventional style in English tries to conceal the repetition.

When a single topic is discussed at length, conventional style has generally preferred to use pronouns, varied forms of a word (for example, singular in one sentence, plural in another, or the noun form in one sentence and the adjective form in the next), varied locations of the word in the sentence, and synonyms for the topic instead of directly repeating the same word in successve sentences.

This painstaking variety in repetition requires a fair amount of skill, but it actually results in a less conspicuous style than one expects from straightforward repetition. The simpler approach is not always the plainest.

*10. Use Common Knowledge and Commonplace Ideas.*   Sometimes commonplace topics and familiar ideas are equated with plainness in style. Considerable artifice in expression or highly colorful language may seem plain when in fact it is the material that is artless and not the style.

*11. Disclaim Artfulness or Ability.*   Authors seeking the advantages of a concealed style may claim to be unsophisticated, may apologize in advance for their lack of polish and fluency, or may in some other way depreciate their writing or speaking ability. Often this apology is sincere and comes out so naturally—hidden in a phrase like "I really haven't thought this through," "I'm not very good at this," "Excuse me, but I'm pretty upset right now," or "Let me try to sort this out"—that we scarcely notice it for what it is. Writers may also explicitly claim to be speaking plainly even when they are not. Sometimes by making the claim, they earn the credit.

*12. Take an Unassuming or Unintrusive Stance.*  It is likewise common in the concealed style for authors to take an unpretentious or unassuming stance, disclaiming expertise, status, or even opinions on the subject. An inconspicuous stance may be deferential and unassertive. It may even hide the presence and opinions of the author.

*13. Avoid Fine Words and Memorable Phrases.*  A concealed style makes no obvious attempt to be memorable. Fine-sounding words and phrases are carefully excised, replaced with less ostentatious prose. Sometimes the style is all the more quotable as a result.

## Making Style More Evident

A conspicuous style calls attention to itself or to the author. It may be stylized, ornate, surprising, graceful, extravagant, idiosyncratic, or ostentatious. It may appear eloquent and poetic.

To make your style more conspicuous, do the following:

*1. Use Unusual or Inappropriate Language.*  A conspicuous style may be created by using language that is in someway out of the ordinary or inappropriate. Diction may seem strange when it is

- metaphorical
- archaic
- provincial
- allusive
- foreign
- used in an unfamiliar or idiosyncratic sense
- used as a different part of speech than usual
- invented for the occasion, either extending or combining familiar words or coining an entirely new word

Diction appears inappropriate when it is not suited to the situation or audience at hand—as when unexplained technical language is used to address an audience of laypersons, when obvious colloquialisms are incorporated in a formal presentation, or when highly connotative words are used in a supposedly objective report.

*2. Use Unusual Word Order or Sentence Structure.*   Word order and syntax become more conspicuous as they deviate further from conventional patterns. Some of the possible variations on the norm include

- omitting words or parts of words
- adding words where they normally would be omitted or where fewer would normally be used (for example, adding extra conjunctions between words in a parallel series, as in "red and white and blue and black," or building up a long series of adjectives before a noun, as in "The *great, gray-green, greasy* Limpopo River")
- rearranging standard word order (as in "Impatient we are")
- doubling or reiteration (as in "Would that this *too, too* sullied flesh would melt, and resolve itself into a dew").

*3. Emphasize the Sound of Words.*   A conspicuous style is likely to emphasize the sound of the writing or speech, sometimes to the detriment of the meaning. The way words sound can be used either to camouflage or to reveal style.

**Strong or Elegant Phrasing.**   An obvious style tries to express ideas in ways that are graceful, powerful, or impressive, selecting words that heighten the impact and phrases that seize the imagination. Such phrasing is often characterized by assertiveness, word play, emphasis, and attention to connotations as well as to sound.

**Motifs and Refrains.**   In stylized writing, key phrases, words, and sentences may be repeated at intervals for effect. This repetition may take the form of a refrain in more poetic discourse, a motif or "touchstone" in prose, or a slogan in advertising. In the process of reiteration, the author hopes to make the message more emphatic and memorable.

**Alliteration and Consonance.**   Alliteration (the repetition of sounds at the beginning of words in succession or proximity) and consonance (the repetition of sounds that occur within successive words) can make the style more euphonious or musical and therefore more obvious. The following line from Shakespeare uses both: "When to the sessions of sweet silent thought I summon up remembrance of things past."

To a certain extent, a transparent style in English also depends on graceful use of alliteration and consonance. Paying no attention to sound is more likely to make your style obvious than inconspicuous.

**Rhymes and Slant Rhymes.**    Rhymes or near rhymes (called "slant rhymes")—the repetition of the same sound, or almost the same sound, at the end of words—can make a style more noticeable. The words *stake* and *mistake* are a perfect rhyme, because exactly the same sound is repeated. *Stake* and *fake* are a more traditional rhyme. *Stake* and *late* or *stake* and *bleak* would be slant rhymes. Hearing a parallel sound reminds us of the similar-sounding word that preceded it and thereby calls attention to the style.

*Note:* The conventional style, even in poetry (though not in comic verse), more often than not attempts to conceal or tone down rhymes, if not to avoid them altogether. Rhyming can be made *inconspicuous* by

- moving rhymes further apart
- placing them in different syntactic roles, as in *make* and *lake* (a verb and a noun)
- rhyming syllables that have differing degrees of stress or emphasis in normal speech, as in *figures* and *stirs* (since the second syllable of *figures* is not as strongly stressed as the first, and the accent on *stirs* is strong)
- rhyming across the boundaries between separate thoughts, as when rhyming a word in the middle of one sentence with a word at the beginning of a new paragraph or sequence of ideas
- rhyming only when particular emphasis or dramatic effect is appropriate (for instance, in a refrain, slogan, maxim, or closing remark)

*4. Use Unusual Syntax.*    There are also numerous ways to change the effect and pattern of syntax, making the sentence structure more obvious or obtrusive. The possible variations are catalogued and named in many works on prosody and the figures of speech. Without venturing too far into technical terminology, we list the following options:

- varying or patterning the meter or rhythm
- varying or patterning the length of phrases
- varying or patterning the length of clauses
- varying or patterning the way sentences begin or end
- repeating words or phrases at invervals or in successive sentences ("I came, I saw, I conquered")
- using parallel or balanced constructions ("United we stand, divided we fall")
- inverting patterns of syntax or reference in successive passages ("Beauty is truth, truth beauty")
- omitting the normal connective words (coordinating and subordinating conjunctions, in particular) or including more connectives than necessary
- purposely leaving a sentence incomplete (with good reason), breaking off one sentence and starting another (usually making some excuse like "what I mean to say is"), or incorporating a pause within a sentence (usually indicated by

three spaced periods [ . . . ], which is the same punctuation used to signal ellipsis, the omission of words from direct quotes)

- putting parenthetical remarks within a sentence
- building a longer than normal sequence or list of modifiers

*5. For Effect, Use a Purposely Incorrect or Awkward Style.* Although it is hardly recommended, style can be made more conspicuous by violating rules of grammar or punctuation, by mixing different styles or voices, by clumsiness in syntax, and by sheer incoherence. There are a few occasions, however, when the ungrammatical or incoherent approach is either more appropriate or more effective than a proper and fluent style.

Incoherence can emphasize strong emotion or (in small doses) can exemplify surprise and spontaneity. An occasionally ungrammatical style can seem more democratic, more fallible, more human and endearing. Though we often respond with frustration to grammatical errors, they can also create sympathy—especially when the improprieties are minor and somewhat explicable, excused by barriers of language and culture, by extreme youth, or by incapacity.

*6. Use Self-Conscious References to Style.* Evident or obvious styles are often ironic, self-conscious, or self-referential. In fact, you can make any style more conspicuous by explicitly calling attention to it, by pointing out to the audience the style of a passage just completed or by telling the audience ahead of time what manner of style or what figure of speech you intend to use. At an extreme, the self-conscious style continually undercuts itself, apologizing for its own assertions, revising in mid-sentence, and digressing wildly. The author may seem to carry on a conversation with himself or herself.

*7. Take Extreme Stands.* Authors who choose a highly visible style may couple it with intellectual flamboyance—with intentional eccentricity in their point of view. They may habitually criticize conventional attitudes or openly flout them. They may rely heavily on extreme, outrageous, or highly inflammatory assertions.

## EXERCISE A

Rewrite the following passages to make the style less obvious. Then compare the results with the original, discussing the advantages and disadvantages of each version.

1. A penny saved is a penny earned.
2. An idle mind is the devil's workshop.
3. I brought in the newspaper. The newspaper was wet. It had been raining. I tried to read the newspaper. I couldn't read the newspaper. The newspaper tore apart. Wet newspaper tears easily.

4. Given a good goal, an attractive, obvious objective, a dream they are fond of to pursue, people will band and bond together.

5. Roses are red. Violets are blue. Sugar is sweet. And so are you.

6. The window panes reflected apples, reflected roses; all the leaves were green in the glass.   —Virginia Woolf

7. It is always painful to part from people whom one has known for a very brief space of time. The absence of old friends one can endure with equanimity. But even a momentary separation from anyone to whom one has just been introduced is almost unbearable.   —Oscar Wilde

8. How dreary — to be — Somebody!
   How public — like a frog —
   To tell one's name — the livelong June —
   To an admiring Bog!                    —Emily Dickinson

9. You can fool too many of the people too much of the time.
                                       —James Thurber

10. Suddenly the whole room broke into a sea of shouting as they saw me rise. Waves of rejoicing swept the place. Women leaped in the air. My aunt threw her arms around me. The minister took me by the hand and led me to the platform.                    —Langston Hughes

## EXERCISE B

Rewrite the following passages to make the style more conspicuous. Expand, compress, or omit where necessary. Compare what you have written to the original, discussing the advantages and disadvantages of each version.

1. We had an early spring. The cherry blossoms came out three weeks before they were expected. Temperatures hit seventy. Then, of course, it snowed.

2. Some kinds of help are worse than none at all. When people want to be useful but get in your way or do the job badly, you wish you had never asked their assistance.

3. Companies ought to take better care of their employees. The company has an obligation to those it hires, the people whose labor creates both product and profit. It is important to the health of an organization to maintain a sense of trust.

4. Some people have a talent for being late. They expect us to be patient, to defer whatever else we could be doing while they finish their own pastimes and errands. Then they show up acting as if nothing had happened. But if they are forced to wait for someone else, they get angry.

5. The telephone has radically changed our lives. We don't write letters anymore, at least not with the same facility or frequency. We can talk to family members a thousand miles away. In the pre-telephone era, it might have been months or years before a message got through. Now we can order

pizza delivered and call a repairperson. No need to send brother Ned into town on the buckboard. Our conception of distances has been altered.

## WHEN TO CONCEAL STYLE

Inconspicuous styles are appropriate

- when you are a newcomer or a subordinate
- when the truth seems self-evident
- when accuracy is crucial
- when you wish to appear mature or dignified
- on social occasions
- when you wish to remove social barriers
- when you wish to appear honest and open

## WHEN TO MAKE STYLE CONSPICUOUS

A conspicuous style is almost never appropriate in the strictest sense of the word. While there have been times in the past when taste encouraged extravagance in expression, present usage is far more conservative. There is considerable social pressure against attention seeking and strangeness in manner.

Nevertheless, stylized writing is expected, appreciated, or useful

- on significant occasions
- to elevate topics not considered significant
- to create humor
- on formal and ceremonial occasions
- in literary writing
- when you wish to attract attention
- when your status is low

---

**GAINS AND LOSSES**

---

### ◀ AN INCONSPICUOUS STYLE ▶

| **Advantages** | **Disadvantages** |
| --- | --- |
| Suggests confidence in the truth of one's ideas | May imply a lack of enthusiasm and conviction |
| Lets the facts speak for themselves | Doesn't "sell" one's views |
| Doesn't distract from the message | Sacrifices the attractions of language |
| Doesn't focus attention on the author | Diminishes opportunity for ethical appeal |

---

## GAINS AND LOSSES

### ◆ A CONSPICUOUS STYLE ◆

| Advantages | Disadvantages |
|---|---|
| Implies vision and insight | May not be clear |
| Sells or enhances the message | Implies that the case is not self-evident |
| May sweep away resistance | May seem more like entertainment |
| Provides emotional and ethical appeal | Generates suspicion |

## *Wider Implications*

We tend to confuse eloquence with either an elevated or conspicuous style, assuming that attractive and effective oratory resides in fine words and impassioned phrases. But eloquence is independent of style. It is defined more by transcendence than by words, by the way an inspired performance sweeps us away, opening our eyes to the world around us, renewing our beliefs, enabling us to appreciate the feelings and experiences of others, transforming our perceptions and understanding.

Either the apparent or inconspicuous style can be eloquent. Either can be attractive.

### LANGUAGE AND STYLE

Transparent and obvious styles reflect different views of language, of the relationship between thought, reality, the author, and expression. Words can represent or illuminate nature, serve either as mirror or lamp.

**Language as Medium.**   A transparent style treats language as a code, a means of conveying information and ideas, a reflection of reality. It acknowledges the limitations of the medium. Words, however detailed, cannot adequately describe reality. They imitate the world. An effective presentation creates an appearance of truth.

**Language as Message.**   An apparent style treats language as part of the message. It blurs the distinction between stance and substance, language and thought.

The style becomes part of the thinking, in much the same way that an artist's brushstrokes and style are part of his or her painting. The performance is part of the subject, in some cases more important than the subject.

## *Conclusion*

Whether a style is apparent or concealed, the goal is the same: to communicate as effectively as possible. Some messages are more effectively and attractively expressed in obvious styles. Some messages are more readily understood and accepted when the style is concealed.

At their best, apparent styles become less obvious; their mannerisms fade from view as artfulness takes over. Even strange and eccentric language is made to appear natural and necessary. Concealed styles, in like manner, may become more effective by employing artifice.

## ASSIGNMENT A: Style That Reflects Meaning

1. Discuss something in such a way that it shows your enthusiasm for the subject—without seeming too gushy or sentimental.

2. Discuss something you are disturbed about, using a style and description that reflects strong emotion.

3. Use obvious repetition to underscore a point, perhaps an ironic truth or satiric jab. The frequency and placement of repetitions will depend on what you are writing about and what you want to accomplish. The repetitions can be exact, partial, or slightly varied.

4. Use obvious repetition to accumulate meanings around a statement, word, or phrase.

5. Write with nostalgia about something or someplace, using melodic diction and phrasing as well as reflective content to suggest and evoke the mood of revery.

6. Use big words and technical language either in an attempt to make a subject sound learned or important or to mock academic, political, and technical styles.

7. Write in praise of an institution, virtue, belief, principle, or right. Treat it seriously without seeming maudlin or chauvinistic, using elements of the grand style (poetic, formal, emphatic, ritual, and archaic diction, allusions, and ornate or contrived syntax, as well as direct proclamations of significance) to reflect the importance of the subject. Don't overdo it.

## ASSIGNMENT B:   Indirection

1. Choose a relatively straightforward or commonplace idea and express it indirectly and at some length, never coming right out and saying what your point is. Justify the indirection by evoking an air of mystery, by implying that the subject is deeper and more inexpressible than straightforwardness would suggest, or by being entertaining in the presentation.

2. Make a request, appeal, or claim in an oblique manner, using indirection for the purpose of easing the way, avoiding abruptness, or softening the blow.

## ASSIGNMENT C:   Ornamentation

1. Take a relatively straightforward or commonplace idea or situation and dress it up, using imagery, allusions, analogies, alliteration and consonance, repetition, rhythmic, patterned, or graceful syntax, and other devices in an attempt to make it entertaining, more attractive, and less commonplace. Be careful, of course, to avoid appearing ridiculous.

2. For the purposes of making someone or something more compelling, ominous, disturbing, attractive, or significant, describe the person or object in an elaborate way. To be safe, it might be best to choose at first a subject you feel you can keep in perspective. If you are too enamored of the subject, you may not be able to judge the originality and worth of your elaborations.

## ASSIGNMENT D:   Concealments and Disclosures

1. Make a proposal for some change or improvement in an organization or procedure, using a plain style to suggest that you are humble and down to earth.

2. In many real-life situations, people have hidden motives or secret agendas, but their public stance must be largely free of apparent self-interest. This is often the case in politics and sales. But it is not absent from interpersonal relations and public service. A person might help the homeless, for instance, but take pleasure in the notoriety it brings. Or a person might campaign against some form of license but enjoy having a degree of power over other people.

This does not mean that the persons involved do not also have good motives, or that they might not accomplish good things if they can avoid abusing their audience's trust and are not controlled by the suspect intention. It simply acknowledges that people may have a number of different reasons for their actions.

Write on a subject where your motives might be questioned, or script a hypothetical argument a politician might make for a project that benefits his or her home district. You might choose either to focus exclusively on the best intentions or to confront charges of self-interest and refute them.

3. Without being too personal, reveal and discuss some hidden motive, secret wish, private agenda, or guilty pleasure. Avoid seeming too eccentric or strange unless you also have good reason, comic or otherwise, to shock and galvanize your readers. Writers who mine this vein often rely on the fact that everyone harbors many of the same feelings, or that childishness lurks in even the most sophisticated soul.

4. Question the intentions of someone or some group you perceive to have hidden motives, and in the process attack and refute the point of view, claim, lifestyle, or proposal being forwarded.

# 18

# Revision
# and Spontaneity

Re-vision—the act of looking back, of seeing with fresh eyes, of entering an old text from a new critical direction—is for women more than a chapter in cultural history: it is an act of survival.          —ADRIENNE RICH

Men grind and grind in the mill of a truism, and nothing comes out but what was put in. But the moment they desert the tradition for a spontaneous thought, then poetry, wit, hope, virtue, learning, anecdote, all flock to their aid.          —RALPH WALDO EMERSON

## Rising to the Occasion

The ability to rise to the occasion is greatly respected. People appreciate ready wit and spontaneous rejoinder. They admire decisiveness and grace under pressure, the cogent reply to a difficult question. Cutting remarks and telling arguments are useless after the fact. But the right thing said at the right time is both effective and entertaining.

Because they appear unguarded, spontaneous and unrehearsed answers may seem not only more artful but more truthful, as well. We feel like we are getting a glimpse of the "real" person.

More than openness or rhetorical dexterity is at stake. Rising to the occasion means responding to crises, challenges, and dangers. It means taking charge when leadership is needed. It means speaking up to prevent injustice.

One must rise to the occasion in less public forums, as well, on matters of conscience, belief, community, and self-interest. One must be ready to counsel and console, to advise with restraint and teach without prescription. One must find time to communicate with others, knowing how to express oneself in such circumstances with tact and understanding.

But spontaneity is not the only virtue. Careful thought, thorough research, and meticulous planning are also accorded high respect. They may seem slow but steady, more likely to wear well in the long run, more genial and dignified, less adversarial, and better suited to normalcy and routine.

A planned and revised style appears to reflect considered opinion rather than prejudice or gut response. It seems to ascribe greater complexity to the situation or subject, thereby reinforcing the audience's values and excusing their inability to understand or deal with it.

We are suspicious of glibness, easy solutions, and stock answers. They seem like lies. They seem insubstantial, ill considered, or dogmatic. Even labored prose may seem more genuine and devout.

Regardless of quality, spontaneous or extemporaneous writing may be perceived as good or bad.

### ◀ SPONTANEOUS STYLE ▶

| **Good Qualities** | **Bad Qualities** |
|---|---|
| authentic | incautious |
| quick witted | scatterbrained |
| fresh, clever | lacking seriousness |
| immediate | immature |

Planned and revised styles may also be perceived as good or bad.

### ◀ PLANNED STYLE ▶

| **Good Qualities** | **Bad Qualities** |
|---|---|
| careful | overcautious |
| thorough, accurate | uninspired |
| measured, mature | stuffy |
| refined | affected |

## Delivery and Revision

The ideal is to combine philosophical depth, practical wisdom, and rhetorical skill, to be able, from a fund of knowledge and experience, to speak extemporaneously and to the point. The appearance of spontaneity or of reflection in style is influenced by the

- degree of polish or refinement
- amount of emotion or enthusiasm
- pertinence of what is said to the situation
- speed with which a rejoinder is made
- length and thoroughness of the discussion
- presence or lack of research and consideration
- methodicalness or dramatic effect of the arrangement
- stylistic wit or creativity

These are matters of revision and delivery.

Revision is the process of changing or refining one's style or meaning, of reconsidering decisions previously made about the form and content of an essay. It should not be confused with line editing, the painstaking process of correcting, regularizing, and formatting an essentially finished piece of writing. It is not something that happens only after a draft of an essay is completed.

True revision goes on constantly as we write and think. Anytime we reconsider a point of view or change an opinion about a subject, a degree of revision is taking place, even if nothing is said or written at the time. We constantly revise and rehearse our ideas, adjusting the presentation to suit the audience or to evoke a better response, adjusting the content to provide better support for our contentions, and adjusting the assertions to accommodate new evidence or to fit the facts.

Delivery instills a sense of performance in the message, dramatizing or re-creating ideas and events to make them seem fresh, immediate, and true. A good performance erases the impression of labor and revision, so the finished essay seems to have been conceived and written in a single moment of inspiration. A good performance is not read, as a speaker might read from a manuscript, but experienced. It seems spoken from the heart.

Whether a style is truly planned or spontaneous is difficult to determine. Some people work very hard and revise at length to create the impression of ease and spontaneity. And some are able, through practice or talent, to speak or write without apparent premeditation and nevertheless appear polished, well prepared, and disciplined.

It is equally possible to plan and appear unprepared, awkward, ill informed, and digressive, or to attempt spontaneity and instead sound contrived.

## *Some Advice About Writing and Revision*

The physical process of developing and refining an essay can be frustrating and exhilarating, the source of panic and pleasure. Understanding the process may make things easier.

## WRITING AND LEARNING

Although it may seem as though you have just one paper to write, just one opinion on a subject, or just one topic to address, in the course of composing most people write many partial essays, making half a dozen or more false starts and twice as many shifts in direction and focus. And each time a person starts over there is a tendency to take at least a slightly different—and sometimes a radically different—point of view on the matter.

Multiple drafts may therefore represent a process of self-education, an exploration of a subject, seeing it through different eyes, in terms of various thesis statements, opinions, or propositions, and in different frames of mind.

## GETTING AN EARLY START

It may be useful to get an early start, to begin writing immediately. Instead of waiting until you have finished researching the subject, you should consider writing *as* you research the subject, changing and developing your ideas as you go along.

The process of framing and supporting assertions helps to focus and direct your thinking.

## WAITING UNTIL THE LAST MINUTE

Some people prefer to produce the final draft at the last minute, even when they have gotten an early start on writing and research. The finished essay may have more immediacy and coherence when it is done in one sitting. And writing to the deadline is like being on stage. It focuses attention and increases the sense of dialogue and performance.

Waiting until the last minute does not work unless you are fairly well informed about the subject in the first place, are able to think well on your feet, and respond well to pressure.

## FIRST DRAFTS

Don't be satisfied with the first draft of an essay, however good it may seem to you. Often the first draft is emotive and self-serving rather than effective. It is written for the author rather than for an audience.

## WORDS ARE NOT THOUGHTS

There may be little relationship at first between what you want to say and what the words mean. As you refine your beliefs and understanding, the correlation gets better.

Writing and reading are generally much slower and much more linear than thought. We think in patterns, circles, pictures, networks, and fields as well as in straight lines. But discourse is more tied down to a straight-line progression, one word or phrase or sentence following another in an extended, one-dimensional chain.

Writing is not the transcription of thought but a representation of it in language.

## REVISION AS STARTING OVER

Revision is difficult or impossible if you only look at what you have already written. Just as the creative thinker must escape preconceptions and common knowledge, the writer must escape his or her established perspective and style.

To revise you must look outside the essay—at all the other interpretations or claims that might have been proposed, all the other material that might have been included, and all the different ways it might have been presented.

The basic questions for revision are "What's not there?" and "How else could it have been written?"

## ROUGH DRAFTS AND SKETCHING

Committing to a single plan, point, or approach too early in the writing process can lead to frustration and wasted effort. It may be useful instead to sketch things out, to write quick, short passages, not attempting to develop, finish, and refine every thought before moving on to something else.

But it can be counterproductive to write rough drafts. You may end up allowing yourself to do sloppy and unpresentable work, on the theory that you can clean it up later. When the time comes to do the final draft, you have nothing worthwhile to build on.

## PERFECT DRAFTING

The opposite pitfall is perfect drafting, the habit of making the first draft as painstakingly complete and polished as possible.

Perfect drafting can make it harder to revise effectively, since the writer who has invested so much time and effort in one form of an essay may be unwilling to make changes, unable to imagine other ways of approaching the subject, and so committed to the ideas already expressed that no alternatives can even be contemplated.

## MENTAL DRAFTS

Some people can do much of their drafting mentally. Instead of putting words on paper, they work out what they are going to say ahead of time. They may produce only one written draft, but it is not for lack of revision and invention.

Relying on mental drafting is useful because it is quicker than actually writing ideas down. But it takes a great deal of discipline, self-awareness, and self-doubt. Just thinking about the subject is not the same thing.

## SUBCONSCIOUS DRAFTING

Some drafting happens on the subconscious level. Given a problem, the mind will work out a solution behind the scenes. An idea appears as if by inspiration. This is usually not an accident. Subconscious drafting occurs when a person has already studied and concentrated on the subject at length.

## TRIAL RUNS

Rehearsals and testing are part of the revision process. Authors learn as they rewrite which ideas work best—which are most supportable, comfortable, and valid on paper. They may experiment with many different opinions and styles, discarding whatever seems false, beyond their abilities, or unattractive.

Sometimes this testing process may be externalized. Ideas may be developed at length and tried out on "safe" audiences, on a friend or colleague whose judgment one trusts. Or hypotheses and interpretations may be tested directly through experimentation—to assess and refine the accuracy of one's assertions.

## WRITING AND BELIEF

Writing things down makes them more permanent, less easy to disclaim. So as we write, we tend to examine our fund of ideas more closely and critically; opinions that normally would matter little to us, issues about which we would normally not trouble ourselves, start to take on more significance when we know our statements will be subject to review and question.

We become more choosy about the opinions we wish to be associated with, the causes we wish to represent and the precise shades of meaning that might be attributed to us. As we write or speak at length, therefore, we may seem to discover, fix, or settle our beliefs, to find out what we think about the subject—where we stand on it and what we stand for.

## Developing a Planned or Considered Style

Planned styles are essentially based on writing and memory rather than speaking and delivery. They rely on the fact that when writing, you can accumulate information, refine the style, and enhance the development of an idea at length, repeatedly adding onto or reworking the same performance. When speaking (without relying greatly on written preparation or memory), the same amount of information can only be conveyed by delivering a series of discrete performances, and these are likely to be disconnected and even contradictory.

A planned style, therefore, is close in effect, if not in fact, to considered opinion, knowledge, and expertise. The following strategies will make your style appear more studied and revised:

*1. Be Thorough.* A planned or revised style is usually fuller, more thorough and complete, with greater attention to detail and to questions of evidence or support. There may be discussion of pertinent principles or definitions, reviews of other research on the subject, re-creations of events or descriptions of methodology, background development, and extensive amplification.

*2. Be Methodical.* Use mechanical, predictable, and foreshadowed patterns of development—indicating in advance exactly what is forthcoming in the next section or in the body of the essay, how many points are going to be made, and the order of presentation. This permits you to simply "fill out the form" as you compose (though there may be considerable spontaneity within the preestablished format).

Categories, lists, and classification systems give the impression of planning. Dividing the issue has a similar effect. It reflects both planning and a degree of analysis or study.

*3. Be Formal, Conventional, and Slow-Paced.* Revision and planning often lead to an increasingly slow-moving, conventional, and dense presentation, particularly when the author is attempting to be as accurate as possible, when effectiveness is being measured in terms of preciseness or scientific and technical truth. A slow-paced, formal style may appear more considered and thoughtful.

*4. Avoid Emotion.* Revised prose tends to be less emotional, more cautious and objective. Authors often filter out their anger, pride, or enthusiasm, their self-interest and subjective perceptions, as they write successive drafts of an essay. The result is an impression of greater distance, impartiality, and reserve.

*5. Suggest a Longer Time Frame Within the Essay.*   The longer time frame necessary for planning and revision may be indicated in the essay: the writer may allude to the duration of his or her study of the subject or to the length of time that has gone into producing the report.

The same effect may be produced by referring to a sequence of discovery, by reporting changes in one's thinking, by including past and present time frames, or by including narratives that show the passage of time.

*6. Use a Style That Suggests Maturity and Experience.*   A stance that implies maturity or long familiarity with the subject can make you appear more thoughtful or composed. Mature styles are generally more abstract, more aphoristic, or more philosophical. Irony, bitterness, world-weariness, and loss of enthusiasm are pertinent but less attractive options.

*7. Qualify Assertions.*   Revised styles often reflect second thoughts and the passage of time and therefore express some doubt or reservation about your claims. Assertions that originally had the force of conviction become first likelihoods and then possibilities.

You can make your style appear more considered by qualifying your contentions.

*8. Define and Distinguish.*   A considered style tends to be more precise about terminology, making fine distinctions between words that in casual conversation might be accepted as synonyms. This pickiness reflects the more permanent and contractual nature of writing, in which an unexamined word can have unfortunate and unintended consequences.

For the same reasons, in planned writing we expect the author to explicitly distinguish his or her point of view from other opinions and theories.

*9. Cite Other Perspectives and Viewpoints.*   Considered styles reflect long study or research. Consequently, they may review other perspectives on the subject. The citations demonstrate that you have read about and discussed the subject at length and are truly conversant with expert opinion, that you can anticipate and refute what might be said in reply, and that you are objective and observant enough to see the issue in different ways.

*10. Take a Complex View of the Subject.*   The appearance of study and careful planning may be created by taking a complex view of the subject. Avoid easy answers and standard solutions, dismissing them as reductive or simple-minded. Focus on significant nuances or difficult concepts. Make the subject hard to understand.

Most matters are more complex than they seem to the layperson, anyway. Common knowledge is usually simplistic.

**11. *Be Reflective.*** A reflective or philosophical stance can make your style look more considered. Reflectiveness in style may include exploring questions, raising doubts, perceiving pitfalls, and seeing truth in both sides of an issue. It is often self-conscious and self-critical.

**12. *Amplify Extensively.*** The impression of planning and revision can be created by careful amplification, by cautiously staying within the parameters of one's original assertion, claim, or proposition and using restatement, division, and explanation to develop it. As long as distinctly new material is not introduced, as long as the author seems to be staying precisely and religiously on the same subject, the danger of appearing impromptu or off-the-cuff will be minimized.

## *Appearing Spontaneous*

Spontaneous styles are related to speaking and delivery, to the extemporaneous development of a subject, without pause for reflection, research, or revision. They risk being identified with simple opinion, prejudice, and emotional response. But at their best, spontaneous styles correspond more nearly with expressiveness, speculation or discovery, and dramatization.

To make your style appear more spontaneous and immediate, do the following:

**1. *Develop a Fund of Stock Answers.*** In the short run, at least, a collection of stock answers to expected questions or problems can give the appearance of decisiveness and sometimes can pass for wit. There is no need for planning or thought. You simply write out or repeat from memory the relevant reply. Of course, when repeated too often, stock answers lose currency.

**2. *Develop A Fund of Ideas.*** One of the hallmarks of expertise is having a repertory of ideas, information, and standard arguments, a fund of material that can be used as the occasion warrants and varied on demand.

This repertory owes something to formal education but is often more directly the result of a person's apprenticeship on the job. In the first few years at a trade, one develops and practices a collection of set pieces, ways of handling the normal questions that arise within the profession and ways of dealing with the issues and problems the profession presents.

These contribute greatly to one's readiness to speak or write. However, they lose the appearance of spontaneity when they are not adapted to the circumstances, when they become dogmatic, when they are too limited in scope (that is, when the author so consistently relies on one or two responses that they become predictable), and when the audience has become too familiar with the author.

*3. Report Common Knowledge.* Sometimes the impression of ready discourse may be gained by simply reporting what is commonly known. Rather than trying to be original or clever, you can respond to questions by reciting generally accepted truths. If your audience is not expert, this report may be appreciated as teaching. Or it may be accepted by a more informed audience as reinforcement of their beliefs.

*4. Force the Discussion Into Familiar Channels.* If a difficult or unfamiliar topic presents itself and an extemporaneous reply is expected, you can sometimes retrieve the situation by pursuing tangents, forcing the discussion or essay onto related issues you feel more comfortable with, for which you have a prepared statement, or about which you have previously written or spoken.

*5. Memorize Telling Quotes, Truisms, and Key Words.* Although it is a maligned skill because it is much abused, the ability to cite maxims and quotations at the right time can be extremely valuable. Not only do the phrases provide testimony to support your point, they suggest that you have a wide familiarity with the subject. People subconsciously assume that someone who can quote a line has read the whole book, that someone who knows a few maxims or principles has commensurate experience.

Key words or "insider" diction can have the same effect. If you occasionally use a technical term, a catch phrase, an allusion, or a slang expression, and use it correctly, you may feel more secure, even when you are speaking extemporaneously, and seem more expert.

*6. Use Vivid and Expressive Language.* Concrete details, metaphorical language, or expressive diction may seem more spontaneous even when they are the result of careful revision.

*7. Use a Conversational Manner.* Spontaneity is a verbal or dialogic style. You can convey a sense of spontaneity by using the style of everyday speech, including features like repetition, intentional sentence fragments, idiomatic expressions, and first- and second-person address.

*8. Use Current Slang or Jargon.* Since colloquialisms and slang are the product of conversation and repartee, a colloquial style can make your writing appear more spontaneous. The danger lies in using phrases that have lost their currency or in using them without proper feeling and delivery.

*9. Be Personal and Informal.*   Any personal note in an essay can make it seem both more informal and more spontaneous. This includes the use of asides or authorial comments, as well as anecdotes, feelings, and personal revelation.

*10. Emphasize Emotion.*   One of the keys to immediacy is the report or representation of emotion in the essay. Writing seems more spontaneous when it appears to come from the heart.

*11. Develop a Fund of Relevant Anecdotes and Examples.*   Pertinent stories, examples, and anecdotes can be used to extend an essay, to fill silence, and to respond immediately to difficult questions. Narrative does not openly assert anything, so it is difficult to challenge. Telling a story may allow you to collect your thoughts while you seek a more concrete answer. It may prove to be a sufficient reply by itself. And people who might have been offended by a direct response may be mollified by an anecdote.

People who speak or write for a living often develop a collection of stories and experiences that they use repeatedly (but not with the same audiences).

*12. Contradict or Refute Whatever Someone Else Says.*   Since anything can be criticized or disputed, it is relatively easy to extemporize by demurring, attacking, or raising objections. This practice, common in both writing and speech, may seem rational, inventive, and entertaining to onlookers, but it is extremely frustrating to the person who must deal with it directly.

*13. Use Associative or Discontinuous Form.*   In extemporaneous writing, we expect some digression, a tendency to drift or dart from one subject to the next. In bad writing, this becomes a lack of coherence. The author loses control over direction and organization, talks around the subject or randomly. In good writing, the digressiveness becomes a form of wit or entertainment: the author makes at least adequate connections between new ideas and previously mentioned subjects.

If the impression sought is not glibness but sincerity, a spontaneous style may contain frequent or obvious breaks in continuity or coherence—since these reflect or suggest a lack of planning or forethought, imply that the author has not carefully rehearsed an answer or statement. Such breaks or hesitation may also reflect emotion.

*14. Cultivate a Certain Roughness in Style.*   A certain unevenness is not only appropriate but sometimes effective and attractive in a spontaneous style. The lack of premeditation it implies may allow the author to justify moments of hesitation and inclarity, slightly inappropriate examples, the occasional excursion into sentimentality, awkwardness, or confusion, and changes of opinion or direction that otherwise would be regarded as weaknesses or defects. The unevenness may be considered aesthetically pleasing—a sign of the author's being down-to-earth, unpretentious, or tough.

*15. Use a Stylized Manner.*   Although it may actually take considerable planning and skill to produce, a stylized manner of speaking or writing is often perceived as more spontaneous and unrehearsed, perhaps because we associate emphatic repetition, refrains, elevated diction, and formulaic expression with oratory and poetry, both of which are more oral and emotive in effect.

Stylized language, if not labored, also may seem witty and hence spontaneous.

*16. Develop Speed in Delivery.*   In an apparently spontaneous style, we expect a reasonable pace—not necessarily a rapid one. In speaking, this pace can be obvious enough just from the speed of talking. In writing, the pace may be implied by the sheer volume of words, by quick, short sentences or cumulative sentences with little embedding (that is, with few subordinate clauses) and an avoidance of balanced sentences. Pace may be indicated, as well, by an appearance of fluency, an ease of expression that seems never at a loss for words.

*17. Invent as You Speak or Write.*   With some effort, you can learn to think on your feet, to analyze, interpret, and judge a subject without premeditation. This ability may be acquired through study of an invention system (see Chapter 11), through training in interpretation (see Chapter 10), and through practice in observation and criticism (see Chapter 12).

*18. Develop a Set of Criteria or Principles.*   Extemporaneous writing or speaking is easier if you develop a set of criteria or principles that apply to the general subject. When faced with a particular situation, you can use these standards to explore and explain it.

*19. Make Rapid Associations.*   Writing seems more spontaneous when it is more inventive. This includes not only verbal wit but also lateral or centrifugal thinking. You can make your style appear more immediate by avoiding categorical thinking, by speeding up the movement from one idea or frame of reference to the next, by making nonlogical associations, and by connecting disparate subjects.

It usually takes practice and premeditation to develop these skills.

*20. Say the First Thing That Comes to Mind.*   Spontaneous styles are often expressive, copious, and surprising, even to the point of seeming scatterbrained or outrageous. The speaker pours out ideas, trying to make the clever material outweigh the dull, but deriving some interest from the randomness itself. This effect is part of the advantage and attraction of free association, stream of consciousness, and freewriting, all of which depend on saying the first thing that comes to mind.

*21. Be Unconventional.* Some of the social niceties may be side-stepped, as well. A spontaneous style can sometimes get away with saying things normally left unsaid. The author slips in a less-than-proper comment, mentions a slightly taboo subject or something inconsiderate or rude, and forges past it so quickly that we are almost not sure it happened. And even after we catch on, we tend to excuse such remarks as unintentional, humorous, or an inevitable part of the style they inhabit.

To a certain extent, all wit depends on saying the wrong thing at the right time.

*22. Be Involved.* The impression of spontaneity often depends on a degree of immediacy or engagement, the sense that the author is at that very moment compelled to speak, without time for forethought or premeditation. Engagement may be indicated by circumstances, by direct claim, by heightened pace, by the inclusion of emotion, by recourse to personal experience, and by arguing for or demonstrating the significance of the issue.

*23. Be Opinionated, Reductive, and Assertive.* Extemporaneous writing is generally more assertive and less qualified than carefully revised and planned discourse. It is likely to be more opinionated and one-sided, with less time spent on subtleties, nuances, or complexities. Issues are usually simplified or brought down to the level of common sense and common knowledge.

*24. Be Brief; Deemphasize Evidence.* There is often less evidence and more emotional or authorial appeal in a spontaneous style. It may rely heavily on judgments and unsupported assertions. Some parts of the discussion may be left incomplete or sketchy—more implied than explained.

## EXERCISE A

Analyze and evaluate the following passages. Which seem more spontaneous? Which seem planned or considered? What elements of style contribute to the effect of consideration or spontaneity in each case?

**1.** Taxes. Nothing sure but death and. You know how it goes. For every buck you earn, the Feds grab a dime or quarter, the state a nickel or dime. For every dollar you spend, the city, county, and state rake off another six percent. You pay taxes on water and taxes on phone calls, taxes on pets and taxes on fishing, taxes on rock concerts and taxes on Kool-Aid, if you can afford it. Luxury taxes, property taxes, school taxes, and utility assessments. It never seems to stop.

I'm not against schools, police, sewers, or highway construction. I'm just against highway robbery.

**2.** I hate paying taxes.

**3.** I've just discovered another misnomer to add to my collection: The Internal Revenue *Service.* What a joke. They call garbage collectors "Sanitation Engineers" and cocktail servers on planes are "Flight Attendants." If the IRS is a "service," then purse snatchers must provide "Handbag Disencumbrance Services" and car thieves must work for the "Automotive Rip-Offment Service."

We're all just indentured servants, coal miners living in company towns, buying our flour and eggs at the company store. The give and take has just gotten more subtle. Instead of scooping up a bushel of grain for every three or four harvested—a feudal system—the modern taxation agencies conceal the transaction. They permit the illusion that you control your own money by allowing choice of where you live or where you spend or what you buy. But instead of owning the houses and stores, they tax the homebuilders and businessperson.

And every check that comes in has run a gauntlet of city, county, state, and federal agencies, each one siphoning off another pint or quart of income, until the net bears so little resemblance to the gross you'd swear they weren't related. But it mostly happens up front, before you see the money. The con in this shell game is simple: they figure that what you don't ever get a hold of you won't ever miss.

**4.** There is some truth to the popular analogy between a family budget and the federal budget. "If I overdraw my bank account or kite a check," says the average person on the street, "I get in trouble. I'm expected to live within my means and to make intelligent decisions about how to spend my money. Why shouldn't government be held to the same standards? You pay as you go or pay the consequences. You don't make frivolous purchases you can't afford. The necessities come first."

By this reasoning, many people become violently upset about how tax dollars are spent. It is hard enough to watch income diminish as taxes, assessments, fees, and levies are subtracted from gross earnings. It is harder still to see that money misspent, to see the government run up bills it can never pay and to purchase what seem like luxuries. The necessities come first and pay as you go. To some this is all that "fiscal responsibility" means.

But it is all too easy to complain about taxes and all too difficult to control them, to understand the difficulties and costs of government, the conflicting responsibilities each legislator may face. The legitimate claims on the public tax dollar can far exceed one hundred cents. And everything seems a necessity.

Should we deny hospital care or police and fire protection to those who cannot pay? Deny education to those too poor to afford it? Deny access to highways to those without the toll? Deny food, water, and shelter to those without money?

Should we take no risks? If an investment opportunity presents itself, a chance to make long-term improvements in the quality of life, should we avoid the prospect to avoid the dangers? Should we buy a lot of things cheap or a few things dear—twenty miles of freeway that will last five years or five miles of freeway that will last for twenty? You get what you pay for. Should we spend on science, on technology, on the arts? What is the comparative worth of military power, entertainment or culture, and the highway patrol? Should police earn one dollar less per hour so that one more missile per month can be purchased? Or one more Matisse?

These are not questions that can readily be answered. Public policy and political doctrines have wrestled with them endlessly—because it is not a simple matter of paying for this and not paying for that. The problem is to get as much of everything as possible, to weigh expediencies. If state-of-the-art fire protection can be had for a price, do you sacrifice sewers and roads to get it? Or settle for a less expensive alternative that gets the job done sixty or eighty percent of the time, and still leaves cash for other needs? The choices are hard, and the answers are seldom obvious.

**5.** What do I think of taxes? I think everyone in Congress should be audited by the IRS and everyone in the IRS should be accountable to us—not to higher agencies or Congress itself but to the people of this country.

## WHEN TO PLAN AND REVISE

A planned style is appropriate

- when you wish to look mature and experienced
- in matters of taste
- when expertise is expected
- on formal and ceremonial occasions
- in organizational communication
- in legislative processes
- when speaking as or for a group
- when formal research has been conducted

## WHEN TO BE SPONTANEOUS

The impression of spontaneity or extemporaneous composition is especially appropriate

- when the subject matter is highly emotional
- when the situation seems urgent
- in lyrical or evocative writing
- in humor
- in public debate
- in casual converstion

## EXERCISE B

Which of the following situations seem to call for spontaneity? For planning and revision? Discuss the circumstances that affect each.

1. An annual report to your employer—specifying the work done in the preceding year and the present status of your office, department, inventory, and/or balance sheet
2. A complaint to neighbors about damage to your car apparently caused by their child
3. A job application letter
4. A newspaper or TV review of an excellent new movie
5. A comparative review of three suggested changes in company/organizational policy or procedures
6. A letter home
7. Asking for a date
8. Responding to a particularly angry or offensive written complaint about your work, your product, your staff, or your organization
9. The results of research sponsored and funded by the government
10. An advertising campaign for an amusement park, for a stock brokerage firm, or for a political candidate

---

## GAINS AND LOSSES

---

### ◀ REVISION ▶

| **Advantages** | **Disadvantages** |
| --- | --- |
| Allows time for planning | Loses freshness and immediacy |
| Increases density and apparent knowledgeability | Leads to second guessing and incoherence |
| Reduces risk | Becomes inflexible |
| Reduces reliance on memory | Seems less inventive |

---

## GAINS AND LOSSES

### ◆ SPONTANEITY ◆

| Advantages | Disadvantages |
| --- | --- |
| Greater immediacy and inherent interest | Seems to lack seriousness and method |
| Seems more genuine, reflecting actual thought processes and revealed beliefs | May not adequately reflect the complexity of one's ideas |
| Unevenness may be attractive | Requires audience to make allowances |
| Less "contractual," more deniable | Seems irresolute or contradictory |

## *Wider Implications*

Very different philosophies are reflected in spontaneity and planning. The two represent opposing views of rhetoric that have been studied and debated for centuries.

### EXTEMPORANEOUS ORATORY

Spontaneity, taken to an extreme, implies that the orator does not need practical experience or education, that the resources of eloquence and invention are enough for success in the forum. A trained rhetorician should be able to lead, adjudicate, or compete in society effectively on the basis of oratory and imagination alone.

Not only that, he or she should have as much authority and understanding of truth as any philosopher. Spontaneity assumes that truth is relative, that there are many correct answers, that either side of an issue can be argued with equal validity, or that truth will emerge from open debate, however flawed or inexpert one's own opinions may be.

An extemporaneous rhetoric values the spoken word over the written word, on the theory that speaking is closer to emotional truths and inspired knowledge, to feelings and insight. According to an extemporaneous rhetoric, the premeditation inherent in writing permits and encourages deception; it falsifies human relationships, creating an unnatural impression of the speaker's ability, expertise, and character.

This view is implicit in sophistry, in the rhetoric of Plato and Socrates, in relativism, in romanticism, and in deconstructionism.

## CALCULATED ORATORY

Planning the speech is favored by Aristotle, Cicero, Quintilian, and modern theories of composition. In a calculated rhetoric, one analyzes the situation and audience, examines precedents and principles, develops arguments and refutations, and prepares the oration in advance, writing it out and memorizing it if necessary.

Calculated oratory assumes that rhetorical training, education, and practical experience are all necessary prerequisites to effective speaking. One must study and apprentice in law to be a lawyer, in political science to be a leader, in protocol and courtesy to participate in society.

Planning depends on generalization, on your confidence that people will act the way you expect them to, that the truth is consistent from one situation to the next, and that what is appropriate for one place and time will be more or less appropriate for another. Instead of generating a speech from the author's present resources and the exigencies of the moment, calculation assumes that the performance can be written out in advance, even delivered on different occasions.

### MYSTICAL AND DRAMATIC RHETORIC

The difference between calculation and spontaneity is like the difference between scripting one's life and relying on inspiration. Planned and revised discourse is crafted and acted out, dramatistic. One's actions and words are prepared in advance and performed, like reading a speech from a manuscript. From the viewpoint of dramatic rhetoric, we "compose" ourselves. Our personalities and beliefs are artistic creations.

Spontaneity is mystical. It presumes that at the right moment, if you are truly ready for it, spiritually, physically, and mentally prepared, the right words will come to you.

Accomplished writers are able to combine the two, calculation and extemporaneity, revision and discovery. They do not sacrifice wit in the process of reflection or precision for the sake of the moment.

## *Conclusion*

The goal of rhetorical training is to make each person not just an effective speaker but a good citizen. The two things are ultimately identical. A good writer is an active participant in public affairs and the world of ideas, articulate and open-minded, sensitive and decisive, experienced and knowledgeable, imaginative and judicious, attractive, ethical, and socially adroit. A good writer is literate in the highest sense of the word, conversant with many ideas and able to discuss them intelligently and effectively, whether speaking in the academy or in the marketplace.

This is the objective of education and rhetoric alike.

## ASSIGNMENT A: Revisions, Concessions, and Reassessments

1. Concede that you have been wrong about something, or that you have either failed or fallen short of expectations. Discuss points of view that seem more correct or courses of action that would have been preferable.

2. Discuss a subject about which you have changed your views. You might want to contrast your former opinions with your present understanding of the subject, perhaps using some narrative to exemplify your views or to dramatize a turning point or moment of insight.

3. Refine someone else's concept or theory.

4. Revise some generally accepted definition, notion, or element of common knowledge.

## ASSIGNMENT B: Literateness and Wit

1. Write on a subject in a manner that suggests wide learning, wit, diplomacy, strength of character, well roundedness, perceptiveness, and courtesy. Avoid being excessively technical or philosophical. Attempt to be interesting, but avoid seeking too exclusively to entertain and amuse.

2. Write in a fairly extemporaneous manner on a subject, trying to speak impressively on an issue or topic without referring to notes or taking excessive time to prepare.

## ASSIGNMENT C: Scholarship and Authority

1. Write as an expert on a subject, in a manner that reflects deep and extended study of the matter; perceptive analysis; familiarity with technical concepts, terms, formats, and competing theories; knowledge of processes, mechanisms, facts, methods, and professional standards; critical distance; and direct experience, reading, and experimentation.

2. Write on a subject in a style that reflects extensive thinking and revision, careful attention to detail, fine distinctions between similar ideas, and a logical or analytic habit of mind.

# Recommended Readings

## I. CLASSICAL AND HISTORICAL RHETORICS

Aristotle. *The* Rhetoric *and the* Poetics *of Aristotle.* Trans. W. Rhys Roberts and Ingram Bywater. New York: Modern Library, 1984.

Blair, Hugh. *Lectures on Rhetoric and Belles Lettres.* London: W. Tegg, 1858.

Campbell, George. *The Philosophy of Rhetoric.* Ed. Lloyd F. Bitzer. Carbondale: Southern Illinois UP, 1988.

Cicero. *De Oratore.* 2 vols. Trans. E. W. Sutton and H. Rackham. Cambridge: Harvard UP, 1979 and 1982.

Erasmus, Desiderius. *De duplici copia verborum ac rerum commentarii duo.* Collected Works of Erasmus: Literary and Educational Writings. Vol. 2. Ed. Craig R. Thompson. Toronto: U of Toronto Press, 1978.

Plato. *Gorgias.* Trans. Walter Hamilton. New York: Penguin, 1988.

Plato. *Phaedrus and Letters VII and VIII.* Trans. Walter Hamilton. New York: Penguin, 1973.

Quintilian. *Institutio Oratoria.* Trans. H. E. Butler. Cambridge: Harvard UP, 1920–1921.

*Rhetorica ad Herennium.* Trans. Harry Caplan. Cambridge: Harvard UP, 1954.

## II. THE HISTORY OF RHETORIC

Berlin, James A. *Writing Instruction in Nineteenth-Century American Colleges.* Urbana: NCTE, 1984.

Bonner, S. F. *Roman Declamation in the Late Republic and Early Empire.* Berkeley: U of California Press, 1949.

Clark, Martin Lowther. *Rhetoric at Rome: A Historical Survey.* London: Cohen & West, 1953.

Corbett, Edward P. J. *Classical Rhetoric for the Modern Student.* 2nd ed. New York: Oxford, 1971.

Howell, Wilbur Samuel. *Eighteenth-Century British Logic and Rhetoric.* Princeton: Princeton UP, 1971.

Howell, Wilbur Samuel. *Logic and Rhetoric in England, 1500–1700.* New York: Russell and Russell, 1961.

Kennedy, George. *The Art of Persuasion in Greece.* Princeton: Princeton UP, 1963.

Kennedy, George. *The Art of Rhetoric in the Roman World, 300 B.C.–A.D. 300.* Princeton: Princeton UP, 1972.

Kennedy, George. *Classical Rhetoric and Its Christian and Secular Tradition From Ancient to Modern Times*. Chapel Hill: U of North Carolina Press, 1980.

Kennedy, George. *Greek Rhetoric Under Christian Emperors*. Princeton: Princeton UP, 1983.

Murphy, James J., ed. *A Synoptic History of Classical Rhetoric*. Davis, CA: Hermagoras Press, 1983.

Murphy, James J. *Rhetoric in the Middle Ages*. Berkeley: U of California Press, 1974.

Romilly, Jacqueline de. *Magic and Rhetoric in Ancient Greece*. Cambridge: Harvard UP, 1975.

Russell, D. A. *Greek Declamation*. Cambridge: Cambridge UP, 1983.

## III. MODERN RHETORICAL THEORY

Bailey, F. G. *The Tactical Uses of Passion*. Ithaca: Cornell UP, 1983.

Bitzer, Lloyd. "The Rhetorical Situation." Philosophy and Rhetoric 1 (Jan. 1968): 1–14.

Booth, Wayne. *Modern Dogma and the Rhetoric of Assent*. Notre Dame: U of Notre Dame Press, 1974.

Britton, James. "Shaping at the Point of Utterance." *Reinventing the Rhetorical Tradition*. Eds. Aviva Freedman and Ian Pringle. Conway, AK: L&S Books, 1980: 61–65.

Burke, Kenneth. *A Grammar of Motives*. Berkeley: U of California Press, 1969.

Burke, Kenneth. *A Rhetoric of Motives*. Berkeley: U of California Press, 1969.

Clark, Gregory. *Dialogue, Dialectic, and Conversation: A Social Perspective on the Function of Writing*. Carbondale, IL: Southern Illinois UP, 1990.

Dillon, George L. *Rhetoric as Social Imagination: Explorations in the Interpersonal Function of Language*. Bloomington: Indiana UP, 1986.

Kinneavy, James L. *A Theory of Discourse*. New York: Norton, 1980.

Kinneavy, James L. "A Pluralistic Synthesis of Four Contemporary Models for Teaching Composition." *Reinventing the Rhetorical Tradition*. Eds. Aviva Freedman and Ian Pringle. Conway, AK: L&S Books, 1980: 37–52.

LeFevre, Karen Burke. *Invention as a Social Act*. Carbondale IL: Southern Illinois UP, 1987.

Markels, Robin Bell. *A New Perspective on Cohesion in Expository Paragraphs*. Carbondale: Southern Illinois UP, 1984.

Ong, Walter. *Interfaces of the Word: Studies in the Evolution of Consciousness and Culture*. Ithaca: Cornell UP, 1977.

Payne, David. *Coping with Failure: The Therapeutic Uses of Rhetoric*. Columbia: U of South Carolina Press, 1989.

Perelman, Chaim, and Louise Olbrechts-Tyteca. *The New Rhetoric: A Treatise on Argumentation*. Notre Dame: U of Notre Dame Press, 1982.

Pruitt, Dean G. *Negotiation Behavior*. New York: Academic Press, 1981.

Toulmin, Stephen, Richard Rieke, and Allan Janik. *An Introduction to Reasoning*. New York: Macmillan, 1979.

Valesio, Paolo. *Novantiqua: Rhetorics as a Contemporary Theory*. Bloomington: Indiana UP, 1980.

Weaver, Richard. *The Ethics of Rhetoric*. Chicago: Henry Regnery, 1953.

White, James Boyd. *Heracles' Bow: Essays on the Rhetoric and Poetics of the Law*. Madison: U of Wisconsin Press, 1985.

Witte, Stephen. "Topical Structure and Revision: An Exploratory Study." *College Composition and Communication* 34 (Oct. 1983): 313–41.

Young, Richard E., et al. *Rhetoric: Discovery and Change.* New York: Harcourt, 1970.

## IV.  THE TEACHING OF WRITING

Elbow, Peter. *Writing Without Teachers.* New York: Oxford UP, 1973.

Kaplan, Robert B. "Contrastive Rhetoric and the Teaching of Composition." *TESOL Quarterly* (Dec. 1967): 10–16.

Lindemann, Erika. *A Rhetoric for Writing Teachers.* 2nd ed. New York: Oxford UP, 1987.

Moffett, James. *Teaching the Universe of Discourse.* Boston: Houghton, 1983.

Murray, Donald. *A Writer Teaches Writing.* 2nd ed. Boston: Houghton, 1985.

Neman, Beth. *Teaching Students to Write.* Columbus, OH: Merrill, 1980.

## V.  STYLE AND COMPOSITION

Christiansen, Francis, and Bonniejean Christiansen. *Notes Toward a New Rhetoric: Nine Essays for Teachers.* 2nd ed. New York: Harper, 1978.

Curtis, Catherine A. "A Study of Conclusions in Expository Prose: Professional Writers versus Textbook Conventions." Diss. Ohio State U, 1985.

Dillon, George. *Constructing Texts: Elements of a Theory of Composition and Style.* Bloomington: Indiana UP, 1981.

Gibson, Walker. *Tough, Sweet and Stuffy.* Bloomington: Indiana UP, 1966.

Group Mu [Jacques Dubois, et al.]. *A General Rhetoric.* Baltimore: Johns Hopkins UP, 1981.

Lanham, Richard A. *Style: An Anti-Textbook.* New Haven: Yale UP, 1974.

O'Hare, Frank. *Sentence Combining: Improving Student Writing Without Formal Grammar Instruction.* Urbana: NCTE, 1973.

Weathers, Winston. *An Alternate Style: Options in Composition.* Hayden, 1980.

Williams, Joseph. *Style: Ten Lessons in Clarity and Grace.* Glenview, IL: Scott, Foresman, 1981.

Zinsser, William. *On Writing Well: An Informal Guide to Writing Nonfiction.* 3rd ed. New York: Harper, 1985.

## VI.  ANCILLARY WORKS

Festinger, Leon. *A Theory of Cognitive Dissonance.* Evanston, IL: Row, Peterson, 1957.

Kuhn, Thomas S. *The Structure of Scientific Revolutions.* Chicago: U of Chicago Press, 1962.

## VII.  REFERENCE

Horner, Winifred Bryan, ed. *The Present State of Scholarship in Historical and Contemporary Rhetoric.* Columbia: U of Missouri Press, 1983.

Moran, Michael G., and Ronald F. Lunsford, eds. *Research in Composition and Rhetoric.* Westport, CT: Greenwood, 1984.

Lanham, Richard A. *A Handlist of Rhetorical Terms.* Berkeley: U of California Press, 1968.

Lindemann, Erika, ed. *Bibliography of Composition and Rhetoric, 1987–.* Carbondale, IL: Southern Illinois UP, 1990.

Lindemann, Erika, ed. *Longman Bibliography of Composition and Rhetoric, 1984–1985 and 1986.* New York: Longman, 1987 and 1988.

# Index